THE NEW HISTORY
OF LITERATURE

THE
MIDDLE AGES

THE NEW HISTORY
OF LITERATURE

Volumes 3, 6, 9, and 10 will be published in 1987,
and volumes 5 and 7 in 1988.

THE
MIDDLE
AGES

.

EDITED BY

W. F. BOLTON

Peter Bedrick Books
New York

First American edition published in 1987 by
Peter Bedrick Books
125 East 23 Street
New York, NY 10010

Library of Congress Cataloging-in-Publication Data

The Middle Ages.
  (The New history of literature)
  Bibliography: p.
  Includes index.
    1. Anglo-Saxon literature—History and criticism.
2. English literature—Middle English, 1100–1500—
History and criticism.   I. Bolton, W. F. (Whitney
French), 1930– .   II. Series.
Pr166.M53 1986   820'.9'001   86–14017
ISBN 0–87226–125–5

Printed in Great Britain

10 9 8 7 6 5 4 3 2 1

CONTENTS

INTRODUCTION

Veiled by changes in the English language over a millennium; decimated time and again by fire, decay, hostility and mere chance; sterilized by alterations in popular taste and critical technique; the literature of the English Middle Ages yet summons to its arduous study a band of enthusiasts whose numbers increase each year. For them this volume offers a guide and a critical testimony. For students of the monuments of later English literature, it describes the pedestal on which those monuments rest.

The volume reviews, in eight chapters by ten experts, the main works and authors during a period that lasted almost the first half of the last thousand years. It begins at the beginning, with the earliest surviving documents of literary importance. It ends with the work of writers whose literary career was already established before the accession of King Henry VIII in 1509.

During this time English intellectual life differed in three major respects from what it has since become. Every writer whose work is a topic in this volume, known or anonymous, was a member of the same international Church. Every writer save the very last few wrote before the invention of printing had revolutionized the profession of letters. And every writer wrote when English was the language of the British Isles alone: they wrote for an audience occupying a small country with a small population whose language was incomprehensible beyond its borders. And they wrote in one of the three literary languages of that small country in preference to Latin and, later, French; English was not a world language, nor yet even the sole literary language of England.

These circumstances combined to impart a substantial conservatism to the literature written down between the early ninth and early sixteenth centuries, and the unity of its outlook is indeed remarkable in view of the expanse of time. But there was change, even progress, and to speak of 'medieval English literature' – whether in praise or otherwise – is to speak of an entity that none of its practitioners, much less its readers, would have recognized.

The earliest English literature is doubly an importation: the literary form and the language from north Germany, homeland of the tribes that had settled in Britain in the fifth century; the literary impulse and intellectual goal from Rome, homeland of the missionary band that had come to convert the Germanic tribes at the end of the sixth century. The achievement of the first five centuries of English literature was the fusion of these two alien components into a single native tradition. When, at the Norman Conquest, the continuity of the Germanic language and hence of the literary form was broken, it was the intellectual content of the old literature – effectively, its religious ideals – that provided the link with the new literature.

Once again an alien force came to bear on the already existing native traditions – traditions that, as we have seen, played an energetic role in the conservative literary milieu. This time the importation was from France, homeland of the new ruling class. It brought with it new literary forms like the romance, new attitudes toward life in the courts where most literature continued to be composed and performed, later even massive new contributions to the literary vocabulary. At its most subservient to this force, English literature lost even its linguistic identity and was written in French; at its most independent it preserved in an artificial literary dialect some of the defunct language of pre-Conquest England; at its most characteristic and influential, it again subsumed the two traditions in a new, vital, eclectic, viable literature that made all forms, native and foreign, its own.

The history of invasion and fusion, invasion and fusion, can be documented to provide the kinetic background to any one work of English medieval literature. Yet such a work, although it is a document in that history and must be seen against that background, derives its properties from a multitude, perhaps an infinity, of sources: the author's learning, experience, and perceptiveness; his control over the verse or prose medium; his capacity for imaginative projection; his talent for the literary embodiment of 'felt life', of human emotion; his ability to synthesize. Hence any account of English medieval literature, while not losing sight of the great movements that crossed and re-crossed the stage, must concentrate on individual writers and their individual works, not simply as particularizations of literary historical trends, but as the stuff that validates literary history. *Sir Gawain* does not derive its interest from its place in literary history; literary history derives its interest from its inclusion of, among other things, *Sir Gawain*.

For this reason the present volume ignores the proportions of time or bulk in arriving at its plan of presentation, and prefers that of demonstrated literary worth; three chapters for the literary master of the English Middle Ages, Chaucer. Yet even here the proportions must not be taken to constitute ultimate judgments. For one thing, a contributive volume on a critical basis is really an anthology of individual essays, not a continuous account, and its organization cannot therefore be regarded as a consistent measure of any kind, merely as a convenient way to bring the essays together. For another thing, critical accounts such as these deal with the intrinsic worth of the literature, not its comparative merits: the 'desert island test' has little or no place in coming to terms with the literature of our own or any former age. And finally, the purpose of the essays is to identify writings and to indicate interpretive directions, not to bring interpretation to a halt.

The bibliographies for each chapter are similarly inceptive. They seek to direct the student to the standard editions of text cited, the standard authorities for facts adduced, the foremost studies for further reading. Some of these bibliographies are shortest where the extant studies are most numerous, for it is easy to list in its entirety a small body of scholarship, but it is necessary to select rigorously where the body is large. A table of dates makes reference to major national and continental events that coincided with the writing discussed.

In drawing up a rough table of contents, the selection of contributors, and the contribution of one chapter, the editor has not sought to fix or prohibit any critical position in the following pages. All the limitations expressed in the first sentence of this introduction deter the tasteful reader from taking a hard-line or monistic view about our older literature. In no field of humane study is there yet so much to be accomplished by individual endeavour and discernment.

WFB

1

THE CONDITIONS OF LITERARY COMPOSITION IN MEDIEVAL ENGLAND

W. F. Bolton

The Differences

We reckon those features in a work of literature the most valuable, which set it apart from all others; we praise originality, not sameness. The distinctive things that works of English medieval literature share with each other are of small interest to us – a common denominator in literature is low indeed. Yet writers do not start anew with each work. They begin with a set of assumptions about what they can do, what is expected of them, what means are at their disposal. Long narrative and drama in the Middle Ages were usually in verse: now we expect both in prose. In consequence, we expect lifelike dialogue; earlier ages also had standards for dialogue, but different ones. Because such expectations are part of an under-standing between authors and their audience, the make-up of the reading public has an important bearing on what writers can do, and this too has changed, along with all manner of tastes, conventions, forms, even material conditions. To gain an understanding of medieval English literature, we must attempt to understand first the historical conditions in which it appeared and which, in large measure, gave rise to it. This chapter is a brief review of those conditions in so far as they differentiate medieval English literature from its later descendants.

The Meaning of 'The Middle Ages'

The name 'Middle Ages' implies that this space of time extends between two others: in this case the ancient (or classical) period and the modern (or, more exactly, renaissance) period. Not surprisingly, those who lived in the Middle Ages had no such view of themselves

– neither 'Middle Ages' nor 'medieval' (from Latin *medium aevum*, 'middle age') appears in English before the eighteenth century, that is, until after the Middle Ages and the renaissance as well. Now the end of the ancient world is often said to have come with one or another of the invasions of Rome in the fifth century; and the beginning of the renaissance with reform movements in the Church in the late fourteenth century, renewed study of classical art and literature in Italy earlier in the same century, or the invention of printing in the middle of the fifteenth century. Like the sack of Rome, these later events had real consequences for English literature; but none of them is an event *in* English literature, and we shall have to redefine the terms and dates for our purposes. The earliest English literature – from about 800 – is far later than the sack of Rome; and we may take any writer already working when Henry VIII came to the throne in 1509 to have begun his career in the English Middle Ages.

But in adopting the chronological limits that the term has for English literature, we need not accept the view of the literature that they imply. When 'Middle Ages' came into the language in the early eighteenth century, the classical world was the object of great admiration, and so 'Middle Ages' concentrates attention on the two ages which delimit the middle one, the glory of classical civilization and the rediscovery of that glory. It implies that the Middle Ages were devoid of classical taste and learning, and that their civilization was consequently barren. Although we do not altogether hold the classical world in such veneration now, we still often use 'medieval' to describe particularly oppressive tyranny, conservative thought, or primitive material conditions.

Study of the Middle Ages, in any case, refutes the notion that classical civilization lost its fascination during that time, or that no civilization at all existed. Over a period of 700 years, even in one country alone, many treaties with the past will be made, and many accommodations with the present. More about medieval classicism will be found below; enough for now to say that our present use of the chronological tag 'medieval' does not carry with it acknowledgement of the implied value judgement.

Finally there is the matter of language. About the time that 'Middle Ages' first came into English, Pope wrote 'such as Chaucer is, shall Dryden be', meaning that the changes which all languages undergo over a space of time would make the early eighteenth century as unintelligible to a later age as the fourteenth century was to them. Such has not happened – we still read Pope and Dryden much as though their language were that of our contemporaries. The sense that language changed during the Middle Ages but not since then may make us feel cut off from the earlier literature. Once again, the change of language – and the apparent cessation of that change – has its consequences for English literature, but the stages of linguistic change do not altogether coincide with changes in literary practice. The linguistic 'differentness' of medieval literature is perhaps the most superficial, and hence the most misleading, of the features which distinguish it from more familiar writing. We can overcome this kind of strangeness with a translation or by studying the earlier stages of the language, but this too is superficial and misleading if we think that by solving the linguistic problems we have come to terms with the literature. Thus the language surface makes medieval writing seem more remote than it is; mere translation makes it seem more familiar than it is.

The Medieval Book

Literature as we understand it today is a matter of the written word; and the written word is recorded and passed on through books. Medieval literature too was a matter of written words and books, but the books themselves were unlike ours, and they profoundly influenced the literature they contained.

The medieval book was written by hand (manuscript), not produced from printer's types on a press. It looked much like our books when on the shelf – scrolls (rolls) were also employed, but almost never for literature. But because it was handwritten, it differed from our books (like this one) in all the four vital points that printing has made us take for granted. A modern press produces as many copies of a work as we require, and after the book has been set in type, the number of copies produced is easy to extend almost indefinitely. So we are used to a plentiful supply of copies; 'economies of scale' make these copies cheap; the printing process can make them all identical; and the rapid turnover of cheap, plentiful, reliable books makes it easy for new books to find a place in the active book trade. But a medieval book took months to copy out. Even when in the later Middle Ages scribes were cheap, or earlier when monks made many of the copies and their labour was in a sense free, the employment of one man on a book for a matter of months greatly inflated prices. And the materials (sheep or calf hide for the pages) were also expensive; perhaps two hundred sheep would give their skins for a single Bible. Such books were not only expensive to produce, they were also scarce, and the law of supply and demand put prices up even higher.

What is more, the scribe invariably made mistakes; when the new copy came to serve as the model for another scribe, those mistakes would almost always be included, along with further mistakes make by the new scribe. And so no two copies were identical, and few were even relatively reliable. The whole question of 'which manuscript *does* give us such and such a poem' enters in here.

When extant books demand such high prices the call for new titles – as distinct from new copies – is going to be slight. The investment in existing books is too high, and the book trade is too slow. The situation is essentially a conservative one. And it is one in which few people could hope to make a living; in fact, writing as a profession hardly exists in the Middle Ages.

Under these circumstances, the publication of a book – that is, its distribution to the book-owning and book-reading public – was not a once-and-for-all matter. It took place continuously, usually (except perhaps for the first few copies) in a place far removed from the author and over a period of years, sometimes centuries. Under these conditions it was impossible for an author to exercise any control over the text of his work, and so once again the question of authenticity arises. We find it hard to know which of a number of different versions of a poem is the 'real' one, and which ones have undergone changes in the text, including additions and deletions.

Until the very end of the Middle Ages, only the most wealthy families had any books at all, and those were chiefly religious service books. The books that existed were mostly in the libraries of institutions with restricted access: monasteries, churches (especially cathedrals), latterly universities. Not everyone could make use of these collections, which were in any case small. Reading, a typical prosperous abbey of the Benedictine Order whose rule fostered the copying and collection of books, took about a century to gather their first two hundred volumes. The library at Canterbury Cathedral, in Chaucer's day one of the largest in England, had at that time about 700 volumes (although, because several works were often bound together, the number of titles was probably considerably greater but even so still smaller than that of a small school library today – no more than 3,000 or so). The University of Oxford managed until the middle of the fifteenth century to house its library in a room only 45 by 20 feet.

In short, the medieval book was a precious object – one volume might cost as much as a student's whole budget for a full year at university. It was consequently a scarce object. Below we shall see the consequences of this for education and literacy, the indispensable preconditions of a flourishing literature in our sense of that word. But, we may say, at least the high cost of manuscript books would guarantee their safe-keeping. Such is unfortunately not the case, especially among books from the English Middle Ages.

In the first place, precious objects attract thieves. Medieval books were so costly that we have records of 'deeds' to them when they changed hands, just as though they were houses, to prove that the change of ownership was legal; but of course books are much more portable than houses, and the common inscription on manuscript fly-leaves, 'let him who takes this book be excommunicated,' was as strong a warning as the devout age could muster. And scarce objects are used and wear out, no matter how much they are prized. Medieval libraries, like other medieval buildings, were especially vulnerable to fire; one such caused great damage in Canterbury in 1067. When books were chained, protection against theft made them especially vulnerable to fire. Such perils existed wherever books were made and kept.

But England had special perils for collections of books. Perhaps the first was the dissolution of the monasteries, 1535–9, during which many libraries were broken up, some to be sold overseas, some to be scattered at home, some to be handed over to bookbinders for use as scrap. Subsequent prohibition of illuminated service books and of traditional scholastic philosophy appeared to license destruction of books of other kinds, and the Oxford library finally sold its bookcases in the mid-sixteenth century, having virtually no further use for them. Already by the end of the sixteenth century historians and antiquaries were beginning to realize how much had been lost, and to reassemble what had survived. One such man, Sir Robert Cotton, built up a magnificent collection including much of what had survived among the Old and Middle English manuscripts. After his death in 1631, his library eventually passed into royal hands; and it was just a century later in 1731 that the collection was ravaged by a fire which destroyed much but not all: only a chance gust of wind preserved the unique *Beowulf* manuscript from more than relatively slight damage, but many others were not so lucky. At least Cotton's collection had been preserved from the iconoclastic uprisings of the seventeenth century which were already afoot when he died, and in which many further old books perished.

As a result of natural and violent events, then, the scare copies of medieval manuscripts were drastically thinned during the renaissance and eighteenth century, and when at last their systematic collection, preservation and study began in the nineteenth century, a meagre and probably unrepresentative store remained. For these disasters had taken no account of literary merit or popularity, and many a unique manuscript today was literally one copy away from extinction when fate spared it. Similarly, the proportions of survival tell us little. The intriguing *Sir Gawain and the Green Knight* remains to us in one manuscript, the humdrum *South English Legendary* in dozens. Is that because the popularity of *Sir Gawain* caused all but one manuscript to wear out, while the *Legendary* attracted no readers? Or rather because the popular *Legendary* kept copyists busy, while *Sir Gawain* went neglected and uncopied? It is probably, in any case, nothing to do with their themes, for *Sir Gawain* is part of a manuscript that also contains – in the same scribal hand and quite possibly by the same author – three long poems on wholly religious topics.

And so a modern edition of a medieval English poem or prose work is likely to be based on one or at best very few manuscripts that differ from each other in enigmatic ways, that were written long after the author's original copy and far from his control, and that survive a series of holocausts that operated arbitrarily without care or regard for literary quality. In most cases, the edition will have many important features of literary form – paragraphs, punctuation, sometimes even line-divisions in poetry – added by the editor in our own times. And of course the editor will have struggled with the accumulation of obscurities and outright errors that litter the surviving versions of the work. Lucky as the work may have been in its manuscript history, and learned as the editor may have been, such an edition cannot have the authority that a modern book, produced under the watchful eye of the author, always has. Present-day readers of a medieval work inherit all that the manuscript book meant for literature in the Middle Ages, and they see as through a glass, darkly.

Authorship, Anonymity and Audience

If we mean by 'authorship' that a work of literature is composed by some person or persons, then all works in medieval England had authors. But in fact we mean more than that: we mean that the composer of the work bears a stable relation with it, one which governs the authenticity of its text, the proceeds from its distribution, and its kinship with his other compositions. As we have now seen, most medieval works lack the first two of these attributes entirely; the third is usually seriously disturbed where it is not lacking. Authors had little control over the production and distribution of their works, and little proprietary interest in them in the sense that modern copyright laws provide for (see below under 'Originality'). They received no proceeds from their sale. And the relation between one work of an author and another is something we can know only when we know who he was and what he wrote.

For much of what was written in the English Middle Ages, we do not know anything of the sort. We have two names of Old English poets, and to one we can attribute positively four considerable works (see Cynewulf in Chapter 2); but to the other, Cædmon, we can attribute only a nine-line prayer. The rest of Old English poetry, including *Beowulf*, is anonymous and almost certain to remain so, given the conditions of its composition and preservation. For Old English prose we are better off, for although we have the names of only a very few writers once again, we can attribute with confidence a really substantial body of work to each. We also have the names of a number of the scholars who produced translations from Latin into Old English. And with these writers we have biographical details in addition to their names; Cynewulf and Cædmon are merely 'brand names' to us.

In the Middle English period we are, naturally, better off, but not immensely so. Brown and Robbins list 4,365 items in their Index of Middle English verse, but only about a hundred authors. Some few of the authors we know to have written more than one poem – Lydgate wrote many, and so did Chaucer – but the vast bulk of the poetry is anonymous. And again among the names are very many that are no more than names: the argument over whether one, three or four authors were responsible for the great *Piers Plowman* is not yet dead, although most scholars accept that all three versions are the work of William Langland alone. But we know almost nothing more about Langland than this, and so *Piers Plowman* is 'a poem nearly anonymous'. *Sir Gawain* is anonymous; so is the *South English Legendary*; the work which survives in most manuscripts, *The Pricke of Conscience*, which outnumbers the next most popular work in this respect (Chaucer's *Canterbury Tales*) by a factor of almost two, is only tentatively ascribed to Richard Rolle. And in prose, although we are once again on surer ground, matters are by no means really clear. The stability which a printed text gives to the relationship between the work and its author is lacking in medieval literature, and our knowledge of that relationship is seriously weakened, with important consequences for our critical approaches.

The other side of the relationship, that of the work with the audience – or of the author with the audience through the work – is also unstable. The question of audience is bound up with that of education and that of performance, and these are topics for discussion below; but it is not premature to say that, so far as we can tell, medieval audiences were 'audiences' in the true sense of the word far more often than we, with our almost exclusive experience of 'private' reading, can easily realize. The cost and scarcity of books played a great role in this. Of course we for our part are literally the audience of plays, sermons, and harangues, perhaps even of the occasional poetry reading; and of course there are references to private reading in medieval literature, such as Chaucer's reading of Ovid near the beginning of *The Book of the Duchess*, or of Macrobius in *The Parliament of Fowls*. But perhaps these are not to be taken as realistic description any more than are the fantastic dream scenes that follow in both poems; and in any case Chaucer was an extraordinarily studious man. In monasteries, where the production, conservation and study of books formed part of the religious régime, monks were read to not only in sermons, but also when they ate and often when they worked. They must have taken in a great deal of what we can broadly call literature that way. But when it came to private reading, a book was given to each monk on a fixed day each year, and he had to return it for another on the same day the next year – whether he had finished it or not. To the degree that the lay audience took their reading habits, as they took so many of their books, from the monastic centres, we can say that private reading was probably rarer than public performance through most of the English Middle Ages. Here again our critical approaches must be realistically in touch with the facts of the matter as far as we can ascertain them. We should at the same time equally avoid the assumption that the literary experience of an auditory then was similar to our own experience of declamations and poetry readings now. We depend heavily on private study of the written word because that is the way we most frequently encounter literature; but those who most frequently encountered it in the spoken word gained quite remarkable facility for maintaining their attention and for grasping matters of individual detail or overall structure: they were primarily 'audiate' rather than 'literate'.

Patronage

Under conditions where the practice of writing brought no direct remuneration, and where there was little social status for a man of intellect outside the Church, writers had either to hold other positions from which they might derive income or at least subsistence, or to obtain reward for their writing by way of a grant. The latter solution constituted literary patronage; the former was sometimes the result of political patronage. Some authors, like Chaucer, benefited from both.

Literary patronage was practised both by secular nobility, especially the crown, and by the ecclesiastical hierarchy, cardinals and bishops, usually in their role as secular powers. It extended chiefly to writers among the laity, because – as we have seen – it was not so necessary to those in the religious life; but the monk Lydgate had many patrons, including secular ones. The important thing to remember is that almost no one was a writer only; all depended on some other means of gaining a livelihood. Patronage, as such a means, was capricious and discontinuous – patrons changed their tastes and favours. Yet the patron was often the most important figure in the author's life: frequently he acted not only as the audience of a book, but in addition as its publisher by showing it to his friends and court circle or by otherwise arranging for its distribution. He gave it not only its currency, but often the weight of his reputation, and hence its authority. Therefore dedicatees can be thought of as patrons even when they gave no direct financial reward. It is hardly surprising that begging letters and other forms of supplication for patronage are common, and that the illustrations on medieval manuscripts often include one that shows the author giving his book to his patron.

In early England, a powerful man could give patronage by including the bard among his retainers bound to him by the oath of fealty; in return the bard shared the protection afforded to the retainers. Later patronage was more often in money, so that only the rich could indulge in it; but this enabled coteries of patrons, such as existed in East Anglia during the fifteenth century (and included the Pastons, the family whose letters form an important collection), to give their collective support to more than one writer. On such a basis 'schools' of literature, writers bound together in their practice by their relation to a patron or group of patrons, were created.

Thus the first effect of the system of patronage was that books were produced at all: they were costly things, as we have seen, and like costly things in any age, were often produced only to order. The patron provided the order. But the patron often provided the specification as well: the subject, which might be the patron himself, was one important specification, for much was made (especially by the writers) of the importance to reputation and lasting fame of his celebration in well-written verse. In the Middle Ages, concern with reputation was great, and this argument obviously had considerable weight. In some cases it must have lead to rather flattering writing, because more than one historian points out that he has written without benefit of patronage, and is therefore to be trusted.

Even when the subject was not the patron, the patron was likely to direct generally the choice of theme. Henry I's first queen, Matilda, encouraged the composition of scholarly works; his second queen, Adelaide, preferred romances. And this writing for an audience of one would have further influence on the choice of style (whether severe or ornate) and even vocabulary (whether full of borrowed French terms or of native English ones). The alliterative revival of northwest England in the fourteenth century, for example, may take its characteristic literary and linguistic form from the instructions of its patrons. Subject, style, and diction in English medieval literature, as well as the very existence of the work, are often the result of the system of patronage.

Education

It goes without saying that many important changes in the pattern of English education took place in the nine hundred years AD 600–1500, but among the schools at least we can distinguish two types and two fostering institutions. The monasteries kept schools for their own novices, and – beginning in the late Middle Ages – for the boys who, though not intending the monastic life, sang in their choirs. The former were as academic as the young monks could manage, and some of them were brilliant; but by no means all the monks attended them because not all had academic talent, and in any case it was a case of monks teaching monks who would go on in their turn to become teachers. These academic monastery schools were virtually never extended to include outsiders, and the trained monks themselves were not allowed by their rule to teach outside the monastery, so the monastic academic schools had little impact on academic patterns among the laity and the secular clergy (priests who belonged to no monastic order) except through the books they produced. The late medieval monastic schools for choirboys were not limited in this way, but on the other hand they were not so academic, and by their late appearance failed to have great influence.

It was not the monks but the secular clergy, especially those living in the precincts of the great cathedrals, who kept the other kinds of school and substantially formed the academic society of the English Middle Ages. Such schools were set up in the very first years after St. Augustine of Canterbury and his missionaries came from Rome in AD 597 to convert the Anglo-Saxons. They too ran schools for the pupils who needed to be trained for the choir in singing the daily services, but these 'song schools' – one is mentioned in Chaucer's *Prioress's Tale* – like their somewhat similar later monastic counterparts, had little academic framework. It was instead the clerical grammar schools that laid the basis for the instruction of most Englishmen who were to get any education at all before 1500. The grammar schools were formed by the cathedral chapters, and although later other bodies – private, municipal, guild, court, university – also set up such schools, it was usually with the authority granted through the bishops and others in power in the secular clergy: the punishment for setting up an unauthorized school, at least where the local church body took action against it, was excommunication. The teachers were almost always priests or others in lower orders.

That does not mean that the pupils at such schools were themselves intending a career in the Church, and the numbers of the laity who had undergone grammar school training were constantly on the increase throughout the English Middle Ages. So was the number of schools, aided by the pervasion of the country by the ecclesiastical establishment with a thoroughness that the secular establishment, the government, could not attempt to match. The earliest grammar schools included the one in York that flourished in the second half of the eighth century; its international fame resulted in the summons of its head, Alcuin, to the court of Charles the Great, there to set up a comparable school system on the Continent. By the end of the Middle Ages, grammar schools in England extended right down to town and even village level. Many of them were free, and those that were not charged very little and usually provided a number of places for pupils who could not pay even the modest fees. At the same time, they were not anything like modern state schools. Only the children of freemen were at all likely to enroll, and only then when they could be spared from family toil. In the early Middle Ages, we must not be mislead by the appearance of a plowman and other members of the rural proletariat in the grammar school Ælfric describes in his *Colloquy*; these are almost certainly freemen playing roles in a school exercise for the purpose of increasing their Latin vocabulary in a way that talking about wholly familiar things would not do. In the later Middle Ages, the serfs – those not freeborn – in effect constituted a valuable asset of the estates to which they were bound, and since a grammar school education gave a serf vastly increased mobility and hence an opportunity to free himself, it was an offence punishable – and punished – by very heavy fines for a serf's child to attend school without the permission of the estate owner.

As a result, literacy never reached a high level in England before 1500. It is difficult to estimate just what the level was among the laity at any given point, but a few anecdotes imply some notion. The Lollard John Claydon had, around 1400, a large number of books in English – we don't know how many – but was illiterate and had to depend on others to read them to him, a strange state of affairs when books were scarce and costly. In 1407 it was said that not three out of any twenty pilgrims could say their 'Our Father', 'Hail Mary', or Creed in any language, an accomplishment that the barest literacy would have secured. And in 1533, the learned and experienced Sir Thomas More thinks that not much more than half his countrymen could read, and this well into the sixteenth century, when it is during the fifteenth that literacy is held to have spread most rapidly. No doubt it did so; but the remark of Sir Thomas reminds us that its spread was from very sparse beginnings, and that through most of the English Middle Ages except for the final few years, anything in writing was closed to the largest proportion of those not clergy or monks.

Such was the position in the schools. The universities in England are not, in the main, an extension of the school system there, but an importation on the model of the continental universities which were already flourishing when Oxford and Cambridge are first reliably heard of in the late twelfth century. In fact one important effect of the foundation of the universities was the down-grading of the grammar schools, for the universities provide a context for some higher studies that had until then taken place in the schools. Since, unlike the schools, the universities were almost entirely composed of the clergy, this effect deprived the laity in the grammar schools of access to some subjects which might formerly have been available to them. The compensation was that increasingly after the foundation of the universities grammar school masters were expected to have the Master's degree, and consequently to be able to mediate the university background which would include subjects that did not formally appear in the school programme.

Our evidence is late, most of it from the period after the change brought about by the foundation of the universities. In theory the school programme would have included the seven liberal arts composed of the trivium (grammar, rhetoric, logic) and the quadrivium (astronomy, music, arithmetic, and geometry), but it is likely that the full set of seven was most often studied only in the monastery novice schools. Indeed the very creation of English grammar schools in the first place, around AD 600, was not to foster the liberal arts – far from it. Although the grammar school programme had something in common with earlier continental and even classical schools, the characteristic of the earliest English schools was that they taught Latin, the language of ecclesiastical culture, in a country where, as nowhere else in the former Roman Empire, Latin had never been fully established as a national language. The need to disseminate this vital skill brought the English grammar schools into being and guided their development throughout most of the Middle Ages.

Thus grammar schools were in the main schools of grammar, and Latin grammar at that; for some time they also included the other members of the trivium, rhetoric and logic, in one form or another, but these subjects were early taken over by the universities (where there existed also the advanced study of grammar). But we should not let our own idea of grammar, whatever that may be, stand in our minds for what occupied the English schoolboy day in and day out for years of his life. The two most common – indeed, virtually universal – textbooks of grammar for medieval schools make it clear that grammar meant not only the study of the parts of speech, syllabification, spelling, and the like, but also the study of the arts of language – figures of speech and so forth – that we should have encountered in universities under the heading of rhetoric, and the study of the use that classical and later Latin authors made of these. In fact grammar quite simply included the study of literature, save that instead of being literary history (like this volume) in which the age or the author provides the focus of interest and organizing scheme of the work, it was literary art, in which the figure (metaphor or the like) or mode (allegory, irony, etc.) or genre (history, epic, etc.) provided the focus and the famous authors of the past provided the models in which these subjects were studied. Hence there are many medieval tracts 'On the writing of prose and poetry', illustrated by copious quotations, but few or none which are critical studies of individual writers themselves.

On the other hand, the study of models implies imitation as one stage of learning one's grammar. And indeed we have not only the statutes that provide for the regular composition, presentation and criticism of Latin prose and poetry; we have in addition at least some examples of the anthologies which provided the models for this kind of practice. The apparent narrowness of the medieval school curriculum hides an intensive and progressive study of the Latin language and its literature, and we can take it for granted that almost all of the writers surveyed in the present-day university study of medieval English literature, and an ever-increasing pro-portion of their audience, had in common this cultivated, rigorous, and largely standardized (for the grammars were few and the anthologies limited in range) education, taught by broadly similar schools under the ecclesiastical authority through clerical teachers. The centralized core of literary knowledge, area of literary ex-pectation, and order of literary sensibility that this system implies, is again of paramount significance for critical approaches to English medieval literature.

Sources, Borrowing and 'Originality'

To repeat: we reckon those features in a work of literature the most valuable which set it apart from all others. So far we have been looking at some of the conditions of literary composition in the English Middle Ages that are common to the literature then com-posed and that set that literature apart in some degree from later English literature. But these common conditions are not the only way in which all medieval English literature is linked. It is further linked because the very ideas behind the opening sentence of this section were understood by medieval English writers and their audiences in a wholly different sense from the one in which we accept them. We praise novelty, originality, inventiveness, and the exercise of the individual imagination in a writer and in a work. Obviously when the physical conditions of book-production enforce literary conservatism, and the narrow unity of grammar school education specifies the range of shared literary experience, the place of literary *tradition* will be far greater than it is today. Participation in the tradition, not departure from it, will form an important part of the understanding between writer and audience. When, in addition, anonymity and doubtful attribution are characteristic of many works, it is affiliation with tradition rather than with the recognized *œuvre* of a known writer that will give a book its identity.

All of which is rather broad and subject to extreme modification: doubtful attribution, for example, often came about when an anonymous work was associated with the name of a writer who had achieved a firm individual reputation. Such reputations show us that medieval audiences did differentiate, and that tradition was by no means all-enveloping. But its role was nevertheless important to an extent we are not accustomed to, particularly through the influence of the Latin classics, the Bible, and continental vernacular literatures. It expressed itself in a wide – and uncataloguable – range of ways, but most notably through the prominent place of translation, imitation, and allusion, which we are apt to find 'unoriginal'.

The Latin classics – and, in the few places where they could be read, some of the Greek classics too – were the object of undimmed veneration and close study and imitation throughout the Middle Ages. The international language of the Church, the vehicle of medieval culture, was Latin, so the classics spoke in a familiar voice. When Aldhelm wrote his treatise *On Metrical Writing* around AD 700, it was the hexameter line of the great Roman poets he described, and he gave examples of the hexameter drawn indiscriminately from pagan and Christian writers: most prominent is Virgil. Pope Gregory the Great, one of the most influential writers of the Middle Ages and the man who initiated the conversion of England in 597, was regarded as an enemy of the pagan classics; yet even he wrote only that their excessive study should not be allowed to distract priestly students from religious reading. The classics, indeed, were held to be a proper source of wisdom for the Christian student even as healing drugs are obtained from the bodies of serpents, or as the Hebrews took for their own use the gold that belonged to their Egyptian captors. Such natural and scriptural analogies prepared the way for the educational system, and in particular for the grammar schools, mentioned above.

As a result, we owe many of our oldest and best texts of the Latin classics to the interest and care of the medieval Church, which saw to their copying and preservation. So too with the various sorts of 'new classics', books about classical forms or themes, that medieval writers added to the inheritance from ancient tradition: schoolbooks like Aldhelm's; adaptations like Chaucer's *Troilus and Criseyde*. To be sure translations from the Latin classics were not so common as translations from later Latin works such as Boethius' *Consolation of Philosophy*, perhaps because access to the pagan classics was thought fit only for scholars whose learning would arm them against undue influence of the original; but we must never lose sight of the state of literacy in medieval England, where few who could read were ignorant of Latin, so a straight translation of, say, Ovid, would be necessary only to an audience who were not only unlearned but positively unable to read. Hence the popularity of the translation-with-commentary form of the *Moralized Ovid* and similar works. Through one medium or another, the Latin classics were ubiquitous in medieval education and literature.

But statements like Bede's, that all the flowers of rhetoric and examples of fine writing that the classics can display are found in greater profusion and elegance in the Bible, are ubiquitous as well: the Bible was not only the prime source of the spiritual life in the Middle Ages, it was also – and by the same token – the literary masterpiece *par excellence*. The matter of its translation, like that of the classics, was in some times and places a delicate one, but portions of it were read out in the vernacular at the beginning of every one of the many sermons that all medieval people attended, often as frequently as twice a week; the Gospels at least were translated into Old English prose and very frequently thereafter, especially in the later Middle Ages; and numberless prose and verse paraphrases and condensations of all Biblical books were produced in every century. Medieval life, and hence medieval culture and medieval literature, was saturated with the Bible, and intimacy with its tales and teachings was commonplace.

Along with the Bible we must consider the vast body of commentaries on the Bible and of other theological literature that developed early, before the conversion of England, and remained a feature of the medieval literary scene until its close. These commentaries sought to give the historical and spiritual (and hence usually symbolic) meaning of every word, often every syllable, of Scripture. They were rarely composed in English and rarely translated into English, but they underlay most of the many sermons mentioned above, which were often no more than a patchwork of translations and adaptations from a number of commentators. This kind of eclecticism was possible because the commentaries themselves were highly traditional and unified in point of view, passing on from age to age in a kind of synthetic progression which collected the writings of former centuries without superseding them. As the Bible was the most important work of literature for the Middle Ages, so these commentaries – and the sermons made up of them – were the most important form of literary criticism. A knowledge of this form and of its traditional content must be expected in any member of a medieval audience not seriously troubled with drowsiness in church.

The continental literature of past and contemporary ages could not, of course, have the esteem of the Latin classics, the Bible, or the writings of the Fathers of the Church, save indirectly when – in common with similar English literature – they followed these models in translation, imitation or allusion. Thus part of the old English poem on *Genesis* is a reworking of scriptural and traditional material, but another and separate part is a translation of a continental Old Saxon poem on the same subject. And Chaucer, who had translated the early Christian writer Boethius, also translated the thirteenth-century French verse *Romance of the Rose*, itself founded on a complex literary tradition with important classical and scriptural sources, and wove paraphrases of Boethius into his *Knight's Tale*, itself an adaptation of a work by the Italian Boccaccio.

But it was in the more distant kinds of influence, imitation and allusion, that continental literary models had their greatest influence on the English Middle Ages. Here a list would be longer than this whole chapter without exhausting the subject; to remain with Chaucer alone, we may point to his debt to Italian and French poetic vocabulary and stanzaic and verse forms, notably the iambic pentameter line; to Italian and French sources like Boccaccio, Petrarch, Deschamps and Oton de Graunson; and to French literary genres like the dream vision and the fabliaux. The language, writers, and types of continental literature were in such ways the shaping influence for materials – whether native materials, classical, scriptural or other – as they took literary form on English soil.

Form and Genre

In the last paragraph above we have seen that Chaucer was a characteristic medieval writer when he borrowed from the famous poets of the Continent not only their themes but – in much the same way – their poetic vocabulary, stanzaic and verse forms, and literary genres, as though those technical or physical aspects of a poem's organization were the same sort of thing as the story it told. We know relatively little about the medieval view of the poem as a

'well-wrought urn' in which the artificial shaping is as important as
the clay, but there is every sign that medieval writers held such a
view.

The distinction between verse and prose itself is an elementary
example. Particularly in Latin, medieval writers – including
Aldhelm and Bede – often followed the earlier practice of producing two versions of the same work, one in prose and one in verse
(Aldhelm wrote his prose version first, but Bede started with the
poem). The implication is that the two versions made different sorts
of statement because the material had been worked up in different
forms; and the further implication is that form is part of the
statement, and that what a prose or verse work *tells* is only part of
what it *says*. Certainly many subjects were handled in verse that we
should now expect to see in prose, including not only history, but
also dietetics, chemistry, and moral theology. Certainly medieval
writers are keenly aware of the formal qualities of both kinds of
writing, as for example whether a work is entirely narrative, or in
dialogue, or mixed. And so, because verse is inherently more formal
than prose, verse was often preferred and underwent more considerable conscious literary development in both the Anglo-Saxon
and the later medieval periods: in both (for there was a considerable
break in the tradition of vernacular composition between the two) it
was only at the end of the period that prose gained any formal poise.

So it is in verse that the evidence for the importance of form and
genre is most abundant, although at the outset the choice of either
verse or prose is itself evidence of the same kind. We may note the
conscious organization of long poems into *fitts* (e.g., *Beowulf*) or
passus (*Piers Plowman*) in a chapter-like pattern. Sometimes other
sorts of organization, like the stanza, reach a high degree of formal
complexity, as – unexpectedly – in the dialogue of plays like those of
the Wakefield Master, where further formal unity is achieved by
intermittent concatenation, that is, the carrying-over of a word or
words from the end of one stanza to the beginning of the next.
Concatenation in turn becomes a 'global' feature of a poem like *Sir
Gawain and the Green Knight*, where the same phrases open and
close the work; and a 'local' feature of a poem like *Pearl*, where they
link each stanza with the next as well as the first with the last,
producing an unbroken chain. A different sort of concatenation
arises in poems like Chaucer's *Parliament of Fowls*, where at the end
of an experience the poet tells us that he decided to write a poem
about it: since the poem we have just finished is the one he decided
to commence, the decision at the end of the poem produces a link

with its beginning. All of these devices shown an awareness of the poem as an object, indeed as a topic in its discussion, which many medieval poems share but which does not appear to have been so common a feature of later verse.

Other formal features of the verse play a role in the 'meaning' of the poem. Both *Sir Gawain and the Green Knight* and *Pearl* are 101 stanzas long, and both show other symptoms of interest in numbers which make a pattern: in *Gawain* there is a long discussion of the five-times-five system in a symbolic pentangle, and the story of the poem involves three temptations, three hunts, and three blows – three-times-three; whereas in *Pearl* the organization of the verse line and the stanza produces a pattern of twelve-times-twelve, which alludes to the 144,000 virgins of *Revelations* 14.3 (who also appear in the narrative of the poem). Such features are especially clear in these two poems, but they exist in other ways in other works: the two poems by the Black Knight in Chaucer's *Book of the Duchess* are, of course, both by Chaucer, but they are set off from their verse surroundings by having many of the same rhyme-words in common with each other.

Another formal feature which is particularly appropriate to an age where the relationship betwen author and poem had not achieved its present-day stability, and where the scrutiny of the poem as a physical object was commonplace, was the interwoven signature. We know of Cynewulf the Old English poet only because in his four surviving poems he used special forms of the letters of the alphabet to spell some of the words toward the end of each poem, and taken together these letters spell his name (Aldhelm had used a somewhat different technique to 'sign' his opus *On Metrical Writing*). The practice was widespread: Chaucer's contemporaries Gower and Langland both demonstrably employed it in one way or another. Such an attribution was less likely to become lost in scribal copying than one appended to the beginning or end of the poem, but its success relied on a scrupulously careful reader who expected the technique. It is hence another evidence of the role of formal features in the understanding between writer and audience. But despite all this evidence, the study of medieval formalism or con-cern for structure in the sense of physical features independent of the 'meaning' or 'story' of the work (but not divorced from them) has only recently begun.

Another aspect of the medieval writer's reliance on form as a vehicle for meaning is the prominence given to genre in medieval works. Today we continue to recognize genre or 'kind' as one sort of literary category: we speak of novels, for example, and may mean thereby a work of prose fiction of medium or greater length, usually concentrating on the external activities of human beings. Sub-species of the novel would include the historical novel, the detective novel, the psychological novel, and so forth. But whereas the category 'novel' is *partly* one of form (the prose medium, the length), it also includes considerations of content or treatment (fiction, human characters); and the sub-species are almost entirely matters of treatment or content. The categories of medieval literature, on the other hand, although they have not been completely listed and defined, refer to *primarily* formal characteristics: the debate, the dream vision, the letter, the play, the short lyric, the complaint, the epic, the romance, and many more. Now whereas content and treatment can be mixed in a single work (it is easy to imagine a historical-psychological-detective novel, for example), the medieval categories do not lend themselves so much to mixing unless the work is of a special kind, the frame story with many stories incorporated, like the *Canterbury Tales*, to name only the most famous. Even here the genres do not mix: they are merely placed together in a fictional container, so to speak, and this sort of organization itself becomes a genre in its own right (cf. Boccaccio's *Decameron*). Such a polymorphous work, far from overcoming the categories of literary genre, demonstrates their importance. When, for example, Chaucer includes several minor genres in the course of his romance *Troilus and Criseyde*, the included forms bring with them all the connotations of their form: the vanity of the complaint against the rising sun, the sterility of the letter to the distant lover, the lopsidedness of the debate on moral responsibility. But Chaucer does not need to spell out these connotations. Because literary genres are classified by their formal properties, and because traditional forms have traditional associations, his employment of these genres gives immediate effect to his intended meaning without his explicit intervention.

This last point raises a subject that lies on the margin of form and genre, and that is the literary or fictional narrator in his relation to his work and to the poet himself. From *Beowulf* (lines 1–2: 'we have heard of the glory of the kings of the Spear-Danes in days of old') onward, story-tellers characterize their relationship with their material; often, as with Chaucer, Gower, Langland and others, they also appear in the story they are telling. But even when they do not, their stance in relation to the material is often artificial . . . they claim, for example, inability to interpret something they have seen, yet the episode is probably fictional and in any case the decision to write about it shows that the writer has already placed a meaning and a value on it. When they also take part in the episode, the 'point of view' in this technical sense becomes all the more complicated. Thus, to mention the most famous example, we have to do with three Chaucers in the *Canterbury Tales*: the pilgrim who was present at the Tabard Inn, and who told the *Tale of Sir Thopas* and the *Melibeus*; the character who now recounts and to some extent evaluates the events of those days; and the real poet, Chaucer the court servant and administrator. Here, and in different ways elsewhere, the variety of viewpoints gives a multi-dimensionality to the telling, which the practice of reading aloud to audiences doubtless heightened.

Some Special Conventions

Despite the promise of approaches to the formal features of medieval literature discussed above – the intrinsic characteristics of the work – recent criticism has paid special attention to other kinds of controlling conventions which, it is said, had an effect on the shaping of the work in terms of outside considerations – an 'extrinsic' effect. To a greater or lesser degree these approaches can point to a measure of critical success, and each of them has, in the light of this success, been encouraged to look on itself as the key-bearer to the closed books of medieval literature. Serious students cannot afford to neglect these recently developed methods; but they may be daunted by their erudition or technicality into accepting them uncritically or dismissing them in panic. They will need to read far more than the following few pages to come to terms with them, but an introduction may temper undue enthusiasm or wrath.

(a) Allegory

Allegory, 'saying one thing by means of another', is a technique frequent in English medieval literature: it is most obvious in personification allegory, where a character stands for a vice (such as Gluttony) or an institution (as in a dialogue between Church and Synagogue), or whatever. It certainly seems that some of the many dream-vision fantasies take that form in order to free the allegory from any restriction of versimilitude. And there are at least some signs that works like Chaucer's *Parliament of Fowls* or *Nun's Priest's Tale* are allegories in which the animals represent persons or classes in society – that they are secular allegories. Allegories continue in diminished use in modern literature: Orwell's *Animal Farm* has affinities with the two last-mentioned works of Chaucer.

But those who put the case for an allegorical interpretation of medieval literature go further than this. They point to the centrality of the Bible in medieval civilization, and remind us that the Bible was habitually studied through commentaries by everyone from the most venerable Fathers of the Church to the humblest village priest who followed in their footsteps. Such commentaries were based on a linked set of meanings for each person, place, thing or episode in the Bible, with anything from two to five levels. Thus the mention of Jerusalem would produce two 'literal' meanings, one linguistic (the name means 'vision of peace') and one geographical. In addition there were three symbolic meanings: the allegorical in the narrow sense (Jerusalem is the Church), the moral (Jerusalem is the soul in a state of grace), the timeless (the celestial Jerusalem). In some cases commentators argued for the simultaneous validity of these meanings – although they saw symbolic significance in the crossing of the Red Sea, for example, they did not deny that it was also literally true as history. But other times, especially when the system was made to apply to non-scriptural writings such as the Latin classics, they would insist that only the 'higher' levels of meaning were valid, and that the literal meaning was merely an attractive but false surface appearance that the wise reader would do well to remove and discard.

Such an attitude is part of a world-view that sees the whole of the temporal material cosmos as a symbolic intimation of eternal spiritual verities. As such it is not only a literary technique but a moral characteristic: those who read an allegory literally are reading with the eye of the flesh and show themselves to be irrational and carnal; those who read the same book symbolically are reading with the eye of the spirit and show themselves to prefer the reason over the body and the soul over the flesh.

Because the allegorical method is so fully developed in medieval writings, in applications to specific books both of the Bible and of the classics, and in general theoretical handbooks of literary method, and because it ties in so well with medieval civilization outside of literature alone, the modern school of allegorists have made large claims for it as the only valid approach to an understanding of medieval literature, including the vernacular, which at their most emphatic took the form that all serious medieval literature was written, and had to be read, along these lines. There is no doubt whatsoever that this approach has made better sense of some very enigmatic medieval works, and some unaccountable aspects of other works, than ever before; and some poems long thought to be on secular subjects really do seem now to be religious.

On the other hand, proponents are almost certainly claiming too much when they say they have the key to all medieval literature. Even the Bible was the subject of medieval commentaries on the literal level alone. Moreover, the difference between literary theory and literary practice needs to be observed *especially* when the theory has been so charged with moral implications that it is incapable of ready adaptation: that is, it is probable that many writers employed this technique only when it seemed convenient, even though they paid it lip-service all along. And finally, no matter what the former theory was, we have still to make our own assessments, and the allegorical approach can show us what a poem means without telling us anything about its value . . . bad poetry as well as good conforms to its rules. Thus the allegorists have given us a tool that is sometimes useful as a necessary preliminary to literary criticism, but it is not literary criticism itself.

(b) Courtly Love

'Courtly love' is the phrase some literary historians use to describe that relationship between a man and a woman which exists outside marriage (although the woman may well be married to someone else); in which the man is the social equal but at the service of the woman; in which secrecy is necessary and a good in itself; in which sexual union is a goal, but not an early incentive; and in which jealousy, anxiety, the pangs of separation, all serve to spice the clandestine passion. Because it makes heavy demands on those who take part in it, it is fitting only for those with refined manners and sensibilities – it is also called *fine amour*. In almost every one of its points it is irreconcilable with marriage between the partners, so it is by no means 'courtship'. It appears as the subject of a few treatises, notably the book *On Love* by Andreas Capellanus; it is referred to in other works of literature; and, without reference, it seems to provide the assumptions that motivate many other medieval love-stories. In its extreme, it becomes a kind of religion which employs the language of the Bible (especially the Song of Songs) and the forms of the liturgy to heighten the literary praise of the beloved.

Some modern students of this system or code believe that it was practised in courtly circles from the twelfth or thirteenth century onwards; that it was held in high respect as a thing finer than either mere promiscuity or the constraints of marriage; and that the literary evidence, which is the only evidence we have of it, reflects this practice and respect. Thus, for example, Troilus is acting according to his highest capacities in loving Criseyde as he does, and Chaucer's *Franklin's Tale* tells of the dilemmas such a high calling can bring about. Our understanding of much of medieval love-literature must depend on whether or not we agree that it is holding a flattering mirror up to life.

Recently doubts have arisen about whether such a thing as courtly love ever really existed outside of the pages of literature; and if it did not, what is its meaning as an exclusively literary phenomenon? The increasing number of scholars who have voiced these doubts now incline to believe that 'courtly love' was a literary vehicle for discussing human love, not infrequently a satirical *reductio ad absurdum* of certain emotional and carnal propensities common enough in every age of human society, and that in this solemnly exaggerated literary form it was intended to laugh to scorn the real-life victims of those propensities. Such a view puts the literature of courtly love in the same category as, for example, Swift's *Modest Proposal*, and goes a long way to restoring our belief in the sanity of medieval writers and courts.

(c) Oral Formulism

The doctrines of the recently developed school of oral formulism are roughly these: a poet who composes through the medium of writing makes his language as he goes along out of individual words; the unlettered poet, composing aloud rapidly and extempore in the physical presence of his audience, has to call on existing formulas of two or more words that fit his metre, because he cannot compose under those conditions from units as small as words. The formulas themselves are the accretion of time and the inheritance of many unknown, unlettered bards. Oral poetry is always fomulaic; written poetry never is. Thus the presence of formulas identifies a poem as oral. Under these conditions, an oral poem has no fixed text so long as it remains an oral poem (although it may be transcribed in one of its spontaneous versions by a 'folklorist'). In our sense, it isn't 'a' poem at all, even when transcribed, because it doesn't arise from one act of imaginative creation or from one poet, but from an accumulation of both. Criticism of such a transcription as if it were a poem in our sense of the word is wholly unrealistic, say those who hold this view, because both the individual words and the all-over structure are not matters of a single purposeful poetic act.

After a period when it was much in vogue, the oral-formulaic theory of literature, which had been widely applied to Old English and somewhat less to Middle English, has begun to attract some scepticism, even from a number of those who were first convinced of it. The criticisms may be simply listed:

1 The shift from 'an oral poem is formulaic' to 'a formulaic poem is oral' has never been substantiated.
2 There is no cultural connection between the ancient Greek and modern Yugoslavian practices on which the theory is based, and medieval English literature. The connection was based on the assumption mentioned under criticism (1) above.
3 What nature of collocation – verbal, syntactical, metrical or a combination – makes a formula has never been properly defined, although a definition has been attempted. As the identification of formulism depends on the identification of formulas, no adequate demonstrations of formulism can be said to exist.
4 External evidence for oral poetry in Old and Middle English has never distinguished between (a) spontaneous oral composition by an illiterate poet and (b) prepared recitation by a literate poet or performer for an audience whether literate or not. As we have seen, there is every reason to think that (b) was common, but it gives no support for (a).
5 The evidence of great literacy and even erudition among medieval English poets, like the evidence for great structural sophistication, as we have seen, is substantial; but it cannot co-exist with an oral formulaic theory of the origin of that poetry.

English Literature in Latin and French

Modern readers assume that language and nation – and hence literature and nation – go together. For England after the Middle Ages this assumption will occasion few omissions. But we may conclude this introductory chapter by taking note that the literature of England before the end of the Middle Ages was not always, often not even usually, in English. It was predominantly a Latin literature before the Norman Conquest, and following the Conquest it was Latin and even more French (more exactly, Anglo-Norman) until English gained dominance during the lifetime of Chaucer at the end of the fourteenth century.

The question of the reputation of English, particularly as a language for literary composition, is really one for a chapter of a later volume in this series, not for the first chapter of the first volume. Here it is sufficient to say how matters stood, not why. Before the Conquest, as we have seen, literacy and Latinity were substantially the same thing, and the Latin of England joined that of the Continent in skill and prestige: one of the works translated into Old English as a result of Alfred the Great's educational reform when a knowledge of Latin had diminished after Danish raids was Bede's *Ecclesiastical History*, which thereby stood on the shelf with the works of Gregory the Great and Boethius among others. And it is little wonder, for – even granting that the conditions for the survival of Anglo-Latin literature were more favourable than those for the survival of Old English – we are struck by the extent to which the Latin literature outnumbers the vernacular, so that, for example, Bede's *History* is larger than all the surviving Old English poetry put together, even though it is only one of his many works, and even though he is only one of many Anglo- Latin writers before the Conquest.

Latin continues in literary use after the Conquest, but the language of the conquerors soon takes its place alongside it and even vies with it for dominance. Much of this development is the result of the special conditions which obtained in Anglo-Norman courts, where the intimate society of a prosperous laity encouraged a special kind of literary circle. Anglo-Norman literature offers in many instances earlier examples of compositions that later became popular in France itself, so that far from being derivative, it was actually original and influential. Needless to say, it also influenced Middle English literature when, in its turn, that came to be written, and it provided the source of many Middle English translations. Even when the laity were no longer French, French writing continued in vogue because, like Latin, it had a substantial and reputable literature behind it. Gower, whom Chaucer knew and admired, wrote three great poems, one in Latin, one in French, and one in English. His work summarizes and in effect ends the era of English trilingual literary history, and reminds us that at no time before his death is it even broadly true to say that literature in the English language is the only literature of England.

The Study of Medieval English Literature

This chapter has concerned itself with features of medieval English literature that are unlike those of later English literature, features with which readers must come to terms if they are to grasp the work they are reading; and it has made some reference to the conditions that dictated such features. Of course modern readers will come across many passages that make a direct appeal to their experience and emotions: the words of the aging Hrothgar to the departing young hero Beowulf, the hectic dreams of the love-lorn Troilus, and many more. But if readers seize on easily available passages of this kind, and reject those whose form, style or content seems irredeemably remote, they will be engaging in an act of disintegration more serious than all the physical calamities that have befallen the texts of medieval English literature, an act that will make finally impossible any significant assessment or appreciation of this literature, even of its seemingly understandable passages. Historical criticism is not the ultimate point in the modern reading of old works, but it is always a fundamental first step.

However difficult and uncertain it may prove, however incomplete its outcome – for no age can ever wholly reconstitute an earlier one – it remains not only necessary but indeed worthwhile, for the literature of medieval England is large, rich, and excellent. Time has diminished its numbers and made remote its survivors, but it has not altered its quality. Some works are of importance because they were the heritage that made possible the literary triumphs of the next age: such are the lyrics and dramas among others. Some are valuable precisely because they did not have descendants, and are hence the last exemplars of their traditions: such are the heroic legends. In all there is the evidence of common human experience, the continuity of the human heart, understood from a point of view that sets a value on experience different from that of our own day, and that formulates the experience and evaluation in different literary modes.

Thus it is the very differentness of medieval English literature that most validates its study. It extends the range of our literary experience; it completes our understanding of literary history; and it provides distinctive views on and syntheses of human experience.

2

THE OLD ENGLISH PERIOD

J. E. Cross

1. The Fusion of Two Cultures

The coming of Christianity to England was the most important single factor for the creation and survival of the Old English literature which remains for us to read. On a practical level it brought writing in documents, and, for us, this means that every extant work passed through Christian hands, whether those of the creator of the work, or of the scribe who copied it. On a higher plane it revealed to the Anglo-Saxons the continental Christian culture, which had developed in the first six centuries after Christ, in the themes and arguments of the Christian exposition and debate. It also opened the way to the pre-Christian classical culture in which the great thinkers of Christianity were trained, men such as Augustine, Jerome, Ambrose and Gregory the Great. This education gave these men the knowledge of the classical ethic and example as well as the means of expressing them. As a result, influences both of content and style seeped from the classical via the Christian Latin to the Christian Old English works.

In many ways, and in a number of individual works, Anglo-Saxon England became a section of the vast area controlled by Christian thought, but it retained distinctiveness, particularly in its poetry, because of the tact of the Christian missions. Both the remembered names of the conversion were sensitive to the nature of the task, Gregory the Great who sent Roman Christianity with Augustine's little band to Kent in AD 597, and Aidan who brought Celtic Christianity at the request of King Oswald from Iona to Northumbria in AD 635. Gregory had advised Augustine to accept and adapt what he could from the pagans:

For there is no doubt that it is impossible to efface everything at once from their obdurate minds: because he who endeavours to ascend to the highest place, rises by degrees or steps, and not by leaps (Bede, *Ecclesiastical History* I, xxx), and Bede reports Aidan's criticism of a previous and abortive mission to Northumbria:

you were more severe to your unlearned hearers than you ought to have been and did not at first give them the milk of more easy doctrine till, being by degrees nourished with the word of God, they should be capable of greater perfection (Bede, *Ecclesiastical History* III, v).

Such statements as these encouraged the envelopment within Anglo-Saxon Christianity of those aspects of pre-Christian ethic which did not oppose the Christian ideal. In *The Seafarer*, for example, the result of good deeds can still be the pagan (and Old Testament) reward of a good reputation after death, but also the attainment of the heavenly glory when the deeds are directed against the devil. Some of the accommodation obviously took a long time. Feuding, for example, which arose from the demand of a death for a death, existed long in Christian England. Alcuin in AD 797 also reproved the remembrance of pagan heroes with his rebuke to the monks at Lindisfarne who had been eagerly listening to heroic song rather than the wisdom of the faith. Little is more dangerous to a growing Christianity than the fond remembrance of and, perhaps, identification with, heroes who live well by secular standards, but without the faith. But usually accommodation took place with some interesting results in the content of Old English poems as we shall see a little later. To judge from the literature, the themes of Christian ethic presented to the English were suited to their harsh and sombre existence on earth. In homily and poetry the cry is often 'Avoid vice, repent, your time is near' – and much of the literature emphasizes the transience and brevity of human life, in echo surely of a reality where man had few aids to a peaceful and long life and where Nature seemed usually to be a mighty opponent. Much of the didactic literature speaks of dangers, of the horror of hell, of the fear at Judgment, for those whose virtue does not outweigh their vice, and of the devil ever ready to ensnare. Struggle is a recurring theme – between men and men, nation and nation, between human and inhuman powers who are at times conceived of in the form of humans as are Grendel and his mother, the monsters in *Beowulf*. These emphases however offer a suitable religion to this people, and there is much to be said for calling the Old English poets particularly 'the doom and gloom boys'.

But adaptation was not needed for pre-Christian matters which had no relationship with religious faith, and some of these could remain. The most significant was the Old English poetic manner, which was of Germanic origin and existed in the other languages of the Germanic group, Old Icelandic, Old Saxon (Continental Saxon) and Old High German. As a result many poems demonstrate Christian dogma and moral theme in the Germanic poetic line, and use stylistic features, which are similar to those in the other Germanic literatures, as well as rhetorical figures which originated in pre-Christian Latin. When we realize too that Christian themes themselves were also accommodated to what may be called the Anglo-Saxon secular ethic, we can see that Old English poetry is in many ways a distinctive body of literature within English literature as a whole.

2. *Features of Poetic Style*

The basic features of poetic style remained in Old English poetry from the poem which, by known date, is the earliest, Cædmon's *Hymn* or *Song of Creation* (between AD 657 and AD 680) to the one which, by known date, is the latest, a piece of verse called *Durham*, which was written in the early years of the twelfth century. This is a considerable period of time, when it is clear that Old English poets thought it poetic to write in a way that their ancestors had, and the earlier Old English poets presumably thought it correct to *write* as their Continental ancestors had *spoken* verse. As early as the fourth or fifth century AD, the runic inscription on the golden horn of Gallehus is carved:

Ek HlewagastiR HoltijaR   horna tawido
                    I, Hlewigast, Holt's son,   made (this) horn

and reveals the same kind of poetic line as the first line of *Durham*:

Is ðeos burch breome   geond Breotenrice
                 This town is famed   throughout Britain

The form of these lines is based on a fact of the language that the main stress fell on the root-syllable of the word, which, in most cases, would be the first syllable. This is understandable since the root-syllable indicated the meaning of the word; and the inflections, which modified that meaning, were unstressed. Since the main stress (and meaning) normally fall on the initial syllable the linking factor in verse was initial rhyme or alliteration.

    The two lines above are printed with a caesura between the two halves (although all the poetry is copied as prose in the manuscripts) because the half-line has been recognized as the unit of verse.

Syllabic patterns repeat themselves in the half-line, but the pattern of the first half appears to have little or no effect on that of the second, so that regular patterning of the whole line is not seen. The two half-lines are linked by alliteration to form the normal poetic line, although in some mnemonic jingles, such as *Hit becwæð*, the verses are not connected by alliteration. If we scan a few lines of *Beowulf*, gaining some help from a literal translation, the major points about stress and alliteration can be demonstrated. The symbols normally used are: main (or primary) stress (´); secondary stress (ˋ); lack of stress (×); vowel-length (-).

wæs se grimma gæst   Grendel haten,   (102)

mære mearcstapa,   se þe moras heold,

fen ond fæsten;   fifelcynnes eard

wonsæli wer   weardode hwile   (105)

siþðan him Scyppend   forscrifen hæfde

in Caines cynne.   þone cwealm gewræc

ece Drihten   þæs þe he Abel slog.   (108)

(The grim spirit was called Grendel, a well-known patroller of the marches, who held the moors, the fen and fastness; the unblessed man lived for a time in the home of the monster-race after the Creator had condemned them in the kin of Cain. The eternal Lord avenged the murder by which he killed Abel.)

We can see that each whole line is linked by alliteration and that the alliterating syllable in the second half-line (also called the *off*-verse or *b*-verse) is the nearest stressed syllable to the caesura, naturally, since this is the linking device. Alliteration is usually of consonantal sound to itself, but l.108 informs us that any vowel alliterates with any other vowel, and l.106 suggests that there were limitations within consonantal alliteration. In the poetry we find that each of the paired consonants *sc*, *sp*, *st* alliterates with itself alone. Lines 106 and 108 also tell us that there need be only one alliterating syllable in each half-line, although usually there were two in the first half-line (also called the *on*-verse or *a*-verse). In our passage we have no extra ornamentation such as internal rhyme at the end of the half-lines, or extended lines, but such occur on occasions, and are lucidly discussed by J. R. R. Tolkien in the introduction to the translation of *Beowulf* by J. R. Clark Hall, revised by C. L. Wrenn (London, 1950).

Main (primary) stress falls on the root-syllables of what Bernard Shaw once called 'the words of power', nouns, adjectives and then verbs, which indicate the main meaning of a phrase, and then, emphatically-used pronouns and adverbs. In line 106 it is likely that *him*, the object of the verb, had a main stress. Some stress (secondary) falls on the elements of compounds which could stand alone as words e.g. *meárcstàpă* (boundary-stepper). One different case is *wéardòde*, l.105 (inhabited), which is a verb inflected as a past tense third person singular, but it has been found that verbs of this kind (Class II weak verbs in the grammars) should have a secondary stress on their penultimate syllable. The number of unstressed syllables in each measure is variable, but this is not disconcerting to those who have enjoyed the metrical experiments of Gerard Manley Hopkins, and it means that narrative poets had some freedom in the creation of rhythmic lines.

Normally, readers who have an ear for poetic rhythm and are aided by a literal translation which gives the sense, can recognize stress, since they are also helped in this by the alliteration; but the actual reading or chanting of the verses has caused debate because deductions have to be made from the poetry itself at a time-lag of a millennium. In *Beowulf* (89–90) and in *Widsith* (103–5) the minstrel (*scop*) sings with harp accompaniment; so, presumably, did the poet Cædmon (see below) but these comments are tantalizing. No one says how the harp was used. Nevertheless J. C. Pope has theorized brilliantly (*The Rhythm of Beowulf*, New Haven, revised edition, 1966) about the recitation of Old English verse, and it seems likely that we should approximate to a chant which emphasizes the stressed syllables when reading, as presumably, King Alfred's mother did when, according to Asser, she read poetry to her son.

At a first reading Old English poetry appears prolix and cumbersome (especially if read in modern translation) yet also strange and exciting. The excitement is caused by the prevalence of poetic alternatives. These included one-word synonyms some of which certainly were metaphors when first used and may carry connotations of their origin, e.g. *freca* ('wolf') for a 'warrior', but also *hælep* ('hero'), *eorl* ('nobleman'), *wiga* ('fighter') can be used as simple alternatives for *guma* ('man'). There were also equivalents in compound words or phrases which were originally metaphors or condensed similes, e.g. *beaduleoma*, literally 'battle-light', which is

used as an alternative for 'sword', but it says in one word that a sword
is, or is like, a light in battle. Other examples include *wælwulf*
(slaughter-wolf =warrior), *merehengest* (sea-stallion=ship), *fugles
wynn* (joy of a bird=feather). Usually the referent is clearly indicated
by the elements of the compound and in context, and the Old English
poetic fancy does not fly so far as to confuse as does that of the skald
in some Icelandic poetry where the reader needs the mental agility of
a crossword fanatic to trace the referent. Other compounds or
phrases are not metaphorical but describe an object in terms of an
attribute, e.g. *beaga brytta*, literally 'distributor of rings', which
presents a leader in terms of his generosity, an idea which is also
expressed by *goldwine*, 'gold-friend'. Such compounds and taut
phrases aid a poet in his continual desire for condensation, and allow
him to add dimensions in the alternatives.

When used thoughtfully, these stylistic features can produce a
tightly-made yet richly-suggestive and subtle poetry, but even here a
caveat must be given that these features, indeed the very words or
phrases, are used so often by poets that they can lose their pictorial or
descriptive content and become merely alternative words for the object.
Obviously, in such cases, the metaphors are dead and the style less
colourful. A clear case of this must be Cynewulf's creation of the
spiritual journey to Heaven in the commonplace image of a voyage over
the sea (in *Christ II, The Ascension Poem*). This concludes in the hope that
God may grant grace:

> þæt we oncnawan magun   ofer ceoles bord
> hwær we sælan sceolon   sundhengestas
> ealde yðmearas   ancrum fæste.   (861–63)

(That we can understand (even) from the vessel's side where we must
tie up the stallions of the sound, the ancient mares of the wave, fast by
the anchor.)

It is unlikely that Cynewulf is visualizing the image of the ships as
horses prancing, and even more unlikely that he would mix his
metaphors by mooring horses to an anchor. I press this to a ludicrous
point of pedantry to emphasize that every seemingly pictorial word or
compound should be considered in its context.

Variation (or the parallel phrase) is the last major feature of the
Old English poetic style that needs description. It may well have
originally been a feature of the pre-Christian oral poetry, since
repetition of an idea is more necessary for a listening than a reading
public, and, even now, is more often a trait of an orator than a
writer. The figure leads to prolixity of expression, sometimes poor

expression, when the word or phrase calls up another by reflex action to the memory without regard to presentation of thought, as in the case of some verbal sequences in Dylan Thomas's weaker poems, and as in *The Battle of Brunanburh* (ll. 13-17). Here the poet is concerned merely to say that the battle raged all day, but the pressure of variant phrases in his memory produces:

siðþan sunne up
on morgentid,   mære tungol,
glad ofer grundas,   godes condel beorht,
eces drihtnes,   oð sio æþele gesceaft
sah to setle.

(After the sun, the famed star, the bright candle of God, the eternal Lord, glided up over the lands in the morning until the noble creation sank to rest.) I fear that God enters this poem merely because the sun is His bright candle. But in the hands of more controlled writers the stylistic device can take the thought forward almost imperceptibly, since variation often extends the initial concept. A minor example may be the description of Beowulf's first approach to the land of the Danes: 'the voyagers saw the land, the sea-cliffs glisten, towering hills, great headlands' (221–23), where the progression of variants gives the impression of movement towards land, first the view from a distance, then the distinguishing of the natural features as the boat moves inshore. Even in simpler use variation can emphasize the dominant concepts (by the repetition), and in a number of cases some technical virtuosity is revealed.

Other devices such as simile (even extended simile) and personification, *paronomasia* (puns) (especially in *The Riddles*) are recognizable as in later poetry, but two figures to which the Anglo-Saxon reaction was probably different from ours is that of *litotes* (negative statement) and *meiosis* (understatement). The figures are now often ones of wry irony and humour. In Old English they may or may not be ironical but they are never humorous, and often are direct statements without undertones. In *The Battle of Maldon*, for example, when the poet comments on the English leader's action in allowing the Vikings to cross the river that he 'allowed too much land to the hateful people' (l.90), he means that Byrhtnoth should not have allowed them to cross; and when the *Beowulf* poet says of Beowulf's return-journey to his home 'in no way did the wind impede the wave-floater from her voyage over the waves' (ll.1907–8), he obviously does not regard this as a cumbersome expression of 'the wind urged the ship etc.', as we might today.

Such different traditions of poetic expression are soon felt by sensitive readers who may judge whether a poet is succeeding in what he is attempting to do.

The language of the poetry is the language of the manuscripts which contain it, not, necessarily, of the poets who wrote it, and this is an obstacle to a critic who can often be helped in his reading by accurate dating and placing of a poem. Almost all the extant poetry is preserved in four manuscripts: *Cotton Vitellius A XV* (also called *The Beowulf MS*) in the British Museum; *Junius XI* (popularly called *The Junius MS*) in the Bodleian Library, Oxford; *The Exeter Book* in the Chapter Library of Exeter Cathedral; *The Vercelli Book*, a codex of homilies and poems, which, at some time during the Middle Ages, was taken to the cathedral at Vercelli, Italy, and now remains there. They are all written in a dialect which is mainly Late West Saxon and all date from about AD 1000, so that we must assume that the poems are at removes of copying from their first writing. Earlier scholars thought that they could determine the provenance and date of some poems from certain features of language which are not common in West Saxon, but it is now accepted that a poetic language existed which included non-West-Saxon features, and in which all poets wrote. On rare occasions individual poems can be dated on other grounds, and we certainly have two named poets, Cynewulf, who worked his signature in runic letters within the text of four poems, and Cædmon, whom Bede describes. But the other poetry is anonymous, and we should assume that each poem was written by a different author. Except within very broad limits, and then debatably, this remaining poetry is undatable and unplaceable.

3. *Cædmon and Scriptural Poetry*

Much verse, some of it poor poetry, was stimulated by the reading or hearing of Scripture, and also by the knowledge of themes and stories which were created to explain or extend scriptural statement. According to Bede (*Eccles. Hist.* IV, xxiv) the simple cowherd Cædmon, who is our first named poet, created a body of such verse on topics listed as the creation of the world and of man, all the history of Genesis, the exodus, the incarnation, passion, resurrection and ascension of Christ, the coming of the Holy Ghost, the preaching of the apostles and the future judgment. Poems are extant in Old English which refer to, or describe, all these subjects but only one, the nine-line *Song of Creation*, is now assigned to Cædmon and this attribution goes with Bede's account of its composition. Nevertheless this poem is important historically since Cædmon did what others might have done but apparently did later

– he presented a Christian theme in the diction and style of Germanic poetry and so created a tradition. The happening is a miracle to Bede who tells the story as one of a prophetic utterance, how Cædmon left the company of his fellows because he could not entertain them by singing to the harp when it was his turn, how an angel appeared to him in his sleep and willed him to sing about the Creation, and how, in the morning, Cædmon remembered his dream-composition and spoke poetically:

Now we must praise the Guardian of the heavenly kingdom (*heofonrices Weard*), the power of the Creator (*Meotod*) and the thoughts of His mind (*modgeþonc*), the work of the Father of Glory (*Wuldorfæder*) as He, the Eternal Lord, established the beginning of every wonder. He first created heaven as a roof for the children of earth, the holy Creator (*Scyppend*). The Guardian of mankind (*monncynnes Weard*), the Eternal Lord, afterwards established the world (*middangeard* 'middle-enclosure') for men on earth, the Lord Almighty (*Frea ælmihtig*).

To us these lines are simple but touching. Technically they fulfil all basic demands, although incomplete control is suggested in some unemphatic repetitions, as if the poet seized on e.g. *Ece Drihten* (Eternal Lord) because the phrase was a metrical half-line and made a sensible statement. But the verses attest the important evolution in the adaptation of secular concepts and Germanic words to the presentation of the Deity and His works. Latin Christian writers had also adapted concepts and words of pre-Christian mythology and cosmology in their descriptions of God and his world, but, according to Bede, no one had done it before Cædmon in English. Bede had said: 'others after him attempted to compose religious poems' but 'none could ever compare with him because he did not learn the art of poetry from men but from God'. Some modern readers, like Bede, no doubt moved by the circumstances of composition and the nature of the subject, rate the poem highly, but we all recognize that Cædmon is 'the bright morning-star of our literature'.

The Junius MS contains poems on the Cædmonian type of subjects, on a section of Genesis, on an episode of Exodus, and on a part of Daniel, all, unfortunately, having textual difficulties which impede a full critical assessment. Manuscript pages are missing at irregular intervals and affect the progress of all the poems. Nor can we be certain that the three poems should end where the manuscript indicates, although they all appear to have their original beginnings. Other complictions affect the poems individually.

Genesis has an insertion at lines 235–851 which is so different in style and some diction from any other Old English poetry that it is recognized as an anglicization of a Continental Saxon poem and is now called *Genesis B* or *The Later Genesis*, while the remaining sections are named *Genesis A* or *The Earlier Genesis*. Pages are missing at the beginning of *Genesis B*, but *Genesis A* l.234 mentions the fourth river of Paradise (Gen. II, 14), and *Genesis B* begins with God's command not to eat the forbidden fruit (Gen. II, 16–17). *Genesis B* ends with the fallen Adam covering his nakedness (Gen. III, 7) and *Genesis A* continues immediately with Adam hiding from God (Gen. III, 8). Obviously the insertion was neat, but the poems are of very different quality, tone and attitude.

Genesis A, technically a very competent sequence of verse, undoubtedly fulfilled a useful function in its day of presenting scriptural narrative in vernacular poetry, in this case from the beginning up to and including Abraham's intended sacrifice of Isaac (Gen. XXII). Omissions of scriptural facts which might need devious explanation, such as Sarah's complaint that God had made her a figure of scorn in her child-bearing (Gen. XXI, 6–7), avoidance of complications by circumlocution, such as the references to circumcision under the name of 'the sign of victory', and some few anticipations, emphasize the poet's aim to present what Scripture his audience could comprehend. But the additions to the events of the Bible in this poem should not be regarded as major elaboration on Scripture. In medieval times, a body of material had accumulated in Hexameral writings, homilies, tracts and verse-by-verse explanation of the text, which was really taken as the story of Scripture, and which was intimately associated with the Biblical text in the medieval mind. It was compounded of scientific lore, of history, of speculation about motive and reasons for the actions and thoughts, of information reaching back to Rabbinic stories, apocryphal legend and early history, and included, on occasions, spiritual interpretations as, for example, that the Ark typifies the Church of the faithful on the sea of the world. Our poet gives no clear hint of interest in spiritual interpretation but he often explains 'literally' or 'historically', in no way to modify the basic narrative but merely to make it more acceptable. At times this is presented in direct comment, e.g. the reason why the raven did not return to Noah – 'it perched on the floating corpses' – which is rationalistic, and commonplace in Hexameral writings; at times by substitution, which also illustrates the close connexion between commentary and Scripture, most notably where, in place of the scriptural 'sons of God' and 'daughters of men' (Gen. VI, 2, 4) whose union produced the 'giants' who were later destroyed by the Flood, our poet speaks of the 'sons of Seth' and the 'daughters of Cain'. The *Beowulf* poet also uses this tradition, when he identifies his giant-monsters as descendants of Cain and adds a dimension to their characters. As a teacher the *Genesis A* poet will moralize, effectively in the image of a tree bearing deadly fruit of sins when pointing out the growth of evil in the world after the murder of Abel, but sometimes in a more pedestrian way by direct comment e.g.: 'Never need any man lack shelter . . . who will serve Him in thought and deed until death', a statement attached to the story of God's support for Abraham.

Both his technical competence and his thought for his audience lead him to present non-scriptural detail to tickle the fancy of the listeners in some purple passages such as the battle of the five kings (Gen. XIV). A producer of 'film-epics' would seize on the scriptural detail of the site – 'the woodland vale had many pits of slime' (Gen. XIV, 10), but our poet creates a different battle in well-known terms and themes of convention:

Then the fierce armies came together – loud were the spears. The black bird, dewy-feathered, sang in hope of carrion . . . There was hard hand-play, exchange of spears, great din of war, loud tumult of battle. From their sheaths men snatched the keen-edged ringed swords with their hands. There buying of battle was easily done for the man who before had not gained his fill of war (1982–95).

The scavenger, the noise, the clash of men appear in similar diction on other poetic battlefields. In this poem, other scenes of violence, the Flood and the destruction of Sodom and Gomorrah, are also much extended in similar diction, suggesting that the memory, not the imagination, was excited by a familiar topic since there would be precedent in secular literature for descriptions of turbulence on sea and land. Even in this, however, the poet entices his audience to accept Old Testament history within their own imagination, since the basic facts of the events are scriptural. In one difficult case we are struck by his competence in presenting an unusual fact within Old English verse, when the Ark remains an ark on an Anglo-Saxon poetic sea (1302 seq.). An earlier critic, probably influenced by an illustration in this manuscript of the Ark as a superstructure on a recognizable ship, described the Ark in the poem as driving 'through stormy ocean surges as a ship flinging back from her bows the spray of Northumbrian waves', but the terminology of the poem is carefully chosen, where possible, to stress the difference.

Admittedly *scip* ('ship'), *lid* ('ship') and *fær* (etymologically something in which a journey is made) are used, and would be difficult to avoid in alliterative verse where nouns often carry the stress, but they are not so common as the loan-word *earc* ('ark'). Other words or phrases could apply to both ship and ark, e.g. *nægledbord* ('nailed board'), *wægbord* ('wave-board'), but many words could not refer to a real Anglo-Saxon ship, and emphasize the peculiar nature of the Ark which contains many beings. It is a *hof* ('a court, a house'), *merehus micel* ('mighty sea-house'), *mereciest* ('sea-chest'), *geofonhusa mæst* ('greatest of ocean-houses'), *sundreced* ('sea-home'), *holmærna mæst* ('greatest of sea-halls'). All of these latter compounds occur only in this passage, and were obviously chosen, perhaps even specially coined, to describe this unique object. Even the inhabitants of the Ark do not sail the vessel, but are voyagers in it; and the sea foams, but not round a prow.

If verse can be functional, this poem is little more than that, but high competence is brought to the task of presenting Scripture as the poet knew it, and as the audience expected it. To us, apart from its antiquarian interest, the poem has impact where Scripture plus commentary impress, or where poetic diction may excite, but is arid (as in the book of the generation of Adam, Gen. V) where Scripture is dull.

Genesis B has vitality and power deriving from its strong but controlled characterization of Satan in vigorous speech, and has humanity which is far removed from the ascetic comment of theologians in its muted sympathy for Adam and Eve. Although only an episode from a longer poem, it gains a unity in the causative link between the two main events, the legendary Fall of the Angels and the scriptural Fall of Man, and also in the simple but effective contrast between light and dark throughout the poem, which has symbolic connotation as well as physical application. As is normal in this kind of literature, this poet inserts moralizations with didactic intent but they seem not to intrude, partly because of the intense emotion aroused by the visualization of Satan where moral ejaculations are not out of place, partly because of concern with the motivations of humans where the moralizations appear to be part of the explanation.

The episode begins with God distinguishing the forbidden fruit, but the poet regresses immediately to the fall of Lucifer. His name 'light-bearing' obviously suggests the source of his pride, his angelic beauty. Lucifer had been made so *hwit* ('bright') that he was like the stars, but he *himself* 'said that his body was fair and bright', vanity leading to pride. Instead of gratitude to his Creator for the gift he offers disobedience. In the manner of a Germanic princeling he considers his own following, thinks them physically and numerically stronger than his overlord's, and states his frustration in passionate speech whose emotion bursts through the poetic rhythms:

'Why should I slave? . . . There's no need for me to have a master' (278–9). 'Strong retainers stand by me . . . who will not fail me in the struggle' (284–5).

But there is no struggle against the Almighty, only punishment, as Lucifer falls headlong to the bottom of hell, 'devoid of light' (333). His pride remains, and now, as Satan (345), he plots vengeance against God who 'has cut us off from the light' (394), unlike man, in moralizing contrast later, who offers humility and penitence after his fall. But Satan is bound in hell. '*Wa la!*' he shouts in torment of frustration, not self-pity, 'if I had the power of my hands and could get out for an hour – a winter-hour – then, with this band, I—', 'but iron bands lie about me' (368–71). Even in translation the vigour of the bitterness is evident in the pride of the man, for he is a man, not devil, acting manfully and intelligibly. His vengeance is to take Adam and Eve from God, and Satan has to persuade a follower to perform the task, with a reminder and a promise which are Germanic, but here, ironic. Forgetting his own disloyalty he asks for service in return for gifts previously made, and unconscious of his own changed condition, he offers as reward the seat next to him in Hell. A retainer volunteers to go to Eden. Here the tempo lessens as the emotion subsides when the poet narrates the persuasion of man to evil. Scripture on the temptation is bare and laconic (Gen. III, 1–7), but the poet draws on tradition known in Latin Christian poetry and Rabbinic writings which consider the motivation of Adam and Eve, thus to create recognizable human beings who are intellectually deceived and deserving of sympathy. The serpent, coiled round the tree of death 'black, dark, full of shadows' (477–8), begins to tempt Adam by claiming to be a messenger of God, bringing a countermand to the order not to eat the forbidden fruit. Adam stands solidly in suspicion of the messenger and puzzlement at the new command, but the rejection gives the tempter levers for the seduction of Eve, helpmeet of Adam and mother of the living. Evil is first threatened on all her descendants if she does not obey, and God's vengeance may be averted from her husband if she does. Eve is seduced by these and other promises, 'since God has created her mind the weaker' (590–1), yet at no point from self-love. She eats, and is shown a 'sign' of the tempter's power (presumably from God, a token which Adam had demanded), the gift of seeing (cf. Gen. III, 7) but supernaturally, and 'the heaven and earth appeared to her more radiant' (*hwitre*, 603). 'A light shines about you' (614), says the fiend, 'tell Adam' that 'I will give him this light' (619). Selflessly, she pleads all day 'with good intent' of regaining God's favour, showing the 'sign' and such 'pledge of truth' to Adam that he too disobeys God. But the sign is 'faithless', the change is made: 'From the woman he took death and hell, although it did not bear these names, but bore the name of fruit' (717–9). The fiend exults, leaving Eve mourning and deceived, 'she saw the light disappear which he had showed her through a faithless sign' (772–4), and the episode ends with a reproach from Adam and preparation for atonement from both.

The speeches which envelop this summary create a most moving situation, but the outline can only hint at the movement in the temptation scene, the sense of structure, the balance and contrast between the two Falls, indeed, the powerful visualization of the whole episode. So imaginative is the conception of the events that some think Milton was stimulated by the poem. Historically this could have been so but the opinion remains a speculation in literary history.

Christ and Satan, in *The Junius MS*, has a different conception of Satan, adds a dimension to hell, and is a very different poem from either *Genesis A* or *B*. Firmly based on theological orthodoxy and acceptable legend, the poem assumes knowledge of the major themes of Scripture and Christian tradition by the audience since it ranges widely through many topics unchronologically (and with backward and forward references to others), beginning with the creation of the world and ending with the temptation in the wilderness. All the major events are related to the power of Christ and the defeat of Satan. The moral is obvious but this does not prevent the poet preaching little homilies directly to his listeners. In the poem this devil however is a dejected being, suffering both the punishments in hell which were distinguished by the old theologians, the *poena damni* (the punishment of loss) and the *poena sensus* (the positive punishments). Without sympathy and with moral aim the poet details the loss in a series of imaginative monologues, none more effective than through the images of sense in:

Alas that I am wholly deprived of eternal joy, that I cannot lay hold on heaven with my hands, nor can I look up with my eyes, nor with my ears shall I ever hear the ringing sound of the trumpet (167–71).

Now for Satan is eternal exile, torture, and diminished power in the devil's rights only to take lost souls (267–8). Even some of his captives are taken when the Lord harrows hell and leads the patriarchs home, and at the temptation, which forms a fitting conculsion to this story, Christ adds to the scriptural 'Get thee behind me!' by sending Satan back to measure the greatness of hell that he may realize the power of Him who created everything.

This is a discursive poem, with touches of imagination, and firm moral aim, in which teaching is done through the situation not through characterization.

A slight connexion of subject matter allowed the discussion of *Christ and Satan*, but manner and method link *Daniel* and *Genesis A*. *Daniel* relies largely on Scripture, in this case Daniel I–V, for its progress, but for one section (362–408) the poet turned to an intermediary, the *Hymnum Trium Puerorum* (Song of the Three Children), a canticle of the Church from the fourth century, which itself is based on Daniel III, 57–88, yet which varies slightly but significantly from the Bible. Wherever the *Hymnum* differs from the Vulgate text of Scripture, the poem agrees with the hymn. A variant version of certain parts of *Daniel* exists in the fragmentary poem *Azarias* in *The Exeter Book*, and scholars have been tempted, by inartistic repetitions of idea in *Daniel* and by seeming difference in style between those sections of *Daniel* which correspond to *Azarias* and the remainder of *Daniel*, to suggest that an earlier version of our extant *Azarias* was interpolated within *Daniel*. But the argument rests on debatable grounds and, with all its faults and emphases, *Daniel* should be regarded as one poem, although incomplete since loss of manuscript leaves causes one break in the narrative and lops off the ending. The emphases suggest some shaping of Scripture and the diction indicates some verbal facility. The poet's rearrangement of Scripture, his moral asides and comment inserted by word or half-line as the story unfolds, present his zeal to emphasize the need to serve God. The enemy of God, Nebuchadnezzar, is unscripturally denigrated when he wakes from his first dream (Dan. II, 1): 'the wolf-hearted lord of Babylon woke from his wine-befuddled sleep' (116–7), and, time after time, his vices, particularly his arrogance, are noted in individual verses or more extended comment. But he and his men are a scourge for God on those Israelites (in the introduction to the poem, 1–32) who broke the covenant. These were prosperous with God 'until pride with devilish deeds came on them at the wine-feast, drunken thoughts' (17–8). In contrast the three young men who refuse to worship the Babylonian idol are 'children of Abraham' (193) who know God, and He preserves them in the furnace. The emphasis is obvious. Scripture is followed but the moral is bludgeoned home, excessively to our taste. This causes some of the repetitions of idea, but others derive from repetition in Scripture itself, and from assumption by commentators on the scriptural text. In Scripture, for example, the heating of the furnace and the burning of Nebuchadnezzar's men is repeated on similar terms (Dan. III, 19–24; III, 46–51), passages which are brought into immediate sequence in the poem. Commentary gives reason for the un-scriptural presence of the angel in the furnace in the English rendering of Daniel III, 23 and 24. Scripturally the three men 'fell down bound' in the furnace, but without apparent release, 'they walked in the midst of the flame praising God'. To explain this, in commentary, the angel's presence, mentioned first at III, 49, was assumed at III, 24, and our poet puts him in the furnace at the outset in order to protect them 'as many learned' (234). Indeed the protecting angel is ever-present and obviously plays his part as representing God's supernatural power. If references to scriptural verses are placed in the margin of the poetic text, we can realize how often the poet repeats and rearranges the separated Biblical verses. His verbal facility in places is worth noting, however; his use of expanded lines (e.g. 232–45) of extended alliteration, e.g.

bæron brandas on bryne   blacan fyres   (245)
> *They bore no brands to the burning of the bright fire,*

and of some play on words.

Azarias appears to be a later version of parts of the *Daniel* poem (not in any direct line with our extant text however), mainly because of the inserted extension, particularly in its presentation of The Song of the Three Children. There is a tested principle of textual criticism that a later version is more likely to extend than to abbreviate. The extensions are competently created and morally uplifting without being imaginatively exciting.

Exodus is an unusual poem in structure, in certain features of style and in its attitude to Scripture. Unlike the poets of *Genesis A* and *Daniel* who rely largely on the progress of the scriptural narrative, the *Exodus* poet seems instead to have absorbed information about the departure of the Israelites, not only from the scriptural Exodus, but from other parts of Scripture (e.g. the Psalms) which speak of the events, as well as commentary, both spiritual and literal, and ancient geography and history (perhaps via commentary), and poured it out in an intensely emotional and richly-suggestive but most uneven poem. His first reference to the departure is a description of the death of the Egyptian first-born (Exod. XII, 29), his last hint of the song of Moses (Exod. XV) when the Israelites are safely through the Red Sea (Exod. XIV). Within these limits he has omitted and juxtaposed much and yet has produced a poem of 590 lines. The number of debated words and meanings in the scholarship on this poem may suggest that the copyists found it too individual and obscure, and, apart from a loss of manuscript leaves in the middle of the poem and a possible lack of ending, it is certain that we do not have the poet's poem in places. Obviously it has been a quarry for philologists and antiquarians but yet it has value for readers of poetry. Startling images, unique compounds, stylistic subtleties, bold but relevant scriptural comparison and apt matching of Germanic phrase to scriptural concept invigorate the reader and impress on him the drama of the events and the wonder in God's awful power to destroy and save, but involved syntax in places perplexes and the unusual structural principle (if it is not lack of principle) needs some explanation. It is perhaps better to share the poet's excitement and rare skills, blame some of the difficult syntax on the transmission of the text, and offer some indication of influences on the structural principle.

Two major insertions (362–446) in the story of the exodus appear to intrude, a brief reference to Noah and the Flood and a longer description of the sacrifice of Isaac (Gen. XXII) whose ending is lost through a lacuna in the manuscript, where the poet might have given reason for the insertions. These scriptural episodes together with the story of the saving of the Israelites at the Red Sea comprise three of the twelve readings from Scripture presented in the ritual for Holy Saturday, a day reserved especially for the baptism of the catechumens, so that the liturgical service may have stimulated the poet to recall Noah and then Abraham's intended sacrifice. Alternatively the stimulus for the linking may have derived from Hebrews XI where the three events are a few of many examples from Scripture used by St. Paul to illustrate the power of faith. But demonstration of influence does not make the insertions organic unless the poet dominantly emphasizes either the spiritual meaning of two savings by sea (as types of baptism) or the power of faith to save. The poem certainly contains hints and statements on both these topics. The unrealistic references to Israelites as seamen, even in the desert, contraposed to the Egyptians as 'landsmen', hint at the typological explanation of the journey to the Promised Land as a Christian's spiritual journey across the sea to Heaven, and the curious description of fighting at the van of the march when the Israelites walk through the Red Sea and scripturally face no enemy, may be influenced by thought of spiritual battle facing the catechumen as he leaves the waters of baptism. Somewhat generally, but also with some direct statement, the poem illustrates the power of faith to save. But neither of these notions is dominant or consistent. The poet's main interest is the scriptural event, elaborated, no doubt, with the additional ideas from discussion about the exodus, and the lengthy story of Abraham and Isaac, particularly, is a wandering from the main purpose.

His evocation of the event is most startling in the description of the Egyptians' destruction by the Red Sea. The sea itself, 'a naked messenger of distress' (475), is vividly personified as a destroyer for God. Sights and sounds of the terrible miracle are heaped together in an inconsequential jumble of notions, which however make powerful impact. Phrases, found elsewhere in Old English poetry, are chosen for their content of violence, and may even be adapted to heighten the violence, e.g. *holm heolfre spaw* (450) ('the sea spewed blood') compared with *Beowulf* 2138, *holm heolfre weoll* ('the water welled with blood'). These jostle with many unique compounds which concentrate the horror, e.g. *blodegesa* (478) ('bloody horror'), *flodblac* (498) ('sea-pale'), the whole description impressing the frenzy of the lashing sea and dying men.

Other touches here and there reveal the poet's interest in style, e.g. the use of the initial sound of the last (and non-alliterating) stressed syllable of a line to form the alliterating sound of the next line (within ll.40–9), and his apt reflection of scriptural phrase, but we are more impressed by the full mind and vigour of fancy in this poem whose main quality is its power to excite.

Judith, in *The Beowulf MS*, is another poem whose structure cannot be confidently considered because of textual uncertainties. Something is lost from the beginning but how much is uncertain. Some scholars, noting that the events of the poem are also found in the last chapters of the Apocryphal Book of Judith, and also that Roman numerals X, XI, XII in the margin of the manuscript may demark sections of the poem as often in other longer poems, suggest that three-quarters of the poem is lost, which would have described the earlier scriptural events. Others argue that the numerals need not have been placed by the poet and that he has adapted, and selected from, the Apocryphal book in order to produce an exemplary episode, and has not intended a paraphrase of the whole Book of Judith.

Certainly the poet relies on Scripture, but as certainly there has been selection and adaptation to idealize the virtuous Judith, to denigrate the evil Holofernes and to bring these two into direct confrontation by omitting the names of all other scriptural characters and the effective actions in Scripture of some of them. The poem at the outset in our text is an opposition between two flat characters which, after Holofernes' death, leads to the defeat of the enemy by the newly-emboldened Bethulians, Judith's people. Such concentration allows dramatic presentation of action and reveals with vigour the example of Judith, chaste handmaiden of God on whom she relies, daring all for her faith and overthrowing God's adversary, himself a figure of vice, an example of drunkenness and lust. The sequence of adjectives and descriptive phrases, together with other changes and attributed motives, far in excess of the brief references of Scripture, reiterate the moral quality of Judith, and the immoral motive of Holofernes. Holofernes' degradation is excitingly portrayed at the feast where the poet both warms to the sound of drunken cacophony and yet places the Assyrians firmly against God, in a sequence of effective phrases. At the feast the noise is loud, the visual images sharp, and the atmosphere charged with doom. Holofernes and his 'companions in misery' are 'doomed' – 'abhorred by the Saviour'. But he shouts and the sound is heard in the verse:

hloh and hlydde,   hlynede and dynede   (23)
> *he laughed and shouted,   roared and resounded*

and he *styrmde ond gylede* (25) ('he stormed and yelled'). Here is emphasized excess at the leader's insistence: 'he drowned his band all day in wine . . . until they lay in a daze; he soused all his company as if they were struck down by death' (29–31) – an ironic anticipation. Later he falls into bed senseless. Judith's moment has come. With medieval Christian relish for the destruction of the enemies of God the poet describes the deed: 'she cut his neck half-through . . . he was still not dead then, wholly lifeless; the courageous woman struck the heathen dog a second time in earnest so that his head rolled out on the floor' (105–11). The women, Judith and her maid, return triumphantly. With dramatic sense of the issues which he is concentrating on, the poet omits and telescopes some scriptural events, and rushes on to the result, the attack by the Israelites. Here, selecting theme and many phrases from the poetic stock and swinging swiftly from Assyrian to Israelite and back again, the poet gives a lively impression of a battle, no doubt to the pleasure of his audience. At this it seems that the poet has told his story since the chapter-long song of Judith is summarily presented and the poet concludes with his own final prayer of gratitude to the Lord. Nevertheless he has made full use of scriptural material and the techniques and diction of Old English poetic narrative to present the example of Judith vigorously and effectively.

4. *Scriptural–Liturgical Poetry (Cynewulf and 'the Cynewulfian School')*

A number of versifications were made because of their relevance to the services and customs of the Church and some still remain. Many of them are scarcely more than exercises in versification and a general survey of titles will reveal the variety of the activity. Basic texts of formal Christian religion exist: three versions of *The Paternoster* (one in *The Exeter Book*); the major part of *The Psalter* in a manuscript called *The Paris Psalter*, together with some quotations in another manuscript; a version of *The Creed*; two renderings of *The Gloria*. Originally in the Kentish dialect there remains *Psalm L*, with an introduction setting the scriptural context of David's confession in the psalm, and a *Hymn* which is a conflation and paraphrase of passages from the *Te Deum* and *Gloria* and presents the dogma of the unity of the Trinity. Two versifications are concerned with the chronology of the Christian year, *The Menologium* whose object was to place liturgical fact in memorable sequence, and *The Seasons for Fasting*. Some religious verses are more personal: *A Prayer*, which is of a penitential nature; also an intercession for a certain *Thureth*; and a poem in macaronic verse (which includes Greek and Latin words) in praise of *Aldhelm*. And some shade off into homiletic or moral verse of little inspiration such as *The Exhortation to Christian Living* and *A Summons to Prayer*. Other pieces of this kind which have more poetic or antiquarian value will be mentioned later, but these last two are enumerated here because, like some of the verses above, they are found in manuscripts associated with the Benedictine monachism in the tenth century.

The texts and concepts of the liturgy had, however, inspired works of imagination, notably among the writers of 'the Cynewulfian school', and to a lesser degree, from Cynewulf himself.

Cynewulf is the only Old English poet to whom a body of work may be assigned, simply because he interwove the letters of his name in runic script within passages of his poems so that his name might be remembered in prayer. All his four poems are associated

with occasions in the Church calendar and the Latin texts connected with these. *The Ascension Poem (Christ II)* derives largely from
the second part of Gregory's *Homily xxix on the Gospels*, which was
read on Ascension Day. *Elene* is a story of the Invention of the
Cross, a festival celebrated on May 3rd in England before the end
of the eighth century. *Juliana* narrates the saint's defence of her
'virginity for love of Christ' and her legend was a reading for her
day, February 16th. The fourth piece, *The Fates of the Apostles*,
recounts the work and kind of death of the apostles in a bare and
pedestrian manner, as a martyrology did.

Cynewulf's poems are more notable for style than their derived
content although, particularly in *The Ascension Poem*, which was
most suited to his talent, a mind well-furnished in Christian
knowledge is displayed. He made comparatively little use of poetic
alternatives in many stretches of his poems, thus producing a more
flowing (and more discursive) but less visually emotive and less
condensed style. Poetic alternatives are, of course, found in compound and phrase, especially in the battle scene of *Elene*, where the
stimulus of a memory of poetry jerks phrases on to the page, but the
scene of violent torture in *Juliana* is little elaborated. In other
sections, many of the compounds appear to have lost the meaning of
their elements and should be translated as alternative simple words.
Often where an image appears it is an image in the Latin original. In
both *Elene* and *Juliana*, which are stories of lively events, much
attention is given to lengthy speeches, in the main presented as
reasonable argument. If we include *The Ascension Poem* Cynewulf
seems to be more a poet of mind than heart.

Juliana is a saint's legend, thus of a genre whose aim was
edification (not delight) by means of a selected and idealized
biography of one of the 'soldiers of God'. The genre adapted
features of classical panegyric and often pressed parallels between
the subject and good Christian predecessors, including the supreme
model Christ, in order to offer an example to the faithful of Christian life and death. Juliana is obviously an example to virgins who
become brides of Christ, although Cynewulf merely presents the
narrative without new bias. Her story is one of resistance to the
pleas and threats of a heathen father and suitor, then to persuasions
of a devil, finally to physical torture, in order to receive 'lasting joy'
with a crown of martyrdom. Heliseus, the suitor, is placed firmly
with the enemies of God in reiterated descriptive phrases. Juliana,
emphatically a woman of unblemished purity and always firm of
faith, speaks boldy and acts strongly, particularly in her rejection

and overthrow of the devil in a lengthy discourse drawn out for clear moral purpose. Often in the days of belief in the devil's rights over sinful man, the saint's life is portrayed as a victorious contest, as here in the speeches, with the forces of evil. But in this poem the imaginative possibilities within the story are neglected in order to reflect the moral nature of the Latin account.

Unlike *Juliana*, *Elene* does not concentrate on the heroine, but the poem is an exposition of that notable event, the finding of the Cross by St. Helena, mother of Constantine. The narrative proceeds from the appearance of the Cross in the sky (which inspired Constantine's victory and his conversion to Christianity), via Helena's journey to the Holy Land, where the poet has made full use of secular poetic phrase, to the major episode of the poem, the prolonged inquisition of the Jews. Here Cynewulf displays his talents by unfolding the arguments. A certain Judas, aided by a miracle, finally uncovers the Cross, is baptized, and the Cross is brought in honour back to Rome. The course of the narrative is clear, although the speeches are overlengthy, but there is some awkwardness in the conception of Helena's character (which Cynewulf took from his Latin source) for when questioning the Jews and torturing Judas she is obviously the dominant inquisitor, but when stating her resolve to find the Cross, her words are those of a martyr.

The Ascension Poem (Christ II) is the most successful of Cynewulf's poems. In this the poet chooses that part of Gregory's homily which explains the mysteries of the Ascension. The Latin homily itself has virtues which are reflected in Cynewulf's poem, notably the clear process of demonstration, enlivened by apt scriptural quotation and presented in fluent rhetorical style. The first part of Gregory's homily explicates the Gospel-reading for the day, Mark XVI, 14–20, with interweaving of reference to the event of Ascension as narrated in Acts I, the Epistle reading for the feast. Gregory then turns to 'the solemnity' itself and poses the difficulty why angels at the Ascension wore white garments, but not at Christ's birth. This is Cynewulf's opening question, but, having presented it, he fills in the background of scriptural event at length from Gospel and Epistle lections, including extra-scriptural concepts which demonstrate his familiarity with the body of material associated with the ascension and its liturgical celebration. Even on return to Gregory at line 547 he enlarges the Gregorian statements, notable extensions or elaborations being the passage describing man's choice, hell or heaven (590 seq.), in which internal rhyme emphasizes the alternatives; the imaginative yet informative elaboration of Christ's leaps (720 seq.) which Gregory had detailed economically (from womb to crib etc.); the non-Gregorian picture of the devil's arrows (759 seq.); the description of the Harrowing of Hell, prelude to Ascension (558 seq.); and the realistic application of Gregory's association of I Corinthians XII, 8 with Psalm LXVII, 19 on the giving of gifts to men (660 seq.). Using the rhetorical figure found in Corinthians (the repetition of the initial word in a clause), Cynewulf here lists a sequence of talents available to individual Anglo-Saxons ('one can . . . stir the harp . . . one can cunningly write the spoken word . . . one can boldy drive the ocean-wood over the salt sea etc.'), instead of the gifts in Corinthians which are more appropriate to God's teachers. This figure and theme stimulated one other poem in Old English, *The Gifts of Men*, which has obvious antiquarian interest; and the figure is the structural principle in *The Fortunes of Men*, which emphasizes the power of the Creator to decide ill or good in numerous imaginatively-conceived vignettes of Anglo-Saxon life. Cynewulf's adaptation at this point however is an excellent illustration of his free use and extension of his main source in elegant recreation from other knowledge.

Another creation from a full mind is the evocative *Advent Poem (Christ I)*, which precedes *The Ascension Poem* in *The Exeter Book* and was once, but no more, thought to be Cynewulf's own. Its story outline is of the Incarnation, but, taking its impetus largely from the 'O' antiphons of Advent, the poem enlarges on these and it evolves a presentation of the Godhead in Trinity in all the rich imagery of Scripture which is abstracted in, or suggested by, the antiphons. Not all the ideas are from the antiphons. The poet adds a dialogue between Joseph and Mary which touchingly expresses Joseph's thoughts, and indicates the part played by the Holy Ghost in the historical act of Incarnation. There is also a lyric sequence in a hymn to the Trinity as part of the general demonstration of the persons of the Godhead in the poem. The poet's power however is in his allusive range of scriptural and exegetical knowledge which serves to produce clusters of concepts fluently displaying the mysteries of Incarnation. Some concepts are startling to us, e.g. the Augustinian idea that Christ chose Mary as his mother, and 'They lived together, mighty Child of God and the Son of Man' (125–6), both statements expressing the consub-stantial nature of Father and Son. Many more exhibit medieval attitudes, particularly the sequence based on the antiphon:

O Jerusalem, city of the highest God, lift up your eyes round about, and see your Lord, for He is coming to loose you from your chains,

the first phrase of which is elaborated:

O vision of peace, holy Jerusalem, best of royal thrones, city-state of Christ, native seat of angels, and in thee alone those souls of the righteous ever rest, exulting in glory. Never a sign of sin is revealed in that homeland but every crime turns away from you, evil and strife. You are gloriously full of holy hope, as you are named (50–8).

Here Jerusalem, to the poet, is a heavenly and earthly city. He expresses the concept of the heavenly Jerusalem, by description of its inhabitants, the angels and the righteous, by emphasis on absence of earthly difficulty, and through the 'etymology' of its name, *visio pacis*, 'vision of peace'. But the etymology of this name, the scriptural context of the later antiphonal phrases which refer to Sion, the habit of multiple interpretation of scriptural text, and a dichotomy used by patristic writers to explain the two but united parts of the Christian congregation, on earth in hope, in heaven in joy of fulfilment, all bear on the poet at once, as he indicates in the phrase 'you are gloriously full of holy hope as you are named'. This was an explanation of Sion representing the earthly Church, 'the hope of the righteous' as Augustine once said, whose 'etymology', *speculatio* ('watching'), prompted the dichotomy. So the poet can continue with the earthly city, to which Christ came in the flesh, in elaboration of the remaining phrases of the antiphon. The richness of interwoven idea and ease of phrase marks this as highly-sophisticated poetry.

The kind of mind and of knowledge illustrated in *The Advent Poem* is also revealed in another 'pseudo-Cynewulfian' poem which demonstrates the Christian significance of that unique bird *The Phoenix* with imagination but didactic intent. The bird was regarded by our poet, and some patristic writers, as a scriptural bird in a reading of Job XXIX, 18 which ran: 'And I said, I shall die in my nest, and I shall multiply my days as the Phoenix', and this, together with the naturalistic descriptions of the Phoenix's peculiar nature among classical writers, prompted Christians to accept the Phoenix as a piece of evidence from nature for the dogma of resurrection of the flesh. Our poem is not an argument against those who doubted this but a demonstration of the dogma through the 'fourfold explanation' of the bird, the method used by some commentators when interpreting an Old Testament text. Because of the nature of the demonstration the poem offers the awful warning to those found wanting at Doomsday, but also the sure hope for those who are faithful in word and deed, yet its very basis of approach to the demonstration allows a remarkable 'historical' or 'literal' description of the bird in its habitat, the imaginative scenery of the Earthly Paradise. For this, our poet drew on the fullest Latin poetical description, Lactantius's *De Ave Phoenice* ('On the Phoenix bird'), adapting it to place the detail from the classical to the Christian conception of history and cosmology, avoiding Latin references which linked the Phoenix with a sun-cult, and adding commonplace Christian ideas about the Earthly Paradise. Within this section there are confidently-handled and delightful passages where the poet is recreating Lactantius's ideas in his own poetic idiom, notably where the Phoenix waits for the sunrise:

The stars are hid, dimmed in the dawn, gone under the waves in the parts of the west, and the dark black night passes away; then, strong of wing, proud in plumage, the bird looks eagerly on the ocean, over the waters under the sky, for when the radiance of heaven may come gliding up over the wide sea from the east (96–103).

If this is 'literal' it is also imaginative, but the poet's main didactic task is to reveal the significance of the bird as a Christian symbol. Even within the 'literal' description he is ready to anticipate by setting the incongruity of a 'warrior' Phoenix in this peaceful scene, because the Phoenix in its rebirth from its own ashes represents the resurrection of the good Christian 'soldier of God', a 'moral' interpretation of Scripture. The Old Testament Phoenix also prefigures the New Testament Christ in the third interpretation, the 'allegorical'; and by the double reference to its nest as a protection in God for Christians on earth and a home for them in heaven, the fourth interpretation, the 'anagogical', is also introduced. This is an essentially medieval way of presenting the meaning of the scriptural Phoenix to Christians, and, in summary here, it sounds a rigid and pedantic method. But the poet has so handled his ideas and his poetic phrase as to create a complex and varied but delightful yet powerful work.

The Dream of the Rood is striking in conception and so sure and controlled in style, so fervent in emotion about the Crucifixion that it has impact on even the modern who is not committed to Christianity. But its full quality is comprehended only through knowledge of the medieval literary conventions and of the doctrine within which it is written, and the precision of style (particularly in the Crucifixion scene) is revealed against the background of Old English poetic diction and theological practice. Its shape is clear-cut and smoothly-finished. The poet gazes on changing aspects of the Cross in a dream as prologue to his encounter with the 'human' Cross of the Saviour at the Crucifixion. This Cross speaks to him of the dramatic event as the central part of the poem, then of its own later fortunes until discovered (by St. Helena), and of its purpose and power within the faith. The poem concludes with the dreamer-poet's prayer to the Cross and to the Lord. But anticipations of idea, and echoes, bind this seemingly simple progression; and selection, change and omission from the scriptural record make this a highly individual poem.

In it Christ Himself is the *Christus Victor* figure in His Divine nature, facing crucifixion as a hero and conquering, but the Cross (which has been humanized in the rhetorical device of *prosopopoeia*, by which an inanimate object is given speech, and, in this poem, freewill) represents the suffering Christ as man. By emphasizing and illustrating the partnership, the dual nature of the Godhead has been conceived poetically and effectively. This has been fore-shadowed in the dream-prologue in the changing Cross seen in the sky, first enveloped with light, bejewelled and golden, a 'Cross of victory', but through the gold the poet sees the agony – and this Cross materializes to a physical Cross which alternates: 'at times it was wet with gore . . . at times adorned with treasure' (22–3). In the body of the poem the consubstantiality of Christ as God and Man is subtly reiterated through the device known as *communicatio idiomatum*, a phrase used by theologians to denote the 'interchange' of the characteristic properties of God and Man in Christ, e.g. 'they took Almighty God, lifted Him from the severe torment' (60–1). Yet the dramatic presentation has personal meaning for the poet, since the Cross, who tells the story, makes the meaning of rede-mption clear to him and thus to every man.

Three more poetic saints' legends complete the group of poems which were formerly assigned to Cynewulf, all of them deriving from Latin sources. Two of these, *Guthlac A* and *B*, are both incomplete but separate poems in honour of the Anglo-Saxon hermit, St. Guthlac, both of which take information from the eighth-century Latin life of the saint by the monk Felix. The third, *Andreas*, narrates the marvellous adventures of the apostle which were originally told in Greek but probably came to the Anglo-Saxon through a Latin account.

Andreas obviously holds the excitement of the fantastic episodes in the original, a tale of Andrew's journey to save Matthew from the cannibal Mermedonians, but infelicities abound where the romantic content clashes with the heroic phrase, and even absurdities where the poet has incongruously inserted phrases found congruously in *Beowulf*, possibly to recall this poem, or to use whatever 'poetic' phrase he could interweave. Much elaboration in the poem is caused simply by the availability of poetic verses, and the content often will not bear the style. But *Andreas* to the Anglo-Saxon listeners may well have been of the same standard and had the same effect as an average thriller of today.

Both *Guthlac A* and *B* are more morally edifying although the supernatural plays its part in both. *Guthlac A* presents the spiritual battles of the saint as *miles Christi* – 'what man was greater than he, the one hero, the one champion known in our times' (400–2) – through a series of attacks by devils whom he has ousted from their home in the wilderness of fenland. Lengthy speeches however lessen the physical action but the moral point of the life is made. And, as a comfort to the listeners as well, Guthlac is given a guardian angel (developed from St. Bartholomew, who is mentioned in the Latin life and in this poem) who strengthens and defends him in his trials. With such aid and such resolve Guthlac must succeed. The devils are defeated and Guthlac lives out his life in his home. The poet has stressed his qualities in moralistic phrase and offered one more example to the faithful.

Guthlac B concentrates on the holy death of the saint although this is introduced by a long explanation why man must suffer death (for Adam's sin), and by a sketchy summary of Guthlac's life. In one section however the poet is interestingly betrayed by his knowledge of Old English poetic phrase and incongruously transforms what is clearly a simple journey by rowing-boat (in the Latin source) into a recognizably traditional sea-journey by ship.

5. *Other Moral [religious] Verse*

A number of moral poems and fragments are interspersed within *The Exeter Book* and other manuscripts. Some are variously entitled in different editions or translations but are named here from the captions in the standard text of *The Anglo-Saxon Poetic Records*. A number of them are read only to extend our knowledge of Anglo-Saxon poetic processes of thought and reading.

Precepts (*Exeter Book*) consists of ten injunctions on morals, discursive in style and repetitive in content, from a Christian father to his son, and includes advice on holding to virtue and to the Lord's decrees, on thinking before speaking, and on avoiding sins such as drunkenness, fornication and treachery towards friends. Some of the comments throw light on certain Anglo-Saxon manners which might not be suspected from the major poetry.

Vainglory (*Exeter Book*) contrasts the arrogant man, drunk with wine at feast, with the humble, loving 'child of God', and points the dangers to the proud man (beset by the 'mental arrows' of the devil which pierce the 'fortress-wall') who is destined for hell as were the proud angels who fell. This could have been an effective fulmination.

The Order of the World (*Exeter Book*) sets its praise of God at the creation of the world in an assumed discourse between two men, although only the expounder speaks. One generally interesting point is made about the Anglo-Saxon conception of the universe, that the sun rotates round a fixed earth.

Almsgiving (*Exeter Book*) is a nine-line exhortation which uses a paraphrase of Ecclesiasticus III, 33: 'Water quencheth a flaming fire: and alms resisteth sins', a common scriptural testimony in homilies on alms-giving.

Two poems are called *Homiletic Fragments* (*HF*), number *I* in *The Vercelli Book*, number *II* in *The Exeter Book*, but they have no connection with each other. *HF II* exhorts the listener to seek consolation in the Lord, not in the world which 'hastens on its stormy way'. *HF I* is merely the ending of a poem, our fragment being a condemnation of slanderers, who are like bees carrying honey in the mouth but a sting in the tail when they speak fair to the face but foul at the back of a man. The fragment continues with a description of the 'old one' Satan inciting evils, and ends with a prayer to hope for heaven on judgment day 'when God will end the life of this earth'.

Anglo-Saxon preachers in prose and verse often stress the dangers of vice through gruesome pictures of the fate of the sinning soul both after death, and at and after doomsday. Besides many other references in poetry, there are three lengthy poems on the events and aftermath of doomsday, one poem still named *Christ III*, which follows Cynewulf's *Ascension Poem* (*Christ II*) in *The Exeter Book*, another *Judgment Day I* in *The Exeter Book*, and a third, *Judgment Day II* in MS 201 of Corpus Christi College, Cambridge. All of these make some impression from the nature of the subject, but *Judgment Day I* is the least imaginative, although recording and using the scriptural statements about doomsday. *Christ III* however presents the destruction of the world in many powerful, and perhaps bombastic, phrases, preaching the fate of sinners when the world burns:

then shall the death-flame seize every living creature, beast and bird; the fire-dark flame shall go through the earth like a raging warrior; where before the waters, the rushing floods, flowed, the fish of the sea shall burn in the bath of fire . . . (981–6).

Judgment Day II is an extended paraphrase of a Latin poem, *De Die Judicii* (attributed to Bede), in which a man sitting alone 'in a grove' and brooding over his future thinks first of the events and warnings of doomsday, but finally of hope in the joys of heaven for the man who serves the Lord. The vernacular rendering exhibits some vigour.

Two versions of the *Soul and Body* are still extant, one in the *Vercelli* and one in *The Exeter Book*, the Vercelli version being the more complete although lacking an ending. In it a condemned soul reproaches its decaying body, whose disintegration is gruesomely presented, then a saved soul thanks its earthly body. The body-and-soul *topos* is well exemplified in medieval literature, although the simple address of soul to body as in our poem is often substituted by a debate in which both body and soul speak.

The Descent into Hell (*Exeter Book*) concerns itself mainly with Christ's harrowing of hell as illustrated first in the Apocryphal Gospel of Nicodemus. The poem begins with the two Marys seeing Christ's tomb empty, but immediately links this with the victorious journey:

open was the grave; the Prince's body received the breath of life; the earth trembled; the hell-dwellers laughed; the Young Man awoke; The Majesty arose, brave, victorious and wise, from the earth (19–23).

But instead of the usual emphasis on Christ's power in the over-throw of the forces of hell, although this is briefly described, the poem continues with an emotional speech of gratitude, most probably from John the Baptist (although there is some scholarly argument about this). This includes apostrophes – O Gabriel, O Mary, O Jerusalem, O Jordan – rather in the manner of the 'O' antiphons, although the prayer which usually ends each antiphon is left until after the last of the apostrophes in this poem.

The medieval exegetical approach to Scripture stimulated the growth of the *Physiologus* or *Bestiary* genre of literature in many languages. In this natural objects are used to point a Christian lesson. Old English has one example of the genre, in *The Exeter Book*, in which creatures from land, sea and air are presented in a rounded sequence, although a page of manuscript has been lost within the description of the bird. As we might expect the creatures are not naturalistically and recognizably described, but the first, the Panther (so named), is presented as the enemy of the dragon and represents Christ who will not harm any creature except Satan; and the second, the Whale, who is so like an island that sailors anchor their ships to it and land, is the treacherous devil who plunges to the depths when the men are securely settled on it. Both these descriptions are naïve but pleasantly medieval. The comment on the bird is too fragmentary for identification, but comparison with a similar Latin cycle suggests that it is the Partridge.

6. *The Elegies*

Five short poems in *The Exeter Book*, popularly known as *The Elegies*, and all concerned with aspects of desolation, physical and mental, make poignant impact on every reader, but unfortunately present problems of detail. Some orientation towards medieval concepts may be needed for full appreciation, but in the case of *The Wanderer* and *The Ruin* this need has been overstressed by literary historians. One emotive theme is that of exile which had many interlocking ramifications in the Anglo-Saxon mind. The desolation of exile could be real as e.g. the adventures of Edwin of Northumbria in the pages of Bede's *Ecclesiastical History* testify. It is often realistic, and used poetically to express an aspect of desolation. Happiness is to stand with one's lord by a 'shoulder-comrade', to drink in the hall, at all times to be with one's fellows. Unhappiness is to be cut off from them in exile, to wander outside the society of men, to be with antagonistic nature. But the concept can be applied metaphorically to the Christian in this world, taking origin from the statements of St. Paul to the Corinthians: 'while we are in the body we are absent from the Lord'; to the Hebrews: 'we have not here a lasting city', 'confessing that they are pilgrims and strangers on the earth'. Christians are those who recognize that they are spiritual exiles as sons of the exiled Adam. 'What is exile?' asks a medieval catechism; 'The whole world' is the Christian answer. But Christ's Advent opened the way home. The Christian is one who accepts temporary exile in order to gain his *patria* in heaven. For the pagans, on the other hand, their grave is their 'long home', and their lot is eternal exile in hell. Grendel, the man-monster in *Beowulf*, is compounded of the realistic exile whose home is outside society and the spiritual exile as a descendant of Cain; but he is a permanent exile who will go direct to hell. The Christian's striving is created in the figure of a journey from earliest times, by land for Bunyan's pilgrim, but usually by sea for the early peoples since the sea was their high road. A further extension occurred in Anglo-Saxon times. Ascetics, particularly the Irish monks, decided to imitate their spiritual exile in reality by going abroad and living there 'for the love of God', and this motive was a factor in the Irish missionary activity on the Continent.

These brief remarks convey the possibilities of connotation available to the poet when referring, even briefly, as in many poems, to exile, and the critic has to consider the context carefully to decide which, or whether more than one meaning, is intended, and may come away without a decision.

This is the major 'problem' of *The Wanderer* and *The Seafarer* at present, although our critical reception of these poems has been clarified greatly in the last two decades. Now we agree that these are poems written by Christians, knowledgeable in the traditions of Old English poetry but also familiar with Latin Christian concepts and style. Both speak of an exile in a first person account, both use the emotional content of cold, and of antagonistic nature, both have Christian moral endings, but the material is used differently to create distinctly-structured poems. *The Seafarer* is clearly didactic with its homiletic ending directed to the audience and its final embracing prayer: 'Let us think where we have a home and consider how we may come there' (117–8). *The Wanderer* is not overtly so, although the same kind of Christian conclusion is offered.

The Wanderer presents the universals of loss and consolation, of poignant deprivation and of ultimate security and, for many, it offers the most powerful argument for the Christian faith in a transient world – all else is in vain. In surface progression it remorselessly unrolls the miseries of the desolate protagonist, now alone, his kinsmen dead or afar, his beloved lord buried long ago, as he speaks out his heart-thoughts; but only to himself, for there is no one in whom he may confide. In the course of the speech the lament is harshened by the abortive attempt to snatch at known consolations prescribed for earthly man – manly precepts of self-control, happy memories of the past – but the memory gives way to the presence of antagonistic nature around him in the unrealistic collocation of

> sea-birds bathing and spreading their wings
> falling hoar-frost and snow, mingled with hail (47–8).

He then generalizes, but the generalization is of death of friend, and of devastation of even the strongest work of man, the ruins of stone – 'the wine-halls crumble, the lords lie dead' (78). Where are they?, he asks, but in rhetorical figure which demands one answer: they are dead long ago: 'How has the time passed away, . . . as if it had never been' (95–6). 'All the realm of the earth is full of hardship' (106). Yet the poem ends on a note of hope and of sure consolation for the Christian 'of the Father in heaven' where 'all security (*fæstnung*) remains for us' (115). This linear progression is deepened and tightened by anticipations and echoes, e.g. the heavenly *fæstnung* of the ending is balanced in one of its concrete meanings of 'stronghold' against the decayed earthly stronghold, and by the use of words of many-faceted meaning. The poem may have some impetus from outcries in the penitential tradition, although we miss the 'I am a miserable worm' tone of the latter which certainly is found in a poem called *Resignation* or *The Exile's Prayer*. Fairly certainly *The Wanderer* has called on themes known in the Latin (and Christian) genre of 'consolation', but poetically it has power from the visualization of the 'lordless man' of Anglo-Saxon society who yet has contact with those who have suffered loss today.

The Seafarer also considers a suffering man in a seemingly-realistic situation, but the final half of the poem is a direct homiletic exhortation and this, together with the other details, radically differentiates it from *The Wanderer*. At the outset it presents a lone seafarer in all the physical difficulties of a cold winter voyage near the coast, where selection from the poetic stock of phrases makes an effective though hyperbolic picture, and where the nature/human society contrast is pointedly visualized:

There I heard nothing but the roaring sea, the ice-cold wave; I made for my entertainment the cry of the gannet, the song of the swan instead of the laughter of men, the sea-gull singing in place of mead (18–22).

His hardship is contrasted with the lot of a man on land who enjoys the delights of drink and company. Yet the seafarer remains a sailor and, when the groves bloom and the cuckoo sings, his thought urges him to sea. Ezra Pound 'translated' this section of the poem to present a heroic figure with 'salt in his blood', a not unreasonable conclusion if the poem had ended here. But a poetic address follows on a Christian hero's actions, on the transience of earthly things, inserting precepts on humility, on the need for penitence, for moderation, and concluding with a prayer. This homily is directly linked with the 'realistic' description by the seafarer's reason for sea-going: 'because the joys of the Lord are hotter to me than this dead life, transitory on *land*' (64–6). If this is the reason the 'man on land' is obviously a figure of a non-Christian who thinks of earthly delight alone, and the seafarer thus represents some kind of Christian. We again consider the opening and realize that the sea-description lacks contact with reality in its convention (as might be expected in Old English poetry) and in its hyperbolic congregation of concept (and because historic Anglo-Saxons ventured onto a winter sea only to escape death). The sea then appears to represent difficulty (in extended metaphor) in contrast with ease on land, and is an obstacle to be surmounted in order to attain an object: 'At all times the desire of my heart urges my mind to go, so that I may seek *elþeodigra eard* far hence' (36–8) – not then simply to be on the sea, but across it. The phrase *elþeodigra eard* can have two different meanings, 'the land of strangers' and 'fatherland of pilgrims'. If it were definitely the first, the protagonist would be going into voluntary exile, and the poem could be a composition illustrating the desires and action of a real-life *peregrinus* (pilgrim) such as the Irish monks. If the second, the poem would be a metaphorical presentation of the Christian's life of exile on the sea of the world and of his desire to be in his homeland in heaven. Both meanings could be present in view of the real-life peregrinus's imitation of spiritual exile, but perhaps this type of ambiguity would need some elasticity of mind to accept voyages in two opposite directions. And since we know nothing about the circumstances of composition, it may well be more likely that this is a metaphorical presentation of the Christian's spiritual exile, a most common image in early Christian literature, than a poetic autobiography of an Irish ascetic's trials, which would then be unique in Old English poetry. But the argument needed here ties this poem to its period, and it is unlikely to affect modern readers in the way that the poet intended.

The Ruin unfortunately is in a damaged section of *The Exeter Book* and the poem has phrases missing in the middle and at the end. Yet the remainder offers a vivid visualization of ruined buildings of stone (possibly Bath which was desolate within the Anglo-Saxon period):

the gaping roofs (are) shattered, decayed, sapped beneath by age; the clutch of the earth, the hard grip of the ground, holds the lords, the builders, perished, vanished (5–8),

where internal rhyme economically emphasizes the inevitability of the corruption of stone and men at *scorene, gedrorene* ('shattered, decayed') and *forweorone, geleorene* ('perished, vanished'). The present decay is contrasted with the bustle of past activity, but war and pestilence took the inhabitants – 'the citadel crumbled' (28). The poet speaks with wonder at the magnificence of the past, and, specifically, in the damaged lines near the end, of hot baths. Those at Bath were named as one of the wonders of Britain in the early ninth century. But the total impression in the poem is of desolation and transience of the greatest man-made objects. 'Ruin' had become a literary theme to express such transience in Latin, in Welsh, and obviously in Old English.

The two remaining poems, *The Husband's Message* and *The Wife's Lament*, are enigmatic to us mainly because they seem to hint at so much more than we are ever likely to discover. Both have a surface simplicity but contain references which suggest a specific set of circumstances for their composition. Yet we can be moved by the desperate misery of the wife in the one poem, and touched by the communion of husband to wife in the other. The woman in *The Wife's Lament* has been separated from her husband and his kinsmen oppress her. Her feelings are expressed in an ebb and flow between the joy of union in the past and misery of separation in the present which is expressed in terms of loneliness and of antagonistic nature. The speaker in *The Husband's Message* is a piece of wood on which apparently is carved a message from a husband, who has been divided from his wife by feud. But now, the message runs, he has overcome his difficulties in a land across the sea and is eager to welcome her.

These may be over-simplistic summaries, and it has been speculated that these poems take their basis from known stories of their age, or, alternatively, that they have Christian signification – but who can decide? If only the poets themselves had entitled their works, instead of leaving this to early editors who named them from what they thought was the content, we might have had a clue. In the case of *The Husband's Message* there is a further argument, whether seventeen lines preceding it in the manuscript, which most of us think to be a poetic *Riddle* which refers to 'a reed', should be attached and considered as part of the elegy. If only *The Exeter Book* scribe had clearly separated these poems! We have to rest safely with the touching expressions of emotion in the two poems.

Other poems or passages which describe the sadness of loss have sometimes been called elegies, including *Deor*, *Wulf and Eadwacer*, *Resignation* (*The Exile's Prayer*), *The Rhyming Poem*, and two passages within *Beowulf*, 'The lament of the last survivor' (2247–66) and a section which expresses an old man's grief for his son on the gallows (2444–62a).

Deor offers allusive glimpses into the Germanic heroic past in a poem designed as a self-consolation in rare stanzaic form. Deor, the minstrel, has been superseded by another *scop* in his lord's favour and has lost his office and his land. So he consoles himself by recalling the far greater misfortunes of Weland the smith who, in Germanic story, had his sinews cut by king Nithhad; Beaduhild, Nithhad's daughter, who was raped in revenge by Weland; the sorrow of Mæðhild; the rule of Theodoric which seemingly oppressed his people, as certainly did that of Eormanric of the Goths 'of wolvish thought' who is next on the list. At the end of each of the descriptions, which vary in length, the poet inserts the consolatory line:

That passed over, so can this.

The final section begins with a kind of Christian fatalism that the Lord apportions both prosperity and misery, and concludes with Deor's own case. The poem is mainly of antiquarian interest.

The enigmatic and brief *Wulf and Eadwacer*, however, fervently expresses the fears of a woman for Wulf who is away from her, in some puzzling references but with poignant emotion:

Then it was rainy weather and I sat weeping when the warrior embraced me in his arms. It was joy to me yet it was also pain (10–12).

Such touches as this need to be cherished since the pangs of love are rarely mentioned in Old English poetry.

The Rhyming Poem experiments and fails but is notable in its attempt. In it the poet not only writes alliterative verse but rhymes the two-half lines to produce a curious sing-song effect which, unfortunately, has little to do with the meaning. It appears to be a poem about a man's fall from prosperity to adversity, furbished with hints suggesting contact between the microcosm (man) and the macrocosm (the world), both of which began in beauty and strength, but both of which are full of miseries in their last age. Some kind of evil, perhaps the sin of avarice, has hastened the change. The poem was obviously created out of monkish knowledge and has moral intent since it concludes with a precept for a Christian to avoid sin and hope for heaven, and an exhortation, 'Let us hasten' to the place where we may see God. Yet the technical demands of the verse-form cause many infelicities.

Resignation has the traits of a penitential prayer, commitment into the hands of God, confession of sin, supplication for grace, and expression of gratitude for favour. The poem is repetitive in some of its pleas, although this gives the impression of an emotional pressure to tell all. The abstractions and generalized statements of the opening section do however appear to give way to a seemingly personal expression of misery, although this includes the well-exemplified misery of exile and poverty, and may well be merely a literary expression, especially where the protagonist says, in effect, I have no money to get a passage on a boat. In such a poem as this the journey is likely to be a spiritual and metaphorical voyage.

7. Beowulf and Secular Poetry

Undoubtedly the mightiest poem of Anglo-Saxon literature is *Beowulf* (3182 lines) in which a Christian poet has created a poem which can be an exciting adventure-story and is also a sombre comment on the human situation. His material is folk-tale, history, legend, both Christian and secular, and his own imagination, and he has worked this into a structure of balances, contrasts and recurrent interlaced themes.

The base points in the surface adventure are Beowulf's three fights with the monsters, against Grendel, against Grendel's mother and finally against the dragon. These are fundamentally folk-tale although imaginatively elaborated and vividly presented, particularly the second fight with Grendel's mother which illustrates the poet's power in creating atmosphere. In the first description of the monster's home, the lake of terror, by Hroðgar, king of the Danes, the poet draws on details from the apocryphal account of 'St. Paul's vision of hell' and joins these with other poetic phrases, none more haunting than the realistic comment:

Though the strong-horned hart, the stalker of the heath, makes for the forest when pressed by hounds, hunted a long way, he will rather give his life . . . on the brink than save his head by plunging in (1368–72).

Beowulf however does dive in to grapple with the she-monster, and disbelief must be suspended while the fight takes place, although a folk-tale pattern shows that there had been a realistic basis to this event. The Icelandic tale of Grettir the Strong has a hero who dived down beneath a waterfall to reach an enemy in a cave behind. In *Beowulf* the realism is not recognizable, but the folk-tale indicates the pattern when Beowulf finally is taken to a hall through the water. Here he despatches the monster with a magic sword whose blade melts in her blood. He then finds the lifeless Grendel and having cut off his head, returns with it and the sword-handle as his only trophies, although treasure lay around the monsters' home. The fights are stirring stuff for romantic minds, but the physical adventures also indicate a structural contrast with moral meaning.

The first two fights take place in Denmark, where Beowulf, as retainer to his own lord, Hygelac of the Geats, combats the first pair, and the last against the dragon in Beowulf's homeland, when he is king of his people. But when he unselfishly goes to the aid of Hroðgar, this Danish king, like Beowulf in the second half of the poem, is old. Hroðgar gladly leaves the young Beowulf to face Grendel, and, as the poet emphasizes, takes no blame for that. The old Beowulf, however, feels it his own duty to face the dragon later, although with the apparently good motive of gaining the dragon's treasure for his people; but he dies without heir, and the result is tragedy for his nation. For the story of nations is the backcloth to the interaction of the individuals, although told in asides and digressions, and a pointed dénouement comes after Beowulf's death. Hygelac had raided the Frisians and a running conflict had been carried on with the Swedes. When Beowulf is dead a messenger forecasts the destruction of the Geats by these avenging nations now that their defence, a strong king, is gone. And the gold will be useless to the ravaged nation. 'Easily may treasure . . . betray every man', the poet had said in comment, when Wiglaf, the faithful companion, gazed on the dragon's hoard, before taking treasure to show to the dying Beowulf at his request.

This ending appears to have been foreshadowed in the serious admonitory 'sermon' to Beowulf by Hroðgar, at a time when joy at the killing of the Danish monsters could have completely filled Hroðgar's heart. Speaking to Beowulf he had warned of the corruption which could come to a man in old age when pride in himself and covetousness might overtake him. But is the unthinking acceptance of what Beowulf sees to be a duty an instance of pride? Is the admittedly short-sighted wish to gain treasure an example of covetousness? Scholars still debate. Yet we recall hints which may be pointers, e.g. the difference in Beowulf's attitude to treasure in the monsters' lake-home and later to the dragon's hoard; that the old king Hroðgar was *not* to blame in not fighting a monster; also that the distress caused to a nation by lack of a strong king had been indicated in the opening episode of the poem, when the child comes across the sea to become a strong king of the Danes. Many such anticipations and echoes occur in the poem and are meant to be a remembered structural feature. Nor should we forget that a Christian poet created the extant poem. Although he was not teaching the stories and beliefs of the faith, he often emphasizes the control of God over even these people, who, historically, were pre-Christian. This is an aspect of Christian belief which is also indicated in other ways in the poem. But in creating his poetic society our poet had no means of research as a historical novelist of today, and no sequential knowledge of the European past since there were no chronicles for this period of Scandinavian history. The past to him was an un-chronological mass and he created as best he could, perhaps taking hints from knowledge of pagans on the Continent whom the English were attempting to convert through such missionaries as Boniface and Willibrord (7th–8th century), possibly thinking of other pre-Christians in the Old Testament, probably drawing on observation of similar vice and virtue around him, certainly accepting traditions handed down in story from the past and in poems of heroes. It is not therefore too surprising that seeming inconsistencies may appear to our brooding modern minds – that the 'good' characters thank God, and that Beowulf himself seems very mild on occasions. They yet remain recognizable pre-Christ-ians whose concern is for things of this world. Indeed our poet visualizes them as Augustine sees the Romans in his *City of God* (Book V) and Augustine's statements could be an accurate com-ment on even the good in the Beowulfian society. Increase in the dominion of Rome and success against their enemies was caused by God, says Augustine, because they put aside baseness, loved hon-our, glory and wealth honestly obtained, willingly offering both life and lands for them. Their desire of praise made them liberal of their goods, but the glory they sought was 'the good opinion of men' and 'they desired to survive after death in the memories and mouths of such as commended them'. Their virtue was great, but their motives were secular (as are all the revealed motives of Beowulf), not those of a Christian as Augustine points out by citing John XII, 43; 'They loved the praise of men more than the praise of God', and God justly gave them the reward which they asked. The Romans were 'honoured in men's mouths and now in most men's writings throughout the world'. Beowulf also was *lofgeornost* ('most eager for praise') and full of manly virtue according to secular standards in order to obtain it, although his 'flaw' is, at least, the lack of *sapientia* (wisdom) which should be the necessity of old age, and which leads to a tragic decision for his nation. His reward is the poem which still recalls his deeds and, as the poet says, that his soul should go to *soðfæstra dom* (the judgment of the righteous). What the judgment may be is left undefined but we may suspect that to the Christian poet and to any Christian listeners it would be the same as Augustine's view of the Romans, that they lived, although by high secular standards, for the world, and their reward is in the world. If this poem is a mirror for princes, as some think, it is yet a warning for Christian princes.

The concentration here on the hero Beowulf is justified since he himself is one of the unifying themes of the poem, but in discussing his situation the poet draws in many other people and episodes. We become conscious of thematic strands woven into the digressions, and that the digressions have relevance to the immediate context but also to the recurrent themes. Homicide, especially murder of kinsmen, is one such theme which begins with the sin of Cain as existing in his descendants, the Danish monsters, and recurs at intervals in Unferth, Heremod etc. to give point to Beowulf's curious self-consolation that no-one may charge him with the murder of his kinsmen. The poem is a most complicated structure which proceeds at leisured pace, with side comments and digressions from the main events, avoiding suspense in favour of anticipation. But it bears reading more than once since it is a wide-ranging comment on secular man in Germanic society from, as I suggest, an Augustinian point of view.

Two other pieces help to illustrate the kind of traditions which the *Beowulf* poet knew and used. *The Battle of Finnsburh*, merely a fragment of 48 lines, yet gives an indication of a swiftly-moving visualization of a night attack. Some of its named characters are Danes also mentioned in the condensed and allusive Finnsburh episode of *Beowulf* (1063–159), but it seems likely that the independent fragment narrates an earlier battle between Danes and Frisians than that described in *Beowulf*.

Other mention of Beowulf characters and events occurs in a mnemonic sequence of verses called *Widsith* after its narrator, a minstrel, who records lists of rulers and their nations, of nations he has visited, and of men he has sought: 'so the minstrels of men go wandering, as is their fate, through many lands' (135–6). The poem obviously has antiquarian interest and gives, for instance, confirmatory information about Hroðgar, king of the Danes.

Another part of a poem on two manuscript leaves indicates that the Anglo-Saxons knew the story of the hero Walter of Aquitaine, which is also told in a long Latin poem. The fragments, named *Waldere*, are too brief to criticize, although they reveal that the original poem could have been an account of the hero in normal heroic style.

Towards the end of the Anglo-Saxon period six versifications are inserted in manuscripts of *The Anglo-Saxon Chronicle* (see later). All of them suggest that a copyist or writer of the Chronicle decided to break into verse to describe certain events. All of them except *The Death of Alfred* (AD 1036) (partly prose, partly irregular rhymed verse), reveal however that the creators knew how verse had been composed, but only one is worth even brief consideration here, *The Battle of Brunanburh* (AD 937), although the others may be named: *The Capture of the Five Boroughs* (AD 942), *The Coronation of Edgar* (AD 973), *The Death of Edgar* (AD 975), *The Death of Edward* (AD 1065). One version of the *Chronicle* narrates the death of Edgar in rhythmical prose with some assonance and rhyme, and this is thought to have been written by Archbishop Wulfstan.

Brunanburh is a patriotic panegyric for the English under King Æthelstan and his brother Edmund on their victory over their country's enemies, the combined armies of Scots, Norsemen from Dublin and the Strathclyde Britons. The poet uses the well-tried phrases to the full, but the poem is different from other poems of heroes in presenting an impression of the action of whole armies rather than implying this through the skirmishes of individuals as is normal, and as is the case in *The Battle of Maldon*.

Maldon is undoubtedly the noblest secular poem of the end of the period. Taking stimulus from knowledge of the real battle in AD 991 when Byrhtnoth, alderman of the East Saxons, heroically opposed the Viking invaders near Maldon, Essex, the poet creates a taut but vivid impression (not description) of the battle as a vehicle for the presentation of the universal theme of responsibility and loyalty even to death, through the actions, but particularly through the speeches, of the English. He idealizes the English (although there is marked contact with reality since these were real people known to history) by a consistent and, on occasions, notedly anachronistic, identification of these with earlier heroes, as well as by echo of earlier poetic phrase and theme. At the outset Byrhtnoth is preparing for a defensive battle against the invaders who have sailed up the River Blackwater, but the river separates the forces. The first clash is verbal when the Viking spokesman insolently and confidently offers peace if Byrhtnoth (as other Englishmen before him had done) will buy them off on their own terms. The tone is brilliantly presented in antitheses, 'treasure for protection' etc., and emotive words. But no less pointed is Byrhtnoth's bold rejection in sarcastic and ironic echo of the Viking's phrases, e.g. 'They (Byrhtnoth's men) want to give you spears as tribute . . . the heriot which will be of no use to you in battle' (46 and 48). This speech reveals the man to whom honour means much, confident in himself and also in enemy slaughter should a battle take place, and even eager to see this: 'it seems shameful to me for you to go abroad with our tax, without a fight, now that you have come so far into our country' (55–8). After a few moments of restiveness on both sides of the water, caught in pointed touches by the poet, the Vikings attack over a narrow causeway but suffer casualties at the hands of three men placed there by Byrhtnoth. The invaders are no fools in war to whittle away their forces in this way and they withdraw. Now Byrhtnoth cannot have his defensive battle, and the moment of decision comes when, as the poet says, he chooses wrongly in allowing the Vikings to cross freely to fight. They 'used cunning' (86) certainly but the implication is that Byrhtnoth was deceived, because of his *ofermod* (89) (either 'pride' or 'over-confidence'). His decision however was one we have been led to expect from the man already presented, and highlights the loyalty of his men, who yet will serve their beloved lord even in error, first with their leader until he dies, then after his death. They encourage each other in a sequence of formalized but noble speeches emphasizing that for each man his is a voluntary choice; and one by one they die. Their inner strength is revealed in the words of Byrhtwold, the old retainer, towards the end of the poem: 'Resolve must be the harder, heart the braver, courage the greater, as our force grows smaller' (312–3). Is the poem merely a commemoration of courage and loyalty in time of need? If it is placed against the time in which it was written, the reign of Ethelred the Unready (*Unræd*, 'no counsel') when England was at the nadir of its power, when the Danes were often bought off with money, and when many Englishmen lacked loyalty, it could be an indictment of some of the poet's contemporaries in this recall of the old poetic and heroic qualities. But whether with political purpose or not, this is no ephemeral battle poem, but a highly skilful presentation of old but recurring ideals and actions.

8. *Other Secular Poetry and Some Curiosities*

Although some secular poetry for entertainment has undoubtedly been lost because of the religious bias of the recorders of extant verse, some lighter verse and some curiosities remain. The most important of these are *The Riddles* in *The Exeter Book*, two of these translating riddles of Aldhelm (640?–709), bishop of Sherborne, viz. Numbers 35, *Lorica*, 'coat of mail' (another version is found in Northumbrian dialect), and 40 *Creatura* 'creation, nature', a number having the same solution and closely resembling riddles in a Latin collection attributed to a certain Symphosius, and another one (number 90) actually written in Latin within *The Exeter Book*. The name of Aldhelm and the certain derivation of some riddles emphasize that the making of enigmas, some of which may seem puerile to us, was the diversion of scholars, something like the solving of crosswords or the writing of epigrams or clerihews is today. But the use of runic letters in some of the enigmas, and, of course, the normal presentation in the Old English poetic line, indicates that native originality played a part. These riddles vary in literary quality from utter banality to delightful sensitivity, in execution from obscurity to simple clarity, in tone from seriousness to dry literary humour or relished bawdiness of the double meaning, but most of them reveal welcome glimpses into medieval life and beliefs, and all, we suggest, should be browsed in translation. Where they can be distinguished the subjects range over natural phenomena, Wind, Sun, Iceberg etc.; birds and beasts including the domestic; man-made objects allied to religion, e.g. Chalice and Bible-Codex; linked with the heroic life, e.g. Sword, Shield, Bow; connected with the everyday life, e.g. Poker, Bellows, Plough. Although dullness outweighs wit in the majority of these enigmas we are fortunate to have this unexpected facet of the scholarly life.

The two poetic dialogues of *Solomon and Saturn* also illustrate interest in the display of knowledge and the testing of ingenuity, but from a much more serious standpoint. In these Solomon speaks with Christian wisdom and triumphs over Saturn the representative of pagan wisdom. *Solomon and Saturn I* exists in a more complete version and also in a fragment, and is a composition in verse and prose. Although there are two speakers, Solomon dominates the poem, speaking on the Lord's prayer which is expounded letter by letter, each one being personified as a warrior-angel who opposes the devil, the letter P, for example, having a long rod with which he whips the old enemy. The magical properties of the Pater Noster in exorcism of the devil which is implied in this poem is also illustrated in *The Charms*. *Solomon and Saturn II* is less simply instructional, more subtle and also better poetry than *I*. In this Saturn is fully pictured as a pagan, knowledgeable in Oriental and Germanic beliefs, who tests Solomon in dialogue, strongly and intellectually. Topics include the interpretation of good and evil, fate and foreknowledge, and Solomon's Christian answers concern the unequal blessings of earthly life, the mingling of joy and sorrow, the wicked man's length of days, and the heavy hand of *Wyrd* (fate, fortune).

Two dialogues in prose between *Solomon and Saturn* and between *Adrian and Ritheus* are more simply catechisms (although some questions are enigmatic) and one example of this in verse is the fragment called *Pharaoh* in *The Exeter Book* which asks and gives answer to the question how many men there were in Pharaoh's army. But all these dialogues illustrate how much miscellaneous knowledge had floated into the consciousness of learned Anglo-Saxons, in devious ways but ultimately from Mediterranean lands.

The Rune Poem is another curious relic, in which the versifier speaks about the names of individual runic letters. Perhaps its purpose was to help memorize the letters although the descriptive snippets sometimes offer simple wisdom as in:

Riding seems soft to every man in the hall, but very strenuous to the one who sits on the strong horse on the roads (13–5).

Such gnomic lore, presented in a seemingly-disconnected way although in verse-form, is also recorded in *Maxims I* and *II* (also called *The Exeter Book Gnomes* and *The Cotton Gnomes*). Christian and secular concepts jostle each other in *Maxims I*, offering basic wisdom about conduct including comment on the ideal woman: 'a woman is in her fitting place at her embroidery; a gadding woman causes talk'.

Christianity had difficulty in ousting pre-Christian beliefs in *The Charms* (many in prose, but twelve in verse) which were incantations of protection against, or cure from, disease or other misfortunes. On occasions there was uneasy adaptation and confusion which is illustrated in the charm 'for unfruitful land'. The first part of this consists of ceremonies in honour of the sun, but includes the saying of Christian prayers, and the second part consists of an apostrophe to Mother Earth, together with practical instructions. In a period when science and medicine were mainly derived and misunderstood from the knowledge of the ancients, obviously charms were to be tolerated.

The last piece of verse written in Old English was composed outside the historical Anglo-Saxon period during the early years of the twelfth century, but has interest in exemplifying that fusion of cultures with which we began. This is the little poem in praise of *Durham*, which follows the conventions of the classical genre of *encomium urbis* (praise of a city), but in regular Germanic alliterative line.

9. *Old English Prose*

King Alfred is scarcely the father of English prose, as he used to be called, since there had been prose translations of Latin before his time and in an area of England outside his influence, but his own delight in literature gave great impetus to writing in English prose. Asser, his Welsh biographer and friend, speaks of Alfred's difficulties, how when he was young and had leisure for learning he had no masters, but when old and had teachers, he was harassed by disease, by the cares of rule and by invasions of the heathen so that he had no time to study.

Yet something was done. Alfred turned first to the works of Pope Gregory, the great Christian teacher who was concerned comparatively little with doctrinal disputes, but more with the expounding of the faith to a practical world. Somewhat strangely to our taste, Alfred asked Werferth, Bishop of Worcester, to translate Gregory's *Dialogues*, a work which is mainly a series of miracle-stories with appropriate moralizing, yet for Alfred these stories were a source of strength 'that', as he says in his preface, 'I . . . might think of divine things in the midst of these earthly cares'. It is likely that this work was translated for the king's own use although one copy, at least, was circulated.

But Alfred certainly intended Gregory's *Cura Pastoralis* (Pastoral Rule) for others primarily since copies were designated for his bishops. Gregory had written the manual for ecclesiastical leaders on the key concept 'the art of arts is the care of souls', but Alfred realized that the book would fit his plan of instilling wisdom into men both of Church and of state. In his own preface to the book Alfred gives reasons, plan and method of carrying it through. He laments the decay of learning from the age of Bede when the great scholars were fluent in Latin, and sees around him the ravages of the invaders, in that the churches, once filled with books, are now burned. Little learning remains; but, taking the example of the Greeks and the Romans, who, in turn, translated the Bible into their own language, Alfred conceives the plan of translating important books into English, so that the young men, leaders of the next generation, can read these in English. He himself is reponsible for the translation, rendering the work 'sometimes word by word, sometimes according to the sense as I had learned it from Plegmund my archbishop, and Asser my bishop, and Grimbald my masspriest and John my masspriest'. This method of 'free translation', where desired, obviously allowed transformation of Latin concepts and stylistic features and gave freer play to the process of composition in English. Unlike the translation of *The Dialogues*, which is often over-literal in its renderings, the English version of *The Pastoral Rule* has a looser style than the Latin, and adds explanations and concrete instances, all these with the unskilled reader in mind. The work was completed no later than AD 896, possibly before, since one of the copies was sent to Swithulf, Bishop of Rochester, who died within the years AD 894–896.

Alfred's method of translation was also applied in two other works, translations of Boethius's *De Consolatione Philosophiae* (On the Consolation of Philosophy), and of Augustine's *Soliloquies*. To the Middle Ages Boethius was the great Christian philosopher, who, while in prison before his execution in AD 524, wrote the dialogue in five books between himself and Lady Philosophy in which she consoles him in his misfortunes, pointing out that the true happiness does not lie in the worldly things which he has lost – wealth, power, fame – but that the highest good is in God. The ideas were clearly inspirational for Alfred in the age of Viking invasions, and in view of his own physical trouble. He absorbed them and produced a controlled argument, particularly of the first four books, although omitting and expanding where he wished. The fifth book on foreknowledge and free-will was a difficult discussion however and Alfred greatly simplified this. It is likely that he was aided in his understanding of the Latin work by the accessibility of a Christian commentary on it.

But Alfred's freedom of choice within his authorities, and, probably, his habit of illustrating from his own experience, is amply attested in *The Soliloquies*, which is really not an accurate name for the Alfredian work. Alfred's first two books are based largely on Augustine's *Soliloquies* although with extensions and illustrations from the contemporary scene, but at the end of Augustine's work, Reason, the personified interlocutor, had referred the writer to another Augustinian work *De Videndo Deo* (On Seeing God) for answer to the question on the life of the intellect after death. Augustinian treatises are often subtle and complicated and it seems that Alfred used *De Videndo Deo* very little, and created distinct answers in his third book, possibly using other writers such as Gregory and Jerome in explication of scriptural texts. Alfred seems to have indicated this method in the well-known preface to the work where he speaks in the extended image of a man selecting trees from the forest for the building of a house. As a result *The Soliloquies* has great originality in composition, and offers good examples of Alfredian prose style.

The last prose work which can be safely assigned to Alfred is his introduction to his collection of laws. Alfred had the conviction that divine law was the source of first principles, and his introduction refers to Mosaic law, the law of the early Church and to early synods. The collection itself is not comprehensive since the main body of law in Anglo-Saxon times was customary and unwritten, and it need be written down only when the custom had to be altered or clarified. The end of the introduction is an example of Alfred's formal style and presents his method:

Then I, King Alfred, collected these together and ordered to be written many of them which our forefathers observed, those which I liked; and many of those which I did not like, I rejected with the advice of my councillors, and ordered them to be differently observed. For I dared not presume to set in writing at all many of my own, because it was unknown to me what would please those who should come after us.

It is possible that Alfred was responsible for the first fifty psalms of the *Paris Psalter* which are in prose, since the style and method of dealing with the text are nearer his known style and methods than those of any other known Anglo-Saxon writer. For this a commentary on the Psalms was used and the English text expands the Latin for clarity. It is also similar in practice to Alfred's rendering of the *Cura Pastoralis* in giving different versions of identical Latin scriptural passages.

Asser states that Alfred kept a commonplace book known to the twelfth-century historian William of Malmesbury as *Enchiridion* or *Handboc*, but this is now lost. The king also broke into verse on occasions. There are metrical prefaces both to the versions of the *Cura Pastoralis* and *The Dialogues*, and metrical versions of the poems with which Boethius interleaved his prose sections. These verses are based on the prose translation of the metres in Alfred's rendering of *De Consolatione Philosophiae*. None of these metrical attempts is especially noteworthy as poetry, but they do show that Alfred knew the principles of native poetic composition.

As Sir Frank Stenton says: 'His unique importance in the history of English letters comes from his conviction that a life without knowledge or reflection was unworthy of respect, and his determination to bring the thought of the past within the range of his subjects' understanding'.

Earlier scholars thought that the English version of Orosius's *Historia adversus Paganos* (*History against the Pagans*) was Alfred's work and that may well be, but it is more safely connected with Alfred's circle. Orosius, a Spanish priest, had been asked by Augustine to write a history opposing the idea that the barbarian invasions of Rome were caused by Christianity, and he did this by emphasizing misfortunes in pagan times. The work was very popular in the Middle Ages since it gave a Christian view of the world history, and though the English translator omits from and adds to his original, this view is retained. There are confusions and misunderstandings of ancient history, but among the mass of information added to the Latin is the valuable account of the geography of Northern Europe, including the economical and factual reports of two voyages, of Ohthere the Norwegian around the North Cape to the White Sea, and of Wulfstan in the Baltic. Both of these reports are full of interesting detail.

Bede's *Ecclesiastical History* was also translated in Alfred's time, and the English versions include the original text of Cædmon's *Song of Creation*. This work was assigned to King Alfred by Ælfric and by William of Malmesbury, but in its very literal translation it is unlikely to be Alfred's own work. But one other important work for historians was begun about AD 890, the compilation of *The Anglo-Saxon Chronicle*, whose composition may have been stimulated by the national pride fostered by Alfred. The Chronicle drew on existing records and stories which were circulating (e.g. the entry for AD 755) for the earliest years of the record, but Alfred's wars with the invaders were described in some detail and various later events are more fully recorded. The content of the various manuscripts of the Chronicle shows that the records were kept at different centres in England and these are obviously of great value to historians. Students of literature usually limit themselves to reading the accounts of selected years where the style is less laconic and staccato, the content fuller, and the story more illuminating of individuals and their actions.

A *Martyrology* is the last relic from the ninth century, a sequence of short notes descriptive of saints and great festivals of the Church year. It is now regarded as an original, although functional, composition, drawing on various sources for its sequence of anecdotes.

But the work of translation and the use of Latin sources was well under way in Alfred's reign and continued in the tenth century. Homilies in English were needed for the edification of Christians and two anonymous collections remain whose contents were composed certainly by the tenth century and perhaps earlier. *The Blickling Homilies* include one which the scribe or writer refers in the text to the year AD 971 and that certainly is the latest date of composition for that sermon. *The Vercelli Homilies* are twenty-three sermons interspersed with the poetic pieces in *The Vercelli Book*. Both are incomplete series of sermons for the Sundays and feast-days of the Church year, and both collections have homilies which vary greatly in style, probably in relation to the degree of dependence on and variation in Latin originals. The Blickling collection has versions of some sermons gathered in the Latin homiliaries of Alan of Farfa and Paul the Deacon, compiled during the time of Charlemagne in France, and the Vercelli series has some which draw on the sermons of the fifth-century Gaulish bishop Caesarius of Arles. These facts illustrate how Christian thought was derivative and sustained in Europe of the Anglo-Saxon period. The collections include general addresses appropriate for a festival, homilies on the relevant Gospel reading for a particular day and for the feasts of saints. These last include, in *Blickling*, the Annunciation and Assumption of St. Mary, John the Baptist, Peter and Paul, St. Martin and St. Andrew; and, in *Vercelli*, the Purification of St. Mary, St. Martin, and St. Guthlac. A more complete version of the prose life of St. Guthlac is also found in another manuscript (MS Vespasian D XXI in the British Museum).

Quite different kinds of material are also presented in English. Much medieval 'medical' knowledge is found in various manuscripts: Anglo-Saxon versions of a *Herbal*, based on the *Herbarium* of Apuleius Platonicus including descriptions by Dioscorides; *Bald's Leechbook* in two books, which includes prescriptions for the outside of the body and then internal organs (some of these recipes are said to have been designated for King Alfred by Elias, Patriarch of Jerusalem, about AD 879–907); a third book which contains a miscellaneous collection of prescriptions; the *Lacnunga*, a medley of recipes, which contain a strong pagan element; the *Peri Didaxeon* or *Schools of Medicine*, which includes more remedies culled from Salernitan writers of the eleventh century. None of these is of literary value, but they have been used effectively by Wilfrid Bonser in *The Medical Background of Anglo-Saxon England* (London, 1963), to which the interested reader is referred.

Byrhtferth, a monk of Ramsey, who was widely educated in the science of his day and wrote mostly in Latin, also produced one book, mainly in English, now called *Byrhtferth's Manual*. This includes varied comments presenting his view of natural phenomena and science, although also considering the symbolism of numbers which mark him as a man of the medieval Church.

But for the first time in late Old English we have prose of entertainment in the English version of the Greek-Latin romance, *Apollonius of Tyre*, where the strange adventures of the hero are transferred with understanding and sensitivity into English. This account, though not typical of Old English literature, is often used as a first reader for students.

Two of the prose texts in *The Beowulf MS* (the third is *The Life of St. Christopher*) are somewhat similar in content, *The Wonders of the East* and *The Letter of Alexander to Aristotle*. The title of *The Wonders* indicates the content, and *The Letter* is a kind of journal in which Alexander describes the marvellous things which he has seen on his campaigns. Thus already in Old English we have the beginning of interest in matters which were used fully in later medieval romance.

Yet the best English prose is presented in works for the faith during the cultural renaissance of the tenth century which was stimulated by the reform and revitalization of Benedictine monachism. The new ideas had originated at Cluny in France but were disseminated in England after the mid-century through two influential ecclesiastics, Dunstan, Archbishop of Canterbury, and Æthelwold, Bishop of Winchester, who arranged a synod at Winchester *ca* AD 963 to which both continental and English monks came. The reformed Benedictine rule, disciplined but not too severe, allowed a great period of learning to flourish, in which knowledge was transmitted mainly in English.

The most prolific writer of this period was Ælfric. He had been trained at Winchester by Æthelwold, but soon after a new monastery had been founded at Cerne Abbas in Dorset in AD 987 he went there as a monk and teacher, and began writing. His first work was probably circulated about AD 991. In AD 1005 he became Abbot of Eynsham in Oxfordshire and remained there until his death. His whole life was devoted to the preservation and transmission of the truth as his Christian authorities had presented it, and his many writings were composed to serve the needs of the Church and of his own friends. First came the two sets of homilies known as *The Catholic Homilies*, which were addresses and exegetical explanations of the scriptural lections for the Sundays and festivals in the Church Year. He also wrote narratives of saints (in *The Lives of Saints*), which were not intended as homilies on saints' days but for private or public reading. Books of the Old Testament were translated in summarized form, and other expository works were written as well as pastoral letters. Obviously for students he produced a Latin *Grammar*, a *Glossary*, and the delightful *Colloquy*, an early example of 'direct method' teaching of Latin. This has an inter-linear version in Old English, not written by Ælfric, which is now used to teach students Old English.

The content of all these works reveals a man learned in Christian knowledge and in the Latin in which this was preserved. His own comments however indicate that he knew and valued Alfred's purpose of providing instruction in English, 'because', as Ælfric says in the preface to *The Catholic Homilies*, 'men have need of good instruction, especially in the present time, which is the end of the world'. Good instruction meant the rejection of error, especially of the heresies, and also the fancies in the apocryphal stories which titillated the minds of many Old English listeners to such as some of *The Blickling Homilies*, but especially the presentation of Scripture, particularly in its spiritual meaning, and the reiteration of important dogmas. He was always ready to depart from a main source by adding and omitting material or by remoulding phraseology, in order to make the ideas clear to his audience. His own attitude as a teacher and his verbal dexterity make him a master of English prose. His ordinary prose, lucid and fluent, has features which are influenced by Latin prose which he read so easily: repetition of words for coherence or emphasis, some play on words, rhythmic balances and some alliteration for the emphasis of dominant concepts. But he also created a rhythmic prose which is thought to be influenced by the patterning of Old English poetry. Ælfric admits greater numbers of unstressed syllables in some of his lines than is found in extant poetry, and is not so rigid in his use of syllables bearing secondary stress, but the linking of two stress phrases by alliteration is common enough in many pieces to demonstrate that he wrote consciously in this way. We print a brief example from *The Life of St. Edmund*, italicizing the alliterating sounds, and marking the main stresses:

Éadmund se *e*́adiga   *E*́astengla c*ý*nincg

wæs sn*ó*tor and *m*úrðful   and *m*úrðode s*ý*mble

mid *æ*́þelum þ*é*awum   þone *æ*́lmihtigan G*ó*d.

('Edmund the blessed, king of the East Angles, was wise and honourable, and always glorified, with noble practices, the Almighty God'). But the real power of Ælfric is seen where, on occasions, he is clearly following a main source and accepts its ideas yet shakes off the shackles of its style in order to produce a pleasant and explicit English passage such as:

Mine gebroðra, hwylce beladunge mage we habban, gif we godra weorca geswicað, we ðe fram cildcradole to Godes geleafan comon?

('My brothers, what excuse can we have, if we cease from good works, we who came to the faith of God from the cradle?'), which is a pointed abbreviation of an ornate passage in a homily of Gregory the Great's. Of Ælfric's work, Professor J. C. Pope has said: 'The thought is scrupulously traditional yet fully digested and feelingly his own', and English prose has become a sensitive instrument in his hands.

Wulfstan, the other major writer of this period, was a public figure and this determined the nature of some of his work. He was Bishop of London from AD 996 to 1002, then Bishop of Worcester as well as Archbishop of York from AD 1002 to 1016 in which year he relinquished the see of Worcester, but he retained the archbishopric until his death on 28th May 1023. As trusted adviser to the kings Ethelred and Cnut, he drafted the later edicts in Ethelred's reign (*Ethelred V–X*), and laws for Cnut (*Cnut I–II*). The content of these reveal his Christian attitude, and his other legislation for the Church is an extension of his work for the state. He wrote the *Canons of Edgar* for the secular clergy, and the *Peace of Edward and Guthrum* to regularize obligations which were due to the Church in Danelaw, besides other shorter pieces on moral and legal points. The prose parts of the so-named *Benedictine Office* are his and, very possibly, the two sequences of rhythmical prose in a version of *The Anglo-Saxon Chronicle* for AD 959 and AD 975 in praise of Edgar and on the death of Edgar respectively. Probably his last work was *The Institutes of Polity*, where Wulfstan gives his views on the duties of different classes of people in his society. Here is seen a firm conception of what is to be done by each class in its order. But students of literature are more concerned with his homiletic addresses, especially the powerful *Sermo Lupi ad Anglos*. Throughout the early years of his high office Wulfstan was writing sermons, not, as Ælfric did, primarily for the feast-days of the Church year although some are on scriptural readings and some are designated for particular occasions, but on favourite topics which indicate his acceptance of his responsibility as a leader in matters of morals and of the faith. He was particularly incited to combat wickedness and moral slackness, warning his audience by continued reference to the last days of the world and the final judgment, preaching on the evils of the times and on evil rulers, but also giving clear information on aspects of the Christian faith and on the duties of priests. For these views he drew on a host of authorities and even used writings of Ælfric, arranging and revising in order to make the greatest impact in public delivery. No doubt Wulfstan was a powerful orator and his prose style indicates this. Characteristic features are the use or intensifying words, or intensifying elements added to words, e.g. *Þeodsceaða* (literally 'national evil-doer'='arch-malefactor'), rephrasing of expressions which might be misunderstood, often introduced by a 'that is', use of favourite tags, of play on words as a means of emphasis, of alliterative and rhyming pairs of words which are often tautological, of rhetorical questions – indeed the many figures of sound which he had learned by reading his authorities and manuals of rhetoric. Rarely did he use concrete illustrations but preferred to thunder out his message in a mass of strong words. The *Sermo Lupi* is both a literary and a historical document, a sermon preached in the difficult times between the expulsion of Ethelred in 1013 and his death in 1016, in which Wulfstan denounces the sins of the nation to which he attributes the calamities which had befallen the English. In it Wulfstan fulminates against their vices but particularly against treachery and disloyalty, beginning with an identification of his age with the last age:

Beloved men, realise what is the truth: this world is in haste and it approaches the end, and it is ever the worse in the world the longer (it is) and so it must grow very much worse before the coming of Anti-Christ because of the sins of the people, and indeed it will then be awful and terrifying far and wide throughout the world. Moreover, consider zealously that the devil has deceived this nation too greatly now for many years and that there has been little faith between men though they spoke fair, and injustice has prevailed too much in the land.

He continues with an unfavourable comparison of the English with the heathen, who pay due homage to their gods, naming the injustices resulting from hatred of God's laws in England. Then comes a reverberating list of punishments which have fallen on the English:

Now for a long time nothing has prospered at home or abroad, but there has been harrying and hunger, burning and bloodshed on every side, ever and often, and stealing and killing, plague and pestilence, murrain and disease, malice and hatred, and rapine of robbers has afflicted us very severely . . .

So Wulfstan goes on reminding his listeners of evils and sins at a high emotional pitch until all must have awaited the ending in stunned silence:

Let us often consider the great doom to which we all must go and save ourselves from the surging fire of hell-punishment, and earn for ourselves the glories and joys which God has prepared for those who work His will in the world. May God help us. Amen.

With Ælfric and Wulfstan it is clear that English prose has become flexible enough both for emotional incitement and for lucid explanation.

3

EARLY MIDDLE ENGLISH LITERATURE

G. T. Shepherd

I

Anyone who has read something of Old English literature will recognize that it has a strange distinctive character of its own. If now he comes on to read what was written in English in the centuries after the Norman Conquest (1066), he will be sharply aware of the difference. Yet however curious the matter of some of this literature, however difficult its language, it will be promptly recognized as early modern literature. Most of its forms, many of its themes will seem familiar. This feeling of familiarity is largely produced by hindsight, by surveying early Middle English literature in the light of later developments. We need hindsight if we want to make sense of English literature as a human achievement enacted over centuries.

Much that was composed in English between the Norman Conquest and the Black Death (1349) is lost. But material to fill some thousands of pages of print survives – very much more than for the whole six centuries of Anglo-Saxon England. If we could survey this material as a whole, we should be struck by its variety. There are substantial pieces of prose, there are vast stretches of verse of many forms. There are many short pieces and many trivial scraps. The quality is as diverse as the forms and kinds; and so is the language and the spelling in which the material survives.

The variety is a clue to understanding. When we think of Old English literature, or for that matter of any modern national literature, we tend to envisage formed literatures with recognizable characteristics, written in a standardized language. With early Middle English literature we are dealing with an unstable continuum, where the débris of an old literature is mixed in with the imperfectly processed materials of a new. The study of this literature has something of the interest and excitement that attends the study, say, of American or of any other ex-colonial literature in the nineteenth and twentieth centuries. The study will uncover processes of literary assimilation, rejection, adaptation, atavism, regeneration, within a novel political and social framework.

In its broadest effect the Norman Conquest accentuated one of the periodic swings of England towards the continental mainland away from the Atlantic periphery. Old English literature as we survey it now had become an insular literature exhibiting a delayed and diluted awareness of intellectual movements overseas. Middle English literature by comparison is amorphous, perpetually responding directly, if often clumsily, to the fashions and movements of Western Europe. And whereas Old English vernacular literature seems to have embodied very adequately the range and thought of Anglo-Saxon England, early Middle English writing is an inadequate instrument. A new literary language had to be reconstructed slowly to accommodate the thoughts and manners of one of the most dynamic periods of history.

The enthronement of William the Conqueror on Christmas Day, 1066, was acclaimed by many Englishmen; Anglo-Saxon England had become used to dynastic change. William claimed to be rightful king and clothed himself with the majesty of the King of the English. In most things he was a deliberately conservative ruler. It suited him to take over the kingdom and to preserve its established ways as it had existed on that day in January 1066 when King Edward was alive and dead.

In the main King William kept his promises. Adjusted to his own fierce will, the institutions and customs of England were maintained. Power and land were taken from the old aristocracy, the war-leaders of the English, and his own followers were rewarded. On the whole he left the Church alone. He had little interest, apart from the use he could make of clerks in secular administration, in its cultural life. He himself spoke a variety of French although he seems to have made an attempt to learn English. No doubt he found English-speakers a nuisance but he had no policy for the suppression of the language. For a time royal writs continued to be issued in English. But Latin was becoming the language of higher government, and in Latin, English clerks were as likely to be proficient as the Normans.

With the fall of the Old English aristocracy, self-conscious and critical patronage for secular literature in the English vernacular largely disappeared. But the need for stories and the unconscious arts of storytelling will always survive political change, so long as a popular audience remains. The tales of Old Germania lingered on:

stories of Wayland and Wade, a great repertoire of confused legend about the Anglo-Saxon kings Offa and Alfred and Athelstan, and about the Viking war-chiefs and Anglo-Saxon saints. After the Conquest too, new stories of new heroes developed – of Wild Edric, Hereward the Wake, of Thomas à Becket, Simon de Montfort – stories recounted often with a strong contemporary political intention, but incorporating the motifs of folk-tale. Most of this material is lost; much of it was certainly sub-literary.

In some monasteries and cathedrals that retained a corporate identity, conditions were favourable for the preservation of the old literary traditions. Some of the Alfredian prose translations survive in post-Conquest manuscripts. The works of Ælfric continued to be transcribed, used and adapted for generations. The vernacular was still being used for utilitarian purposes, for medical recipes, for legal and historical documents. A twelfth century MS from Peterborough (Bodleian MS Laud Misc. 636) contains, with other vernacular material, a transcription of the Anglo-Saxon Chronicle with the famous English continuation up to the year 1154. At Worcester at the end of the eleventh century there was sufficient confidence in the vernacular for Colman, chaplain to Wulfstan, to compose the life of his master in English.

But Worcester is a special case. In the tenth century it had been one of the three dioceses held by the great reforming bishops. Their revived monasticism gave strength and character to all late Old English intellectual life. From Alfred's time the West Midland diocese had come to exist as a strong redoubt of the culture of Wessex. It cherished its old literary inheritance after the Norman Conquest, long after Winchester and Wessex had ceased to dominate national life. The West Midlands constituted a more stable area in the late tenth and throughout the eleventh centuries than other parts of England. Moreover at the end of this period the diocese of Worcester had as bishop the Englishman Wulfstan who had been consecrated in 1002 and retained his see until his death in 1023. He kept going the liturgical and organizational methods of the Old English Church, preached in English and encouraged composition in English.

An interest in systematic history seems to have been developed at Worcester. The D text of the Anglo-Saxon Chronicle is usually referred to as the Worcester Chronicle and it is well-informed on mid-eleventh century events in the West Midlands. The Chronicle is thought to have been used by Florence of Worcester (*fl.* 1100), the first of a great line of English monastic historians writing in Latin during the twelfth and thirteenth centuries.

This development at Worcester suggests how new ways in letters transformed and yet fulfilled the old. In composing his universal history Florence looked back to the example of Bede. He set English history in a larger context and the historical impulse which had sustained the Anglo-Saxon Chronicles now blossoms into Latin. Other monasteries now produced their own historians. In the same mould, Simeon of Durham in *Historia Regum* is also indebted to Bede and to the Anglo-Saxon Chronicle, as well as to Florence. The high literary gifts and wide range of learning of William of Malmesbury (*d.* 1143?) found their habitual expression in historical works. William had a special interest in Anglo-Saxon hagiography and translated Colman's life of Wulfstan into Latin. He probably knew something of Old English poetry and cherished the vernacular traditions, rather sentimentally and patronizingly. There are many other monastic latinists of the twelfth century who produced histories – Henry of Huntingdon, Eadmer of Canterbury, Benedict of Peterborough, for example – talented writers with individual gifts, monks interested in the past as well as in the contemporary scene.

It is these historians who interpreted the Norman Conquest to later generations. To them the world of the Anglo-Saxons had acquired the distance of an *ancien régime* over which they are inclined to moralize. The last king of the English is turned into the saintly figure of Edward the Confessor. Duke William becomes an instrument of the wrath of God upon a sinful people. Looking back from the mid-twelfth century when it must have been usually quite impossible to say who among their contemporaries was of pure Norman or pure English stock, these historians dramatize the Conquest and use it to explain the social stratification of their own times.

For our purpose in studying literary history the recognition of the change that had come over English life is more important than identifying the events that caused it. In many ways it is the reign of Henry I (1100-35) not of William the Conqueror that is the turning point. It is from the early years of the twelfth century that the novelty of their world astonished and perplexed people, not only the historians. Men saw all about them at this time a dissolution of old traditions and a confusion amidst which they could not as yet clearly distinguish the new. And the changes occur at all levels of social, religious, intellectual life.

Society hates anarchy as nature abhors a vacuum. The old bonds of society had loosened but there is a new assertion and realization of sovereignty. The state was becoming a much more in-stitutionalized expression of the royal will, maintained by sub-ordinate layer after layer of administrators and executives. This separation of the machine of government from the society to be governed is accompanied by the development of a new court literature. This literature does not reflect the actual bonds knitting a whole society together; rather it delineates and mirrors the aspira-tions and fantasies of those who already occupy a station within the feudal pyramid of power. Knighthood initiated a man into the power structure. In return for his promise of military service to his feudal lord, the knight was given opportunity to acquire and exploit a measure of power and honour for himself. To the young and ambitious, it afforded a splendid opportunity.

Many young landless men from France had made their own fortunes and their descendants' by participating in Duke William's venture in England. Many of them married well-born Englishwomen. For sexual activity like war itself was not only a means of satisfying youthful appetites, it was also a means of acquiring status and honour. Whatever we make of the psychology of 'courtly love' in its refined and literary manifestations, the modes of behaviour that developed between the sexes had also a distinctly public and political function. To be the lover of a noble and beautiful woman was to expropriate something of her nobility and worth. To win such a woman, who in addition possessed both wealth and alliance, could bring solid worldly power.

In England in the twelfth century it was still possible for a young, free and vigorous man to carve out a career of honour and profit in the Marches, in Wales, in Scotland or in Ireland. He needed an appetite for honour and great place, he needed physical strength and an expertise with horses and weapons. These qualities would do well enough to begin with. Later, as success came, add practical sense, an ability to manage men, wealth and possessions, and sufficient address to win a wife, who preferably should have higher status and more possessions than oneself. The true career of Will-iam Marshal, first earl of Pembroke and Striguil (*d.* 1219), is more fully instructive of the ethic that produced and in turn fed upon court literature than any single English fiction of the time.

In the twelfth century the young men of France may have had less opportunity than the young men of England in pursuing such careers. But in France at this time they were producing much better fictions, and the poets there were polishing the new fashionable stories at leisure in lively and clever courts. Early French literature is a brilliant and rapid growth.

The narratives in verse which embody the life, adventures and values of aspirant knighthood we call romances. It is in origin and destination primarily a literature for youth: indeed this is one respect in which the new romance of France can be clearly distinguished from the old heroic poetry of Germania. The old poetry was essentially memorial verse which by showing the achievement of a representative leader glorified the communal identity. Romance delineates instead individual aspiration and shows that a young unencumbered man can seek fame and status in an institutionalized system of which he may be part but of which he is never in control. The basic situation in these later fictions is a quest.

In French the word *romans* was used at first to refer to compositions in the vernacular, to distinguish them from compositions in learned Latin. Soon the word implied the vernacular compositions that were particularly characteristic of contemporary French society – these verse tales of love and war. This specific use does not seem to have been commonly employed in English before the end of the thirteenth century. Before this time the developed genre was known well enough in England but only in French. From the mid-thirteenth century onwards there are many adaptations into English of French romance, but these English pieces have lost something of the keen social relevance of earlier romance. English stories categorized as romance are mixed with older memories of another social order and with more restricted social ambitions appropriate to English speakers. That they were composed in English means that they would not reflect the social values of the established aristocracy. The attitudes are less refined, less liberal; the interest more communal, more physical.

Some scores of Middle English vernacular verse-narrative romances survive. Less than a dozen of these seem to have been in circulation before 1300. It is in the earlier part of the fourteenth century that most of the popular English romances were composed and welcomed. Most of them are entirely derivative, many of them are written in tail-rhyme stanzas. Discounting the irony of presentation, Chaucer's *Sir Thopas* demonstrates fairly faithfully what these popular romances were like. Chaucer's parody of course carries a sophisticated judgment on early romance. By his time, there were new fashions and new developments. The alliterative poets of the late fourteenth century bring more than a new style to their handlings of romance themes. In the fifteenth century prose comes into use. Romance was to be given often a moral purpose or an allegorical function. It is sometimes a vehicle for a new realism in later times.

King Horn, usually considered to be the earliest English romance, survives in three MSS: the earliest text is a south midland dialect in Cambridge University MS Gg.4.27.2 (*ca.* 1250). The metrical form is curious but successful. The underlying rhythmic structure is that of the old four-stress long alliterative line, reorganized into brisk rhymed couplets with an irregular syllable count. In handling his story the composer harmonizes different elements. Horn is of royal birth, but his parents count for little in the story: they are early dispossessed of the kingdom, his father slain by Saracens – the convenient universal enemy in Middle English romance (here we may guess that the Saracens replace Vikings in earlier tellings of the story). Horn is abandoned in a boat with a band of youthful companions. Only two of these enter into the action, one as loyal friend, the other as treacherous enemy. The party is cast up on Westerness.

Þe children ʒede to tune,	*went inland*
Bi dales and bi dune.	
Hy metten wiþ Almair king	
(Crist ʒeue him His blessing!)	
King of Westernesse	
(Crist ʒiue him muchel blisse!)	
He him spac to Horn child	
Wordes þat were mild:	
'Whannes beo ʒe, faire gumes,	*young men*
Þat her to londe beoþ icume?' (lines 153-62)	

'We beoþ of Suddenne	
Icome of gode kenne,	*kin*
Of Cristene blode,	
And kynges suþe gode.	*exceeding*
Payns þer gunne arive	*Pagans . . . arrived*
And duden hem of lyve.	*put them to death*
Hi sloʒen and todroʒe	*tore apart*
Cristene men inoʒe.	*in fair numbers*
So Crist me mote rede,	*So help me Christ*
Us he dude lede	
Into a galeie	*rowing-boat*
Wiþ þe se to pleie,	
Dai hit is igon and oþer,	*One day passed and a second*
Wiþute sail and roþer:	*rudder*
Ure schip began to swymme	*float*
To þis londes brymme.	*shore*
Nu þu miʒt us slen and binde	
Ore honde bihynde;	*our*
Bute ʒef hit beo þi wille,	
Helpe þat we ne spille.' (lines 175-94)	*do not perish*

Horn is adopted by the royal court and instructed in simple courtly duties. Rimenhild, the king's daughter, falls in love with Horn, and Horn, cautiously reciprocating her love, uses it as a means of obtaining knighthood. Thereby he acquires his right and obligation to advance his honour and make his fortune by war. The lovers are tricked by Horn's evil companion and Horn exiled to Ireland where under the *nom-de-guerre* of Cutbeard he does great deeds in King Thurston's service.

But Rimenhild at the end of seven years is promised in marriage to a foreign king and in desperation she calls Horn back. He comes disguised as a beggar, discloses himself through signs and riddles and slays the presumptuous suitor. But he goes abroad again, this time to win back his father's kingdom.

Horn sed on his rime	
'Iblessed beo þe time	
I com to Suddenne	
Wiþ mine Irisse menne.	
We schulle þe hundes teche	*dogs*
To speken ure speche	
Alle we hem schulle sle	
And al quic hem fle.'	*flay alive*
Horn gan his horn to blowe—	
His folk hit gan iknowe.	
Hi comen ut of stere	*from aboard*
Fram Hornes banere.	
Hi sloȝen and fuȝten,	
Þe niȝt and þe uȝten.	*morning*
Þe Sarazins cunde	*race*
Ne lefde þer non in þ'ende.	
Horn let wurche	*caused to be built*
Chapeles and chirche.	
He let belles ringe	
And masses let singe.	
He com to his moder halle	
In a roche walle.	*wall of a cliff*
Corn he let ferie	*ordered corn brought*
And makede feste merie.	*feast*
Murie life he wroȝte,	*lived*
Rymenhild hit dere boȝte. (lines 1363-88)	*paid dearly for it*

For Horn has now to return in haste and in disguise again to rescue his bride Rimenhild from the advances of the old false friend Fikenhild. Fikenhild is slain, the marriages are made and the various kingdoms sorted out happily.

However bald the plot may sound in summary form the romance itself is put together cleverly and entertainingly; the two-fold move adds interest without repetitiousness. Much of *King Horn* illuminates the history of romance in England. The tone throughout is well maintained but not distinctly courtly. The love theme provides the mechanics of the plot but scarcely the motivation of Horn's activities. That the woman takes the initiative in love, as Rimenhild does, is usually considered to indicate a pre-courtly ethic. But the author is not unaware of the obligations that courtly romance imposes. In the treatment of incidental material, in the exoticism, in the creation of expectancies, and in the simplification and miniaturization of time and place and real societies, *King Horn* conforms to the genre.

King Horn is the best example of early English romance, both in its performance and its promise. Less central in the development of romance is *Havelok*, composed in Lincolnshire it would seem, and preserved in the late 13th century Bodleian MS Laud Misc. 108. As with *King Horn*, the setting in which the story grew up appears to be that of the old Danish invasions. Once more we have the story of an orphaned boy who wins his way to knighthood and establishes his right to rule. But in treatment the English *Havelok* emerges as a deliberately popular piece, aimed at an uncourtly audience which is interested in athleticism, responsive to piety, harsh justice and a simple love-match, and accustomed to the values and cultural standards of the provincial household.

Two long romances, each with local interest, probably best illustrate the ordinary, not over-demanding taste for vernacular romance at the end of the thirteenth century. Both *Guy of Warwick* and *Beves of Hampton* derive from Anglo-Norman romances. Both make use of the two-move structure observable in *King Horn*. Beves, captured by pirates, has various adventures among the Saracens in Armenia from which he eventually brings home his bride Josian. When success is assured and rest seems won, the adventures are triggered off again by an incident involving his great warhorse Arundel.

In somer aboute Whit-sontide	
Whan kniʒtes mest an horse ride,	*on*
A gret kours þar was do grede	*had been organized*
For to saien here alþer stede,	*test all of their horses*
Which were swift & strong.	
Þe kours was seue mile long;	*seven*
Who þat come ferst þeder, han scholde	*have*
A þosand pound of rede golde.	

Þer wiþ was Beues paied wel: *pleased*
Meche a treste to Arondel.   *Greatly he trusted*
A morwe, whan hit was dai cler,
Ariseþ boþe kniȝt and squier
And lete sadlen here fole   *had their horses saddled*
Twei kniȝtes hadde þe kours istole,   *made a flying start*
Þat hii were to mile before   *two*
Er eni man hit wiste y-bore.   *any living man*
Whan Beues wiste þis, fot hot   *hot foot*
Arondel wiþ is spures a smot   *his/he*
& is bridel faste a schok.   *his/he*
A mide þe kours he hem of tok.   *overtook*
'Arondel', queþ Beues þo,
'For me love go bet, go,   *run faster*
And I schel do faire and wel
For þe love reren a castel!'   *build*
Whan Arondel herde what he spak,
Before þe twei kniȝtes he rak,   *raced*
Þat he com raþer to þe tresore,   *sooner*
Þan hii be half and more.
Beues of his palfrai aliȝte   *from*
& tok þe tresore anon riȝte.
Wiþ þat and wiþ more catel   *money*
He made þe castel of Arondel.   *Arundel (in Sussex)*
    Meche men presisede is stede þo   *his; then*
For he hadde so wel igo.
Þe prince bad, a scholde it him ȝeue.   *asked/he*
'Nay', queþ Beues 'so mot y leue,
Þouȝ þow wost me take an honde   *though thou wouldest I take*
Al þe hors of Ingelonde!'
Siþþe þat he him ȝeue nele,   *Since he will not give*
A þouȝte þat he it wolde stele.   *He*
    Hit is lawe of kinges alle
At mete were croune in halle,   *to wear*
& þanne eueriche marchal
His ȝerde an honde bere schal   *staff of office*
While Beues was in þat office
Þe kinges sone þat was so nice –
What helpeþ for to make fable?
A ȝede to Beues stable   *He went*
And ȝede Arondel to niȝe   *too near*
And also a wolde him untiȝe;
And þo Arondel fot hot
Wiþ his hint fot he him smot   *hind*
And to-daschte al is brain –
Þus was þe kinges sone slain.
    Men made del & gret weping   *lament*

For sorwe of þat ilche þing.   *same*
Þe king swor for þat wronge
Þat Beues scholde ben an-honge
& to-drawe wiþ wilde fole.
Þe barnage it nolde nouȝt þole   *baronage/endure*
& seide hii miȝte do him no wors
Boute lete hongen is hors;   *than have his horse hanged*
Hii miȝte don him namore
For he servede þo þe king before.
'Nai', queþ Beues, 'for no catele
Nel ich lese min hors Arondele,   *lose*
Ac min hors for to were   *in order to defend*
Ingelonde ich wil forswere.' (lines 3511-78)

He is again obliged to leave England for the second round of
adventures which at length conduct husband and wife to old age
and a pious end.

Guy starts life in a humble way and aspires to the love of Felice,
daughter of the Earl of Warwick. He is knighted, successful in great
exploits and marries Felice. He sets out again as a pilgrim knight to
atone for his past pride of life, kills a variety of giants and other
villains, and like Beves dies in sanctity. Only the reaction of an
audience could determine where or whether romances of this
scope, loaded with incident like beads on a thin string, should come
to an end. Successful heroes beget sequels. There was to be a
lengthy derivative romance on the deeds of Guy's son Reimbrun.

Of the other thirteenth-century English romances little needs to
be said. Idealized face-to-face relationships provide themes for two
of them: *Amis and Amiloun* tells the tale of the undying loyalty of two
sworn brothers; *Floris and Blanchflower* shows again how true love
never did run smooth. Both stories are pretty, almost as pretty as
their titles, but neither is worked out with the elegance and
tenderness that a modern reader would think the stories deserve.

Examined alongside their analogues, broken down into themes
and motifs or plot-functions, there is almost nothing in any of the
romances that is original. The story of *Floris and Blanchflower* exists
in much older form in Byzantine and Arabic tales. There are
versions of *Amis and Amiloun* in French, Spanish, German, Old
Norse, Danish, Welsh and Latin. The story of Beves acquired a
circulation from Ireland to the Urals. Stories were told and retold
and refashioned. Any version that survives is in a sense an
accidental epiphany in a constantly moving process. We have to
generalize about a whole industry from the few products that survive.
We must assume that from the eleventh century in England there

was a demand for and a sufficiently effective method of circulating these stories. By the thirteenth century they have been worked over again and again by professional versifiers. The dozen romances of date earlier than 1300 cannot represent anything like the full range of familiar material. It is certain for example that the story of Tristram is ancient. Yet the only version of the story in Middle English, apart from Malory's, is in the mid-fourteenth century Auchinleck MS. With the romances composition, revision and performance is nearly always anonymous. There is however a group of long romances of early fourteenth century composition, *Arthur and Merlin, King Alisaunder* and *Richard the Lionheart* which may well be the work of one man. Whether this be true or no, each of these romances will demonstrate the range of material, the breadth of shallow learning, the patience and industry that the composition of extended romances was coming to entail.

Romance is the most characteristic genre of medieval composition. Probably the most important single fact about it in literary history is its bulk. It stretched out vast and shapeless, but with immense and continuing influence all over Europe. Don Quixote's hundred books and more, some large, some small, including only four of the twenty-one volumes of *Amadis of Gaul*; four huge parts of the *Mirror of Knighthood*, all the *Ten Books of the Fortunes of Love*; all these represent only a specialist's anthology of old romance. Yet at any time through the Middle Ages it would have been difficult to put together a large collection of masterpieces. There were few good writers. Medieval England had no more than three or four – all of them fall outside our centuries – but in the main composers of Middle English romance are competent within the terms of their own intentions. Medieval romance is essentially – like most modern fiction – a literature of entertainment, a wish-projecting and fantasy- fulfilling diversion. And the nemesis of this kind of writing in any age is unfortunately oblivion in the age that comes thereafter.

Romance invaded public life as well as private fantasy. Many of the French and Anglo-Norman romances were 'ancestral romances' where the historical careers of founding members of great families were embellished with magic and gallantry. In the *Song of Roland*, which was certainly known in England in the twelfth century, the presentation was designed to glorify a whole national community. As European peoples began to identify themselves as nations, so great myths arose to underpin their new self-consciousness.

In England a new perspective of the national destiny was set out most successfully by Geoffrey of Monmouth (1100–54), a monk who worked at Oxford and became eventually Bishop of St. Asaph. His great work *Historia Regum Britanniae, completed ca.* 1136, traced the descent of the princes of Britain from Brutus, the grandson of Aeneas who, escaping from the destruction of Troy, had founded Rome. Geoffrey's book ends with the death of Cadwallader, the last British king of the seventh century, but it tells the story of Arthur at length and the long struggles against the Saxons. The power of the book lay in the use that could be made of its underlying scheme as political myth, and the myth remained potent until the Commonwealth. It linked the foundation of Britain with the story of divine Troy and the mission of Rome the great. Arthur emerges as a figure to be set among the heroes and emperors of the world. Indeed in story he was to become the Emperor of all the western world. In this history the Saxons become the local enemy; but the general impression of the book is that the Saxons are pushed to the periphery of history, and that the mighty past as well as the present and the future belong to the imperium of Britain – the inheritance of the Norman and Angevin kings. This view of history was relevant. The Angevin kings were to pursue their dream of empire on the Continent, but also in the insular domains: in Wales, in Scotland and in Ireland. In conquering them, Englishmen saw that they were returning them to their old associations of glory.

The book was immensely successful and the myth powerful. It represented as much an assimilation of old, half-forgotten traditions as an imposition of policies. Many stories from the old Celtic lands flowed back into England and France. Most commonly they are known to us in their earliest form in French. So Thomas the Englishman is named as the author of the first Tristram – in Anglo-Norman. Marie of France drew upon Breton *lais*, which were composed in England and show a knowledge of the English language and the English scene.

What is more curious is that it was possible for an English poet, born not much more than a century after the Conquest and writing in English and retaining some knowledge of Old English poetic methods, to take over the whole story of Brutus's Britain and present it without irony as the heroic record of his own race. Layamon, a priest of Areley Kings on the Severn in Worcestershire, after a reading of old books decided

Þat he wolde of Engle þa æðelæn tellen;
Wat heo ihoten weoren and wenene heo comen
Þa Englene londe ærest ahten.

(That he would tell of the noblemen of the English; what they were called and whence they came, who first held the land of the English.)

His narrative is a version of the Anglo-Norman *Roman des Bretons* by Wace, itself a version of Geoffrey of Monmouth's Latin *Historia*. In his *Brut*, Layamon we must believe thought he was writing a national story closer to what we should classify as history than to romance. And yet the past is so remote to him that the relevance of any of the events to the recent history of the English is altogether lost. What comes out of his telling is the fierce glory of the past.

The *Brut* survives in two MSS: MS Cotton Caligula A. ix and MS Cotton Otho C. xiii, both of which are now taken to be of the period 1250-1300; but the date of composition is considerably earlier, probably about the year 1200. The Otho text was shorter than the Caligula and looks like a revision; and as we have it, was still further reduced by the fire of Cotton manuscripts in 1731.

The Caligula text contains over 32,000 short alliterative lines. It follows Wace's story fairly closely, but with many omissions and reductions, and some additions. Layamon composed in the style of a public narrator rather than in that of chronicler and often uses direct speech in place of report.

The story falls into three unequal parts: the foundation of Britain after the fall of Troy up to the begetting of Arthur; the story of Arthur; a brief post-Arthurian history of the Britons. The Arthurian material is of course best known. Arthur is presented not as we have come to know him in later story, as the benign but passive presence behind the individual adventures of his knights, but as himself the war-leader, the captain of his host. In many ways the treatment is pre-chivalric. It may be a new myth but it is told with nostalgic passion. It comes over as a story of military triumph and disaster, of valour and narrow loyalties, of hate and revenge. The culminating action is the great battle between the arrogant Lucius, Emperor of Rome, and the heroic national king.

Æfne þan worde . þa sturede þa uerde	*moved the army*
Bi þusend and bi þusende . heo þrunnggen to-somme;	*pressed together*
Ælc king of his folke . ȝarkede ferde.	*each/prepared his army*
Þa hit al was iset . and ferden isemed,	*moved in readiness*
Þa weoren þar riht italde . fulle fiftene ferden.	*counted*
Twein kinges þere . æuere weoren ifere,	*together*

Feouwer eorles and a duc . dihten heom to-gadere,   *four/arranged*
And þe Kæisere himseolf . mid ten þusend kempen.   *warriors*
Þa gon þat folc sturien . þa eorðen gon to dunien;   *began to resound*
Bemen þer bleowen . bonneden ferden;   *trumpets/summoned armies*
Hornes þer aqueðen . mid hæhȝere stefnen.   *spoke out with loud voices*
Sixti þusende . bleowen to-somne;   *together*
Ma þer aqueðen . of Arðures iueren   *More/A's companions*
Þene sixti þusende . segges mid horne.   *warriors*
Þa wolcne gon to dunien . þa eorðe gon to bivien.   *heaven/shudder*
To-somne heo heolden . swulc heouene wolde vallen.   *as if*
Ærst heo lette fleon to . feondliche swiðe,   *very savagely*
Flan al-swa þicke . swa þe snau adun valleð.   *arrows/snow*
Stanes heo latten seoððen . sturnliche winden.   *after/grimly let fly*
Seoððen speren chrakeden . sceldes brastleden;   *cracked/clashed*
Helmes to helden . heȝe men vellen;   *rolled off/tall*
Burnen to breken . blod ut ȝeoten;   *corslets were smashed/poured out*
Veldes falewe wurðen . feollen heore marken.   *Fields were stained/banners*
Wondrede ȝeond þat wald . iwundede cnihtes ouer-al.   *wood*
Sixti hundred þar weoren . to-tredene mid horsen;
Beornes þer swelten . blodes at-urnen.   *Warriors died/ran out*
Stræhten after stretes . blodie stremes;   *flowed along paths*
Balu wes on volke . þe burst wes unimete.   *Disaster/panic was total*
Sva al-swa suggeð writen . þæ witeȝen idihten:
    writings; which wise men compose
Þat wes þat þridde mæste viht . þe avere wes here idiht.   *fight/decreed*
(C text, lines 27424-81)

Clearly Layamon knew something of the old alliterative poetry. The rhythms and diction seem to have lingered confusedly in his ear. He reproduces many of the old stress patterns of Old English verse, but the taut firm structures have been eroded, largely no doubt in consequence of the loss of inflexion in the living language. A syntax such as Layamon used, more dependent upon order, inevitably reduced the functional importance of alliteration of verse structure. Layamon commonly makes use of rhyme and half-rhyme to mark and knit his verse units and sometimes the stress pattern is scarcely recognizable at all.

The Caligula text in particular shows a similarly remarkable but indistinct retrieval of the old verbal style and diction. The poet will use old heroic terms, particularly in compounds, but often as if they were fixed epithets or honorifics, as if neither he nor his audience should be expected to have a clear idea of their meanings. They give an evocative sonority to the narrative. Many talented English poets have on occasion used words in this way. Many of the tricks and traditions of oral composition and oral delivery were familiar to

Layamon, but the existence of the two distinct texts affords conclusive evidence that the work was read as well as heard.

II

These men in England who wrote history and the myths of history show that profound and disturbing change was occurring. They regarded their present with anxiety, the past with regret, the future they see only dreamily. Few of them communicate the vivid excitement of the age. They do not describe in direct terms the great cultural and intellectual movements in twelfth-century Europe which seem so prominent to us as we look back.

A few writers less devoted to history seem to have had a sense of what was happening. Walter Map (*ca.* 1170) saw that he stood in a position very different from that of his forefathers in the eleventh century and talked about the *modernitas* of his own time. Chrétien de Troyes (*ca.* 1135–*ca.* 1190) writing in French self-consciously welcomed the new world of chivalry and learning which was replacing in its eminence the glories of the ancient world. Adam the Scot (*fl.* 1180) saw the new personal piety of his generation as the consummation of all Christian endeavour. Where clever people talked in court or school or cloister there were voices asserting that an old world was dead, that old methods were nerveless and old books so much lumber. The intellectual world was being renewed. There is a new grammar, a new logic, a new poetry, a new devotion. By the end of the thirteenth century these self-styled novelties are no longer novel, but in learning and literature the momentum generated by these twelfth-century activities was to drive onwards until the Reformation.

When the word medieval is used nowadays with any particularity it usually refers to something which first took definite shape in the twelfth century: romance, as we have seen; the orders of knighthood, tournaments and the Crusades; Gothic arches and dreaming spires; the love-songs of troubadors and the great stone castles; the wandering scholars and the universities; the schoolmen with their rediscovery of Aristotle and his Arabic commentators. In religion the impress is still heavier. Many people who today aspire to reject Christianity are doing no more than doubt the adequacy of the formulations and systematizations of the faith that were initiated in the twelfth century.

There had been great changes in Northern Europe as a whole. In the record of these changes the Battle of Hastings is only an incident. By the end of the eleventh century the outer barbarians, the Western and Northern peoples, had come to feel fully at home in the Latin Christian world. The twelfth century is a time of social consolidation, developing a firm confidence in a new social order. Trade begins to flourish and towns to grow in north-west Europe. Beneath the superstructure of power even something of a money economy begins to emerge.

The early career of Godric (1065?–1170) is often cited as illustrative if not entirely typical of new economic man in the twelfth century. Godric was born on the east coast of England and as a young man successfully engaged in mercantile trade around the seas of Europe. His later life is also symptomatic. About the year 1120 Godric left trade and took to religion. After arduous pilgrimages to the great shrines of Christendom, including the Holy Land, he spent his long latter years in a hermitage at Finchale, Co. Durham. In his choice of an eremetical life, in the manner of his devotions, Godric was still in tune with his age. This strange impressive man is also referred to sometimes as the first vernacular composer of religious lyric verse. Some few stanzas with musical accompaniments are preserved of his compositions at Finchale.

The career of Godric, and the comparative freedom with which he could move on his own business about Christendom, suggest the increasing stability of European states. The theory as well as the institutions of Church and state could be more clearly examined and more sharply defined. The conditions for intellectual life existed. There were more opportunities for clerks. Travel grew easier. More men read more books.

Closer to the heart of change perhaps was something that can be sensed throughout all the stages of Godric's career: a powerful sense of liberation. Often in reading about the Anglo-Saxons, and reading what they wrote, one is led to think that this remote people viewed existence as if it were a small pool of light within an immense obscurity, as if they were squatters in a metaphysical void. But in the twelfth century men have suddenly been made free in great fields of thought and experience. They acquired a sense of the size and unity of Europe. They encountered the Muslim world beyond, powerful and real; and rediscovered the Greeks and the science of the ancients.

The schools turned these new experiences and attitudes into words. Education was of course at this time almost entirely in the hands of the Church. Schools had to be licensed by the diocesan bishop and were attached to the cathedrals and to larger monasteries. In all schools the basic instruction was Latin grammar leading to a close study of a few old authors, starting with Aesop, proceeding to Virgil and Ovid, and of parts of the Bible, particularly the books of proverbial literature, and of course, the Psalms.

Theobald of Etampes, who taught at Oxford at the beginning of the twelfth century, observed that trained schoolmasters were to be found not only in the cities of England but even in the small towns. This seems an enthusiastic over-statement. Probably few English schools grounded their pupils very thoroughly in all the subjects of the *trivium*, for right through the twelfth century the best and most aspiring students took themselves off to make the rounds of the great schools of France – Chartres, Laon, Tours and Paris.

The school of Chartres has an importance in English literary history. It had been founded in the early eleventh century and had built up a strong tradition of literary humanism. The great literary figure of Chartres in the mid-twelfth century was Bernard Sylvestris, who wrote an influential commentary on Virgil, taught the arts of composition, and philosophized in the style of Boethius, in mixed verse and prose, in *De Mundi Universitate*, an exposition of the natural order and the divine forms which owed as much to Virgil and Ovid as to Plato. To Bernard's work many later poets were indebted, notably Alan of Lille (*ca.* 1128–1202), known as *doctor universalis*, who in addition to his theological works composed *Anticlaudianus*, a richly allegorical poem on nature and faith, and in a style more directly imitative of Bernard, in mixed verse and prose, *De Planctu Naturae*, an extraordinarily elaborate composition, abstract yet sensuous, mythological and schoolmasterly. It fascinated the later Middle Ages. Chaucer knew it well and so did Spenser.

The learned schoolmasters had a more general influence on the way in which English writers in Latin, and eventually by Chaucer's time in the vernacular, were to use words. The authors of the twelfth century Arts of Poetry were legatees of the school of Chartres. A number of them were English born: Gervase of Melkley, Geoffrey of Vinsauf and John of Garland. Both Geoffrey and John seem to have studied at Oxford for a time and Geoffrey taught in English schools, but most of their careers were made in France.

Geoffrey's main treatise in Latin verse, *Poetria Nova* (1210), is a manual, with full exemplification of the teaching, on verse composition. Its success depended upon its adaptation of the aims and methods of ancient rhetoric to the needs of medieval poetic com-

position. The poetic tradition that Geoffrey and his fellows inau-
gurated was not to be rejected in English poetry until Wordsworth's
day.

The main changes wrought by these new theories of poetry are
directly visible to anybody who sets a piece of Anglo-Saxon poetry –
a passage of *Beowulf,* say – beside a passage of Chaucer, who was
direct if distant heir to these twelfth-century rhetoricians and had a
first hand knowledge of *Poetria Nova.* There is lucidity, apparent
coherence, visible structure, liveliness, verbal grace in Chaucer's
work. The virtues of Anglo-Saxon poetry are different. Chaucer
used a syntax which reproduces relations of cause and effect, of
logical and observable sequence. His vocabulary is an instrument of
objective perception as well of inner self-consciousness: it can be
used for description and analysis. He has a variety of styles which
can be adjusted to his audience and to his subject matter.

The Arts of Poetry taught poets how to write in this lucid, bright
and varied fashion. A modern reader may find the doctrine rather
ordinary, but in the late Middle Ages it established a new mode of
poetry. The prime appeal for understanding is coming to be made
to the inner eye which demands 'imagery' in poetry, not to the inner
ear. In late medieval poetry the typical figure is simile: in earlier
poetry it was metonymy which Geoffrey considered a dull and
exhausted device. The new interest was in saying what things were
like: hence the concern with description and amplification.

It took generations, even centuries, for European poets to learn
these lessons, especially in the intellectual milieu of the later
Middle Ages where what we nowadays call original creative writing
had very little esteem. Advanced learning in the universities did not
encourage this kind of writing. In the English universities there
seems to have been no positive wish to develop vernacular literature
until the 1570s. Much more important for the early history of
vernacular literature are the lower schools in towns and villages, run
by clerical schoolmasters. Boys' schools where grammar was taught
seem to have been the real nurseries of English literature.

Probably even at a fairly low level of grammatical instruction
some stimulus was given to vernacular composition. In all schools,
then as now, there were appropriate occasions for literary displays.
Schools at all times like producing plays. Early in the twelfth
century, there is a note that a clerk and schoolmaster, Geoffrey of
St. Albans, prepared a play about St. Katharine for a performance
at Dunstable. Schools of cathedrals and monasteries were involved
in the dramatic representations of the liturgy on the great occasions

of the Church's year. But vernacular texts of English drama belong to the later medieval centuries.

Where Latin was well taught, schools produced Latin *comediae*: verse pieces often in dialogue, apparently for declamation, not for stage presentation. They are display compositions, modestly learned, often strenuously comic or coyly coarse or sentimental. Some of these pieces were very popular. Often they are highly rhetorical versions of stories which appear elsewhere, particularly in French *fabliaux*. The stories out of which Chaucer made the *Miller's Tale* and the *Reeve's Tale* give the best idea in English of what *fabliaux* were like. In the thirteenth century, an English piece, *Dame Siriz*, using comparable material, is the solitary representative of the genre. *Dame Siriz* in form and colouring suggests clerkly composition in a small-town milieu. A clerk Wilekin attempts to seduce Margery, wife of a merchant away at Boston fair. Failing in a direct assault, Wilekin seeks help from Dame Siriz, who doses a little dog with pepper and successfully uses it to arouse Margery's fear for her own safety and eventually to move Margery to respond to Wilekin's advances. It is an old story, set out here in loose dialogue form. By chance there survives also, from a slightly later date, a fragmentary piece in 85 lines introduced into its manuscript with the title *Interludium de clerico et puella* and dealing with the same story.

The schools also developed fable literature, a genre of short narratives, usually about the animal creation, to which a sharp didactic point is added. The origins of fable composition were remote, but the genre was familiarized in the West through the Latin reworkings of Aesop by Phaedrus and Avianus which were used as the first reading book in schools. There were great new collections of similar stories freshly put together by Odo of Cheriton (*d.* 1247), Alexander Neckham (1157–1217), and others, pedagogues all. Their fables are by no means childish apologues. They are witty, often topical, often cynical. There is no vernacular collection of this sort, but it is plain from Chaucer's *Nun's Priest's Tale* and from sermons that this kind of material was in common use and abundant supply.

There is an early thirteenth-century English *Bestiary* preserved in a late thirteenth-century miscellany, MS Arundel 292. This is a difficult text in 802 lines, written in a puzzling mixture of measures, in short alliterative lines, split septenaries and octosyllabics. The genre is old but this Middle English treatment depends upon the eleventh-century *Physiologus* of Thetbald and presents a select menagerie of creatures, the lion, eagle, serpent, ant, etc., including

the mermaid and elephant. First the nature of the beast is described; then the *significatio* is given. The interest of the writer is
morality, not zoology.

Natura formice [The nature of the ant]

Ðe mire is magti, mikel ge swinkeð	*ant/mighty/you*
In sumer and in softe weder, so we ofte sen hauen.	
In ðe heruest hardilike gangeð,	*autumn/go bravely*
& renneð rapelike, & resteð hire seldum,	*run in haste*
& fecheð hire fode ðer ge it mai finden.	
Gaddreð ilkines sed,	*all kinds of*
Boðe of wude and of wed,	*tree/plant*
Of corn and of gres,	
Ðat hire to hauen es.	*that is hers to collect*
Haleð to hire hole ðat siðen hire helpeð,	*drags/what afterwards*
Ðar ge wile ben	
Winter agen	*to face the winter*

Significacio

Ðe mire muneð us mete to tilen,	*reminds; to procure*
Long livenoð, ðis little wile	*long-lasting sustenance*
Ðe we on ðis werld wunen.	*dwell*
For ðanne we of wenden, ðanne is ure winter.	*depart hence*
We sulen hunger haven and harde sures	*storms*
Buten we ben war here. . . .	*unless/careful*

Bestiary material is used to illustrate all kinds of composition,
stories, love-poetry, sermons, meditations. Many Elizabethan
writers continued to exploit this medieval inheritance.

Every medieval schoolboy who had acquired some knowledge of
Latin would have worked through some of the *Disticha Catonis*, an
accumulation of Latin moral proverbs which had reached a final
form in the Carolingian schools and was to continue in school use
until long after the Renaissance. The collection offered single-line
or couplet injunctions, memorable on account of their concision
and worldly good-sense. Often in medieval writing the authority of
Cato reinforces a truism about life. Gnomic material is of course
common in all early literary cultures. The schools transformed this
traditional lore into a semi-learned kind of writing.

In early Middle English there are two fairly extended bookish
presentations of gnomic material: the twelfth century *Proverbs of
Alfred* (in four versions); and later the *Proverbs of Hendyng*. The
ascription of proverbial wisdom to King Alfred – as legendary as the
ascription of the Wisdom books of the Old Testament to Solomon –
gives authority to familiar morality. The proverbs are presented as

the direct utterance of the worthiest and wisest of kings sitting in council with his thanes. They are composed in alliterative lines, mixed with rhymed couplets. Successive exhortations to 'my dear sons' teach the duties of the estates of man, and offer reflections on the nature of life and human destiny. The *Proverbs of Hendyng*, a shorter piece in some 300 lines, is usually thought to be of mid-thirteenth century composition. The figure of Hendyng is unidentifiable, and the hoary, featureless spokesman is invoked, it would seem, to sustain a kind of satiric disillusionment and moral cynicism.

Mon þat wol of wysdam heren,	
At wyse Hendyng he may lernen,	*from*
Þat wes Marcolves sone;	*Marcolf, a mythical sage*
Gode þonkes & monie þewes	*virtues*
forte teche fele shrewes,	*good-for-nothings*
For þat wes ever is wone . . .	*his custom*
Þis worldes love ys a wrecche,	*misery*
Whose hit here, me ne recche,	*Whoever/I'm not bothered*
Þah y speke heye;	*shout aloud*
For y se þat on broþer	*one*
Lutel recche of þat oþer,	
Be he out of ys eȝe.	
'Fer from eȝe, fer from herte,'	

Quoþ Hendyng. (lines 1–6; 201–9)

In a world of education where books were precious, most of the teaching, especially at the lower levels, was done by spoken question and answer. And at all levels of writing in Latin prose, the form was familiar to English readers: in Boethius's *Consolation of Philosophy*, in several of Alcuin's treatises, in Æfric's *Colloquy* and his *Interrogationes Sigewulfi*. The catechetical method retained its popularity both in teaching and as an expository device in formal composition. It was used for example in philosophical and psychological treatises by Anselm and by Ailred. One of Anselm's scholars at Canterbury, Honorius of Autun, employed it in his lengthy popularization of doctrine, the *Elucidarium*. The work had an enormous success and was translated into most vernacular languages. Only a fragment remains of the early English translation. The same form is used in another fragmentary piece, *Questions between the Master of Oxford and the clerk* in MS Harley 1304, and also in a more substantial piece, though also incomplete, the southern *Vices and Virtues*. This gives psychological analysis and moral classifications at a high level of sophistication in the form of a discussion between Reason and the

Soul. The dialogue form continued to be used in a succession of Middle English pieces in elaborating a theme which had attracted Old English monastic writers – the debate of the body and soul. The device injected a certain dramatic quality and sensationalism into a common homiletic theme.

The catechism is a rudimentary form of dialectical exposition. Higher education elaborated the same method. The formal disputation became the chosen instrument of advanced schools in late medieval times. A thesis was proposed, debated *pro* and *contra*, and in light of the debate the thesis was successively modified to ensure that it was as valid or truth-saying as possible. The method was not only incorporated into the techniques of teaching and examining in schools, but in many respects was taken as showing how all intellectual enquiry was to be conducted. The development of this strictly dialectical, basically oral method of thinking was natural enough in an intensified programme of study which was grounded in the *trivium*. It exploited all the arts of the *trivium*. It required fluency and correctness in verbal expression. The balancing of probabilities was an essential part of logical training. The finding and the persuasive presentation of arguments was the essence of rhetoric. In general terms all medieval literature was shaped within the matrix of this programme. But in particular we may note here that the debate as a form had a powerful and inevitable attraction for medieval writers.

Happily, all the disciplines of the schools find a justification in one brilliant early Middle English debate poem. *The Owl and the Nightingale*, 1794 lines of four-stress couplets, is preserved in two manuscripts: as the first item in the second and separate part of the mid-thirteenth century MS Cotton Caligula A. ix (one of the MSS of Layamon's *Brut*); and also in the second part of Jesus College Oxford MS 29 of slightly later date. It seems likely that the poem was written somewhere near Guildford in Surrey, a town linked in the poem with a Master Nicholas – and his title suggests that he was a schoolmaster. The opening of the poem narrates how the poet overhears an altercation in the hedgerow between a nightingale and an owl. The nightingale attacks the song and general manners of the other bird. At nightfall the owl in turn defends herself against the assault which has been maintained by the nightingale. The birds agree to submit their case to this Master Nicholas, an excellent and judicious authority on the matters in dispute, we are assured. One suspects that this is the poet himself.

But before the birds betake themselves to his judgment, they rehearse their cases against each other. They do this quite formally. First the nightingale elaborates on her charges against the owl on the two major counts. Then the owl delivers her countercharges on the same issues and defends herself against the nightingale's attack. The shape of the argument becomes clear. The owl is charged with being a dismal, life-denying perversity, preoccupied with dirt, disaster, and dangerous knowledge. The nightingale is charged with general uselessness and the possession of a one-track mind concerned solely with self-indulgence and sex. In self-defence the owl claims for herself a judicious common-sense, foresight, a concern for the public as a whole and a special concern for the welfare of individual unfortunates.

Of none wintere ich ne recche,
Vor ich nam non asvnde wrecche.   *enfeebled*
& ek ic frouri uele wiȝte   *comfort many*
Þat mid hom nabbed none miȝtte.   *have no strength*
Hi boþ hoȝfule & uel arme,   *are miserable & very poor*
An secheþ ȝorne to þe warme.   *eagerly*
Oft ich singe uor hom þe more
For lutli sum of hore sore.   *in order to reduce their pain*
                                                    (lines 533–40)

The nightingale counter-asserts the absolute value of her own *joie de vivre* which she can communicate to those superior people who desire it.

Ac ich alle blisse mid me bringe,
Ech wiȝt is glad for mine þinge
& blisseþ hit wanne ich cume,   *when*
& hiȝteþ aȝen mine kume.   *look forward to*
Þe blostme ginneþ springe & sprede,
Boþe ine tro & ek on mede.   *tree*
Þe lilie mid hire faire wlite   *beauty*
Wolcumeþ me – þat þu hit wite! –   *knowest*
Bid me mid hire faire blo   *colour*
Þat ich shulle to hire flo.
Þe rose also mid hire rude   *blush*
Þat cumeþ ut of þe þornewode,
Bit me þat ich shulle singe   *Asks*
Vor hire luue one skentinge.   *song of desire*
                                                    (lines 433–46)

Within this confrontation there are many turns and arguments which make it difficult for a modern reader (like a juror in a court case) to follow the drift. The poem is an exhibition of the skills involved in presenting opposing views. Once the narrations are examined a medieval technique of organization becomes plainer. On each side the case is made up of particular points designed to illustrate the general line of attacks or defence. These particulars may be simple assertions, or scraps of abusive language, or anecdotes, or analogies, fable-material, embryonic fabliaux, tags of conventional wisdom on the authority of Alfred. Each point made in this manner is in turn answered or turned back upon the other party, not immediately always, sometimes after some hundred lines in a later speech.

At the same time the scope of the argument deepens as the piece continues and neatly incorporates a discussion as to whether there is a special faculty of predictive knowledge in the human mind and another discussion on the role and forms of love in human society. These were current issues under debate at the end of the twelfth century. Indeed throughout, the poem is full of allusions to contemporary issues: on the definition of virtue, on the new schools of music, and the new style of song-verse, on the Northern European missions, on the new theology of confession. But the poet is concerned only with the play of these issues on the surface of the poem, with the result that the modern reader must work not only to unravel the threads of agrument, but also to activate the cultural life of the time in order to see the relevance of some of the material.

There is no message in *The Owl and the Nightingale*. The argument ends on a technicality. No judgment is given. The birds fly out of the poem to seek Master Nicholas's decision.

'Bihote ich habbe, soþ hit is,	*Promised*
Þat Maister Nichole, þat is wis,	
Bituxen us deme schulde,	*judge*
An ȝet ich wene þat he wule.' . . .	*expect*
'Ah ute we þah to him fare,	*But let us*
For þar is unker dom al ȝare.'	*judgment on us all prepared*
'Do we', þe Niȝtegale seide,	
'Ah wa schal unker speche rede,	*who*
An telle touore unker deme?'	
'Þarof ich schal þe wel icweme',	*fully satisfy*
Cwaþ þe Houle, 'for al, ende of orde,	*from beginning to end*
Telle ich con, word after worde.	
An ȝef þe þincþ þat ich misrempe	*distort*
Þu stond aȝein & do me crempe.'	*check*
Mid þisse worde forþ hi ferden,	
Al bute here & bute uerde,	*without armed escort*

To Portesham þat heo bicome.   *Portisham in Dorset*
Ah hu heo spedde of heore dome   *succeeded in their suit*
Ne can ich eu na more telle.
Her nis na more of þis spelle.

(lines 1745–8; 1779 to end)

The poem is to be taken as about what it purports to be: the debating of two birds. The poem is certainly not solemn; it is often comic. But it is serious in that as the poet elaborates arguments for and against, he draws out of the experience and the moral and intellectual milieu of his own society issues which he acknowledges to be important.

The tone of the poem may suggest Chaucer's in *The Parliament of Fowls*: it is that of elegant and inventive celebration, relating to a real world which is taken for granted. Unlike Chaucer's poem *The Owl and the Nightingale* is not courtly. It is humorously learned but not refined. It is a poem of the town invaded by the countryside. It is clerkly, but not monastic or even ecclesiastical, nor particularly pious. There is throughout an acceptance of the normality of ordinary secular life. The poem is a striking tribute to the vitality and literacy of what, when we think of the range and richness of Angevin culture as a whole, must still be regarded as a vernacular sub-culture. It is a sub-culture which had sprung up round English schools by the beginning of the thirteenth century.

III

The most profound changes that come over literature in the twelfth and thirteenth centuries are the result of changes within religious life. We are not concerned with matters of ecclesiastical organization and structure, but with the inner life. In their deeper thoughts about life and death, men came to a recognition that a more intimate relationship was possible between God and the individual worshipper than traditional religion had provided. The new relationship gave subject matter for many writings throughout the rest of the Middle Ages. Indeed once started the movement was irreversible. From our narrower point of view, the recognition of this relationship is important because it demanded self-explanation and self-expression. The keener awareness of the individual character of the encounter between God and man was accompanied by a heightened emotionalism and an increased power of self-analysis and introversion; and these have consequences for the development of literature. To put the complex matter over-simply:

the new spirituality built up an enormous potential for imaginative activity.

Although the new experiences of religion were essentially personal, the monasteries were still the seed-beds and the forcing-houses for its cultivation. Earlier reform movements, especially that associated with Cluny in the early eleventh century, had produced an ideal of a busy ordered community organized best to conduct decorously a full daily round of monastic worship. All other activities which had accrued richly to monastic life, reading, writing, gardening, housekeeping, farming, had been counted subsidiary to this highly organized corporate worship.

But in the twelfth century among the best spirits of the age grew a new desire for singlemindedness in religion, a desire to reduce the accumulation of subsidiary activities, a desire to simplify and intensify the dependence upon God. It was the Cistercian Order which at the beginning of the twelfth century best represented this movement. The Cistercians gained their particular influence through the power and representative quality of Bernard of Clairvaux (*ca.* 1090–1153), a man in many ways, in personal style and in religious force, like John Wesley. The man and his writings were of a piece, austere, formally elegant, passionate, personal. The influence of St. Bernard is imposed on almost every piece of devotional writing in the later Middle Ages.

The direct links between Bernard and England were few; but there were many Cistercian foundations in England. Though there were some Cistercians of distinction as writers, notably Ailred of Rievaulx (*ca.* 1110–66), the Cistercians were never an order famous for learning or for literary activities. Their influence was overpoweringly strong in giving a peculiar intense quality to the devotional life. Their hour of immediate influence was brief. By the end of the twelfth century some men thought they had acquired a strong odour of sanctimoniousness.

A more systematic attempt to intellectualize the new attitudes in religion was made by a school of writers on the fringes of the University of Paris in the abbey of St. Victor. The Victorines explored and charted the minds of men and drew great maps of knowledge. The vast-ranging writings of their greatest scholar, Hugh of St. Victor (*ca.* 1096–1141), were speedily available in most large libraries in England. In all fields of high intellectual speculation, in theology in all its branches, in Biblical interpretation, in psychology, in epistemology, the Victorines were busy and influential.

In the later medieval centuries the most remarkable demonstration of the hard-worn ability to express the inwardness of exalted experience is to be found in the literature of mysticism. Men
learned the language of rapture from St. Bernard, especially from
his sermons on the Song of Songs; they learnt the language of
mystical theory from Richard of St. Victor. But the vernacular in
England is not used systematically to treat mystical experience
before Richard Rolle in the fourteenth century.

More than a century earlier, however, the new religious attitudes
were prominent in vernacular writing which though not mystical
had an avowedly devotional character. Of the greatest importance is
the lengthy prose treatise, the *Ancrene Riwle* (The Rule of
Ancresses). In eight parts the work gave instruction to a small group
of young women who had withdrawn from the world to live in a
range of individual cells in order to devote themselves to a life of
physical hardship, self-knowledge and religious observance for the
love of God. The first and last parts of this treatise deal with the
externalities of the life, and give instruction and advice on the
formal devotions that they should use, on living conditions and
outward behaviour.

Hwa se is unheite, forkeorue of uhtsong tene, of euch of þe oþre fiue, þe
haluendal of euchan ʒef ha is seccre. Hwa se is ful meoseise, of al beo ha
cwite. Neome hire secnesse nawt ane þolemodliche, ah do swiðe
gleadliche, & al is hiren þet hali chirche ret oðer singeð. Þah ʒe ahen of
godd þenchen in euch time, meast þah in ower tiden þet ower þohtes ne
beon fleotinde þenne. ʒef ʒe þurh ʒemeles gluffeð of wordes, oðer mis-
neomeð uers, neomeð ower venie dun ed ter eorðe wið þe hond ane. Al
fallen adun for muche misneomunge & schawið ofte i schrift ower ʒemeles
herabuten. (end of Part I)

(Whosover is unwell, let her cut ten [paternosters] from matins, and five
from each of the other hours, and half the total from all of them, if she is
decidedly ill. If she is seriously ill, let her be excused the lot. She should
accept her illness not only patiently, but very gladly, and all is hers that holy
church reads or sings. Although you must think of God at all times, most
intently think of Him during your hours, so that your thoughts are not
wandering about. If through carelessness you stumble over your words, or
say a wrong versicle, make a *venia* [plea for forgiveness], bending down to
the earth and touching it with the hands only. Prostrate yourselves completely for serious error, and frequently disclose in confession your carelessness in these matters.)

The intermediate parts, parts two to seven, deal with what the
author thought much more important, the Inner Rule; and it is in
this area of the book that we can see the new spirit of religion

thoughtfully anatomized. He begins part two with instruction on how to keep strict and watchful control upon the senses, and then upon the feelings and emotions. He proceeds to show how the temptations to sin which originate on the level of instinctual life can be identified and resisted. He explains how the surest defence against sin is through frequent self-examination which should issue as verbal confession. Then he goes on to show how a life of pain and humiliation can serve as a constant discipline and produce habits of purity. Finally in part seven of the Inner Rule he describes how a life of self-control fulfils itself in a purified life of love.

When the argument of this central area of the book is set out thus, the unfolding coherence, perhaps also the grimness of the programme is evident. Yet the book does not read like this, either simply or grimly. Each part of the work has a distinct flexibility. Often the argument can appear to digress and draw in subsidiary material or linger to introduce further schemes of classification. It can leap forward or back across the whole work. Everywhere there is art concealing art. The total effect is of sustained conversation, animated and witty, always controlled by an awareness of the quality and effectiveness of the words and rhythms that are used.

Sometimes the prose takes wings, as in the wooing speeches of Christ:

Sete feor o þi luue. Þu ne schalt seggen se muchel þet ich nule ȝeoue mare. Wult tu castles, kinedomes, wult tu wealden al þe world? Ich chulle do þe betere – makie þe wið al þis cwen of heoueriche. Þu schalt te seolf beo seoueuald brihtre þen þe sunne, nan uuel ne schal nahhi þe, na wunne ne schal wonti þe; al þi wil schal beon iwraht in heouene & ec in eorðe, ȝe & ȝet in helle; ne schal neauer heorte þenchen hwuch selhðe þet ich nule ȝeouen for þi luue, unmeteliche, vneuenliche, unendeliche mare: al Creasuse weole, þe wes kinge richest; Absalones schene wlite, þe as ofte as me euesede him, salde his euesunge – þe her þet he kearf of – for twa hundret sicles of seoluer iweiet; Asaeles swiftschipe, þe straf wið heortes of urn; Samsones strengðe, þe sloh a þusent of his fan al ed a time & ane bute fere; Cesares freolec; Alixandres hereword; Moysese heale. Nalde a mon for an of þeos ȝeouen al þet he ahte? Ant alle somet aȝein mi bodi ne beoð nawt wurð a nelde. (Part VII)
(Set a high price on thy love. Thou canst not name so much that I will not give more. Wilt thou castles, kingdoms, wilt thou rule all the world? I will do better for thee – make thee with all this queen of the kingdom of heaven. Though shalt thyself be seventimes brighter than the sun, no evil shall come nigh thee, no joy shall be lacking thee; all thy desire shall be fulfilled in heaven and also in earth, yea and also in hell; nor shall ever heart imagine the kind of happiness that I shall not give thee in return for thy

love, immeasurably, incomparably, infinitely more: all the wealth of Croesus who was the richest of kings; the shining beauty of Absalon, who as often as one trimmed his hair, sold the trimmings – the hair that was cut off – for two hundred shekels of silver in measure; the agility of Asael who competed with deer in running; the strength of Samson who slew a thousand of his foes at a time and, alone without help; the nobility of Caesar; the prowess of Alexander; the vigour of Moses. Would not a man give for only one of these all that he possessed? And all of them together in comparison with my body are not worth a needle.)

The author is not identified. He was a cleric, a canon rather than a monk, a well-read and travelled man with experience of the world, probably something of a scholar. He knows the Bible well and many of the aids to Biblical study. He draws often upon Gregory and Augustine and a range of later authors including Anselm, Bernard and Ailred; and shows a rather surprising familiarity with the ideas of university scholars teaching at Paris around the year 1200. But his bent is always literary rather than strictly theological. His prime concern is with life not dogma.

The *Ancrene Riwle* was written in the early decades of the thirteenth century. But all questions of date and provenance are involved in the confusion of the surviving manuscripts. There are five thirteenth-century manuscripts which contain the Rule in some form or other in English, and two substantial English versions from the fourteenth century; but extracts and adaptations continued to be made into the sixteenth century. There are also French versions and Latin versions of the Rule. Although it is now certain that the Rule was originally composed in English, none of the surviving texts gives it in its original form. The text in MS Cotton Nero A.xiv is the fullest early text and it was this Nero text which was used first in modern study of the Rule. But there is a text in Corpus Christi College Cambridge MS 402 which has acquired a special importance and is usually distinguished from other texts of the Rule by the title given to it in the manuscript – *Ancrene Wisse* (Guide of Ancresses). This manuscript can be linked with Wigmore in Herefordshire where the priory had been ruled for some years (*ca.* 1147) by Andrew of St. Victor, in his generation a leading Biblical scholar. The text of the *Ancrene Wisse* was extraordinarily well transcribed. There is consistency about the spelling, grammatical usages, punctuation, vocabulary and style which is remarkable among Middle English texts. Moreover there is another manuscript, MS Bodley 34, which contains a group of different texts written out by a different scribe who nevertheless produces exactly the same consistent characteristics of spelling and language of the text of *Ancrene Wisse*. The dialect exemplified in both manuscripts is of the West Midlands, probably of Herefordshire, somewhat formalized in transcription. But is seems that in these two manuscripts we have evidence of the existence in the West Midlands in the early thirteenth century of an organized centre for the production of religious pieces in the vernacular. Again we are confronted with the literary vitality of the West Midland area in the early Middle English period.

The Rule was written for the edification of young women; so were the pieces collected in MS Bodley 34. There is a prose exhortation to virginity called *Holy Maidenhood*, which sets out the disadvantages of worldly life and human marriage, and the inestimable advantages to be had by withdrawing into the religious life and a spiritual marriage with Christ. It is an eloquent, often vivid, but in the main deliberately, matter-of-fact persuasion. This work is also found in another manuscript, MS Cotton Titus D. xviii, not of this same West Midland scriptorium, but containing an imperfect text of the Rule.

Another prose treatise, *Sawles Warde* (Guard of the Soul), appears in both MS Bodley 34 and MS Cotton Titus A. xviii, and in another closely related manuscript, MS Royal 17 A. xxvii. *Sawles Warde* is an adaptation of some chapters of scholastic dialogue on the nature of man, *De Anima* by Hugh of St. Victor. The vernacular treatment concentrates on the moral allegory where, in the house of the mind, Wit and Will are represented as man and wife struggling for mastery. Again the peculiar virtues of West Midland religious prose are in evidence. There is a similar control of word and phrase as is found in *Ancrene Wisse*, a similar ingenious use of detail and of a sub-comic tone, even when the issues are most serious.

Ant Warchipe hire easkeð: 'Hweonene cumest tu, Fearlac deaðes mungunge?' 'Ich cume' he seið 'of helle'. 'Of helle?' 'ʒe' seið Fearlac 'witerliche ofte & ilome.' 'Nu' seið þenne Warschipe 'for þi trowðe treowliche tele us hwuch is helle ant hwet tu hauest isehen þrin.' 'Ant ich' he seið 'Fearlac, o mi trowðe bluðeliche, nawt tah efter þet hit is – for þet ne mei na tunge tellen – ah efter þet ich mei & con, þertowart ich chulle reodien. Helle is wid wiðute met & deop wiðute grund, ful of brune uneuenlich, for ne mei nan eorðlich fur euenin þertowart; ful of stench unþolelich, for ne mahte in eorðe na cwic þing hit þolien; ful of sorhe untalelich, for ne mei na muð for wrecchedom ne for wa rikenin hit ne tellen. Se þicke is þrinne þe þosternesse þet me hire mei grapin. For þet fur ne ʒeueð na liht, ah blent ham þe ehnen þe þer beoð wið a smorðrinde

smoke, smeche forcuðest, ant tah i þet ilke swarte þeosternesse swarte
þinges ha iseoð, as deoflen þet ham meallið ant derueð as & dreccheð wið
alles cunnes pinen, ant iteilede draken grisliche ase deoflen þe forswolheð
ham ihal & speoweð ham eft ut biuoren & bihinden, oðerhwile torendeð
ham & tocheoweð ham euch greot, ant heo eft iwurðeð hal to a swuch bale
bute bote as ha ear weren.'
(And Prudence asks her, 'Where do you come from, Fear, who put us in
mind of death?' 'I come' she says 'from hell'. 'From hell?' says Prudence,
'and have you seen hell?' 'Yes' says Fear, 'most assuredly and often'. 'Now'
says Prudence then 'tell us truly on your honour what kind of place is hell
and what you have seen therein.' 'And I, Fear', she says, 'gladly on my
honour, yet not exactly as it is – for that no tongue can tell – but as far as I
can and know, I will inform you about it. Hell is wide without measure and
deep without bottom; full of incomparable burning, for no fire on earth may
be put alongside it; full of unendurable stench, for no living thing on earth
could endure it; full of inexpressible misery, for no tongue for very
wretchedness and distress could talk about it. So dense is the gloom there
that a man may clutch at it. For the fire gives no light, but it blinds the eyes
of those who are there with a smothering smoke, the foulest of fumes, and
yet in that same black gloom, they see black shapes, such as devils who
thrash and hurt them for ever and torment them with all kinds of pains, and
dragons with tails, horrible as devils, who swallow them whole and spit
them out again before and behind, sometimes tear them to pieces, and
chew up each particle of them, and again they become whole, as they were
before, for a similar punishment without respite.)

The pieces that stand first in MS Bodley 34 stand first also in
MS Royal 17 A. xxvii. These are three prose lives of saints: Saint
Katherine of Alexandria, Saint Margaret of Antioch and Saint
Juliana. All three lives are very similar. They are stories of virgin
martyrs, with little basis in history, offered as edifying entertainment. They were designed to please the ear in their use of
alliterating rhythms – rather in the style of Ælfric's *Lives of the
Saints*; and designed moreover to capture easy attention by their
portrayals of shining heroic maidens triumphing over the most
outrageously cruel villains. In each there is a fair crop of sensational
horror to make the flesh creep; entries by the sliest and most
picturesque devils; and all the sweet savour and red roses of a
martyr's triumph. These Katherine Group legends are excellently
told.

They are specimens of an immense medieval output of legendary
lives. Saints' lives and passions in all medieval languages, learned
and vernacular, mirror very faithfully the available literary fashions
and also the changing patterns of piety over the centuries. In many
respects they are sanctified romances: sometimes in their treatment,

even in their material scarcely distinguishable from unsanctified romances. But the form of the saint's legend in Latin acquires a certain standardization in the *Legenda Aurea* of Jacobus à Voragine (1230–98), an Italian Dominican friar. In England also the same process of accumulating and rewriting – usually abbreviating – the old legends into short, brisk narratives, gathered up into massive collections, was already producing the metrical *South English Legendary* and a *Northern Passion*. From the middle of the thirteenth century such collections begin to snowball. By the end of the thirteenth century composition in English is dominated by the pulpit.

A century earlier the situation was quite different. Preaching seemed to have developed little since Anglo-Saxon times. As already noticed, Ælfric's sermons were still laid under contribution and we know by report of the vernacular preaching of Wulfstan of Worcester and of Abbot Samson of St. Edmunds at the end of the twelfth century. There are a few small early Middle English sermon collections which show that something of the Anglo-Saxon skills was kept alive. But on the whole the twelfth century in England despite its general intellectual activity, in fact probably because its intellectual activity was at a level which could be maintained only in the Latin language, has little to show.

At the end of the twelfth century a great bishop of Paris, Maurice de Sully, established a new style of vernacular preaching in France. His mass sermons were brief, simple, well-constructed on a regular plan: narration of the gospel incident, short spiritual commentary and exhortation: a plan not unlike Ælfric's, but in Maurice's sermons worked out with more precision to achieve a sharper impact. Some of Maurice's sermons were translated rather laboriously into English: these are the so-called *Kentish Sermons* in Bodleian MS Laud Misc. 471.

The movement at the end of the twelfth century towards a revival of preaching was accelerated by the coming of the Friars. The Franciscans in particular can be thought of as diffusing to all members of society, to laymen as well as to the secular clergy, the attitudes of devotion and the new piety, the new inwardness of religion which had been the concern of the monasteries and of people with special religious gifts in twelfth century. 'About this time,' wrote Roger of Wendover, 'there sprang up under the auspices of Pope Innocent, a sect of preachers called Minorites [Franciscans] who filled the earth, dwelling in cities and towns, by tens and sevens, possessing no property at all, living according to the Gospel, making a show of the greatest poverty, walking with naked feet, and setting a great example of humility to all classes. On Sundays and feastdays they went forth from their habitations preaching the Gospel in the parish churches. . . .'

Both the Dominicans and the Franciscans set great store by preaching and trained to this end. Much of their preaching may have been extempore, and during the early thirteenth century much of it was no doubt in Anglo-Norman, for the Franciscans recruited an élite. What survives of their compositions in English does not fully measure their importance in English literary history. It is plain that they brought a new liveliness and persuasiveness into the religious uses of the vernacular. They would employ any verbal device to arrest the hearts and imaginations of their listeners – impassioned rhetoric, paradox and startling imagery. They would take popular songs and use them as texts for sermons and they extended the technique of introducing *exempla* and ransacked all sources sacred and profane for the purpose. Thirteenth-century material of certain Franciscan origin occurs in the main in commonplace books, and is largely made up of scraps of useful information, odd verses, religious parodies and hymns, usually assembled indiscriminately by a variety of hands in any of the three languages, Latin, Anglo-Norman, English. Although individual pieces may be detached and identified, for instance the *Luue Ron* in which Friar Thomas of Hales teaches a young woman in religion that Christ is the sweetest of lovers, or the English translations of familiar Latin hymns by Friar William Herebert (*d.* 1330), Franciscan influence was sufficently powerful to transcend the vernacular and to work downwards from the highest level in the intellectual life of England. Their great achievement was in the development of the late medieval scholastic disciplines in the university at Oxford. The work of such men as Duns Scotus, Roger Bacon, William of Ockham contributed to the formation and expression of English thought over centuries, but the English vernacular of their own times was incapable of response.

Without the profound intellectual influence of the friars, the Augustinian canons contributed more directly to the revival of English literacy. The canons were particularly active in the minor schools. Some of them wrote as well as taught. A canon Orm gave his name to the *Ormulum*:

Þiss boc iss nemmnedd Orrmulum Forrþi þat Orrm itt wrohhte.

This book is called 'Ormulum' because Orm wrote it, and it is a compilation in English of the mass Gospels for the year in 10,000 long, unrhymed septenaries. The work exists in Bodleian MS Junius I, transcribed probably by Orm himself in a North-east Midland dialect for which he devised an elaborate and scrupulously accurate notation, presumably to facilitate reading aloud. In all respects Orm laboured to present the Gospels in a full, simple and unambiguous form. His attempt at fulness in content and at standardization in presentation are evidence of what the breakdown of the Anglo-Saxon tradition entailed.

The collapse was not so total as this work may suggest, for it reads rather like the composition of a diligent and ingenious missionary in foreign parts struggling to put Scripture for the first time into a barbarous tongue.

Orm's activities demonstrate that when a writer, even one of only moderate literary gifts deprived of the support of a literary tradition, takes on an extensive piece of composition, he is obliged to confront and solve some problems of form. In some communities of the West Midlands as we have seen the habits of literary prose were sufficiently preserved to permit highly successful adaptation for some specialized needs. In many places these habits in prose did not exist. The translator of the *Kentish Sermons* for example was groping for a syntax and style. Very often there was nothing to fall back on but verse forms. So Orm used the Latin septenaries. Sermons, homiletic tracts and saints' lives employ a variety of verse forms rhymed and unrhymed. Often in our eyes the intention is prosaic enough. A Biblical paraphrase, *Genesis and Exodus*, uses four-stress rhymed couplets; another, *Jacob and Joseph*, a mixture of ecclesiastical septenaries and French alexandrines.

During the late thirteenth century scriptural and homiletic material was gathered together in collections which continued to be copied out and expanded into the age of printing at the end of the fifteenth century. These collections merge with the collections of saints' lives and are minor products of that spirit of encyclopedism which marks much of the intellectual work of the late thirteenth century.

A Northern work, *Cursor Mundi*, for the most part in four-stress couplets, contains nearly 24,000 lines in its fullest version. It presents a composite survey of world history, pivoting on the Incarnation of Christ. It is based on the work of the twelfth-century scholastic writers who had harmonized ancient, Biblical and apocryphal history into a continuous narrative. For an understanding of the design read into human history by late medieval writers this is a useful work. As illuminating of their conception of the moral order is *Handlyng Synne* by Robert Mannyng of Brunne. *Handlyng Synne*, an adaptation of the Anglo-Norman *Manuel de Pechiez* of William of Waddington, deals with the precepts and practice of morality, treating in turn the Ten Commandments, the Seven Deadly Sins, the Sacraments, and the elements of confession. This scheme is elaborated at length (the work has more than 12,000 lines in four-stress couplets) with stories and social comment designed to illustrate the categories. It assembles popular anecdote, fable, fabliau, saint's life, Scripture and apocryphal Scripture, legend and history: a reduction of the world's experience to a comprehensive moral scheme.

Robert Mannyng was author also of an English version of a popular Anglo-Norman chronicle by Peter of Langtoft, another derivative of Wace's *Brut* into which a mass of later material had been worked. Robert Mannyng lived far into the fourteenth century. He was still alive in the third Edward's reign, as a canon at Sixhill in Lincolnshire. In his writing Robert tells us something about himself and enables us to infer much more about how he thought of his role as an English writer. He wrote, he claimed, in plain English for the edification of simple men who knew no French. He recognized that the vernacular was in common use for romances and popular rhymes. He wanted to do something better. The same point is made at greater length by the author of *Cursor Mundi*. Men love to hear stories and read romances of Alexander, Brut, King Arthur, Gawain, Tristram and many more. They relish the appeal of stories of courtly lovings. Both Robert Mannyng and the author of *Cursor Mundi* cherish the hope that they can turn these interests in the vernacular to loftier ends. English they see has already become a literary language with a wide appeal and application. Indeed by the end of the thirteenth century we can detect the decline of Anglo-Norman – a decline that is speeded up during the next century with the surge of national feeling in the French wars. Already in the early years of the century a more self-conscious and deliberately artistic use is being made of English. The public for the great verse *King Alisaunder*, composed in the South-East of England shortly after 1300, was looking for something that could reflect, though still palely, the learning and the literary dignity of the medieval Latin epic and of the aristocratic French versions of ancient story. In some ways a work such as *King Alisaunder* looks forward to the high literary achievement of Chaucer and his contemporaries. But fourteenth century literary history is not a simple matter. There were to be many checks, cross-currents and innovations. By 1300 the English vernacular was re-emerging. The clearest and most distinguished testimonies to the re-establishment of a native style are some of the shorter vernacular poems in MS Harley 2253.

4

ALLITERATIVE POETRY IN THE FOURTEENTH AND FIFTEENTH CENTURIES

D. J. Williams

From about the middle of the fourteenth century, and beginning, it seems, with baffling suddenness, there was a rapid growth of poetry composed in a metrical form inherited from Old English alliterative verse. Because of this ancestry and because of the suddenness it is usually referred to as the Alliterative Revival, and its impetus survived into the sixteenth century. There are some difficulties about treating all the poems of this movement together in a brief space. They include some of the finest and best-known poems in Middle English, comfortably comparable in quality with Chaucer's: *Sir Gawain and the Green Knight, Pearl, Piers Plowman*. They cover in any case such a wide variety of styles and subjects that the integrity of the category assumed in this chapter is threatened. However, most of the poems to be considered have enough in common, beyond their verse form, to justify certain generalizations. The first part of the chapter attempts such generalizations and conjectures about the history and relations of the poems and the circumstances of their composition. The second gives a critical account of individual works.

I

The Alliterative Form

The common denominator of these poems is their use, in some form, of an unrhymed line whose structure is not unlike that in Old English poetry, although to call a Middle English poem 'alliterative' generally has further implications.

The principle behind the line is different from the alternating strong and weak accents of the more widely used English iambic metre. Its structure is based on the balancing of four stressed and any number of unstressed syllables about a medial pause. This usually means two stresses in each half-line. The function of

alliteration is to give unity to the two halves of the line, usually by
pointing stressed syllables. The Old English pattern of alliteration,
linking the first three stresses but not the last, remains typical:

Now the *ký́ng* of this *ký́the* ‖ *kéfe* hym oure Lórde

But the flexibility of the line is greater in Middle English because of
the freedom with which further stressed syllables can be introduced, usually of varying weight, and because of a much freer use of
alliteration:

His *bé́de* grehównde and his *bró́nde* ‖ and nó *bý́erne* élls

And *bó́wnnes* over a *bró́de* méde ‖ with *bré́th* at his hérte

A line may have as many as six or seven main and subsidiary
stresses, while alliteration may at one extreme be reduced to a
couple of syllables, or at the other be multiplied to point more than
three stresses, or even be shifted onto unstressed syllables:

Mí́st múged on the mór ‖ mált on the móuntez

Uch *hílle* had a *hátte* ‖ a mýst-*hakel hú́ge*

Brókez bý́led and *bré́ke* ‖ *bi bónkkez abó́ute*

In origin this metre with its chiming initials is a native growth
quite separate from the syllabic and rhymed verse of French and
Latin, but by the fourteenth century the meeting of the two
traditions had made possible some striking combinations. End
rhyme could be added to alliteration and the alliterating lines
grouped into stanzas, often of a breathtaking complexity.

A great deal of Middle English verse employs alliteration while
depending on rhyme and syllable for its main structure – a large
number of the lyrics for example. Although the blurred boundaries
of such categories are interesting they are outside the scope of this
chapter. On the other hand most of the poetry to be considered
here is, in following the alliterative tradition, carrying on rather
more than the mechanism of a verse line.

A reader of Middle English alliterative poetry soon notices the
presence of a distinctive vocabulary. Numbers of the words are
rarely to be found outside alliterative poetry, and many words and
phrases cluster about certain subjects. There are, for instance,
numerous synonyms or near synonyms for 'man' and 'horse' and for
their activities in typical contexts of hunting or combat. The reader

also becomes familiar with a large stock of phrases and rhythmic and alliterative combinations which all the poets use with slight variations. Much of this stock is identical, allowing for changes in the language, with that of Old English poetry, and this has often been explained rather vaguely by reference to a cultural memory preserving in a later and quite different society the traditional ideas and attitudes of an earlier 'heroic' age. But an account in purely literary and artistic terms is more satisfactory and tells us much about the nature of alliterative poetry.

It is true that not only words, phrases and patterns, but even topics such as heroic conduct recur in this poetry to the end of the Middle English period. Some of these topics were as alive as ever to the later poets, but what they thought about them and how they used them were different. Verbal patterns and vocabulary continue because they are as much part of the medium of expression as of what is expressed. They are embedded in the substance of the verse itself. Rather as in rhymed verse a poet is likely to use some rhymes more often than others, so the alliterative poet has his stock patterns, but more noticeably perhaps since alliteration infects the whole line, not only its close. But we should not regard these patterns necessarily as the alliterative poet's 'moon and June', as refuges for flagging invention. They are the available mechanisms and materials of his chosen form and he will show his quality as often by his use of them as by abandoning them.

The long life of these 'formulae', as they are frequently called, was no doubt encouraged by the probability that much alliterating poetry in its earlier years was transmitted orally as often as by manuscript – stock phraseology is easier to retain in the memory. But such considerations are irrelevant in the poems considered here, all evidently composed 'in the study'. It remains true, though, that alliterative poetry is in other important senses 'oral'. Its most characteristic effects can really only be appreciated by the ear. This is obviously so in the case of ornate and sonorous passages of description or vigorous action for which some of the poems are famous. An important factor in the work of many alliterative poets is the display of their art itself. The audience were expected to appreciate rhetorical and metrical skills, often amounting to bravura, which are manifested through recitation aloud.

On the other hand it is a great mistake to regard the medium as a cumbersome one only useful for battles and noisy arguments. An essential way in which it is an oral verse is its closeness to the rhythms of natural English speech. Its most typical patterns are stereotypes of some of those rhythms, so that as well as the rich artificiality the medium is almost too well known for it is capable of an easier, natural style, often underlying the other. The range from the splendour of *Fortune* to the efficient seriousness of *Mum and the Sothsegger* is wide. Only the best of the poets command more than a part of it. Such generalizations as it is possible to make about the numerous subjects and preoccupations they cover are best considered together with what we know of their original audience. A sense of responsibility towards audience and subject, coupled with a certain impressive competence, are qualities often to be found in the humblest of these works.

Background and Audience

It is probable that the tradition of composing alliterative poetry in some form continued uninterrupted from the Old English period to the fourteenth century. Evidence is scanty, probably because many manuscripts have been lost, and just possibly because something of the tradition was kept alive only orally – though it is hard at this distance to imagine what. At any rate even the earliest poems of the sudden new growth were composed by men with books within reach. Until we can prove the loss of great predecessors, and provided we do not imply a consciously archaizing reversion to old forms, the name Revival will do well enough to refer to the new growth, whatever its causes (no doubt it is partly to do simply with the growth of all serious writing in English); while we can at least say something about the particular milieu in which the poets worked.

The great majority of their compositions are associated with the western and northern regions, away from the capital and the South and East generally. The strangeness of their language to a modern reader who finds Chaucer easy enough is largely accounted for by their having been written in a form of English which survives only in provincial dialects, whereas Chaucer's was to become the standard. But this regional distribution was not exclusive, and the modern implications of the word provincial are quite inappropriate. Some of their poems were copied in dialects other than those of the North and West. Chaucer knew alliterative poetry, and even if the Parson, being a 'Southren man', could not compose '"rum, ram, ruf", by lettre', his creator gives occasional signs that he himself could (*cf. The Knight's Tale*, 2605–13). The alliterative poets were well read in foreign and Latin literature – the *Gawain*-poet possibly as widely so as Chaucer – although they were not led thereby to forsake their *traditional metre. Their interests and preoccupations were by no means provincial. The politics of Winner and Waster* and *Piers Plowman* have as much to do with London and the court as with the country.

Still, the West and North are the home of this poetry, and in these areas its patrons seem chiefly to have been aristocratic households and families of some substance. Several important exceptions must be noticed, but the typical alliterative poet may be imagined as an educated man, clergyman or layman, in the service of one of the great nobles or of a lesser knight in his provincial estates.

There is almost no evidence of particular cases, but the families of the de Bohuns, the Beauchamps of Warwick, and the House of Lancaster and their dependents may be taken as likely examples. John of Gaunt, Duke of Lancaster, was one of Chaucer's patrons and his sphere of influence included a large part of the northern alliterative area. The de Bohuns were patrons in the fourteenth century of a famous group of manuscript illuminators, and Sir Humphrey de Bohun, Sixth Earl of Hereford, had commissioned, so its author tells us, *William of Palerne*, one of the earliest alliterative romances. Such households display an active interest in the arts and literature, and a poet would have access to his patron's library which, if that of Guy of Warwick early in the century is any indication, might contain a wide variety of religious and secular books in French and Latin.

The poet may have been himself a courtier, or possibly, like Chaucer at the royal court, his main employment may have been administrative. If he were a clergyman he might be chaplain to the household. His poems would be read aloud, perhaps he read them himself, to the courtly audience. This probably accounts for the in most cases small number of manuscripts in which each alliterative poem survives. There would be little need for more than a couple of copies. In this rather intimate way a poem might still get a surprisingly wide distribution.

All these circumstances affect the literature. Even when a poem has not been specially commissioned it is likely to be influenced by the interests and preoccupations of the patron and the court as well as of the poet. Many of the poems present, often in idealized form, details of courtly life and knightly combat. But they are concerned in depth too with moral and political issues that occupied the higher ranks of the laity: the paradoxes set up within a Christian ethic by divergent ideals of human love and the need for a man to make his way by physical prowess.

The ambitiousness of these themes should not be a surprise. The alliterative poems may have been, with some calculation, locally based, but they were rarely inward-looking or narrow as this implies. Some poems, like *Sir Gawain* and the *Awntyrs of Arthur*, make deliberate references in wholly fictitious contexts to places familiar to their audience. The appeal of this is easy to understand, and part of the poet's function was to entertain and to compliment his hearers. There are probably many more such references to people and places than we shall ever be able to detect, but they are never the main point. Similarly, although the special understanding between a poet and his audience might be thought to have fostered the continuance of tradition and convention, a good poet could always employ these for the particular task in hand and even transcend their apparent limitations.

There is perhaps a further danger for the modern reader of assuming that the alliterative poet's consciousness of tradition corresponds to his own. The poet of *Sir Gawain and the Green Knight* says he will tell a story

With lel letteres loken,	*true/fastened*
In londe so hatz ben longe	

('as has long been done in the land'), implying his interested awareness of the traditional, national character of the alliterative form. But his attention even in speaking of the Arthurian past is on contemporary manners and morals. Alliteration is not a nostalgic but a living form, appropriate for matter of immediate relevance. *Morte Arthure* must have succeeded not by reminding its hearers of ancient heroic epics, as it does some modern readers, but by reflecting their own aspirations and doubts about a present heroic ideal. It would not have seemed irrelevant to them to consider alongside it the actual military campaigns of Edward III, in which some of them may have taken part.

By no means all alliterative poetry is aristocratic, and even some which is would have a much wider appeal than the word implies. The ideals of the aristocracy were of interest and relevance to quite other social groups – as much in the *Canterbury Tales* will show. Where alliterative poetry flourished it must have done so at several levels, and some of the poems we now read may well be courtly by imitation rather than by exact origin.

History and Relations

With very few exceptions both the authors and the patrons of the surviving poems are anonymous. It is difficult to be certain or very precise about the place of origin of any poem from indications of its dialect or other evidence. In all but a handful of cases our dating of the poems remains conjectural and so approximate as to make a chronological arrangement impossible. Because of this, and because so many poems share the same conventions even down to small details of vocabulary, it is still impossible to be certain when two poems are the work of one author, or to know the direction of any relation between them: which came first? Did one influence the other or are similarities caused by the tradition? There is therefore no point in attempting a systematic history here, although a few things can be said beyond mere conjecture. In the next section an often very approximate date will be given for each poem, but the comparisons suggested will usually be of a critical rather than an historical nature.

The later history of the alliterative movement may be mentioned first, since in some ways it affects our estimate of the earlier. Many of the poems, even of the fourteenth century, have been preserved for us only in copies from the fifteenth, sixteenth and even seventeenth centuries. Partly this is to be regretted since evidence of the date and provenance of the original becomes increasingly tenuous in late copies. But on the other hand it is instructive to observe a kind of continuation of the tradition at the hands of scholars and provincial landed gentry. Our copy of *Morte Arthure* was made by a Yorkshire gentleman in the fifteenth century while new alliterative poetry was still being composed; and our copy of the *Destruction of Troy* is owed to a gentleman writing in Cheshire in the following century, when the movement was long spent. The copying was not indiscriminate, for several of the copyists and collectors showed an interest in the nature of the poetry, and one motive for their activity was no doubt the kind of local pride that moved the gentleman of Baguley, Cheshire, to compose as best he could an alliterative account of the battle of Flodden in which the House of Stanley distinguished itself on the English side.

That poem *Scottish Field*, composed soon after 1515, may be considered the last of the movement. Alliterative poetry continues to be written into the sixteenth century in Scotland where it is often of a high order, especially in the hands of Henryson, Dunbar and Douglas, but these are not to be dealt with here. The earliest poems are harder to fix in time. *William of Palerne* is among the earliest we can date with any certainty, the Earl of Hereford for whom it was made having died in 1361. We even have the Christian name of its author, William (like his hero). But a number of works may be earlier. The Alexander poems called *A* and *B* may date from about

1350, while one opinion would put *Joseph of Arimathie* earlier than 1340. At any rate this decade is usually taken roughly to see the start of the Revival. The earliest poems are not all romances. There are good reasons for dating *Winner and Waster* to about 1352–3 since it is a topical poem about contemporary economic conditions. It also presents something of a problem by its confident use of what are clearly already well-established conventions of alliterative poetry although few of the possibly earlier texts can show them. In between the earliest and the latest, matters are more difficult, but it is perhaps worth saying that the greatest of the remaining poems belong to the latter part of the fourteenth century: all three versions of *Piers Plowman,* the *Gawain* poems and very likely *Morte Arthure.*

II

The order and grouping of the poems to be discussed is a matter of convenience and is neither chronological nor in any consistent way thematic. *Piers Plowman* and the *Gawain* group are set somewhat apart because of their preeminence.

Attention has been drawn to the number of poems that use alliteration but which do not fall within the scope of this chapter. They must be mentioned, however, since their development was not entirely separate from the poems of the Revival and influence may have passed in either direction. A special case is *Pearl*, which is usually treated among alliterative works but whose rhyming stanzas and reduced alliteration make it close to the pattern of many of the lyrics. Alliterating forms are also much used in the Miracle Plays, and in the immense *Metrical Paraphrase of the Old Testament*. Although the method and feel of the medium in these is normally rather different, the possible connexions should be remembered.

There are also many minor works in verse, closely related to the alliterative tradition, but which would take up space disproportionate with their quality if mentioned individually. These include various kinds of 'everyday' verse – a category much larger than it could be today: political prophecies, poems of practical and moral advice, and various comic and satirical pieces.

Some short poems deserve more attention. There is a group in rhymed stanzas, satirical or critical of contemporary conditions, which, although they are so early (*ca.* 1300), are a useful indication of the presence of alliterative skills in poets not necessarily belonging to aristocratic circles. Still, we should not call these poems popular if we mean that, say, the controlled and movingly particular

Song of the Husbandman was actually written by one of the oppressed farmers it describes, although they may have been part of its audience. Another good example from this group is a *Satire on the Consistory Courts*. It is a piece of bravura alliterative writing in an intricate stanza, and although it purports to be the complaint of an ignorant man about the learned who sit in judgment on his activities among local women, its highly conscious artistry reminds one of the work of Scottish poets some two hundred years later.

Another comic poem of later date and fully alliterative is the *Blacksmiths*. It uses the noise-making capabilities of the line with extra alliteration to voice the complaint of one disturbed at night by the blacksmiths, whom he calls 'horsetailors:'

Swarte smeked smethes, smateryd wyth smoke,	*smoked*
Dryve me to deth wyth den of here dyntys.	*din/blows*
Swech noys on nyghtes ne herd men never:	*such*
What knavene cry and clateryng of knockes!	*knaves'*

These summary references would not be complete without a mention of the patriotic songs which Laurence Minot and others wrote in various combinations of rhyme and alliteration in the fourteenth and fifteenth centuries. The best have an infectious rhythm and are full of satisfying insults to the enemy.

Fortune or *Summer Sunday*. This too is a short poem but one which, whatever its date, belongs firmly to the alliterative mainstream. It is usually referred to as a lament for the death either of Edward II (*d.* 1327) or of Richard II (*d.* 1400). But it reveals no names and although it was quite possibly occasioned by a particular death, either of king or lord, its meaning is of designedly more universal dimensions.

The setting belongs to the medieval convention of dream or vision poems. The narrator says that he rose with the sun on a summer Sunday and joined lords and ladies hunting in a forest. Separated from the others he crosses a river and comes at last upon a woman with a wheel, Fortune in her familiar medieval guise. The poet had in his mind's eye one of the contemporary pictures of Fortune and her wheel, depicting the impermanence of earthly glory. On top of such a wheel sits a crowned king saying, *regno* – 'I am reigning.' On the left and reaching up towards him another figure says, 'I shall reign.' On the right and at the bottom are a falling king and one without power. The rest of the poem is a sharp, visually and dramatically realized account of this wheel and its troublesome meaning, closely following the pictorial image.

The traditional words of the figures on the wheel are expanded into separate, inserted stanzas addressed in carefully judged tone to the narrator. The figures are before us in turn to the last detail: the reigning king boldly crosses his legs in the manner of monarchs in numerous contemporary pictures. The surviving text is incomplete, but the last three lines of the manuscript begin to depict the desolate image of the fallen king:

Yeth I say soriere, sikyng ful sare,	*saw/sighing/sorely*
A bare body in a bed, a bere i-browth him by,	*bier/brought*
A duk drawe to the deth with drouping and dare.	*drawn/dismay*

Not counting the speeches of the wheel-figures, the stanza used is a variety of one met with frequently in alliterative poems. Compare, for instance, the *Awntyrs of Arthur*, the *Pistill of Susan* and the *Quatrefoil of Love*. Eight long alliterative lines rhymed *ababab* are followed by what has come to be called a 'bob', or line of only one main stress, and a 'wheel' of three-stress lines, all five rhymed *cdddc* :

Erly risinde in the est ende;	*rising*
Day daweth over doune, derk is in towne;	
I warp on my wedes, to wode wolde I wende.	*put*
With kenettes kene that wel couthe crie and conne,	*hounds/skill*
I hiede to holte with honteres hende.	*hastened/wood/noble*
So ryfly on rugge roon and raches ronne	*often/hills/deer/hounds*
That in launde under lynde me leste to lende –	*glade/tree/rest*
And lenede.	*stayed*
Kenettes questede to quelle,	*bayed*
Also breme so any belle –	*loud*
The deer daunteden in the delle –	*frightened*
That al the downe denede.	*resounded*

Form serves meaning closely, with the encrusted alliteration and flexible rhythm giving a proper splendour to the theme. This goes with an often elliptical density of expression and much play on words. The hunt which begins the poem is a recognized image of the prosperous courtly life in contrast to what follows; and the narrator's change of mood when Fortune looks at him reinforces the awareness of passing prosperity.

In general the theme is a common one, especially among the more aristocratic alliterative poems. There is a complete wheel of Fortune scene, similar but more complex, in *Morte Arthure*. The exact meaning and emphasis given to the topic varies a good deal. It can be very simply moralistic, but in *Fortune* it is subtly ambivalent, aware of the dangers of ambition and pride in the rising and reigning figures, but conscious that they are a part of kingship, and full of regret at the affliction and passing of the great.

Winner and Waster, The Parlement of the Three Ages, and *Death and Life*. These three poems may be usefully grouped for comparison since they have some similarities of subject and form. They probably all belong to approximately the same North Midland area and have often been connected for further reasons. The first two are found in the same fifteenth century manuscript, and some have thought they are by one author. There is no evidence for this, and another theory, that these two were known to the author of *Death and Life*, is also not very likely.

Each consists mainly of a 'debate', an allegorical form in which personifications engage in argument, and in each the setting for the allegory follows the dream convention. But in each these devices serve different purposes. *Winner and Waster* dates from 1352-3, and bases on the political and economic situation of that time a statement of rather wider significance.

In his dream, the poet says, he saw two opposing armies facing each other on a plain. Above on a hill is encamped the king, Edward III, who sends his son, the Black Prince, to prevent the battle and to call upon the leaders to explain their cause. The forces are those of Winner, the principle of amassing wealth, and Waster, that of prodigal spending. But the issues are not the simple opposition of ant and grasshopper we might have expected. On Winner's side we find the Pope and the notoriously profit-conscious friars, on Waster's the nobility and soldiery. The arguments they use also take some unexpected turns. Although Winner argues prudence and thrift, Waster manages to monopolize the justification by Christian virtue, since he spreads his wealth about so that the poor benefit, and is not concerned to lay up treasure on earth and so to endanger his soul. Waster is accused, however, of excess and pride, especially in his extravagant feasts. Their luxury so appals Winner, he says,

that tenys my hert	*it troubles*
To see the borde overbrade with blasande disches	*spread/glittering*
Als it were a rayled rode with rynges and stones.	*decorated cross*

Either's case is full of subtlety and covers all grounds, economic and moral. The king's verdict is to allot each one a dwelling where he is most loved: Waster to the markets and shops of London to keep the money moving, and Winner abroad to be looked after by cardinals and the Pope – but to be ready to return whenever he is called for. The poem breaks off during this judgment speech so that something important may well be missing.

Whether this is so or not, the precise meaning of the debate and conclusion is anything but obvious. Both Winner and Waster have a bad side and, since the king acknowledges them as his servants, Edward and his son are being criticized on both counts. The apparently laudatory descriptions of king and prince are not without irony, and the debate gives a full picture of all the wrong in the country caused by either principle. But it seems that each is somehow necessary – as Waster and Edward point out, they complement each other. The king's judgment, presumably deferred to, is itself a satire on the state of affairs rather than a remedy. It indicates his good will but not his power to change things.

The poem has an extra dimension whose significance may also be a little obscured by the lack of a conclusion. In a prologue, the poet has used the style of apocalyptic prophecy to warn about the dangerous state of the kingdom. This effective way of suggesting the urgency of the problems dealt with in the dream is also heavily ironic, ending as it does with a complaint that in these times real poetic talent is no longer rewarded – anyone who can tell a few funny stories fares better. The poet renews the comic desperation of this appeal, and also ironically the real urgency, by mock appeals for refreshment from his audience as the first two sections of the poem end. We would be denying the sophistication of this poet's art to see these as simply the call of a thirsty man – as if he could not ask for a drink in prose on the night but must write his *ad libs* in advance.

The Three Ages is generally considered rather later in date, although still in the fourteenth century. Again the preliminaries to the dream, and the poet's creation of a character for himself, are important. In May he goes into the forest in hopes of shooting himself a deer. He comes upon a fine hart which he stalks and kills. Then, hiding his kill from foresters, he sets himself to watch over it till nightfall, but he falls asleep and dreams. In his dream Youth, Middle-Age and Old-Age are arguing for their respective ways of life. Youth is a young knight, lover, hunter and warrior. Middle-Age scorns him for frivolity. He is a landowner, a sober and prosperous householder. But their dispute is in effect only a prologue to Old-Age who silences both with a long exposition of the transitoriness of both pleasure and wealth. Where their arguments remained worldly and expedient, his have a death-shadowed spiritual base. His words are mostly occupied with an account of the Nine Worthies, nine great heroes from Joshua to Godfrey of Bouillon, as an example that all, however powerful, are subject to death. He enjoins them to prepare for death since all here is vanity, and then departs:

Dethe dynges one my dore, I dare no lengare byde.

A bugle blows and the dreamer wakes as the sun sets, and returns home.

At first the connexion between the hunting dreamer and the substance of his dream seems slight, unless we are to connect his activity with the hunting of reckless Youth. That connexion is appropriate, but the dreamer also has something in common with Middle-Age since his hunting is perhaps more practical in purpose. But it should be remembered – the poet reminds us again at the end – that it is in spring that he dreams this timely admonition that all will fade. So too the unexplained bugle, and the fading day at the close reinforce the theme of death and judgment.

The poem has been accused of a lack of proportion, in particular that the Nine Worthies take up too much space. The fault is rather that the actual treatment of them lacks interest. Like many a medieval poem, the *Three Ages* has parts whose intrinsic interest, or the space they occupy, seems to detract from, or even run contrary to a main design. Partly it may result from a division of aims. To a courtly audience and to the poet himself the Nine Worthies had a special fascination. From the early fourteenth century the catalogue of heroes, three pagans, three Christians, and three Jews, formed a favourite motif within the topic of transitory earthly glory, perhaps especially relevant for an audience with pretensions to power. The subject is similar to that of *Fortune*, and the two motifs, Worthies and Wheel of Fortune, are combined in *Morte Arthure*. This could justify the length of the treatment but not its method which is haphazardly either unnecessarily detailed or hastily allusive. Only the refrain-like reminders of the power of death keep the catalogue moving. But the poem seems to survive this, and the other main developed section, on the poet's hunting, justifies itself beautifully. Much of the savoured detail of the sport and the kill is part of a convention, but its familiarity would enhance its reality for the audience, even without such fine passages as the hunter's long wait to catch the deer unawares, when he dared not move:

For had I myntid or movede or made any synys,   *aimed*
Alle my layke hade bene loste that I hade longe wayttede.   *sport*
Bot gnattes gretely me grevede and gnewen myn eghne . . .   *eyes*

It is the enjoyable, physical concreteness of this setting that provides such a disturbingly contrasted background for the theme which casts doubt on all such pleasures.

Death and Life is a much later work, perhaps as late as 1450. Its author might have derived his leading idea, a contest between a personified Life and Death, from *Piers Plowman*. There are certainly moments which remind one of Langland's poem. But considering the general availability of such a theme and treatment to many medieval authors, the nature and even the fact of the debt must remain uncertain.

It is altogether a sparer and less leisurely affair than the two earlier debates. The dreamer's state of mind giving rise to his vision is important as always, but it is conveyed in very few lines. In a brief prologue the poet considers how man's life is threatened by death 'with his darts keene', and advises obedience to Christ's will and prayers for God's grace to gain eternal bliss. Later on, some of the poet's emphases and the richness of his style suggest a courtly background. But here at least, as well as in total effect, the lessons of transitoriness and hope in God are stated more generally and with less concern for the particular kind of life which is beset by death in the *Three Ages*. It is a religious poem, almost without any element of lament.

Thinking his devout thoughts, the poet wanders in the usual flowery wood and lies down to sleep and dream. He sees from a high place country, towns and people – the whole world. From the East approaches a lady, Life, whose progress brings joy to the world.

The world rejoices in the presence of Life and her entourage till noon. But then from the North comes the terrible and grotesque Lady Death whose look kills. Her destructive course is halted by God at Life's appeal and the debate begins. The climax of it comes when Death rashly claims victory even over Christ on the cross. Life here assumes a more exalted role. She tells how Christ raised her up and, with this renewed, eternal life, invaded hell itself. The contest over, Life restores her people and departs. The dreamer, unable as yet, naturally, to join eternal Life, wakes sadly but with hope.

As is nearly always the case with these debates the opposition is not total as it appears. Winner and Waster exist together, and so do the Three Ages. Life eternal must 'defeat' Death but both are servants of God's will. Death, at the very moment of claiming Christ as a victim, kneels humbly as she speaks His name. Thus Death's defence is perfectly sound up to that point: fear of her compels men to virtue, and she is able to claim all the great ones of history as her exemplary prey. One can compare – many of the actual arguments are related – the debate imagined in the Middle Ages and used in *Piers Plowman*, between Mercy, Peace, Righteousness and Truth, the so-called Four Daughters of God, the result of which is not a victory but a reconciliation.

William of Palerne is a translation of the French *Roman de Guillaume de Palerne* which was composed late in the twelfth century for Yoland, daughter of Baldwin IV, Count of Hainault. Comparison can tell us much about the character of each version, but to compare them merely in order to judge the translation as one might do with a modern book is of little profit. It was no part of the English poet's task to 'capture the essence' of his original. He was making available an entertaining and interesting story for the use of his English hearers, and does so with great efficiency. Many of the virtues of his version are those of the original. Occasionally he seems to have been discontented with the lack of concrete visual detail in the French and added a little of his own.

The *Roman* is a courtly poem of course, and the English version remains so even though its patron, Humphrey de Bohun, seems to have had in mind an audience other than the normally bilingual nobility. The courtliness appears in all its emphases and preoccupations. The familiar idea of inborn nobility showing through in humble circumstances is a main motive in the story. The treatment of military prowess as a test of such nobility, and the intense, almost painful concern with the sentiments of lovers are also characteristic. But if the reader is familiar only with the usually 'historical' and designedly realistic alliterative romances, the story of *William of Palerne* will come as a surprise.

William, son of the King of Apulia, is rescued from the wicked designs of his uncle by a werewolf who looks after him in the wild. The werewolf, who is Alphouns, son of the King of Spain enchanted by his stepmother, from here on engineers almost all of the story. William is adopted by the Emperor of Rome and falls in love with his daughter, Melior. To avoid an arranged match for Melior the lovers flee, disguised first as white bears and later as deer. They are protected and aided in their adventures by the ever resourceful werewolf until William finally arrives at his home in Apulia, in time to save his mother and sister from a siege mounted by the King of Spain. This plot with a number of further complications is such that of the five thousand or so lines of the poem, a good thousand consist of dénouement. The part dealing with the disenchanting of the werewolf by his stepmother is worth special mention for its beautiful and moving combination of comedy and mystery.

It is an easy story to like at a fairly simple level, but it is much more difficult to know exactly what its original audience might have found in it. There is certainly no need to suppose them either naïve or credulous. But much of its content could be called highly theoretical: its concerns with love and a noble code of behaviour are seen isolated by quite deliberately artificial and extraordinary circumstances. It is a kind of compendium of entertainment with something for everyone. There is plenty of attractive sentiment, an abundance of incident, and a good deal of battle – generally of the less worryingly lethal sort one sees in an early Western, as distinct from a modern war film. The less frivolous members of the audience would have been pleased with the several occasions on which one character gives another advice on how to behave, usually with particular application to the governing class: how to treat one's servants, how to preserve humility by caring for the poor while one is prosperous. Such expressions of an acceptable ethical code are an important part of what is primarily a literature of amusement.

In *Chevalere Assigne* (late fourteenth century) we see an attempt to harness a similarly fantastic story to a more determinedly moral or religious purpose. The poem, only a few hundred lines long, is an adaptation of an extract from the much longer French romance, the *Chevalier au Signe* (Knight of the Swan). Queen Beatrice is persecuted by her husband's mother, Matabryne, who substitutes seven whelps for the seven children the queen gives birth to. Matabryne then poisons her son's mind against Beatrice so that he agrees after some years to punish her. Meanwhile six of the children had escaped Matabryne's clutches by changing into swans, and the seventh is brought up by a hermit until, summoned by an angel, he comes as a mere child to defend successfully the honour of his mother.

The explicit intention of the narrator in all this is to illustrate the providence of God. But although the purpose is pious, the story is calculatedly sensational, rather in the way that many a religious writer or preacher in the Middle Ages – Mannyng, for instance –

made stories precisely to impress ideas on a certain audience. The poet wastes little time on detail. The verse is perfectly adequate to the unambitious task and reveals little about its author. Whatever the poet's station, there is nothing to suggest that his audience was courtly.

The Alexander Poems. One of the central secular themes in medieval literature is the story of Alexander the Great, told in an immense variety of interrelated legends and histories which had been developed since his lifetime. The story or stories were always popular and were turned to account in every possible way by different writers, for sheer sensation, for moral or satirical purpose, for grand tragedy. Three of the Middle English Alexander works are alliterative.

The two earliest (*ca.* 1340–70) are fragments only and neither is very impressive. They are called *Alexander A* and *Alexander B* (or *Alexander and Dindimus*), and are based on a Latin version of the Alexander legend called the *Historia de Preliis*. *A* starts with an account of Philip of Macedon's conquests and marriage, and then tells the early history of Alexander beginning with the flight of his magician father, Nectanebus, from his kingdom in Egypt. It tells how Nectanebus tricks Philip's queen by magic and fathers Alexander upon her. It tells of the prodigies which precede the hero's birth and some of the deeds of his early manhood, including his abrupt and callous killing of his father and his taming of Bucephalus. The story breaks off soon after this, and a gap in the manuscript also means the loss of the account of Alexander's education.

Alexander B may just possibly be another part of the same translation of the *Historia*, of which *A* represents the start, but it is unlikely to be by the same author. *B* is taken from two episodes late in the hero's life. First, in the East, he encounters the Gymnosophists, a people who live a simple life in caves and go naked. Then he reaches the Ganges and conducts a correspondence with Dindimus, king of the so-called Brahmins who live on the farther shore. In both episodes the point is the contrast between Alexander's way of life, active and worldly, and the unwordly and self-denying life of the two peoples. The correspondence with Dindimus amounts to a typical 'debate' on the subject. The story is a mere extract with no proper beginning and end. It was interpolated by its scribe to fill what he wrongly supposed to be a gap in the story in a famous manuscript of the French *Roman D'Alixandre*, now in the Bodleian Library.

Compared with the author of the third poem, the *Wars of Alexander* (late fourteenth – early fifteenth century), the poet of *A* is a hack working to stereotyped patterns. The *Wars* is also a translation of one version of the *Historia de Preliis*, but its rendering of the Latin, although much closer, is concentrated and imaginative where that of *B* is wastefully diffuse. It is a nearly complete version of the *Historia*, with some additional material, and therefore includes the episodes which also occur in *A* and *B*. The description of the preparations for Alexander's entry into Jerusalem is an impressive piece of original elaboration by the English poet, but otherwise he contents himself with bringing to life his source in accomplished alliterative verse, and in such a way that we see the whole sweep of the story as the stirring and nobly tragic one that his courtly audience would find it.

Formally the story as the English poet received it is simply a series of episodes and he did nothing to impose further order upon it. But despite its length, the vigour of the verse and the frequent finely judged scenes keep the narrative in movement. The death of Philip combines a prosy directness with an ironic pathos as Alexander mourns for one who was only his mother's husband:

With that he blothirs in the brest and the breth stoppis	*gurgles*
And in a spedful space so the sprete yeldis,	*short/spirit*
And Alexander ay onane angirly he wepis	
And gretis for him as grevously as he him geten hade.	*mourns*

There are nearly epigrammatic lines such as that in which the young hero expresses his wise choice of old rather than young men to advise him, his preference being rather 'The sadnes of slike (such) men than swyftnes of childir'.

As the story accumulates we begin to see a kind of pattern being made out of repeated episodes and recurring preoccupations. At several points we find Alexander warning or being warned against excessive ambition and pride. This is an important concern especially in the exchanges between Alexander, proud but a hero making his way against odds, and Darius, proud and in the wrong and luxuriously secure. When the latter is defeated his words take on a newly righteous tone:

Heves noght your hert up to highe, take hede to your end.	
It limps not always the last to licken with the first.	*befalls/accord*

Darius' death in the magnanimous Alexander's arms is occasion for elaboration of the same theme. In all this running discussion of

Alexander as he goes, the hero is under criticism but is still the hero. He stands for the limits of worldly attainment – he explores the sea bottom and the upper air as well as the remotest and strangest regions of the world – and the inevitability of his urgent striving is eloquently expressed in his words to the Gymnosophists:

Ye se, wele seldom is the see with himselfe turbild,
Bot with thir walowande windis. My will ware to riste,   *were/rest*
Bot anothir gast, and noght my gast, tharof my gast lettis.   *spirit*

He sees himself as a part of God's providence. Although this particular explanation has no place there, we find in *Morte Arthure* a similar concern with the admiration or doubts that may be felt before such achievements.

The Destruction of Troy (probably fifteenth century) is a version of one of the other great medieval stories. The story of Troy for the Middle Ages was not Homer's, but was derived from the much later accounts ascribed to Dares and Dictys. The complete history was given in the late twelfth century French *Roman de Troie* by Benoit de Saint Maur, and this was translated into Latin about a century later by Guido de Columnis. These two are the principal sources of medieval Troy stories, and the alliterative poem is a close translation of the Latin and makes a vast work of some fourteen thousand lines.

It is important to bear in mind the descent of the story for two reasons. First, for the writers and their audience the matter of Troy, like that of Alexander and, in varying degrees, many other stories, was a piece of history rather than a fiction. Not that parts of it were not considered critically and sceptically, but the various accounts were valued according to their fidelity to events. Hence the English poet's prologue in which he affects to argue the case for his version against accounts derived from Homer (which he himself could only have known by hearsay). Homer, being a Greek, gave a biassed picture. Dares and Dictys were Trojan and Greek respectively and accounts based on them must be fair. In fact, in all medieval versions the Trojans are the favoured side, and more than one European nation, on the pattern of Aeneas and Rome, had a legend of its founding by one or other of the fugitives from Troy – in the case of Britain, one Brutus. Therefore the Troy history was specially significant.

The second reason for considering the descent of the history and the serious attitude to it is that it tells us much about the intention and therefore the success of the English translator. He was not selecting, like Boccaccio and Chaucer, one interesting episode for development in his own way. Presumably his patron required the whole history in English, to which the only proper solution was to render one of the two most complete accounts. The poet was competent and conscientious, not in the same class as the translator of the *Wars of Alexander*, but the patron could hardly have complained at the result: he would have on his shelves 'The Complete Troy, from the Best Authorities'. It was required reading for the well-informed in any case, but to have commissioned a whole new English translation reflects further credit on the anonymous patron.

The English has been called monotonous and dull, but this seems unfair and is perhaps based on attempts to read too much at once. It was no doubt read normally an episode at a time. The story, which begins with Jason's expedition for the Golden Fleece long before the seige, is compelling and often moving, and the English copes with it adequately enough. Special mention is often made of the descriptions of storms at sea where this well-trained alliterative poet was able to use his stock of noisy formulae, but he can be effective as well in less obvious contexts. Of course, large scale adjustments of the structure for artistic purposes were not part of his job. Even his comments on the story as it proceeds are translations from those in Guido – authorized and acceptable views of the history, as it were, as well as simply the story itself.

The Siege of Jerusalem and *Joseph of Arimathie*. In different ways these poems occupy border positions between secular and religious. The *Siege* has been considered to depend in part on the *Destruction of Troy*, and therefore to be later, but there could be other reasons for the few closely similar passages in them. Its poet combined a number of versions, legendary and historical, of the destruction of Jerusalem by Titus. As he explains at the start, the point is that this is God's delayed but terrible revenge for what the Jews did to Christ. However, once the point has been made, there are few explicit reminders of it. Most of the poem is a full account of the siege, where the enthusiastic concentration on details can be seen as fulfilling the main point: the audience will enjoy the dealing of justice. But it would also probably be appreciated for the acceptable, bloody commonplaces of alliterative war poetry:

Baches woxen ablode aboute in the vale   *brooks/with blood*
And goutes fram gold-wede as goteres they runne.   *gold armour*

Even in so destructive an event the poet has found room for the polite custom and magnanimities of noble warfare. It is a good poem in which to observe the typical techniques and formulae of this aspect of the alliterative movement. Typically too, the narrative must pause now and then for an elaborate description, but in this poem there is a reason for each one (it is not always so). In order that the fall and loss shall be great, we must see the exalted richness of Jerusalem and the Old Law beforehand. Hence one of the more splendid passages is the description of the first advance of the exotic Jewish army, reaching a climax with an armed elephant,

Kevered myd a castel, was craftily ywroght,	
A tabernacle in the tour atyred was riche,	
Pight as a paveloun on pileres of selvere,	*fixed*
A which of white selvere walwynde therynne	*ark*
On four goions of gold that hit fram grounde bar,	*pivots*
A chosen chayr therby on charbokeles twelfe,	*carbuncles*
Betyn al with barnd gold with brennande sergis.	*burning candles*
The chekes of the chayr wer charbokles fyve,	*side-pieces*
Covered myd a riche clothe ther Cayphas was sette.	

Caiaphas is surrounded by priests singing psalms of the great deeds of Jewish heroes – all to no avail.

Joseph of Arimathie (*ca.* 1350 or earlier) is an extract from the Arthurian romance of the Holy Grail, but it treats the story of the conversion of the King of Sarras by Joseph and his son rather as if it were the legend of a saint, the purpose being to demonstrate the power of God in His servants. This it does briefly and unpretentiously, and somewhat at the expense of Joseph who, as the king says, is plainly no scholar and fails to give a convincing defence of the Gospel he preaches.

The style is simple but achieves a quite disconcerting realism when rendering conversations, with their casual courtesies and easy transitions. Joseph is arranging lodgings for his followers with the king, when the latter points to one follower in particular:

'I trouwe that beo thi sone,' bi Josephe he seide.	*to*
'Ye, sire, so he is, forsothe as I the telle.'	
'Con he out of clergye?' seis the kyng thenne.	*is he learned*
'Leeve me forsothe, sire, ther lives no bettre.'	*believe*
The kyng lette lede hom into town lowe	*had them led*
To a feir old court and innes hem there.	*lodges*

The Quatrefoil of Love, The Pistill of Susan, St. John the Evangelist, St. Erkenwald. These four are religious poems. The first three are in a variety of the rhymed stanza found in *Fortune*, but belong as do most of the stanzaic poems to the northerly part of the alliterative area. *St. John* (late fourteenth century) is the story of the saint's life told, curiously, in the second person as an apostrophe to John himself. The *Quatrefoil* (1350–1400) is a skilfully written allegorical poem exhorting to penance and devotion to the Virgin Mary. In it a lady pining for love is told by a dove of the truer love of God. The dove's discourse tells (briefly!) the whole story of the world from Adam to the Last Judgment, using throughout the quatrefoil or four-leafed clover as an image for the three persons of the Trinity plus the Virgin. The complex stanza works well, and the poet uses the device of echoing the last line in the first.

The Pistill (*Epistle*) *of Susan* (*ca.*1350–60) simply tells the story of Susannah and the Elders from the Vulgate, without any additional moral. The narrative is none too satisfactory in the original, with Daniel unaccountably condemning both elders before producing his evidence. But the poet makes no major changes except for simpliflying a little and adding the touching reaction of Susan's husband as she is led to punishment.

Thei toke the fetteres of hire feete,
And evere he cussed that swete: *kissed*
'In other world schul we mete,'
      Seide he no mare.

St. Erkenwald (*ca.* 1386) is written in the unrhymed line and is a poem of considerable distinction – especially in comparison with the usual popular pious saints' legends. It has been attributed to the author of *Sir Gawain* but, while it would not disgrace him, the attribution is most unlikely. Although it is a North West Midland work, the saint it celebrates was a Bishop of London. During the rebuilding of St. Paul's on the site of a destroyed pagan shrine, the workmen find a tomb containing a richly clad, undecayed body. No one can interpret the inscription nor find any record. Bishop Erkenwald is fetched and prays for help to understand the mystery. He conducts a service and then proceeds to ask the corpse, in Christ's name, to tell its story.

He was, he says, a great and much honoured judge in King Belin's time. By God's will his body had remained uncorrupted, but his pagan soul was forfeit and not rescued from limbo. The Bishop decides to baptize the body but he is forestalled. His own tears falling on the corpse already effect the baptism and release the soul to bliss:

Wyt this cessyd his soune, sayd he no more,
Bot sodenly his swete chere swyndid and faylide   *expression vanished*
And alle the blee of his body wos blakke as the moldes,   *colour*
As rotten as the rottok that rises in powdere.   *decayed thing*

The narrative is realized with great conviction and tact and perfectly controlled, from the prologue, which explains the history of London – New Troy – and its temple up to the coming of St. Augustine, to the unemphatic close, explaining the reason for the decay of the now useless body, as the congregation thoughtfully depart:

> Meche mournynge and myrthe was mellyd togeder.   *mingled*
> Thai passyd forthe in procession and alle the pepulle folowid,
> And alle the belles in the burghe beryd at ones.   *rang together*

Morte Arthure (late fourteenth or early fifteenth century) is one of the masterpieces of alliterative poetry. The poet works entirely within the tradition but commands the medium and the favourite themes with assurance and panache. The hero is not the Arthur we see in one familiar cycle of stories, helplessly regarding the decline of his court and the adultery of his queen and Lancelot. He is the great conqueror and ruler, and the story tells of his rise and inevitable fall, caused here by the treachery of Modred, his nephew. The themes and motifs found separately and repeatedly in the *Wars of Alexander*, in *Fortune*, in the *Three Ages*, appear again in combination and in compelling form.

The story begins, after a summary of Arthur's conquests to date – from Ireland to Greece, with the king holding his Christmas feast at Carlisle. He is visited by an embassy from the Emperor, Lucius, to demand the king's appearance before him in Rome to answer for his occupation of lands belonging to the Emperor and for withholding tribute. The consequence is that Arthur must march on Rome to assert his rights, leaving Modred in charge in Britain. Most of the rest of the narrative concerns his exploits and those of his knights, especially Sir Gawain, abroad. The king fights and kills the giant of Mont St. Michel, and his army defeats that of Lucius in France. He has reached Rome when news of treason calls him home to a last fateful battle with Modred and his death.

This story would have been called a 'tragedy' in the Middle Ages, when the term was used of any narrative of a fall from prosperity and success. Such a fall was not necessarily a judgment on the character of the hero, since Fortune is fickle and in any case all worldly success is temporary. In the first part of the poem such considerations rarely if ever arise, but when Arthur is encamped before Rome he has a dream of the Wheel of Fortune whose interpretation puts in doubt the value of all his acts of prowess:

Thou has schedde myche blode and schalkes distroyede *men*
Sakeles, in cirquytrie, in sere kynges landis: *innocent/pride/many*
Schryfe the of thy schame and schape for thyn ende. *confess*

He has reached the peak of his attainment. Decline and death are inevitable, but the honour Arthur sought and the way he sought it remain admirable, as does he himself. Nevertheless the coming of this dream is like the coming of maturity. It is time now to think of saving his soul. On the one hand Arthur stands for the best an earthly ruler can achieve, but on the other he is a sinful man whose ambition has caused suffering and destruction, and whose achievements will be wasted and lost. The case is like Alexander's but more poignant since Arthur is a Christian. The poem expresses not an ideal religious judgment of him but the simultaneous awareness of ultimately opposed imperatives and sympathies. Similarly the poet pictures chivalrous warfare with approval, even of its most terrible ferocity, and with pity at the loss that results.

The dream of Fortune shows the measure of Arthur's achievement as well as warning of its end. It is movingly done, for Arthur is one of Nine Worthies but, as only the first of the three Christian ones, he could hardly have known this, since the set was incomplete. The poet has Lady Fortune reveal it to him in the prophetic dream. She shows him the wheel upon which appear in this case not four figures but eight, six falling – the past Worthies – and two rising. Arthur himself she puts in the ninth place, the throne atop the wheel, and he sits in state until noon when, despite his cries, 'Abowte scho whirles the whele and whirles me undire', and his back is broken.

The visual and dramatic power of the poet is well shown in the scene which follows the dream. Arthur makes no answer to the wise men who interpret the vision. He rises and arms himself and goes out, alone but for his greyhound:

And bownnes over a brode mede with breth at his herte. *goes/anger*
Furth he stalkis a stye by tha still evys, *walks/path/wood-side*
Stotays at a hey strete, studyande hym one. *hesitates/brooding alone*
Att the surs of the sonne he sees there commande, *source/coming*
Raykande to Romewarde the redyeste wayes, *going*
A renke in a rownde cloke with right rowmme clothes, *man/wide*
With hatte and with heyghe schone homely rownde;
With flatte ferthynges the freke was floreschede all over . . . *man*

As the striking figure approaches more and more details of his appearance become clear. He is of course a pilgrim, which sorts well with the penitential note struck by the interpreters of the dream. Indeed with this pilgrim the action of Arthur's decline begins, for he is Cradoke, a knight come to summon the king to return and save his threatened kingdom from Modred's treachery.

The prevailing tone in the poem is stern and sublimely heroic. There is plenty of courtly splendour but women play a small part. Arthur's queen, Gaynor, however, expresses early the essential pathos of the story in lamenting that his necessary course must cause her to lose him. There is considerable humour, but usually of the kind that goes with soldierly heroism, as when Arthur cuts off the legs of a giant in battle:

'Come down,' quod the kynge, 'and karpe to they ferys.   *talk/mates*
Thowe arte to hye by the halfe . . .'

A modern reader may well find it hard to come to terms with some important aspects of the poem. No doubt part of the intention in the realism of bloody battle scenes was to convey the horror:

Bot Floridas with a swerde as he by glenttys   *slips by*
All the flesche of the flanke he flappes in sondyre,
That all the filthe of the freke and fele of the guttes   *many*
Foloes his fole fotte where he furthe rydes.   *horse's feet*

But there is often in it something nearer delight than we should now want to admit. Perhaps too, the poet's virtuoso technique is hard to appreciate at first, as he indulges, for instance, in alliterative displays using the same letter for line after line. But in neglecting to take account of these aspects we may lose much of what the first audience found in the poem.

The rest is more easily communicated, even the patriotic partisanship, say, at the discomfiture of Lucius' emissaries. There are the awkward contradictions of a character like Gawain, with a hero's necessary recklessness ever going just too far. There is Arthur himself, terrible in wrath but acting only upon consideration:

To warpe wordez in waste no wyrschipe it were,
Ne wilfully in this wrethe to wreken myselven.   *Wrath/revenge*

And then deeply pitiable in defeat, mourning the loss of his knights in whom all his honour consisted:

'Kyng comly with crowne, in care am I levyde;   *left*
All my lordchipe lawe in lande es layde undyre,   *low*
That me has gyfen gwerdons, be grace of hymselven,   *rewards*

Mayntenyde my manhede be myghte of theire handes,
Made me manly one molde and mayster in erthe.   *on earth*
In a tenefull tym this torfere was reryde,   *troubled/conflict*
That for a traytoure has tynte all my trewe lordys.   *lost*
Here rystys the riche blude of the rownde table
Rebukkede with a rebawde, and rewthe es the more.   *rebel*
I may helples one hethe house be myn one,
Als a wafull wedowe that wanttes hir beryn.   *children*
I may werye and wepe an wrynge myn handys   *curse*
For my wytt and my wyrchipe awaye es for ever.

There is, too, the special affection between these two, uncle and nephew, also reaching its fulfilment in the last battle.

The Awntyrs of Arthur and *Golagros and Gawain* are two courtly Arthurian romances in rhymed stanzas. The first (late fourteenth – early fifteenth century) shows the influence of *Morte Arthure* in its way of referring to Arthur's career and change of fortune. It has been said also to show the influence of *Sir Gawain* but the only evidence for this is its opening hunting scene which is quite likely to be independent.

It is a genuinely courtly poem, showing the earnest moral concerns we have seen in many others. It consists of two episodes. In the first, during a royal hunt, Gaynor and Gawain are accosted by a dreadful apparition from a lake. It is the ghost of the queen's mother and its message is both a *memento mori* and an appeal for prayers to save the soul from torment. It warns against pride and luxury in Gaynor and, in answering Gawain's question about those like himself whose calling involves conquest 'agaynes the righte', it blames Arthur for covetousness. In the second episode a knight comes to claim lands which Arthur has wrongly seized and given to Gawain. Gawain wins the ensuing combat but magnanimously restores the knight's lands. All are reconciled and the queen offers prayers for her mother's soul.

The episodes are connected thematically rather than structurally. We see on a small scale in the second a successful resolution of the kind of problems raised more profoundly in the first. But the first, which is interesting incidentally as a kind of contemporary commentary on the issues of *Morte Arthure*, casts a gloom over the second so that it is hard to believe one is to approve entirely of either Arthur or Gawain, whose victory is by no means decisive.

The poet has no mean skill, not only in details but in their arrangement. When Arthur is asked a boon, instead of an immediate answer comes a description of the king sitting in manly splendour, with his gorgeous robes and his great grey eyes. And we are aware as we wait for him to speak that the value of all this is in doubt since Arthur has been called covetous.

The poem is also interesting because it contains references to what were evidently places locally familiar to the audience. The Tarn Wadling from which the apparition rises existed in Cumberland almost to this day (it has been drained). The same kind of reference, perhaps even complimentary to the houses of local nobles, occurs in *Golagros and Gawain*.

This fifteenth century Scottish poem is still very similar in its deep concern for noble ethics and behaviour, including again some reflections on the shifts of fortune. Arthur and his knights are on an expedition to the Holy Land. The journey is hard and they are short of food. Arriving at a city they send messengers to ask for hospitality: first Sir Kay who is offensive and ill-mannered and receives a rebuff, and then Sir Gawain whose courtesy is more successful. Later the expedition comes to a castle whose owner owes no allegiance to Arthur. The king decides to lay siege despite advice to the contrary. The fighting culminates in a single combat between the owner of the stronghold, Golagros, and Gawain. The result is a delicate problem of honour which is solved only by Gawain's magnanimity. The souce was a part of the French prose *Perceval*, but the author adapts the story to his own purpose. Again there are two episodes thematically connected, but the structure is far more ingenious.

The whole first episode of Gawain and Kay's contrasted success is a sort of curtain raiser, showing in a small matter the way of courtesy and reason which is developed further in the second. But within the second, in turn, Kay again provides a sub-plot as a humorous foil for the story of Golagros and Gawain. Before the great single combat which ends with Golagros's defeat and wise reflections on the uncertainty of fortune, Kay engages an opponent who, seeing himself at a disadvantage, unexpectedly surrenders, to Kay's immense relief, concluding resignedly,

'Quhair that fortune will faill,
Thair may na besynes availl.'

This compromise with fortune looks forward to the result of the main contest.

Arthur is advised throughout by one Spinagros, who seems to know all about the mysterious Golagros. In the French story there is a realistic reason given for this knowledge, but the Scots poet, in dispensing with this, throws a special emphasis on Spinagros as a deliberately-placed prophet and wise authority. From him come some of the most important statements in the poem about knightly conduct and morality. Indeed, in general it is clear that much of the interest, outside the vigorously described action of battle, is meant to consist in the substance and manner of the speeches between chivalrous protagonists.

Rauf Coilyear and the *Book of Howlat*, two other fifteenth century Scots courtly poems, must be mentioned briefly. The first is again about the courteous behaviour expected of a knight, but in this case, with didactic irony, embodied in Ralph the charcoal burner in his encounter with Charlemagne. There are some amusing details and the language is lively, but the main theme, slight, obvious, and insisted on rather than developed, becomes tedious.

The *Howlat* was composed by Richard Holland, for Elizabeth Dunbar, Countess of Moray, and is a moral allegory in which birds play human beings. It is an attractive work which, apart from its moral theme, is also a gracefully designed compliment to its patroness and to the House of Douglas into which she married. It is an instance of the kind of background we may envisage for the more numerous anonymous cases among alliterative court poems.

Piers Plowman

Almost nothing in other poems of the alliterative movement explains *Piers Plowman*. It is written in the unrhymed long line but it is not in any sense courtly and its audience was immediately a much wider one than other alliterative works can have had. More than fifty manuscripts survive, many of which, not all by professional scribes, show by their enthusiastic tampering with the text the interest of the writers in its subject. It was read in all parts of the country.

About the author nothing reliable is known except that he was probably called William Langland and came originally from a West Midland region, perhaps near Malvern which he mentions. This is farther to the South than the birthplace of most alliterative works. It seems, again from the poem itself, that Langland knew as much about London as the country. It is significant for our view of the role of alliterative poetry that Langland found this medium suitable when writing, it seems, for a mixed audience of clerics and a newly prosperous middle class laity, and not for the aristocracy. There is even evidence that some of his ideas, perhaps too some of his actual lines, came to the ears of a virtually illiterate lower class audience who found in them echoes of their own unrest and dissatisfaction. But Langland, though he deals critically with the contemporary scene, including the lot of the poor, is no revolutionary. Yet his traditionalism is, and must have seemed then, challengingly idealistic. Politics are not his real concern and his ideas and art would mean little to a wholly unlearned man. As a poet too, Langland is a disturbing combination of innovator and profound traditionalist – though not alone in this among contemporary English authors.

We speak of *Piers Plowman* for convenience as one poem. But it is really three, composed during the last thirty or forty years of the fourteenth century and known now as the A, B, and C texts. Scholars have disputed but most now agree that all three are the work of Langland. The A-text, between two and three thousand lines, was composed before 1370. The B-text is a thorough remaking and expansion over seven thousand lines long, composed late in the 1370s. In the 1390s came the C-text, a revision of B consisting of numerous small omissions and additions and rearrangements, apparently with a view to increased clarity of the main ideas and development. The B-text is usually the most quoted, and I shall follow this custom, the differences between B and C being of small moment in such a sketch. But this curious history of the composition of *Piers Plowman* has important implications.

Some of the minor differences in the three texts are explained by changes in the immediate historical context. Langland's examples are often highly topical. But what is more important is that his own ideas seem to have been developing and deepening, especially between A and B, and that he decided to incorporate these developments not in a new work but into what is ostensibly the same poem. If this makes us think of more recent examples, such as Wordsworth or Ezra Pound, of poets who have spent much energy on revising or expanding the same main works, the comparison may not be entirely inappropriate. Langland's revisions are not 'polishing', but if we conclude from this, rightly enough, that his leading interest is in content rather than form, we also discover how profoundly the form matches the poet's exploration of meaning and what a conscious artist Langland is.

Piers Plowman is a multiplication of the usual allegorical dream form. Instead of one dream there are ten altogether (two of these are dreams *within* dreams) interspersed with brief waking periods. It is divided into some twenty sections called Passus, but also into two main parts. The first, called for short the *Visio*, begins mainly from a critical view of society, of the world of men, and of its government. A solution is sought through the individual conscience and responsibility, and is pictured in an image of labour in the field of the world led by Piers the plowman, a symbolic figure of the ideal servant of his God and his fellows. But the *Visio* ends with doubts and confusions about whether such virtuous toil guarantees any kind of safety from the evil which seems a match for good in the world. The conclusion seems to be that to 'do well' is the first requirement and for the rest to trust in God.

In the second and longer part, called the *Vita*, the *Life of Dowel, Dobet and Dobest*, the dreamer, previously more of an observer and critic, is the central figure. The idea of doing well has become an entity and the subject of the dreamer's search. The enquiry is no simple presentation of pious truths. The dreamer questions everything, not only what is Dowel and how it is done, but is it possible, is it even worth the trouble? The answers are uncompromising and the dreamer, full of opinion, learns slowly. In this part Piers is mentioned rarely and seen only briefly, but he is the motive and goal of the quest, an ideal of perfect human life as close as possible to the divine. But the *Vita*, as well as being an enquiry after that ideal, is also about the scheme of God's grace without which the enquiry is useless. The first climax, therefore, is reached in the great allegorical vision of the Crucifixion and redemption in which Christ takes on the nature of Piers. A second, of a different kind, comes in the last Passus. Taking up the apocalyptic note prevalent in the *Visio*, it depicts the world in extremity and man (the dreamer) in desperate old age, with the Church assailed by Antichrist – in the all-too-recognizable form of the friars. The situation seems hopeless, but in the last lines of the poem, with an appeal for grace, the search begins again for Piers Plowman.

But such a summary can tell one nothing about the nature of the poem. It must be selective, and selection is dangerously misleading in a work that proceeds by detail and pursues not one but a number of related courses. This summary in particular implies a story or progress, like a journey with a conclusion, whereas the reader finds that each dream, instead of simply picking up where the last one ended, begins from a different position, and introduces a different perspective and different forms to deal with it. Neither continuity of place nor chronological time are governing factors. Hence the final Passus is not the first in which old age has assailed the dreamer, nor is its picture of the world meant to be later in time than the one in the Prologue. Rather it is another view of the present in changed terms. Langland is not writing to show a known and ideal solution achieved after difficulty. He is concerned with the difficulty itself of seeing and pursuing the ideal in the present world.

The form of *Piers Plowman* reflects this concern with often disconcerting exactness. Its structure is best thought of not as an externally imposed unity, but in more detailed terms of characteristic patterns and images in the argument as the reader experiences them. More significant than any totally resolved order are the repeated movements towards order by which the poem progresses. Throughout the *Vita*, Dowel and its comparative and superlative are defined and redefined over and over in different terms, adjusted on each occasion to the circumstances of the dreamer and his changing understanding. In the *Visio* the development is partly characterized by a series of parallel crises giving rise to recurrent apocalyptic images of destruction and the kingdom to come. At each such crisis, precipitated by mounting evil and natural disasters, fundamental standards of truth are reaffirmed, in each case showing up the distressing distance between ideal and reality.

The dream form gave a medieval poet access to a number of chiefly allegorical modes and to a conventional freedom in their use. But no one ever exploited its possibilities to the extent Langland did. Almost nothing he does, taken singly, is without its traditional parallels, but the combinations are unique. He begins with a deceptively simple and distinguished example of a dream setting:

In a somer seson whan soft was the sonne,
I shope me in shroudes as I a shepe were,   *dressed*
In habite as an heremite unholy of workes,
Went wyde in this world wondres to here.
Ac on a May mornynge on Malverne hulles   *but*
Me byfel a ferly of fairy me thoughte.   *miraculous adventure*

I was wery forwandred and went me to reste   *travel-weary*
Under a brode banke bi a bornes side,
And as I lay and lened and loked in the wateres,
I slombred in a slepyng it sweyved so merye.   *flowed*

His first sight is of a symbolic world, the field of people dominated by the tower of Truth and the dungeon of Falsehood. The panoramic view, with the people 'Worchyng and wandryng as the worlde asketh', becomes detailed as the dreamer picks out small scenes within the great one. All this is satirical and realistic until without warning we see a king and his knights, the commons, Kind Wit (Natural Intelligence) and Clergy working together to organize a human society. The dizzying shift of perspective and the association together of figures that a primmer notion of allegory might keep apart are typical of Langland. This particular allegorical tableau proceeds to a series of pronouncements about the rights and duties of a ruler and his people. Suddenly there enters a crowd of rats who hold a parliament, the implications of which threaten the fabric of the orderly kingdom. Again there is no transition (to say nothing of the problems for a reader who insists on knowing where, visually speaking, the rats and Kind Wit are in relation to one another), but the main line of thought is aggressively clear. In all this and for its underlying echoes or explicit references to the Bible, the Prologue is a foretaste of what is to come.

Although some variety of personification is often the basis, the range of Langland's allegorical method is huge. It is less important to distinguish between the types of allegory than to appreciate how each is part of one complex figurative language and way of thought. Its sources range from already traditional allegorical interpretations of the Bible to original creations such as the figure of Piers himself. Allegory is a means of compression, of associating and connecting ideas and images from several levels, as is shown in the Prologue. The figure of Piers derives its energy and significance from a number of sources. He is an obvious symbol of honest toil and a common denominator of human society. But already in Biblical allegory he has a meaning similar to that of the Good Shepherd. His role in the *Visio*, leading people and directing their work, is made to remind us of an Old Testament leader like Moses.

The variety in the allegory may be taken as an instance of the all-inclusive range of the whole subject and form. In Passus II–IV the attempted marriage and trial of Lady Meed is a brilliantly developed series of allegorical actions showing the crippling power of the profit motive at work in the law and government. It gives simultaneously an incisive satire on the actual state of affairs and a picture of an ideal solution. The next vision moves from a social and political scene to the case of individual morality, combining again fact and ideal in the confession of the Seven Deadly Sins. Its incongruous ironies are famous: Gluttony, on his way to confess himself (literally), is diverted by the delights of a pub and takes two days to sleep them off. Sloth begins his confession by falling asleep. In the midst of what appears to be a basically abstract allegorical framework, the reader can be overwhelmed by an unwelcome onslaught of physical detail:

And seten so til evensonge and songen umwhile	*sometimes*
Til Glotoun had y-globbed a galoun an a jille.	*swallowed*
His guttis gunne to gothely as two gredy sowes;	*began to grumble*
He pissed a potel in a paternoster-while	
And blew his rounde ruwet at his rigge-bon ende,	*horn/back-bone*
That alle that herde that horne held her nose after	
And wissheden it had be wexed with a wispe of firses.	*corked*

The confession provides deliberately startling uses of Langland's method. But the same sort of combinations and associations occur too when he is treating the idea of Christian charity and God's grace, the high point of which is perhaps the rich and intricate Tree of Charity vision in Passus XVI.

Allegory is a means of expository clarity and also of mystery and concealment, and Langland uses it for both. The concealment is not only a matter of disguising dangerous ideas (which he implies is the case with the fable of the rats). The poem is full of densely meaningful statements, usually in some allegorical or symbolic form, whose significance is only learned later after much questing and explanation. This is true, for instance, of the often quoted description, by Holy Church in Passus I, of Christian love as the 'plant of peace':

For hevene myghte noughte holden it, it was so hevy of hymself,	
Tyl it hadde of the erthe yeten his fylle;	*eaten*
And whan it haved of this folde flesshe and blode taken,	*earth*
Was never leef upon lynde lighter therafter,	
And portatyf and persant as the poynt of a nedle,	*light/piercing*
That myghte non armure it lette ne none heigh walles.	
Forthi is love leder of the lordes folke of hevene	*therefore*
And a mene, as the maire is, bitwene the kyng and the comune.	*mayor*

In a way this mystery, which the dreamer accepts rather than understands, already contains the answer to much of his later puzzled questioning. On the other hand, Holy Church also teaches him in terms of simple clarity, and this institutes another of the poem's typical internal movements, from abstract statement to an understanding through experience. In the early part of the *Vita* which appears to contain so much abstract doctrine, the really significant development is in the character of the dreamer from obstreperous or despairing discontent to a sometimes comically delayed acceptance.

It is notoriously difficult to account for *Piers Plowman* by assigning it to a single genre – other than the infinitely expandable envelope of the dream convention. In Passus I the dialogue between the dreamer and the Church looks very much like the familiar pattern of a *consolatio*, the medieval form in which a mortal trouble is resolved by the discourse of an authoritative symbolic figure. The classic example is Boethius' *Consolation of Philosophy*, and *Pearl* too is comparable. But however complete, Holy Church's teaching appears to resolve nothing and the genre changes to satire as the dreamer's attention returns from himself to his surroundings. The very variety of genres Langland brings together must tell us something of his intentions. Satire, *consolatio*, complaint, prophecy, sermon, commentary – each belongs with a particular line of thought. We must ask why he refuses to accept the single resolution offered by any one artistic form?

Langland's subject is, or gradually turned out to be, unavoidably comprehensive. It is a search for truth and meaning whose answer must be found, not in an abstraction but in the awkward contradictions of actual human experience. This is reflected in the poet's creative search through poetic forms to cope with the awkwardness and variety without falsifying or suppressing it. It is also reflected in the erratic course of the dreamer who, as well as being a representative of all men and a personification of the wayward human Will, stands also for Will Langland the poet. In this role he is reproved by Imagination in Passus XII for writing poetry instead of performing religious duties. He is not even allowed to plead the serious theme of his work in excuse – there are enough books to teach such things. Will's reply is in two parts. First he simply enjoys doing it and he has observed that even saints have recommended recreation amongst more serious pursuits. Then he says that if he knew what it meant to do well he would gladly give up poetry for religious devotion. His poetry is synonymous with Will's quest for understanding, and the passage expresses, with a candour unusual in medieval literature, the deep personal necessity of that search. But the disarming irony of the scene should also correct any notion we may have of Langland as a dourly humourless moralist.

Some Political Poems

Inevitably *Piers Plowman* was to have some influence on other poets in the alliterative tradition, but rather less than we could expect. It seems from the few imitators that its involvement with the contemporary political and social scene is what most affected its audience. Imitation is in any case not very close and it is perhaps better to think of a body of writing on such matter of which *Piers Plowman* is a very important but rather untypical part.

A poem which declares its allegiance to Langland openly is *Pierce the Ploughman's Creed*, composed towards the end of the fourteenth century. It is an attack on the friars, simple enough in design but effective and cleverly written in detail. The speaker, seeking to know his creed, asks the four orders of friars in turn and receives an answer from each in the form of abuse of one of the other three. When all four have thus convincingly damned themselves and each other, the speaker applies to Pierce the Ploughman who sums up the case against the friars and delivers a creed based on the beatitudes. The poet ends charitably with an acknowledgement of the few virtuous friars and prayers for the rest.

The descriptions of the friars are good, especially the fat Dominican in his splendid refectory:

A greet cherl and a grym, growen as a tonne	*tun*
With a face as fat as a full bledder.	*bladder*

The picture of the Ploughman and his wife is of a different dimension. The accumulated description of his threadbare and comfortless clothing achieves a moving and symbolic quality – the real poverty the friars only profess:

I seigh a sely man me by opon the plow hongen.	*saw/poor*
His cote was of a cloute that cary was y-called,	
His hod was full of holes and his heer oute,	*hood/hair*
With his knopped schon clouted full thykke.	*knobbly/soled*
His ton toteden out as he the londe treddede,	*toes stuck*
His hosen overhongen his hokschynes on everiche a side,	*gaiters*
Al beslombred in the fen as he the plow folwede.	*muck*

Much of the dialogue is sharp, with a use of speech rhythm and vigorously colloquial image we associate with Langland himself.

Two partly allegorical fragments, written during the last years of Richard II and the beginning of Henry IV's reign, may well be two parts of one long poem. They are now usually referred to together under the title *Mum and the Sothsegger*. The first fragment, sometimes called *Richard the Redeless*, examines the failure of the government under Richard II, with particular attacks on the extravagant Richard's rule through favourites, and his corrupting influence among young men who spend too much on frivolous dress:

Thilke lewde ladde oughte evyll to thryve   *that ignorant*
That hongith on his hippis more than he wynneth.

In a neatly ironic passage Wit (i.e. wisdom) is banished ignominiously from court as soon as it is discovered that neither the king nor his knights are acquainted with him.

This fragment ends abruptly. The second lacks a beginning, but it is difficult to see how the connexion between the two was made, if it ever was. The main idea in the second fragment is the problem of good counsel in public affairs – how shall a king be well advised, for instance, if those who depend on him for advancement refuse to speak the truth openly before him? In a dream the narrator finds that Mum, the principle of keeping quiet from misplaced prudence or deliberate sycophancy, holds sway everywhere. He can find no one who knows or will countenance Truthteller: it is rejected as some disagreeable new fad, 'sum noyous nyceté of the newe jette'. The poem ends with the poet trying some particular truthtelling of his own.

Even if the fragments were complete it would probably not be the most illuminating approach to treat the work as an artistic design. Not because the writing is not skilled, but because the purpose was so clearly practical. *Mum* was presumably written by someone who was, in a perhaps minor way, concerned in public affairs and government. His work would probably be circulated among his acquaintance in manuscript, and it is obvious from his own remarks that he expected some notice to be taken. As a work of political theory designed for practical, present effects it shows remarkable literary accomplishment. Because of this it rises above its occasion in a way that, for instance, the group of tracts of religious controversy beginning with *Jack Upland* do not. They deserve only a mention, for being after a fashion partly alliterative. *Crowned King* (*ca.* 1415), as a piece of advice to Henry V near the Battle of Agincourt, is ostensibly similar to *Mum* but is very short and far less ambitious.

The Gawain Group: Cleanness (or Purity), Patience, Sir Gawain and Pearl

There is no proof that these four poems were written by one man, but the feeling that they were dies hard among most readers of them, including myself. But in any case, since it is not impossible, it can be very illuminating to consider them together. They are preserved in the same manuscript, were all probably composed in the same North West Midland dialect between 1360 and 1400, and show certain similarities of theme and attitude. Therefore, even if they are the work of a 'school' rather than one poet, the close association makes them a striking instance of the range of the best alliterative poetry. Between them they cover a variety of religious and secular matters in a way designed for a sophisticated courtly audience, but so as to transcend any limitations that may have imposed. The range is typical of alliterative poetry, and one is led to wonder by the hair's breadth survival of this one manuscript, whether the awesomely consistent quality is also typical of what we have lost. Nothing certain can be said about the order of composition. This account begins with the least well-known of the four.

Cleanness is often compared to *Patience*. Both are didactic, religious poems which make their impact chiefly through superbly told versions of Biblical narratives. Both take as their nominal theme the idea named in their modern titles. But the differences between them are quite as striking, especially the difference of scale. *Cleanness* is nearly two thousand lines long, between three and four times the length of *Patience*, and contains four main narratives instead of the latter's one.

The narratives are linked by a didactic discourse, and introduced rather in the way that a contemporary preacher might have used examples or stories to illustrate his theme, except that in *Cleanness* the narratives take up most of the space. This basic structure of narratives or other disparate elements united by a discursive or dramatic frame is common in medieval poetry. Dream poems like the *Book of the Duchess* are one variety of it, as are the *Confessio Amantis* and even the *Canterbury Tales* at another extreme.

The speaker of the discourse recommends purity – that is purity of heart, saying that it is necessary in order to deserve a heavenly reward, and showing God's hatred of its opposite. The proof is the first story, a version of the Parable of the Wedding Feast, in which the man in the unclean garment is punished by his angry host. We are then told that being clean consists of avoiding sin of all kinds. But the speaker chooses to continue his argument through the example of a particular uncleanness which God seems to have punished with a particular severity, even more severely than the pride of Satan and the disobedience of Adam, namely filth of the flesh. By this is meant 'unnatural' sexual practice, and the first instance is the story of the Flood, in which even innocent animals were destroyed. Only Noah and his family were saved, for their adherence to God's natural law.

After this, says the speaker, God in his mercy resolved never to destroy the whole world again, but his punishment of sexual sins was as fierce as ever. The instance now given is the destruction of Sodom, after which the region of the Dead Sea, where the usual courses of nature are reversed, was left by God as an example to this day. But Lot was spared, again for adhering to natural law and, even more important, his uncle Abraham's marriage was blessed with a son from whom Christ descended. The speaker now describes the purity of Christ, king of nature, whom we must emulate. He then explains how even impure man can do this through the sacrament of penance. The last story in the poem is a warning against returning to former uncleanness after such purification. Here, instead of sexual sin, the uncleanness is the sacrilege of Belshazzar in defiling the vessels from God's temple.

The four stories cover a range of narrative style and method, each a masterpiece in its own right. They have in common the author's imaginative sensitivity to his Biblical original, as sometimes he renders closely the words before him, while at others he boldly expands or combines different stories. The Wedding Feast combines two similar parables and recreates in the best courtly, alliterative style the setting of a lordly feast and the wrath of its host at the disruption of the decorum in his court.

The last story echoes the first: Belshazzar's impious feast over against God's heavenly one. In both feasts too there occurs a judgment (in the Middle Ages both Bible stories were interpreted as images of doomsday). But the last story develops in much greater detail the scenes of courtly splendour. And the feast is only part of this narrative, for the poet also tells of the sack of Jerusalem and the capture of the vessels by Nebuchadnezzar in the first place. The two episodes together are made to embody variations on the traditional themes of tragic fall and the importance of fidelity. The noble Jews are made slaves for their falsehood to God, 'To sytte in servage and syte (sorrow) that sumtyme wer gentyle'. Nebuchadnezzar learns the lesson of one fall from power, and his death is marked by a noble regret at the inevitable, while Belshazzar, despite his honourable treatment of Daniel, is beaten to death in his bed, and the narrator reflects: 'Now is a dogge also (as) dere that in a dych lygges'.

The scene in the two intervening stories is very different. The Flood story is done in narrative and visual symbols with almost no development of human characters: the helpless ark, a mere box tossed on the waters, demonstrating God's care for the few he has chosen to save; the final scene of animals rushing from the ark to repeople the world. Much stronger in most readers' minds than that last picture of God's mercy is the terrible one of His wrath at the heart of the story. Here even a mention of the sinfulness of the people is suppressed in a deep expression of pity, and the animals are in any case innocent, as they flee to high places from the rising water:

Summe styghe to a stud and stared to the heven,	*climbed/peak*
Rwly wyth a loud rurd rored for drede.	*fiercely/voice*
Harez, herttez also, to the hyghe runnen;	
Bukkez, bausenez and bulez to the bonkkez hyghed,	*badgers/hastened*
And alle cryed for care to the kyng of heaven,	
Recoverer of the Creator thay cryed uchone,	*rescue/each*
That amounted the mase – his mercy watz passed	*arose/tumult*
And alle his pyté departed fro peple that he hated.	

With pitiful leavetakings, men and women die with the creatures:

Luf lokez to luf and his leve takez,
For to ende alle at onez and for ever twynne.

The sexual sin which is at issue in this and the next story is not in itself the poet's main concern. It is a powerful image of impurity in general, and impurity is equated with infidelity to God's law, the law of nature. This law, as it applies to sexual matters, involves less narrowly puritan prohibition than we might have expected. The animals are said to be paired for the ark not merely to reproduce but 'to plese ayther other'. The whole complex of themes is dealt with in detail in the story of Sodom. Here God explains to Abraham how the Sodomites have rejected nature and have preferred their uncleanness to the 'play of paramorez' that He himself invented for them, and which He describes in surprisingly intense terms. In contrast to the previous story, this one is full of restrained but humorously sympathetic treatment of human characters. The poet's Abraham, deeply concerned for the fate of his nephew Lot, is entirely his own.

It can be seen from even this selective account that the stories have a richer thematic development and the poem as a whole a more complex unity than is provided by the sermon frame alone. The independent directions taken by the stories are united by a certain parallelism and above all by the main themes. *Cleanness* relates the decorum and purity of the ideal earthly court to that of God's heavenly one, and to the order and natural law of His creation. The narratives give a kind of history of God's treatment of His subjects, balancing His great punishments against the mercy represented by Christ and the sacraments.

Patience again consists of a story and discourse but in a simpler two-part structure. But again there is a thematic unity transcending the explicit connexions made by the speaker. He associates patience and poverty by using the Beatitudes from the Sermon on the Mount. He finds patience and poverty of spirit appropriate virtues for his own situation which is also called poverty. He pictures this as comparable to having to obey an all-powerful lord. The result of disobedience, he says, can be seen in the case of Jonah. The situation of poverty is not merely literal but is also a metaphor for the state of all human beings before the Almighty. The Jonah in the story is so presented as to be a representative figure, a man on God's errand in a difficult world. We will sympathize with his difficulties, but Jonah is a comic figure too, laughable for his foolish resistance to God.

Like those in *Cleanness*, this story is an imaginative development and animation of the Biblical original, in which each emphasis is calculated to serve the poet's own purpose. At every stage Jonah is shown avoiding the (admittedly great) hardships of his life. When God charges him with the mission to preach in Nineveh, he runs away to sea, testily justifying himself on the grounds that God is too remote to care. His short-sighted delight in his escape is expressed in the busy scene of the boat departing from the harbour.

Even the swallowing by the whale, which the narrator himself admits is incredible, is rendered with conviction. Jonah is wafted through the vast jaws 'like a speck of dust through a church door', and then,

Ay hele over hed, hourlande aboute,
Til he blunt in a blok as brod as a halle.   *staggered/place*
And ther he festnes the fete and fathmez aboute,   *wades*
And stod up in his stomak that stank as the devel:
Ther in saym and in sour that savoured as helle,   *grease/filth*
Ther watz bylded his bour that wyl no bale suffer.

He learns of the mercy of God through his misery in the belly of the
whale, as he listens to the sea beating on its back. But his humble
submission is temporary, and he is soon angrily objecting to God's
sparing of the Ninevites after he, Jonah, had foretold destruction.
God has made him a liar.

There follows the subtle and comic scene in which Jonah removes himself to sulk and watch over the city. God shades him with
a 'woodbine' to his great but not entirely uncritical delight:

And ever he laghed as he loked the loge alle aboute,
And wysched hit were in his kyth, ther he wony schulde,   *homeland*
On heghe upon Effraym other Ermonnes hillez.   *or*

When God causes the shelter to wither Jonah is peevishly angry.
His wish to die is the extreme of his unwillingness to suffer the
difficulties of living in this world. With irony, God compares
Jonah's lack of patience with His own restraint and forbearance
despite the immense destructive power He wields. The comparison
returns the poem to the theme of the prologue. There the poet had
quoted the Beatitudes, a text symbolic of the mercy of God which,
although the speaker did not actually say so, is the other side of the
less comfortable truth that to resist is in any case profitless. The
lack of confident emphasis on God's grace is part of the prevailing
tone of realistic, humorous stoicism:

For he that is to rakel to renden his clothez   *hasty*
Mot efte sitte with more unsounde to sewe hem togeder.   *discomfort*

At first sight the difference of *Sir Gawain and the Green Knight*
from these two seems complete. But although it is an elaborately
wrought secular romance it has in common with them an intense
concern with certain aspects of private and public morality of a
necessarily Christian kind. It also shares, and surpasses, their
virtuosity and formal ingenuity.

The opening of the poem indicates a consciousness of history of
the kind we have met before in alliterative poems. The first stanza
summarizes events from the sack of Troy to the founding of Britain
by 'Felix Brutus', and the next takes us to Arthur, the noblest of all

the kings of Britain. This consciously splendid beginning provides both a historical setting for the events to follow and also a thematic one, since the adventures deal, in a changed perspective, with similar issues, of fidelity and treachery, conflict and happiness, to those affecting the noble history of Britain.

The story begins with a description of Arthur's court at Camylot during Christmas. It is rich and realistic. Every detail would be recognized and appreciated in a fourteenth century noble house, but Arthur's is an ideal. It is the best that could be, as are Arthur himself and his knights and ladies. The court are 'in their first age', that is, a youthful prime whose potential and whose dangers are perhaps suggested in the description of Arthur's restlessness and 'somewhat boyish' temperament. The impatient but glorious youth of the hero in the *Wars of Alexander* has something of this.

Arthur is delaying the start of the meal, according to custom, until something interesting or amusing should happen. What does happen is therefore both expected and unexpected, wanted and unwanted – the breathtaking entrance on horseback of the strange, half-giant knight; fine figure of a man for all his stature, admirable indeed but for his being a bright green colour (and his horse too). While the court stares, so do we, for with masterly assurance the poet devotes three stanzas of detailed description to the Green Knight and his strange equipment:

Whether hade he no helme ne hawbergh nauther,	*yet*
Ne no pysan ne no plate that pented to armes,	*breastplate/belonged*
Ne no schafte ne no schelde to schwve ne to smyte,	*thrust*
Bot in his on honde he hade an holyn bobbe,	*holly-bough*
That is grattest in grene when grevez ar bare,	*woods*
And an ax in his other, a hoge and unmete,	*monstrous*
A spetos sparthe to expoun in spelle, quoso myght,	*cruel axe*

before the frozen action begins to move again.

The court recovers its composure as Arthur asks his errand. The Knight, scornful of the 'berdles chylder' of the youthful court, proposes the famous game. Someone must strike a blow at the Knight with the 'spetos sparthe', and then receive one in return in a year's time. After some delay, in which the Knight continues to malign the court's reputation, Gawain accepts the challenge and strikes off the Knight's head so that it rolls among the onlookers' feet, spraying blood. The Knight, however, picks it up and as he holds it up by the hair it tells Gawain he must seek the Green Knight himself for the return blow. The Knight gallops from the hall. The close of this first section makes the paradoxical situation clear: Arthur and his court must put on a brave face of unconcern, and indeed the whole ghastly incident is incredible, even ridiculous, but for all that Gawain is bound by his knighthood to fulfil the rest of the agreement.

Since the poem is accessible in many editions and translations it seems unnecessary to spoil the pleasure of anyone's first reading by summarizing the rest. Already in this section we have a sample of the poet's narrative and dramatic powers and his unerring control of rich visual and concrete detail. We see too the use of the curious stanza, not found in any other poem. It is obviously related to that of *Fortune* and *Golagros*, but since it has no rhymes on the long lines, and since they vary in number from stanza to stanza, it has a paragraph-like freedom, while retaining the pointed concentration available in the swifter, often elliptical lines of the 'bob and wheel'.

It is also unnecessary to draw attention in detail to the remarkable structure of the narrative, with its obvious and overt patterning of events and images, assisted by numbers; for instance, where groups of three events at the castle are seen to bear on those at the chapel. The poet also uses formal means to emphasize the 'circular' pattern of the plot with its year-long time scale and blow answering blow, finally returning to the historical setting with an almost word for word repetition of the opening, such as we saw in *Patience*.

Sir Gawain belongs to the medieval genre of courtly romance, but other really comparable examples are hard to find in English. *The Knight's Tale* matches it for seriousness and sophistication but is informed by a different spirit. It may be sensibly compared to the great French romances of Chrétien de Troyes written some two centuries earlier. But *Sir Gawain* is a more highly developed work. The intention to entertain an aristocratic circle remains but, despite its stately richness, *Sir Gawain* is not self-indulgently leisurely. All is purpose, and the courtly ideals which are the subject of romance, although basically much the same as those of the twelfth century, are under a closer critical scrutiny. This does not mean that in *Sir Gawain* the rightness of the highest of those ideals as such is under fire. But they are treated with a subtlety and ironic profundity that reaches beyond their immediate context. The whole paraphernalia of romance literature too is treated with magnificent ambivalence – rather as was Jonah's escapade in the whale.

When Gawain sets out to fulfil his promise, the poet presents with careful clarity the issues at stake. In an elaborate description of the hero's arming, he uses Gawain's shield-device of the pentangle to show precisely what his knighthood means. The key is fidelity and truth both to knightly virtues and to God. The testing he is about to undergo, then, is by the highest standards possible for the noblest kind of man. But one of the difficulties he must contend with – perhaps in a sense it defeats him – is that to others, and even at times to himself, his actions seem less important than that.

Nothing is taken for granted in this agilely self-aware romance. Therefore as Gawain sets off there are some people even suggesting that the quest is trivial and only foolish pride insists that so good a man should commit suicide for a promise made at a Christmas entertainment. He should stay at home and do something practical like leading men and governing lands. Of course such arguments cannot prevail. Were Gawain even to consider them, not only his high ideals but the whole poem would collapse. But they have an attractively reasonable sound, and only a poet in complete control of his theme and medium could introduce so dangerous a note simply to define by contrast the world of high achievement in which his hero moves.

A rather similar ironic method is employed during Gawain's stay in Bertilak's castle. We have been told by what standards Gawain lives and that to him this quest is no game, but from the courtiers at the castle we learn what such a high reputation may mean to the world. They are delighted at his visit because from one so famous they will learn the most refined fashion in courtly speech and manners, and the elegant forms of paying court to ladies. This is doubly ironic since in many romances Gawain does have the reputation of a skilled womanizer. It is alluded to again with great lightness of touch when Bertilak's wife is wooing Gawain by challenging him to live up to this more frivolous fame. He denies that his knowledge and skill in such things is the equal of the lady's, thus rejecting, as it were, his own literary reputation which she may well know better than he (from romances!).

Even Gawain, so responsibly conscious of his calling, is unable to see the significance of all his own actions. Convinced of the inevitability of his fate at the chapel, he discovers that in fact he has himself determined it. This is designed by the poet as a revelation for the audience too. The deftly dramatic and psychologically satisfying dénouement sorts out the differences between Gawain's and other people's understanding of his success and failure. Arthur and the court, for instance, are able to share in both, although only Gawain himself was at the humiliating heart of things. It is easy to be over-specific about the poet's 'thesis' in all this, especially when he chose not to reveal one explicitly. But in general one might say that he has made, in Christian and aristocratic romance terms, a comment on human limitation and the relation between ideal and real. The comment is serious, but not in any way pessimistic, and the treatment is comic in a way that is reminiscent of *Patience* and *Pearl*.

The detailed texture of *Sir Gawain* is a contributor to its meaning. Its most decorative effects are never purely decorative. The success of its simultaneous consideration of ideal and real depends on the wholly convincing realism of events in the overtly literary context. This shows especially in the dialogues with their precisely judged atmosphere and tone: the oddly menacing heartiness of the lord of the castle as he diverts Gawain's thoughts from the quest; the nervy haste of Gawain's exchanges with him on the last night of his stay; the delicate twists and turns of Gawain's verbal contest with the lady where, though both know that her purpose is to cause the knight to sin, nothing appears on the surface but polite conversation.

A realistic density is given even to the summary account of Gawain's extraordinary adventures on his journey; not, however, by describing at length his encounters with monsters, but by naming some features of his route through North Wales and the Wirral, and by picturing the cold season and the discomfort that was with him even between adventures:

For werre wrathed hym not so much that wynter nas wors,	*battle*
When the colde cler water fro the cloudez schadde,	*fell*
And fres er hit falle myght to the fale erthe.	*pale*
Ner slayn wyth the slete he sleped in his yrnes	
Mo nyghtez then innoghe in naked rokkez	
Ther as claterande fro the crest the colde borne rennez	
And henged heghe over his hede in hard iisse-ikkles.	

The solidity of the setting, both indoors and out, acquires, beyond realism and the expected diversion of an audience familiar with its details, a symbolic resonance. It was there too in the concrete naturalism of the stories in *Cleanness* and *Patience*, but here the metaphoric implications are harder to assess. The way the tangled wood through which Gawain approaches the castle reinforces his troubled mood and the spiritual dangers of his journey is clear enough. But it might be a mistake to seek only for exact symbolic relations between the famous hunting scenes and the bedroom dialogues they alternate with. Part of the value of those exciting hunts is the unease they create in the listener – the feeling that they must have something to do with Gawain, but what?

Nevertheless, throughout *Sir Gawain*, the particular adventure and its abstract meaning are echoed, enriched and expanded by metaphoric and formal patterns. The most striking instance is the passage at the beginning of the second section, where the narrator's solemn reminders of the seriousness of what Gawain undertook that Christmas gradually give rise to an extended picture of the passing year. In some ways this picture resembles the 'history' that opened the poem. Despite the repeat and return of the seasons, the year is never the same. No one can tell the end by the beginning.

Pearl shows a formal skill of the kind found in *Sir Gawain* but carried much further. The use of numerical patterns, whose significance in the romance is problematic, is here an obvious part of the structure and meaning. Who knows why *Sir Gawain* has a hundred and one stanzas? The reason for the same number in *Pearl* is easier to understand.

Pearl is a dream poem. The dreamer mourns the loss of what he calls his pearl, which seems to have been a young child. Weeping over the grave in a garden he dreams he is in a beautiful country by a stream, whose banks he follows in hopes of being able to cross because the farther shore is even more beautiful. At last he sees across the river a girl wearing a crown and whose dress is ornamented with pearls. It is his own Pearl. She greets him, but then rebukes him when he expresses delight at having found her again, and for supposing they can now live together.

They cannot meet for he is mortal and she in heaven. She rebukes him further for his naïve belief in the real existence of what he seems to see with his mortal eyes. Most of the rest of the poem is a conversation between the Pearl and the dreamer. He seeks to know how she, so young, is crowned in heaven, and persists, despite her words, in his protests at the injustice of God, who rewards so richly an innocent child and yet gives nothing more to men who have lived and suffered long on earth. His protests finally subside, but he asks to see something of the heaven she lives in, and the poem reaches its climax with a description of the Heavenly City, appearing as it did to St. John in the Apocalypse.

The sight is too much for him and, forgetful of the girl's words, he wades into the stream to cross, and wakes. The poem closes with his reflections on the lessons of the dream: regretful still at his loss and that his worldly desire itself deprived him of a continuing vision of the city, but more calmly resigned to the truth and to deserving that reward while he lives.

The structure of the poem is a *tour de force*. The lines are in general rather shorter than the usual alliterative ones, but still with four stresses, and having sometimes much alliteration, sometimes none at all. They are arranged in twelve-line stanzas, rhymed *ababababbcbc*. These are arranged in groups of five, linked together by having their *c* rhymes (lines 10 and 12) and the actual rhyme word of the last line in common, and by *concatenatio*, repetition of the whole or part of the last line of each stanza in the first line of the next. Repetition also links group to group, and the last line of the poem repeats the first. This ought to mean twenty groups of sixty lines, but an extra stanza was added in the fifteenth group to give a total of 1212. The numbers are symbolic, being associated with the twelve-fold structure of the Heavenly City. The poem itself therefore reflects and symbolically imitates the eternity which is part of its subject. The 101 stanzas suggest completeness and fulfilment rather as does the expression 'a year and a day'.

Pearl also reflects the jewelled beauty of the city of the Apocalypse in its texture, most obviously in the passages where the narrator actually describes the splendour his eye sees, such as the 'ornament' of the rich landscape he wanders in by the river:

> The dubbemente of tho derworth depe
> Wern bonkez bene of beryl bryght.
> Swangeande swete the water con swepe,
> Wyth a rownande rourde raykande aryght.
> In the founce ther stonden stonez stepe
> As glente thurgh glas that glowed and glyght.
> As stremande sternez, quen strothemen slepe,
> Staren in welkyn in wynter nyght;
> For uche a pobbel in pole ther pyght
> Watz emerad, saffer, other gemme gente,
> That alle the loghe lemed of lyght,
> So dere watz hit adubbement.

(The adornment of those precious depths were the fair banks of bright beryl. Swirling smoothly the water swept with a whispering murmur flowing evenly. In the depths there stood glittering stones that glowed and glinted as a beam of light through glass; as stars streaming light, while men sleep, shine in the heavens in a winter night; for every pebble set in those pools was emerald, sapphire or noble gem, so that the whole water gleamed with light, so precious was its ornament.)

But the richness is maintained throughout. It is obvious that to repeat words is difficult without changing the meaning, and this the poet does so that, far from being confined by the complex form, it actually enables him to push the expressiveness of his language to its limits. The use of the word 'deme' in the sixth section, referring to God's judgment and to man's thought and speech, is a subtle instance, showing how even in dialogue this elaborate artificiality helps rather than hinders the argument.

The imagery is under tight control, and is part of an intricate symbolic development. The pearl stands, on the one hand, for the bodily perfection of the girl as the dreamer saw her, and on the other for the innocent purity that is required for a soul to enter heaven, free of earthly defilement. The garden where the poem starts is a place of growth and decay, of death and regeneration, and the narrator enters it in the crucial harvest time:

I entred in that erber grene   *grassy place*
In Auguste in a hygh seysoun,
Quen corne is corven wyth crokez kene.   *sickles*

The harvest image is picked up and developed with other references to the Last Judgment (the Apocalypse itself), while the earthly garden becomes a heavenly one in which nothing is cut down nor decays.

Pearl is a Christian *consolatio*. Its twofold purpose is to celebrate and mourn some trouble or loss, and to offer consolation, to show indeed that excessive mourning is unprofitable and foolish. In this case the loss is kept deliberately mysterious. It is some time before we know that the girl was but two years old, and the narrator hints but never says directly what was his relation to her. One thinks of the concealment of identities in Chaucer's *Book of the Duchess*, and it seems likely that *Pearl* contains a similar compliment to a patron bereaved. That the grief should be expressed also as the poet's own is entirely proper.

At first a modern reader may miss the relevance in this context of the debate between the dreamer and the Pearl, especially since the treatment is partly comic. It is concerned with the discrepancy between earthly and spiritual understanding. The dreamer is getting an answer for his grief in Christian terms of God's grace and the promise of eternal life. But, being human, in his trouble he cannot see this. Despite the Pearl's first warning, he sees everything – even finally the Heavenly City – as something gained or lost in worldly terms. Hence the importance of visual images, which the dreamer sees without appreciating their meaning. It is he himself who introduces irrelevance, by questioning the propriety of the child's reward in heaven. But all the time the debate appears to be pursuing this rather special case, points are being made about the dreamer's own.

Consolation must ultimately mean reassurance for the bereaved about his own position. The dreamer's first concern for the Pearl's fate has already become more selfish. But the special case of the innocent is brought directly to bear on his trouble in the thirteenth section where he is told that to enter bliss he must become like the Pearl, like an innocent child. The humour with which the dreamer is treated during the urgent debate is never allowed to damage the sympathetic expression of his grief. Rather it intensifies it. Humour, the Christian consolation, and the sense of loss all come together in the ironic resolution.

Apart from its extensive use of the Bible and medieval religious writings in Latin, *Pearl* is closely related to continental religious and secular literature. It is not unlikely that the poet knew Dante's *Divina Commedia*, and much in *Pearl* can be explained by reference to it. It seems appropriate to close this chapter with perhaps the best single example of the alliterative poet's combination of local, native tradition with a wide outlook and contacts.

5

CHAUCER
(i) CHAUCER'S LIFE

W. F. Bolton

By the nature of his public life and by the nature of the literary profession in his age, we have much evidence about Chaucer the courtier, diplomat, and civil servant, and very little – outside the poems themselves – about Chaucer the poet. The literary allusions to him before his death are confined to a few lines by Thomas Usk, two passages by John Gower (one in Anglo-French), and a ballade by the French poet Deschamps in honour of the 'grant translateur noble Geffroy Chaucier'. It is only after his death that we find any quantity of testimony about him as a writer, and then it is usually praise and not information. Hence we have much documentary information about Chaucer – far more than about Shakespeare, born about 220 years later – but scarcely any materials for his literary biography.

Chaucer was born about 1343, the son of a prosperous wine-merchant already known at court. The records first reveal the young Chaucer in the service of Elizabeth, Countess of Ulster, the wife of Lionel, son of the reigning king Edward III. In 1360 the king paid Chaucer's ransom, along with that of some others, to release him from captivity in France; from this we learn both of Chaucer's participation in the war, and of the favour already being shown him by the crown. Indeed from 1357 to the end of his life, Chaucer retained his connexion with the court, and especially with the household of another of Edward III's sons, John of Gaunt, with whom he was campaigning in Picardy in 1369.

Chaucer survived the plague year of 1362 as he had that of 1349, and about 1366, aged perhaps twenty-three, veteran of court service and foreign wars, he married a lady-in-waiting to the queen. In the next year we find him in the king's household. The plague returned to England in 1369; again Chaucer survived, but Blanche, the wife of John of Gaunt, died. On this occasion Chaucer wrote his earliest datable poem, *The Book of the Duchess*, a work in which his courtly connexions and literary powers fused. (If, as is sometimes said, he wrote the short poem *An ABC* for Blanche, it must of course be even earlier.)

But he did not then or ever take up the literary profession as a livelihood. Instead he was abroad again in the service of the king in 1370, and still again – this time in Italy – in 1372–3. He continued to make official journeys to the Continent (mostly to France but sometimes to Italy and at least once to Spain) as late as 1387, and on the king's business within England until 1398, but increasingly from the time of his return from Italy in 1373 he was taken up with his offices at home: Controller of Custom and Subsidies on Wools, Skins and Hides in the Port of London; Controller of the Petty Customs; Justice of the Peace for Kent; Knight of the Shire (i.e., Member of Parliament) for Kent; Clerk of the King's Works; Deputy Forester of the Royal Forest at North Petherton. And all the time he was writing: even before the first Italian journey of 1372–3 he had translated at least part of the vast French *Romaunt of the Rose*.

In 1376 Edward III's enormously popular son, the Black Prince, died, and the plague returned again to England. Edward III himself died in 1377, and Richard II, the ten-year-old son of the Black Prince, came to the throne. Of this period, or at least before 1380, are Chaucer's incomplete *House of Fame*, the *Anelida*, and the stories which became *The Second Nun's Tale* and *The Monk's Tale*.

In 1381 came the uprising known as the 'Peasants' Revolt'. Like so many of the events in England already mentioned, it must have coloured Chaucer's life deeply, for it involved his county and challenged the class of which he was in so many ways a part; yet like those other events too, it has little or no place in his poetry. It is as though the life of his imagination were really as separate from his official life as the distribution of the surviving documents implies. Or did his political links become chains that restrained his choice of poetic subject-matter?

Chaucer's wife Philippa died, it appears, in 1387, when he was about fifty-four. By this time he had already translated Boethius' *Consolation of Philosophy* and written two works in which the influence of the *Consolation* is great, *Troilus and Criseyde* and the early form of *The Knight's Tale*. Already complete too were the *Parliament of Fowls* and the *Legend of Good Women*, dream-visions like the *House of Fame*. The beginning of *The Canterbury Tales*, left unfinished at his death, also dates from the late 1380s. Although his poetic career began early in his life with his works for Blanche, the period of his greatest activity and most perfect achievement followed his fortieth year.

The official documents from the same period begin to tell a different story. Although Chaucer continued to hold public office, perhaps to the end of his life, and received various official loans, grants and annuities, he fell on increasingly difficult times. Actions against him to recover debts date from 1388 onwards. In 1390 he was robbed and beaten several times, and on one occasion lost over £20 of the king's money to the highwaymen. In the last year of his life he was granted the tenancy of a dwelling in the garden of Westminster Abbey, in the company of others who had long connexions with the court. All this while he was continuing with his work on the *Tales*, some of the shorter poems, and, it seems, with the prose works on astronomy.

Toward the close of Chaucer's life yet another king, Henry IV, took the throne, this time on the abdication of Richard II in 1399. But Chaucer's own part in public affairs was at an end. In October 1400 he died and was buried in Westminster Abbey, not as a poet – that tradition followed his burial there – but as a resident of the abbey precincts. He was not yet sixty years old.

(ii) *THE MINOR POEMS AND THE PROSE*

S. S. Hussey

Some authors, like Donne or Wordsworth, write a consciously new style of poetry because the contemporary tradition appears to them sterile and lifeless. Others, like Shakespeare or Pope, start by appealing to current tastes, however much their poetry later outgrows these fashions. Chaucer, although his earliest work was contributing something new to English poetry, was writing in a well-established French tradition of verse. Given the situation in England in the second half of the fourteenth century, it could hardly have been otherwise. As the introductory chapter to this book and the brief Life of Chaucer have made clear, his early education in royal households would have been in the sort of courtly accomplishments, largely French in origin, which he describes in the portrait of his own squire in the *General Prologue* to *The Canterbury Tales*. When in later life he united the present-day professions of senior civil servant at home and diplomat on his travels abroad, he would have been in regular contact with men brought up in the same European tradition. His own social position, midway between the aristocracy and the rising middle class, made him able to appreciate the views of both, as the debate in *The Parliament of Fowls* for instance makes clear.

His poetry must have been a largely spare-time occupation. In *The House of Fame*, probably written while he was at the Custom House, one of his characters upbraids him for leading a kind of all-work-and-no-play existence:

And noght oonly fro fer contree
That ther no tydynge cometh to thee,
But of thy verray neyghebores,
That duellen almost at thy dores,
Thou herist neyther that ne this;
For when thy labour doon al ys,
And hast mad alle thy rekenynges   *accounts*
In stede of reste and newe thynges,
Thou goost hom to thy hous anoon;
And, also domb as any stoon,
Thou sittest at another book
Tyl fully daswed ys thy look.   *stupefied*

The early poems, in their concern with dreams and books, seem a world away from Chaucer's public life. The picture he gives of himself in them is clearly a deliberate poetic creation: that of a rather bewildered man doing his best, but not very successfully, to understand the puzzling world around him. And that world was one of social, political and religious ferment of which Chaucer's poetry gives hardly any direct hint, in contrast to the work of his contemporaries Langland and Gower. The Peasants' Revolt, for example, was taking place in London at about the time Chaucer was working on *The Parliament of Fowls*. The insurgents were sacking the Savoy palace, the house of his patron, John of Gaunt, but Chaucer is writing a poem ostensibly about birds.

There were two other reasons for Chaucer's beginning his poetic career with translations, both of which are mentioned in Chapter 1 of this book. The first was linguistic. From the Norman Conquest until the thirteenth century, English had been largely in eclipse as a vehicle for polite literature (although religious and didactic prose and alliterative verse continued to be composed in English in the conservative West and North). When, in the fourteenth century, English was once again felt to be the natural tongue for English poets to use, they had no large native body of verse to start from. The court where Chaucer was a squire spoke English but more often read French, for French literature enjoyed great European prestige throughout the Middle Ages. The second reason is the medieval respect for tradition. A new poet hoped to contribute something, but within the already existing conventions; new wine was expected to arrive in old bottles. It follows that personal revelations in poetry are few; the Dreamer, although he speaks in the first person, is not necessarily or wholly Chaucer. It is also not surprising that fifteenth-century critics set higher store than we do on Chaucer's earlier poems and correspondingly less on the more original or colloquial of the *Canterbury Tales*. In praising him for his 'morality and eloquence ornate', his 'sweetness of rhetoric', for being 'universal father of science (*learning*)', they are simply showing that they recognize his great contribution in adapting this tradition to the needs of English poetry.

The more important of Chaucer's two early translations is unquestionably part of the immensely popular French poem the *Romaunt de la Rose*. This had been started about 1237 by Guillaume de Lorris and continued some forty years later by Jean de Meun. The influence of the whole poem can be seen at all periods of Chaucer's career, but of the three long translated sections included in most editions of Chaucer only the first is generally agreed to be by him. This represents about one twelfth of the original and covers the first part of de Lorris's work. But several features found here reappear in Chaucer's own early poetry. The *Romaunt* is cast in the form of a dream which takes place on a morning in May, the season for loving. Its setting is a large walled garden inhabited by allegorical characters. The Dreamer (who is also the Lover of the poem) enters the garden and wanders about admiring its beauty, its birds who sing so melodiously, its gently running river, its mild (*attempre*) weather, its orderly rows of trees with their shadowy foliage under which docile animals sport and play. (The ordered and rather general view of nature would have appealed to the early eighteenth century.) He sees and falls in love with a rose on a bush reflected in one of the wells in the garden. At this point the first of the three Chaucerian passages ends, just before the God of Love, who has been following the Dreamer at a distance, pierces him with the twin arrows of desire and longing. The remainder of this very long poem becomes an endeavour on the part of the Dreamer/ Lover to pluck the rosebud. His first attempt is only partially successful; he kisses the bud but is immediately banished from the garden. De Lorris ends here after some four thousand lines. His great achievement, which Chaucer must have recognized, was to portray the charming naïveté (in the best sense) of young love, for the beautiful garden clearly represents the court (the proper setting for a love affair) and the allegorical figures who assist or oppose the Dreamer portray the varying moods of the loved one. She never appears in the poem in her own person, but her love is symbolized by the Rose of the title.

It would be difficult to imagine a man more different from Guillaume de Lorris than Jean de Meun. He was an encyclopedist and something of a cynic. Conseqently he gets away from the subject of the poem for hundreds of lines at a time – and he added eighteen thousand. There is much good poetry here, and Chaucer used some of it later, but it will not be our concern in this chapter. Finally, however, the castle in which the Lover's chief helper Bialacoil ('Fair Welcome', allegorically the Lady's encouragement to the Lover) has been imprisoned is stormed and the Lover wins the Rose.

It is likely that Chaucer translated some of this poem before writing *The Book of the Duchess*; he had certainly read it. He had also perhaps already translated *An ABC to the Virgin* from another long French poem, Guillaume Deguilleville's *Pèlerinage de la Vie*

Humaine, for there is an early tradition that this translation was made at the request of the Duchess Blanche. Each of its twenty-three eight-line stanzas begins with a letter of the alphabet excluding j, u and w – hence the title. The whole is a prayer to Mary, the intercessor between God and Man. Although Chaucer's translation is more varied than its French source, it is hardly a remarkable poem. Its chief use may be to remind us that, though his poetry is predominantly secular and though he later on satirized churchmen, his wider view was fixed on Heaven. The Retraction at the end of the *Canterbury Tales* may appear less strange in the light of an early poem like the *ABC*.

So the description of Chaucer by his contemporary Eustace Deschamps as 'grant translateur' is merited, even though Deschamps would have included in it later translations (e.g. of Boethius) and what we should now call adaptation of a definite source. Chaucer composed short poems throughout his life. Some of them have pretty certainly been lost and the few which remain are difficult to date. But his first long original poem, *The Book of the Duchess*, is likely to have been composed not long after 1368 when its heroine Blanche, the wife of John of Gaunt, died. Gaunt remarried in 1371 so that an elegy for his first wife would hardly have been tactful then or later. Between this date and the *Romaunt de la Rose* in the thirteenth century, French poets like Machaut, Froissart and Deschamps had kept many of the same conventions of love poetry, although their work had lost a good deal of the freshness of their model. Chaucer generally avoided their artificialities and excesses whilst retaining the main features of the tradition. One of Machaut's poems, *Le Jugement dou Roy de Behaingne*, is a source of sorts for Chaucer, but our interest is less in what he borrows from Machaut or anyone else than in what he transforms in the borrowing.

The Book of the Duchess, written in octosyllabic couplets like the translation of the *Romaunt*, has the form of a dream. At the beginning the poet is unable to sleep, so he takes up a book to pass the night away. The story, the tragic episode of Ceyx and Alcyone from Book XI of Ovid's *Metamorphoses* (Chaucer was a fervent reader of classical as well as of French authors and the Eagle in *The House of Fame* calls Ovid 'thyn owen book') is paraphrased. But Chaucer omits much of Ovid's rhetoric: the description of the shipwreck in which Ceyx meets his death, the lament of his wife Alcyone when she hears the news, and the final change of the pair into birds. He did retain, however, Ovid's description of the cave of sleep (lines

592–615 in Ovid, 153–77 in Chaucer), and Morpheus, the God of Sleep, finally makes the Dreamer fall asleep over his book. The walls of the room in which the Dreamer finds himself are painted with scenes from the *Romaunt de la Rose*, but he soon leaves it – transitions in both literary and real-life dreams are made with a minimum of fuss and logic – to join a hunt he hears outside. However, he is soon distracted to follow a puppy who, having lost the scent, leads him down a woodside path until he comes upon a young knight clad all in black sitting in a glade with his back to a large oak. The dream setting hitherto might have come straight from the *Romaunt*: the same spring-like weather of May, the same birds singing sweetly, the same flowers, the same huge leafy trees with the same woodland animals running about beneath them. But attention from now on is concentrated on the Knight in Black. He is lamenting the death of his lady and seems ready to die for grief. In answer to the Dreamer's question whether he can help to relieve his sorrow, he recounts at length his devotion as a youth to the service of the God of Love, his courtship of the most beautiful and courtly of ladies, their marriage and his eventual loss of her. But the Dreamer still does not realize that the Knight's loss is through the death of his Lady:

> 'What los ys that?' quod I thoo;   *then*
> 'Nyl she not love yow? ys hyt soo?   *will she not*
> Or have ye oght doon amys,
> That she hath left yow? ys hyt this?
> For Goddes love, telle me al.'

and later still:

> 'Sir,' quod I, 'where is she now?'

Although he has heard the Knight lamenting her death (479) and has had one or two hints of this later (e.g. 577), it is not until he hears the blunt words 'She is dead' that he realizes what has happened. And then the encounter is ended, the Knight rides back home, and the sound of a bell rouses the Dreamer with his Ovid still in his hand. In Chaucer waking up is much briefer than falling asleep.

The main story is clearly an allegory. The Lady is called White (i.e. Blanche) at 948 and the identification of the Knight in Black with John of Gaunt is clinched by some rather excruciating puns in lines 1318–9. Their marriage is seen as the culmination of a courtship conducted according to the rules of courtly love (for which see Chapter 1). As the Knight recounts this to the Dreamer, we see that the woman is traditionally the superior of the man. At first he sees no hope that she will return his love and she actually refuses him once (1243), but subsequently, 'another year', seeing the Knight's devotion and concern for her reputation, she relents and shows him her mercy (1270). Continental theorists had argued that marriage, in which the male was unquestionably the master, was inimical to courtly love, but here and elsewhere in Chaucer this is not the case: Palamon and Emily marry at the end of *The Knight's Tale* and in *The Franklin's Tale* the lovers are married from the beginning. Devotion and fidelity to the lady do not presuppose adultery on the part of the lovers. The whole picture is idealized, yet occasionally we are made to share vicariously in the Knight's real sorrow for his dead wife:

> for be hyt never so derk,
> Me thynketh I se hir ever moo.

and

And yet she syt so in myn herte,	*remains*
That, by my trouthe, y nolde noght,	*would not want to*
For al thys world, out of my thoght	
Leve my lady; noo, trewely!	

Although this main story does not begin until line 443, what has come before is by no means irrelevant. The episode from Ovid is a mirror image of the Knight's own case, for there the man dies and the woman lives on to mourn him. But the connexion is implicit, and it is our job as readers to make it. The setting in the wood, so like the garden of the *Romaunt* and no doubt of a hundred derivative poems, is a signal that this is to be a poem about love. It should be noticed too that here the Dreamer is not, as in the *Romaunt*, himself the lover, but listens to the Knight's lament. This was also true of Machaut's poem, where there are two people sorrowing, a lady mourning the death of her lover and a knight whose own love is unrequited: the question posed is, which is the harder case and the decision eventually goes in favour of the knight. Why, it may be asked, does the Dreamer take so long to discover that the Lady is dead? Is he, as has been suggested, simply being tactful in concealing his knowledge? In fact he contributes little to the conversation. It is the Knight in Black who does the talking and who praises Blanche. The almost therapeutic function of the Dreamer is simply to lead him on to remember the happiness of his past life and by so doing to divert his attention away from the sad present. He gradually comes to accept the bereavement, as people must in real life. The obtuseness of the Dreamer is therefore perhaps necessary (and medieval dreamers often seem very literal-minded in their questions to those they meet) but there would appear to be no real connexion with Chaucer as his contemporaries knew him. The 'I' of *The Book of the Duchess* is a fictional character. Or, it could be argued, Chaucer is here beginning to develop the detached position characteristic of his later poetry: the Narrator of *Troilus and Criseyde* or the appearance of Chaucer as one of the Canterbury pilgrims, involved, but not too directly, and free to comment on the significance of what he sees.

The overwhelming impression of *The Book of the Duchess*, however, is of a formal, sophisticated poem, seen in a kind of middle distance, 'drenched in a leisured melancholy' as Professor Coghill has put it. The formal elements are indeed considerable, and recur (but with variations) in Chaucer's earlier poetry. Chapter 1 of this book will have made it clear that to the medieval mind poetry was something to be learned the hard way. Whatever may be our impression now – and the function of art has always been to conceal as well as to demonstrate art – few poets then seem to have regarded poetry as wholly inspirational, a kind of leaping up of the heart at the appearance of rainbows. The rhetorical devices of *The Book of the Duchess* are easy to discover: the opening of the Knight's lament is a series of paradoxes (599–615). He uses an elaborate chess metaphor – which the Dreamer totally fails to grasp – to show how false Fortune has captured his 'queen'. When he describes Blanche he proceeds according to the text-books, from top to toe; hair, eyes, face, mouth, neck, throat, shoulders, arms, hands, nails, breasts, hips, back – and the remainder, he adds, equally in proportion. Idleness, in the *Romaunt*, is described in the same fashion (538–61). Although she is evidently kinder than some medieval highborn ladies – Blanche does not send her suitor on wild-goose chases half across the world – the effect is to show her less as a person than as a paragon of all the virtues, the embodiment of ideal womanly beauty. (As yet Chaucer's description means what it says and no more. The surface picture of the Prioress in the *General Prologue* is that of another lady full of courtly behaviour and sensibility, but we are expected to supply the ironic counterpart by remembering that this is a portrait of a *nun*.) Another (of several) rhetorical figures is the series of illustrative comparisons or *exempla*. The Knight is urged not to commit suicide because of unrequited love, like others whom he names 724–39; he would go on loving Blanche even if he had all the virtues of the heroes of antiquity listed at 1056–74. And these rhetorical figures are now and then gratuitous to an extent they are not in the later poetry. Together with them goes an occasional diffuseness in the writing. Lines 294–320, for instance, really say very little beyond 'The birds singing sweetly in the morning woke me up'. The pleasure comes in decoration for its own sake. It is a young man's poem to his patron.

There is some doubt whether *The House of Fame* or *The Parliament of Fowls* followed *The Book of the Duchess*. But *The House of Fame* is surely the more likely. It is once more written in octosyllabic couplets, which Chaucer did not use afterwards, whereas the *Parliament* is in the seven-line stanza (rhyme royal) used for the later *Troilus and Criseyde*. It shows a new Italian influence supplementing but not superseding the more important French tradition. This influence, however, comes from Dante and not yet from Boccaccio who was to supply Chaucer with the source material for his two longest poems, *Troilus* and *The Knight's Tale*, and also for part of *The Parliament of Fowls*. There is no event comparable to the death of Blanche the Duchess which will help to date *The House of Fame*. In the last few lines there is a reference to 'a man of great authority', but it seems pointless to speculate which if any public or literary figure he was intended to represent (John of Gaunt, Boccaccio, Boethius, even Christ who dispenses eternal fame, have all been suggested). If the passage quoted earlier does indeed refer to Chaucer's tenure of the controllership at the Custom House, the poem may be dated between 1374 and 1385, but these are wide limits.

For its first half at least *The House of Fame* gives the surface impression of a very well organized poem. It is divided into three books, the third unfinished. Both Books I and II have a proem (or formal introduction) and an invocation, Book III an invocation only. The proem to Book I deals with the nature and causes of dreams, so it is not strange when this turns out to be another vision poem. This time, however, the Dreamer falls asleep 'wonder sone' and there is no previous bedside reading. But the glass temple of Venus in which he finds himself has its walls covered with the story of Virgil's *Aeneid*, the telling of which takes up the whole of Book I, so the structure is not very different after all. In the summary of the *Aeneid* especial attention is paid to Book IV, the story of the love of Aeneas and Dido, his desertion of her and her eventual suicide. The stress on this part of the *Aeneid* is not surprising. In the Middle Ages it was regarded as one of the great love stories, and it showed how a man's deceitfulness could cause a woman to become, in the religious imagery characteristic of courtly love, one of Cupid's martyrs. Men like this who delude women into believing that the world is well lost for love of them are the villains of the stories in *The Legend of Good Women* in which Chaucer once again tells the story of Dido. Here he cites several other *exempla* (383–426) so that no one is likely to miss the point. His sympathy is entirely with Dido, whereas Virgil's had been with Aeneas who had more important things to do than linger in Carthage. Book IV of the *Aeneid* also contains the impressive allegorical figure of Rumour (*Fama*) who, like some gigantic ever-growing creature from science fiction, spreads over the whole world the story of these tragic events. Chaucer does not mention this in Book I of *The House of Fame*, but in Book III Fame becomes the chief figure. Yet already this is not quite the usual love vision. Its dream does not take place in May but on the 10th December, a date which – to us at least – carries no special significance. When, at the end of Book I, the Dreamer goes outside the temple, he finds not a beautiful garden but a desert. As he looks up into the sky he sees a huge eagle who comes soaring downwards towards him and in Book II this bird carries the Dreamer (whom he addresses by Chaucer's own name of Geoffrey) in his claws up through the heavens.

Near the beginning of Canto IX of the *Purgatorio* Dante dreams that he has been snatched away by an eagle, and the suggestion for this new character may have come from there. But although the influence of Dante is clear in *The House of Fame*, its extent should not be overestimated. Usually it is a matter of a few lines (especially close in the invocations) and not of the whole poem as was to be the case with Boccaccio later. Perhaps Chaucer recognized in Dante the nature of sublimity in poetry, but felt his own genius closer to the more straightforward narrative technique of Boccaccio. Again, the eagle who becomes the Dreamer's guide in Book II of *The House of Fame* may be modelled on Virgil, Dante's guide, but there were many other parallels for an allegorical journey to the next world or a flight through the heavens, and Chaucer mentions some of them in Book II. In one respect this eagle is most unlike such guides. He explains that the Dreamer has been granted the privilege of visiting the House of Fame as a reward for his devotion to the God of Love. But this, we are told, has been a purely literary devotion. In accordance with his presentation of the Dreamer as a puzzled and somewhat ineffectual character, Chaucer now describes him as being unskilled in love (248, 627–8). The Dreamer, too, plays as little part in the conversation with the eagle as he had in that with the Knight in Black in *The Book of the Duchess*. He has little chance to give more than monosyllabic replies to this talkative bird who spends the journey lecturing him on such things as gravitation and the nature of sound waves – all this to demonstrate that speech (which is sound) naturally makes its way to the House of Fame in mid-air. Whatever his literary origin, the guide has clearly been developed far beyond the touching but brief picture of the puppy in *The Book of the Duchess*. He dominates Book II but disappears after he has set down the Dreamer at the entrance to the House of Fame. He returns later on at 1990–2033, but is much less colourful on his second appearance.

Despite the mention of 'this lytel laste bok' in the invocation to Book III, it is almost as long as Books I and II put together. From its beginning Chaucer has let his talent for fantasy indulge itself. The symbolism of the opening is promising. Fame's palace stands on foundations not of rock but of ice; the names engraved on one side have been almost obliterated by the heat of the sun, whilst those on the other remain as sharp as if newly carved. But the building is over-decorated and over-full with musicians, en-tertainers, heralds, and above all with petitioners to Fame who sits on a dais and presides over everything. At first she is like Virgil's Fama, growing ever more enormous as she feeds on rumour, but soon it becomes clear that what she dispenses is in fact reputation. Furthermore she grants it on impulse without any reference to the justice of the request:

And somme of hem she graunted sone,
And somme she werned wel and faire,   *refused*
And somme she graunted the contraire
Of her axyng outterly,

so that Fame with her fickle nature is close to Fortune (who, we learn a few lines later, is her sister). Yet the reputation she grants is to be spread abroad on the winds just like rumour. Nine different companies in all approach the goddess's throne and are variously rewarded. This is surely too many; we have long since taken the point about Fame's capricious judgments. The Dreamer is now asked to account for his presence there. Not surprisingly, what he has seen in Fame's palace seems to him to bear little relation to the reward he has been promised for his service to Cupid:

Quod y, 'That wyl y tellen the,
The cause why y stonde here:
Somme newe tydynges for to lere,   *learn*
Somme newe thinges, y not what   *don't know*
Tydynges, other this or that,   *either*
Of love, or suche thynges glade.
For certeynly, he that me made
To comen hyder, seyde me,
Y shulde bothe here and se,
In this place, wonder thynges;
But these be no suche tydynges
As I mene of'.

So he is led to the House of Twigs which constantly whirls about
and lets *tydynges* escape through its innumerable apertures. This
house, made of wicker twigs, is far more confused than the House
of Fame had been. There the arrangements were ordered, even if
the fate which Fame meted out was uncertain. When he gets inside
this new house he discovers that it too is full of people all busily
spreading rumours. The direct source here is Ovid, *Metamorphoses*
XII, but we have clearly returned, by a roundabout route, to Virgil's
Fama. This house has no presiding deity, but all the rumours that
escape fly straight back to Fame:

Thus out at holes gunne wringe
Every tydynge streght to Fame,
And she gan yeven ech hys name,
After hir disposicioun.   *according to*

Soon after this the poem breaks off, just as the Dreamer catches
sight of 'a man of great authority'.

The poem has been getting steadily wider and wider, so that by
the middle of Book III it is almost out of hand. It is dragged back
towards the close, but if the final message is meant to be that
reputation is based on rumour it is not made as clear as it might
have been. The difficulty seems to be at least partly a semantic one.
The classical Fama, when personified, meant primarily 'rumour',
and at the end of Book II the House of Fame (like the later House
of Twigs) rumbles with *tydynges* compounded of both truth and
falsehood. But in Book III *fames* (1139, 1154) means 'reputations',
and when Fame appears in person this is the signification she
usually bears. The situation is scarcely helped by synonyms like *loos,
name, laude, renoun*, all used in this same sense. At 1406 the goddess
is called

Goddesse of Renoun or of Fame.

She is evidently no longer the unprepossessing *monstrum horrendum* or *dea foeda* of Virgil, but a powerful deity who decides the worldly reputation of many men. In both Boccaccio and Petrarch Fame appears as the goddess of renown and this is the significance the word usually bears in Chaucer's own translation of Boethius. By Book III of *The House of Fame*, then, 'reputation' is the overwhelming sense of Fame and the idea of rumour seems to have been relegated to the House of Twigs. Her fickle nature is akin to that of Fortune, and some at least of the suppliants before her throne are concerned.with love, the apparent reason for the Dreamer's visit in the first place.

It is difficult to avoid the conclusion that Chaucer's reach has exceeded his grasp. He has evidently been using the dream poem to explore something more philosophical than the consolation for the bereaved John of Gaunt sought in *The Book of the Duchess*. The insubstantial nature of much of what he encounters in his quest is clear: the temple of Venus is constructed of glass, the House of Fame built on ice and the House of Rumour made of twigs. But the insubstantial and the capricious are notoriously difficult to provide with a local habitation and a name, and perhaps this is why we feel the sense slowly slipping away from us. Furthermore the poem is bursting at the seams. Chaucer's imagination has been allowed to run riot and has peopled the two buildings he describes with a bewildering array of gossips and status-seekers. Almost as a by-product he has drawn his first great comic character, the eagle, exulting in his own loquacity and affability in the manner of the later great comic creations, Pandarus, the Wife of Bath and Chaunticleer. But all this machinery in *The House of Fame* becomes top-heavy. Perhaps that is why, like *The Squire's Tale*, he never saw his way clear to finishing it.

The Parliament of Fowls is unquestionably a poem about love. Its opening lines say so in typical rhetorical fashion. How to begin your poem was one of the fundamental problems in text-books of rhetoric, and one of the recommended methods was by using a *sententia*, a wise saying. The first line of the *Parliament* is a Middle English translation of the old Latin tag *ars longa, vita brevis*, but Chaucer has cunningly expanded this in lines 2 and 3 by paraphrase – another rhetorical trick – and in line 4 comes the explanatory statement 'Al this mene I by Love'. But (says the following relative clause) the poet is bewildered by love, and in any case what he knows about love is not first hand but only from books.

The lyf so short, the craft so long to lerne,
Th'assay so hard, so sharp the conquerynge,   *attempt*
The dredful joye, alwey that slit so yerne: *fearful/slips away so quickly*
Al this mene I by Love, that my felynge
Astonyeth with his wonderful werkynge
So sore, iwis, that whan I on hym thynke   *truly*
Nat wot I wel wher that I flete or synke   *I am not sure*
                                      whether I float

For al be that I knowe nat Love in dede,
Ne wot how that he quiteth folk here hyre,   *pays people their wages*
Yit happeth me ful ofte in bokes reede
Of his myrakles and his crewel yre.
There rede I wel he wol be lord and syre;
I dar not seyn, his strokes been so sore,
But 'God save swich a lord!' – I can na moore.   *Anything except*

In these first two stanzas Chaucer has launched himself into his poem. Once again the poet appears as a bookworm; recently he spent the whole day reading one particular book 'a certeyn thing to lerne'. As we have by now come to expect, he falls asleep over this book. Once more poet becomes Dreamer, but a Dreamer who is not himself a lover but anxious to learn about love.

The book this time is the *Somnium Scipionis*, originally part of Cicero's *De Re Publica*. When this work was lost the text of the Dream of Scipio was preserved embedded in a much longer commentary on it made by Macrobius about AD 400. The Middle Ages came to regard Macrobius as an authority on dreams; the proem to the first book of *The House of Fame*, which distinguishes the various types of dream and their probable causes, may well be indebted in part to him. In the summary of the dream which he (as usual) provides here, Chaucer stresses the 'commune profit' (47, 75), a phrase which may be translated as 'the general good', 'concern for one's fellow men'. (Griselda in the later *Clerk's Tale* is praised for having regard to the 'commune profit' of her husband's subjects.) The *Somnium* also shows Africanus, one of its two chief characters, pointing out to the other, Scipio the younger, how insignificant earth and earthly values are in comparison with heaven, a common medieval lesson and the one which Troilus comes to learn at the very end of *Troilus and Criseyde* (although there the single earthly fashion discussed is courtly love). In the dream of *The Parliament of Fowls* this same Africanus appears as guide to the Dreamer and leads him up to the gates of a walled park over which there are twin inscriptions:

'Thorgh me men gon into that blysful place
Of hertes hele and dedly woundes cure;
Thorgh me men gon unto the welle of grace,
There grene and lusty May shal evere endure.
This is the wey to al good aventure.   *fortune*
Be glad, thow redere, and thy sorwe of-caste;   *throw off*
Al open am I – passe in, and sped thee faste!'

'Thorgh me men gon,' than spak that other side
'Unto the mortal strokes of the spere
Of which Disdayn and Daunger is the gyde,   *Scorn and Haughtiness*
Ther nevere tre shal fruyt ne leves bere.
This strem yow ledeth to the sorweful were   *weir*
There as the fish in prysoun is al drye;
Th'eschewing is only the remedye!'   *avoiding it*

As the Dreamer stands in doubt (his usual indecisive pose)
Africanus pushes him through the gates and disappears. Inside is
the usual *Romaunt*-derived park with its allegorical characters with
names like Youth, Pleasure and Nobility. Walking through the park
the Dreamer comes upon a temple of Venus. The interior is dark
and some of its inhabitants seem questionable, at least to the extent
that they represent a voluptuous, illicit, corrupted love; Venus
herself is pictured lying half-naked on a bed of gold. The whole
scene is beautiful but somehow repulsive, and the Dreamer seems
glad to get outside again into the good fresh air of the garden. He
wanders about until he comes upon Nature sitting on a mound of
flowers in the middle of a clearing, surrounded by all kinds of birds
who have assembled there to choose their mates on St. Valentine's
Day. In particular a formel (female eagle), perched on Nature's
hand, is sought by three courtly tercels (male eagles) each of whom
stakes his claim to her in impeccable courtly terms. The birds of
lower rank who act as judges are however impatient to choose their
own mates and be gone. Several of them can see little point in this
long-drawn-out procedure, and Nature is obliged to intervene to
keep the peace. She eventually hands over the choice to the formel
herself who begs for a year's intermission to make up her mind.
The other birds gladly disperse with their mates, and the noise they
make as they fly away wakes the Dreamer up.

The poem clearly lends itself to a division into three. First comes
the episode with Africanus, drawn from the *Somnium Scipionis*.
Next is the garden, indebted in general to the *Romaunt* and its
successors but for the description of the temple of Venus to
Boccaccio's *Teseida* (the source of *The Knight's Tale* too). The third

section is the assembly of the birds – which gives the poem its title –
and the ensuing debate presided over by Nature. The figure of
Nature is taken from the twelfth-century Latin *De Planctu Naturae*
by Alanus de Insulis (Alan of Lille) where the birds appear as part
of the decoration on Nature's robe. In Chaucer they become not
only alive but very vocal. Various sources are possible for the
debate: the contemporary *Songe Saint Valentin* by the French writer
Oton de Grandson is another Valentine poem, whilst in Boccaccio's
Il Filocolo a lady has to choose between three suitors who are
respectively brave, courteous and wise. But the debate form has a
long history in both literature and university life, so the scene in the
Parliament may be either Chaucer's own idea or a composite from
several sources. Particularly relevant, however, is the courtly *demande d'amour* where a choice has to be made between different but
superficially equal positions. A convenient illustration is that at the
end of the first part of Chaucer's own *Knight's Tale*. There Palamon
may see his lady each day, but only from the window of his prison.
Arcite, his rival in love, has his freedom, but if he returns to Athens
– where she lives – he risks losing his head. Chaucer poses the
question to the section of his audience most expert in such affairs:

Yow loveres axe I now this questioun:
Who hath the worse, Arcite or Palamoun?
That oon may seen his lady day by day,
But in prison he moot dwelle alway;
That oother wher hym list may ride or go,   *he wishes*
But seen his lady shal he nevere mo.

In the *Parliament* the birds are asked to choose between the three
tercels, each of whom advances his own good claim to the formel.

These sources occasionally overlap. For instance, Jean de
Meun's conception of Nature in the second part of the *Romaunt* is
clearly influenced by that of the earlier Alanus, and Chaucer is
probably remembering both. We are approaching the situation in
some of his later work (such as *The Wife of Bath's Prologue*) where his
sources are so interwoven and interdependent that it is frequently
very difficult to judge which part of his wide and varied reading
inspired a particular passage. Nor is the language of the *Parliament*
entirely divorced from life. Prof. Brewer has pointed out in his
edition how certain terms from parliamentary procedure (e.g. 'de-
lyvered' or 'charge') are used to give a proper colour to the conduct
of the debate. At the other end of the scale, the talk of the non-
courtly birds, with its 'com of', 'holde thy pes', and 'by myn hat', is
as colloquial as anyone could wish.

The three sections of the poem are formally linked in that Africanus, the chief figure in the first, acts as the Dreamer's guide up to the gates of the garden, and it is in one part of the garden that Nature, who presides over the debate at the end, is discovered. They are also written in general in rather different styles. That of the meeting with Africanus is fairly straightforward, the tone of exposition with plenty of *and's* and *then's*. The garden is appropriately described in a rather slower, more obviously 'poetic' syntax. In the debate the style varies according to the speaker, from the formal courtly tone of the three eagles to the colloquial vocabulary and rhythms of the speech of the lowest class birds. Although Chaucer had always been good at conversation in verse – there are some good examples in *The Book of the Duchess* – this is the first poem in which he shows such a variety of styles deliberately chosen to reflect a corresponding variety of subject-matter.

Furthermore, the three parts of the poem seems to be expressing differing views about the nature of love. For Africanus what matters is love of one's fellow-men, the 'common profit'. Later on, Nature too appears to be pursuing the same aim. She is described as 'ful of grace', a phrase normally applied to the Virgin Mary (319), and as God's deputy ('vicaire', 379); she is the symbol of the order and stability of His universe. She therefore wishes the birds to mate in accordance with their natural and proper inclinations. The garden, perhaps more purely decorative than usual, personifies 'romantic' love, and the temple of Venus carries this much further to show the sensual, corrupted love to which an exaggerated romantic approach can lead. In the debate the eagles, and especially the first, are the epitome of courtliness. He addresses not his equal but his 'sovreign lady' (416), reflecting the fact that in courtly love it is the female who makes the final choice of whether to accept the love offered her by the near-despairing male. The speeches of all three eagles illustrate both the positive and negative aspects of the code: the tercels will be discreet but no boasters, attentive and self-abasing but neither jealous nor cruel. The one thing they hope for is the formel's 'mercy'. The lower class birds proceed in a much more natural fashion; in their courtship the male is the dominant partner. There is probably some element of social conflict here. Courtly love had always been recognized as the province of the aristocracy, but the opposition between 'gentil' and 'cherl' should not be taken too far. Some birds, like the sparrow-hawk and the turtle, accept courtly love although they themselves do not practise it.

What are the lower-class birds in fact discussing? Not really which suitor the formel should choose. There can be very little debate about this. The betting from the start is heavily on the first eagle, the 'royal' bird (394, 633), and he is Nature's favourite. The question is rather what is the *sense* in courtly love? Can it find any place in real life? Supposing the formel does in the end accept one of these three tercels, what are the two others to do? So much medieval love poetry is ideal and theoretical, operating in a perfect world where courtly love is naturally the best of all possible states. Chaucer is much more practical and realistic. Here we may profitably return to the inscriptions above the twin gates to the garden quoted earlier. The first gate leads the way to 'all good fortune', 'the heart's delight' and 'green and pleasant May', a love which is not specifically 'courtly'. The inscription above the second gate seems to show an extreme courtly love (and the references to the person-ifications *Disdayn* and *Daunger* clinch the identification) as an un-attractive, indeed arid occupation. Both trees and fish are dying of drought, and the only safe course is total abstinence. The three tercels, the later practitioners of this kind of love, appear self-centred, as well as refined and noble. But before we rush to make a too modern judgment in praising the 'common sense' of the lower-class birds, we should remember that the cuckoo is even more selfish; the turtle, in advocating lifelong devotion even if unrewarded, is impractical; and the goose ('If she won't love him, let him love somebody else') is guilty of the grossest over-simplification.

Love, in fact, is neither a simple nor necessarily a wholly pleasurable business. The opening two stanzas of the poem say that Love is wonderful, yes, but domineering and sometimes cruel too. A full appreciation of Love, we are told, is fraught with difficulties. Not only courtly and 'natural' love but the 'common profit' – and even Venus – if taken alone can make out a realistic case for itself. Set side by side, as they are in the *Parliament*, they show up the advantages and disadvantages of each. Chaucer does not press the point; he invites us to make the comparison. Whatever it was that he had been looking for in his reading of the *Somnium*, his last remark before falling asleep is that he failed to find it but found something else instead:

For bothe I hadde thyng which that I nolde,
And ek I nadde that thyng that I wolde.

('For I both had something which I hadn't wanted, and also I didn't have what I had wanted'.) The end of the poem likewise expresses a failure to discover the perfect, all-embracing answer. What is Chaucer to do then? Typically, he goes on reading:

I wok, and othere bokes tok me to,	
To reede upon, and yit I rede alwey.	*still*
I hope, ywis, to rede so som day	*indeed*
That I shal mete som thyng for to fare	*find*
The bet, and thus to rede I nyl nat spare.	*won't stop*

The date of *The Parlament of Fowls* may perhaps be 1382, on the somewhat dubious interpretation of an astrological reference at lines 117–8. The poem might, as Prof. Brewer suggests, have been intended for recitation at court on St. Valentine's Day 1383, possibly in conjunction with some game in which lovers (like the birds) on that date chose their 'partners' for the ensuing year. The first eagle, called 'royal', may well refer to Richard II, but those who have tried to probe the allegory further cannot agree on the identification of either the formel or the other two tercels. The other birds are divided into classes – birds of prey, waterfowl, seedfowl and wormfowl – and these might represent the classes of medieval society. What is much more important than either exact date or allegorical interpretation, however, is the way in which Chaucer has manipulated the traditions. In the *Parliament*, the shortest and best integrated of his three main early poems, we are led down from the heavens, through a conventional garden of love, to witness a *demande d'amour* where the judges, far from deciding which suitor is the most desirable, challenge the validity of courtly love itself, and include among their number some most uncourtly birds.

It is likely that in the early 1380s Chaucer was again translating, but this time from Latin not French, and into prose not verse. The book was the *Consolation of Philosophy* (*De Consolatione Philosophiae*) of Boethius, a work which enjoyed immense prestige in the Middle Ages because it discussed questions in which they were still vitally interested. Before Chaucer King Alfred had also translated it, and so had Jean de Meun who had composed the second and longer part of the *Romaunt de la Rose*; later on Queen Elizabeth also tried her hand at 'Englishing' this work. It is possible that Chaucer knew the book quite well before settling down to translate it – parts of the *Romaunt* owe a good deal to Boethius.

Boethius lived after the classical period proper when the Goths were in power in Italy. He had enjoyed a successful public life when he was charged by the Gothic leader Theodoric with attempting to restore the power of the Roman Senate, and was cast into prison. He was put to death in 524. His book, perhaps written in prison, tells how he was visited there by the Lady Philosophy, an allegorical figure, who attempts to convince him that a wise man would view the contrast between Boethius's present misery and former happiness in the wider context of God's scheme for the government of the universe, and would come to recognize the true and enduring values. The work is in the form of a dialogue between Boethius and his visitor, although, apart from a long speech in the fifth and last book, Boethius's contribution is confined to brief questions and even briefer agreements to the propositions Philosophy puts forward by way of answer. Boethius was almost certainly a Christian, although he was influenced by pagan writers, especially Plato, Aristotle (whom he had translated) and Cicero. In the Middle Ages his death was sometimes wrongly attributed to his Christian faith. In the Retraction at the end of *The Canterbury Tales*, Chaucer classes his translation of Boethius with 'other books of saints' legends, and homilies and morality and devotion', but in fact Boethius deals scarcely at all with the life to come and his emphasis is on man's behaviour in this world.

Most of the first three books is taken up by Philosophy persuading Boethius that he has lost merely the trappings of life (such things as possessions, dignities, fame, beauty – what Chaucer later calls 'false felicity') and that these are not, as men wrongly imagine, self-sufficient, but corrupting and transitory. True happiness is found in the sovereign God who alone is good and whom all things naturally desire. It is in the last two books that the great question, modern as well as medieval, of the relationship between predestination and free will is raised. Boethius questions why God, who is good, allows evil to triumph and why He seemingly acts like Fortune in rewarding men indiscriminately. Philosophy replies that God's foreknowledge (*purveaunce*) orders all things and Destiny carries out this plan in detail on earth. Fortune is the executrix of Destiny, and being therefore twice removed from the stability of Providence, Fortune is mutable and fickle. The true dispositions of Providence may be hidden from men to whom their earthly manifestations (via Destiny and Fortune) may seem unjust and unreasonable. They must believe that all is in reality directed towards good. In Book V Boethius asks about the connexion between God's foreknowledge and man's free will. If God is both omniscient and omnipotent, how can man have any free will? Or how can he be blamed for his sins? Or why should we bother to pray to God? Philosophy distinguishes God's knowledge from man's. God knows no temporal restrictions of past, present and future, but exists in an eternal now. Hence God's foreknowledge does not imply necessity. But to us on earth there are two kinds of necessity: simple necessity (universal laws, such as 'the sun must rise' and 'all men must die') and conditional necessity. (To explain the latter we may use an illustration which Chaucer employed again in *Troilus*: a man seeing someone else sit knows that that man is sitting, but the beholder was not responsible for the sitting, i.e. he did not foresee it and consequently did not necessitate it. The man sat of his own free will and the necessity followed this. But to the beholder all this is present at one and the same time, and this is how God's seeing works.) Hence our change of purpose, our exercise of free will, does not invalidate the foreknowledge of God, because God knows when and how our actions may happen. Therefore, since free will is available to man, earthly laws rightly exist and we may legitimately pray to God. And since man does have free will, he should choose virtue. The end of the book does not refer back to Boethius's imprisonment.

The Latin original is divided into 'proses' and 'metres'. Each metre repeats the ideas of the preceding prose, but the poetry raises the tone of the argument. Chaucer keeps these divisions, but the whole of his translation is in prose. However, besides the Latin original, he used a Latin commentary and also a French prose version (perhaps Jean de Meun's). The result is a prose style sometimes diffuse, with glosses which at times illuminate but now and then merely irritate: ' . . . with the oportunyte and noblesse of thyne masculyn children (that is to seyn, thy sones)', and 'Homer with the hony mouth (that is to seyn, Homer with the swete ditees)'. Not surprisingly, the metres are more rhetorical and metaphorical than the proses and their sentences are longer. The first metre of Book III provides a by no means extreme example:

Whoso wole sowe a feld plentevous, let hym first delyvren it of thornes, and kerve asondir with his hook the bussches and the feern, so that the corn may comen hevy of erys and of greynes. Hony is the more swete, if mouthes han first tasted savours that ben wykke. The sterres schynen more *unpleasant* aggreablely whan the wynd Nothus leteth his plowngy *stormy* blastes; and aftir that Lucifer, the day-sterre, hath chased awey the dirke nyght, the day the fairer ledeth the rosene hors of the sonne. And ryght so thow, byhooldyng ferst the

false goodes, begyn to withdrawe thy nekke fro the yok of
erthely affeccions; and afterward the verray goodes   *true*
schullen entren into thy corage.   *mind*

Yet elaboration of this kind is partly offset by an occasional welcome
brevity, usually of a proverbial kind:

'But tyme is now,' quod sche, 'of medicyne more than of compleynt'.
'Knyt forth the remenaunt', quod I.

The influence of the *Consolation* can be seen especially in
Chaucer's two longest single poems, *Troilus and Criseyde* and *The
Knight's Tale*. The characters in both, nominally pagans, are apt to
blame Fortune for their unhappiness without having any clear
perception of Fortune's true role as a being subordinate to a
benevolent Providence (Troilus does finally achieve a correct
perspective, but only after his death). Theseus's closing speech
(*Knight's Tale*, 2987 ff.) stresses the impermanence and mortality of
all earthly things, including man who is advised to 'maken vertu of
necessitee' (3042). In Book IV of *Troilus and Criseyde*, lines
953–1078, Troilus considers that 'divine purveyaunce' has predestined his separation from Criseyde. He cannot see how the free will
which some men allow can square with God's absolute power and
foreknowledge. Nor is the converse any better, that predestination
itself brings about God's prescience. Either way, it is a deterministic
universe to Troilus, and free choice seemingly has no place in
deciding events

For although that, for thyng shal come, ywys,
Therefore is it purveyed, certeynly,
Nat that it comth for it purveyed is;
Yet natheles, bihoveth it nedfully,   *none the less*
That thing to come be purveyd, trewely;
Or elles, thynges that purveyed be,
That they bitiden by necessite,

And this suffiseth right ynough, certeyn,
For to destruye oure fre chois every del.   *bit*

The final plan of the despairing lovers, that Criseyde will find a
means to return to Troy, is Criseyde's, not Troilus's, and has
nothing to do with the question of predestination. But she does
advise patience in order, like Theseus, to 'make virtue of necessity'
(IV, 1586–7). But Troilus is a tragedy, and the happy ending to the
Knight's Tale is a patched-up affair, a diplomatic solution to the
factions of quarrelling deities.

In both these books Chaucer is using his Boethian material to provide a philosophical-religious background to his story and so give it greater depth and significance. The same perception of the possibilities of his wide reading was seen earlier in the use of the *Romaunt* -like garden as the setting for two of his love poems, although there our interest is rather in his adaptation of the tradition than in the tradition itself. Where Chaucer got his scientific and particularly his astronomical knowledge, another interest evident in all his work, it is now impossible to say. But since we have just been considering a translation into prose, it may be better to depart from chronology and look at his two prose scientific works written at the beginning of the last decade of his life.

The *Astrolabe* and the *Equatorie of the Planetis* may be taken together. An astrolabe was an instrument designed to assist in calculating the positions of the sun and the stars, whilst an equatorie (which was evidently more complex and of which only two models have survived) was concerned with the complementary task of ascertaining the position of the planets. Both texts testify to Chaucer's practical interest in astronomy and astrology, for after describing the construction of the instrument they give worked examples showing its operation. Since the examples are for 1391, and the equatorie was constructed on (or more probably set for) 31 December 1392, these two works date from late in Chaucer's career, after the beginning of the *Canterbury Tales*. Incidental references to these sciences are common throughout Chaucer's work, in the *House of Fame* for instance, but detailed technical information of this kind is unusual in Middle English at this date; Latin was far more likely to be used for any work of scholarship. The main source of the *Astrolabe* is an eighth-century Arabic treatise, although – like other scientific material – this had already been translated into Latin before the Middle Ages. It is probable that the *Equatorie* reached Chaucer by a similar route.

The *Astrolabe*, however, begins with an original prologue in which Chaucer says he is writing for 'little Lewis my son' who had apparently already shown some proficiency in mathematics and had especially asked to be taught about this instrument. Since Lewis was only ten years old and not very advanced in Latin ('for Latyn ne canst thou yit but small') Chaucer apologizes for his simple language ('rude endityng') and for his repetitions ('superfluite of wordes'). Indeed to those of us who are not historians of science, the charm of the work rests in two things: the clarity of Chaucer's expository prose and the occasional direct intervention of the teacher ('Now have I told the twyes'; 'Tak kep of these latitudes north and south, and forgat it nat'; 'Take this manere of settyng for a general rule, ones for evere'). Yet Chaucer is here the most modest of expositors. He calls himself a 'lewd (inexpert) compilator of the labour of olde astrologiens', and clearly envisaged the book as an elementary treatise, intended principally for the amateur astronomer. It is not fanciful to imagine that a small portable model such as this gave intense pleasure to the little boy, about whom we know nothing certain: 'Wayte bisely (watch carefully) aboute 10 or 11 of the clokke' and 'let A and F goo fare wel tyl ageynst the dawenyng a gret while, and com than ageyn'. The book is unfortunately incomplete. The Prologue promises five parts, but only the first two and a few additional and perhaps spurious sections appear in the extant manuscripts. The missing part might well have contained astronomical tables as the *Equatorie* does.

We cannot be certain that the *Equatorie*, discovered only in 1951 in a unique manuscript at Peterhouse College, Cambridge, is really Chaucer's work. True, the name *Chaucer* is written in the inner margin of one of the folios, but we need further clearly identified specimens of Chaucer's handwriting to establish that (as its editor believes) the text and the first set of tables were not only composed by Chaucer but written in his own hand. The hand is not a formal scribal one, and there are numerous erasures and interlinings, as if the text was in course of composition or revision. Eleven of the words used are recorded only in Chaucer, and the Oxford English Dictionary cites twenty-four more as appearing first in the *Astrolabe*. The spelling and phonology are remarkably consistent, and no forms appear which cannot be paralleled in the best manuscripts of *The Canterbury Tales*. But similar consistency could be true of other contemporary works composed in London but not by Chaucer, and in dealing with the vocabulary of the *Equatorie* we must remember the paucity of such works in Middle English. There is nothing in the language of the *Equatorie* against Chaucerian authorship, but we simply do not know enough about his individual linguistic usage – as opposed to that of his scribes – to be sure. The case for the Peterhouse manuscript as a Chaucer holograph is even less proven.

As well as the text, the *Equatorie* contains some brief notes, a Middle English cipher and astronomical tables. The latter are a modification of the famous Alfonsine Tables to suit the position of London (as the astrolabe is constructed to the longitude of Oxford): the magician in *The Franklin's Tale* used similar, perhaps earlier, tables to calculate the most propitious time for 'removing' the rocks around the coast of Brittany. And the growing sophistication of mathematical tables made them increasingly useful for routine astrological calculations, so that by the sixteenth century the astrolabe and the equatorie must have begun to seem something of the curiosities they now are.

The probable date of *The Legend of Good Women* comes as something of a shock. It is later than *Troilus and Criseyde*, possibly as late as 1386 which would place it immediately before *The Canterbury Tales*. Towards the end of the Prologue to the *Legend* the God of Love accuses the Dreamer of slandering his servants by having translated the *Romaunt de la Rose* and written about Criseyde who had been deceitful in love. On the intercession of Queen Alcestis he is allowed as a penance to write *The Legend of Good Women* (or, as its earlier title has it, the 'Legend of Cupid's Saints', that is, those women who were true according to the 'religion' of courtly love):

Thow shalt, while that thou lyvest, yer by yere,
The moste partye of thy tyme spende
In makyng of a glorious legende
Of goode wymmen, maydenes and wyves,
That weren trewe in lovyng al hire lyves;   *their*
And telle of false men that hem bytraien,
That al hir lyf ne do nat but assayen   *do nothing but try*
How many women they may doon a shame;
For in youre world that is now holde a game.   *considered a joke*
And thogh the lyke nat a lovere bee,
Speke wel of love; this penance yive I thee.

This is the same Dreamer we have met before who, for whatever reason, is not a lover himself but who knows how to write about lovers. When the book is finished it is to be presented to the Queen 'at Eltham or at Sheen' which were two of the royal residences. Lydgate in the following century says that the *Legend* was composed at the request of Anne, wife of Richard II. After this command the Dreamer awakes and prepares to start writing.

After the 'psychological realism' that critics have pointed out in *Troilus and Criseyde*, we are perhaps prepared to see the *Legend* with its dream construction and May-morning setting as a retrogression to the much earlier poems *The Book of the Duchess* and *The Parliament of Fowls*. Yet we should be careful on two counts. First of all, even if we allow this view, we surely ought not to regard a poet as an automaton who progresses inevitably towards his best poetry and then conveniently stops writing or dies. Literature is full of evidence to the contrary: the second version of Wordsworth's *Prelude*, for instance, is different from the first but hardly superior to it. And then, as historians of literature, we must be wary of our comparative judgments of Chaucer's works. Most of us think of him first as the poet of *The Canterbury Tales* and as a master of realism and characterization. Fifteenth-century critics considered him an exemplar of poetic diction and the great love poet. When Lydgate, in his *Fall of Princes*, recounts the Chaucer canon, he gives no indication that *The Canterbury Tales* is the most important work in it, and when he does come to discuss the *Tales* he praises them for their language and variety of subject-matter, picking out for special mention *Melibeus, The Clerk's Tale* and *The Monk's Tale* – scarcely our choice! Caxton, in the Prologue to his edition of Chaucer in 1483, says:

He comprehended hys maters in short, quyck and hye sentences, eschewyng prolyxyte, castyng away the chaf of superfluyte, and shewyng the pyked grayn of sentence (*theme*), vttered by crafty and sugred eloquence.

This point of view, with its emphasis on selection of material and appropriate rhetorical expression of it, would hardly minimize Chaucer's early poetry or find it strange that after *Troilus and Criseyde* he returned to the old manner in *The Legend of Good Women*.

The Prologue recounts how only one thing can draw the poet away from his books (*books* again) and that is his great devotion to the daisy. He gets up early to watch its petals open and, after spending the whole day looking rapturously at the flower, sees them close at sunset. Then he goes home to fall asleep on a bed made up in his own garden – which will enable him to wake up early the next morning once again to watch the flower open. This absorption in the daisy perhaps reflects a contemporary debate between the devotees of the 'flower' and the 'leaf'. There exists a poem with the title *The Flower and the Leaf*, probably composed in the fifteenth century but once thought to be Chaucer's. This controversy is literary and artificial in tone, rather like the Valentine cult in *The Parliament of Fowls*, and although Chaucer mentions it at this point of his poem it is clearly not of great importance. In any case, Chaucer's devotion to the daisy would not accord with this later poem which supports the chaste and faithful followers of the Leaf against the idle and pleasure-loving devotees of the Flower. Although the Prologue of the *Legend* is set in early May when the weather as usual is 'attempre' and the earth has shaken off its winter torpor, there is no preliminary bedside reading as there had been in the earlier poems. Yet the chief characters in the dream are the God of Love and his queen Alcestis who is dressed in green and wears a crown of white, so that the daisy motif is repeated. Alcestis, too, according to the legend, chose to die in her husband's stead and is therefore the pattern of wifely devotion, a true 'saint' of Cupid. She was eventually brought back from the underworld and returned to her husband. No metamorphosis into a daisy is mentioned in classical sources and her tale is not reached in the *Legend*, but some of Ovid's other heroines were changed into flowers. Not only is she the subject of a *balade* which the Dreamer recites in her honour, but she stands at the head of a whole procession of women who were true lovers and who worship the daisy which symbolizes their devotion. When the God of Love argues that the *Romaunt* and *Troilus* prove that the Dreamer is a heretic, unfit to join in honouring the daisy, it is Alcestis who tries to excuse him: perhaps he acted in ignorance in composing the offending works or was commanded to write by some patron he dared not refuse; he has written other poems more acceptable to the God of Love, and, in any case, those in authority should not behave like tyrants. It is because Alcestis is so charitable as well as so devoted that the God of Love hands over the erring Dreamer to her, much as Theseus in *The Knight's Tale* spares Arcite and Palamon at the request of Hypolita and Emily, or Arthur in *The Wife of Bath's Tale* allows sentence to be passed by his queen. Thus did rulers preserve their dignity and show their mercy. In this case the result is the 'penance' of writing the *Legend*.

The Prologue is preserved in two versions. One is shorter than the other, omitting some of the detail of the poet's adoration of the daisy and the presentation of the completed book at court, and making a few transpositions of material to improve the structure. On the other hand, this shorter version, which is probably (but not certainly) the later, has the God of Love point out to the Dreamer books containing stories of good women, and some of these books Chaucer used in his other works. But the two versions do not differ in essentials. Their subject-matter is indebted to Deschamps, Froissart and Machaut, but not so obviously as in *The Book of the Duchess*, and this growing subtlety in incorporating his borrowings is a measure of Chaucer's developed poetic skill. The *Legend* is new in one other way: it is almost certainly the first use in English of the decasyllabic couplet, the metre which Chaucer found so useful for narration in most of *The Canterbury Tales*.

Only nine of the nineteen legends promised actually appear, and even the ninth is unfinished. They tell of classical heroines who suffered (and sometimes died) out of love for worthless men. The stories are mostly taken from Ovid and Virgil, although Chaucer seems also to have drawn upon Boccaccio and on the twelfth-century Guido delle Colonne whose Latin prose work was largely responsible for medieval knowledge of the legend of Troy. They demonstrate an ability to ignore the realities of life: all women are true and all men are heartless deceivers – except Pyramus, and Chaucer apologizes at the end of that tale for including one faithful man. How serious was he in writing them? We must disabuse ourselves of any modern view of, say, Cleopatra as enchantress or Medea as child murderess. In the religion of love they stood as sufficient examples of martyrdom. Dido had already been prominent in Chaucer's summary of the *Aeneid* in *The House of Fame*. In the *Legend*, too, Aeneas, pictured as a typical courtly lover (1264–76), treats the whole affair as a delightful interlude. No allowance is made for his destiny spurring him on towards Italy. His tears are false and he steals away to his ships 'like a traitor'. In these stories no opportunity is wasted of pointing up the moral. Antony, having left Octavia, is already a deceiver when he loves Cleopatra. Thisbe creeps out of her house to meet Pyramus by night; alas that any woman should trust a man before she knew him better! Scylla becomes enamoured of Minos and betrays the city of Megara, for which act of devotion Minos later rewarded her cruelly. None of these comments is essential to its tale. Perhaps Chaucer really *was* commanded to write such a series and the Prologue is not so much fiction as we suppose. If so, he proceeded to carry out his penance in such a way as to be sure of giving ample satisfaction. Theseus and Tarquin are the blackest villains, and it takes some effort to visualize this Theseus as the future just ruler of *The Knight's Tale*. But it is Jason who is the most unbelievable cad. The double story of Hypsipyle and Medea opens with a diatribe against Jason – 'There (*where*) others falsen oon, thow falsest two!' He agrees that his companion Hercules should praise him to the skies; he acts coy, but bribes Hypsipyle's courtiers; he marries the queen, appropriates her goods, begets two children on her and sails away. After he has later left Medea, he marries his third wife. He is a 'devourer and dragon of love' (1581) with a sexual appetite bidding fair to rival that of the Wife of Bath herself.

Even granting the constraints imposed on Chaucer by the pattern of these tales, all this seems too great gilding of the lily. Sometimes his devotion to his task seems less than fervent. Ariadne is a little too concerned with her own and her sister's future position in Athens to be quite the pathetic figure she appears, looking out to sea from the uninhabited island on which Theseus had left her. In her case it had not been quite all for love. The legend of Phyllis – the last but one – is largely padding. It is the only case where Chaucer, like Ovid in the *Heroides*, quotes from the actual letter in which the deserted woman enshrines for posterity the treachery of one of its heroes. And in the same tale Chaucer says he has no time to dwell on the passion of Phyllis for Demophon:

But, for I am agroted herebyforn
To wryte of hem that ben in love forsworn,
And ek to haste me in my legende,
(Which to performe God me grace sende!)
Therfore I passe shortly in this wyse.

What does 'agroted' mean here – 'had enough of'? And is the parenthesis meant to be ironic or dutiful in its tone?

Yet, whether or not his heart was fully in his work, Chaucer is incapable of writing really bad stories. One trouble is that they are not long enough for us to become involved in the fate of their characters. Another is that the whole idea is too restrictive. None of these heroines shows anything approaching the infinite variety of that later Cleopatra. Perhaps, as in the *Monk's Tale* (where the stories are all medieval tragedies in which a successful man is brought low by the fickleness of Fortune) Chaucer was experimenting, in *The Legend of Good Women*, with a structure within which he could tell a number of tales. Perhaps he did not finish the *Legend* because with the idea of the Canterbury pilgrimage he simply hit upon a much better framework. So what we finally remember from the *Legend* is the detail. Pyramus and Thisbe, shut up in the seclusion of their own houses, learn of the existence of each other through gossiping neighbours. Lucrece's husband having conceived the plan of the ride back home entirely on impulse (which is in itself convincing), knows how to get into the house quietly – and so does Tarquin on his second visit. Ariadne wakes and gropes around in the bed to find Theseus gone. In the first of the legends there is really not very much about the love affair, and Cleopatra dies not from the asp's bite but by jumping into a pit full of snakes. Yet the battle of Actium, with its grapnels, shearing-hooks and quicklime, comes to life as a naval encounter of Chaucer's own day, a description fit to compare with that of the tournament in the *Knight's Tale*. It is this eye for the dramatic detail (although not every one is original with him) and the desire to use direct speech wherever possible that make Chaucer's legends occasionally soar above the narrative competence of Gower who also told the stories of Thisbe, Medea and Lucrece. There are few really memorable lines in the *Confessio Amantis*, but Gower would probably have finished *The Legend of Good Women*.

Chaucer's early translation, *An ABC to the Virgin*, has already been mentioned. In fact, he continued to write short poems throughout his career. Not all of them are datable with any degree of confidence, but some at least were certainly written in the 1390s, that is after the *General Prologue* and most of the *Canterbury Tales*. In the *Complaint of Venus* and the *Envoy to Scogan* there are half-humorous references to approaching old age and declining poetic powers. But a late adaptation of the lover's complaint to his lady – a stock rhetorical topic in contemporary French poetry – to the poet's complaint to his empty purse:

Now voucheth sauf this day, or yt be nyght	*guarantee/before*
That I of yow the blisful soun may here,	
Or see your colour lyk the sonne bryght,	
That of yelownesse hadde never pere.	
Ye be my lyf, ye be myn hertes stere,	
Quene of comfort and of good companye:	
Beth hevy ageyn, or elles moote I dye!	*must*

with its recognition that money as well as ladies' complexions can be shining and golden, shows that the second of these laments does not have too much basis in fact. The least attractive of these short poems to us are those which are allegorical in manner and heavily dependent on courtly love, such as this extract from *A Complaint to his Lady*:

Thus am I slayn with Loves fyry dart,	
I can but love hir best, my swete fo;	
Love hath me taught no more of his art	
But serve alwey, and stinte for no wo.	*cease*

The references to Cupid's arrows, the paradox of the beloved as the man's enemy ('swete fo'), the determination to serve his lady continually and uncomplainingly – all these are standard in late medieval love poetry, but their expression here does not come to life. If this kind of writing represents a norm in fourteenth-century courtly love literature, at least we can see how far Chaucer often rose above it. Although in the main these poems are artificial and somewhat pedantic in manner, there are one or two attempts to relate literature to life, as was so triumphantly done in the later works. Such short poems with their fashionable French forms are probably more acceptable to us when they appear as set pieces in Chaucer's longer compositions, like the *rondeau* as the birds fly away at the close of *The Parliament of Fowls* or the *balade* to Alcestis in *The Legend of Good Women*.

Other verses, like those on Fortune or Gentilesse ('Nobility'), deal with medieval commonplaces which Chaucer refers to again and again and in which we can see the growing influence of Boethius on his philosophical thinking. Perhaps the most interesting of all these minor poems is the unfinished *Anelida and Arcite* which was possibly composed about the same time as *The House of Fame* with which, as Clemen notes, it has a good deal in common. Here too there is a massive apparatus in the form of the epic background which does not easily coalesce with the other style in the poem, that of Anelida's formal love complaint. In its mixture of styles *Anelida and Arcite* is both structurally and metrically complex. It represents perhaps Chaucer's first use of Boccaccio's *Teseida*, the epic of Theseus and the source of *The Knight's Tale*, in which Arcite (but an Arcite who behaves very differently) is one of the chief characters. 'False Arcite', as he is called, who deserts Anelida, is in the pattern of Aeneas in *The House of Fame* or the men in *The Legend of Good Women*. Like *The House of Fame*, *Anelida and Arcite* is interesting more for what it promises than for what it performs.

It would be wrong to regard the early poems and translations simply as forerunners of *Troilus and Criseyde* and the *Canterbury Tales*. One might argue, for example, that Chaucer first mastered and then outgrew the dream convention, that whereas the dream gave a certain re-moteness and introduced characters and behaviour impossible in the real world, he finally abandoned it as a structural device, having become increasingly concerned with ordinary people. Or that the development of the Dreamer becomes a way of achieving objectivity, so that he gradually turns into the detached observer of *Troilus* or the persona of Chaucer the Pilgrim (one might also contrast the political concern of Gower's narrator or the passionate engagement of Will in *Piers Plowman*). Or that Chaucer begins in octosyllabics and graduates via rhyme royal to the decasyllabic couplet of *The Legend of Good Women* and most of the *Canterbury Tales*. But although this approach to Chaucer's early work is in a sense inevitable, if these poems are to continue to be read they must stand or fall in their own right.

Chaucer's search is first and foremost for suitable subject-matter. The closing stanza of *The Parliament of Fowls*, as has been mentioned, seems to show a certain dissatisfaction with the result to date. Earlier in the same poem, the *Somnium Scipionis* has provided at best a partial answer (90–91) and Africanus suggests the garden may furnish a better:

And if thow haddest connyng for t'endite,   *the ability to put it into shape*
I shal the shewe mater of to wryte.

The Prologue to *The Legend of Good Women* appears to suggest that little new material remains for the fourteenth-century poet:

And I come after, glenyng here and there,
And am ful glad yf I may fynde an ere
Of any goodly word that ye han left.

This is partly the poet's innate modesty. The study of rhetoric advocated such an approach as one means of gaining the sympathy of the reader. But we should remember how many of these works are translations (the *Romaunt*, the *ABC*, the *Boethius*) or direct borrowing of material from other writers (the Ceyx and Alcyone story in *The Book of the Duchess*, the tales in *The Legend of Good Women*, and several other instances). Plagiarism, it has been emphasized, was no crime in medieval eyes. On the contrary, it was a tribute to the excellence of the original. The increasing breadth of Chaucer's source material, the French tradition of *The Book of the Duchess* being supplemented – but not replaced – by the influence of Dante in *The House of Fame* and of Boccaccio in *The Parliament of Fowls*, is a mark of his widening interests and growing assurance of manner. So too is the better integration of these borrowings into Chaucer's own work; the *Legend*, with all its limitations, is a big advance on *The Book of the Duchess* in this respect. But books are always important to him. Not only are they, as the *Legend* says (25–6), the repositories of all that is valuable from earlier ages; if we are to believe the eagle, Chaucer himself, as well as his Dreamer, is apt to pore over them until lack of light or sheer weariness sends him to sleep.

In this poetic climate convention is highly regarded and originality is not, as it so often is today, at a premium. It has been the chief aim of this chapter to show that such respect for poetic tradition does not presuppose an unimaginative or second-rate poet. In Chaucer's early poems the accepted tenets of courtly love are regularly measured against the demands of life itself. The interlocking roles of rumour and reputation are examined in *The House of Fame*, and it was the perennial question of how far free will is consistent with predestination or an apparently completely fickle

Fortune that seems to have attracted Chaucer most in Boethius. The dream vision is seen to be capable of comedy as well as high seriousness – witness the lower-class birds of the *Parliament* and above all the Eagle in *The House of Fame*. Where the convention becomes too restrictive, as in *The Legend of Good Women*, Chaucer seems to lose patience with his poem. In developing these conventions beyond the state in which he inherited them Chaucer also found himself introducing a variety of styles within the one work. The *Parliament* is the best example here, although *The Book of the Duchess* showed an early facility with conversation in verse. (The philosophical and scientific prose is less remarkable stylistically, but in these areas the English language had had less practice.) The connexion between different parts of the poem is usually implicit. It is we who have to set the Ceyx and Alcyone story beside the Black Knight's own tragic tale or let one kind of love in the *Parliament* counterbalance another. The Dreamer would not presume. He may be on occasion obtuse, but he is also tactful, a man who is sure his audience will know more about love (and perhaps even about life) than he does, the reflex of a poet who, having shown how old traditions are capable of leading to revised judgments, is content to leave the last word to his readers.

(iii) *TROILUS AND CRISEYDE*

D. S. Brewer

I

The very first line tells us the whole story in outline, if we did not know it before:

The double sorwe of Troilus to tellen.

We realize immediately that a simple narrative of suspense is not intended, though we shall in fact find a surprise ending to the poem. The interest of the poem lies in the significance with which it invests the story, both deepening its implications and enlivening the narration. The general manner of enlivening lies in the word *tellen* which looks forward to the briefly delayed 'my purpose is' (I,4). These first few words move us out of the isolation of modern print, to group us with an *audience*, which in the first instance, possibly, included the young king, sixteen years old, Richard II, and his younger wife, the universally beloved Anne of Bohemia, 'Young, fresh folks!' as the poet later addresses them. We are placed in this group, and in many others down the ages and across the world, by the relationships established by the poet between him and us. It is a poem of direct address; *I* (whom you know) am telling *you*. The relationship suggested here is that of the primal 'literary' group, before even writing existed, when the family, or the larger house-hold, or the village, gathered round the known story-teller, the repository of the history and traditions of the group. His re-telling helped to create recognition and self-identity, separated past from present and so contributed to hope and resolution for the future. For if the past is dead to us we lose our own identity and are lost in the flux of the present; we are directionless, helpless, the sport of wanton force and chance, solitary.

Chaucer is no primitive, however. The primal group is only suggested. Probably the first fourteenth-century royal group really existed, in actuality, as the famous *Troilus* frontispiece suggests; but that picture is itself an imaginative reconstruction of the very early fifteenth century, painted after Chaucer's death, as far as we know.

It might itself even be a product of the poem's power to create the sense of a listening group. In this very first stanza Chaucer also refers to himself, in a curious conceit, as *writing* – he says 'These verses, that weep as I write'. This balance between the spoken and written word is very characteristic of the poem, and source of much of its strength. The poem draws both from the emotional communal world of 'oral' culture, and from the more precise, intellectual, individualized, even solitary world of 'written' culture. Chaucer occupies the region best descriped as 'manuscript' culture, and the nature of manuscript, near to but not the same as print, has special effects. The written word is as it were the platform of the spoken, conditioning but not denying the spoken word. The effect is transferred to us even through print in our modern editions, but it is worth making the imaginative effort to recreate more consciously the conditions of manuscript culture in Chaucer. Someone who read *Troilus and Criseyde* soon after it was completed in 1385 would be a courtier, high official, lawyer, rich merchant, or country gentleman – a well-educated man of the world. He read his manuscript in Gothic script, which may look awkward now, but was as easy to him as print is now to us. He had no notes, but did not need most of them, nor a glossary. Nor did the spelling look quaint to him. The book probably contained *Troilus and Criseyde* alone, and if like the manuscript now in St. John's College, Cambridge, was a large but comfortable book, though the splendid manuscript in Corpus Christi College, Cambridge, made for some nobleman, is bigger and fatter. In either case the book was pleasant and easy to read, and the reader was in much the same situation as anyone who nowadays takes up, with pleasant anticipation, a new, well-produced novel by a famous author. The style was fresh and new, both more splendid and more realistic than he was used to in English, but it was not anti-traditional, the story was known in outline, and the tradition was one in which authors preferred to please rather than shock. The reader probably read aloud, either to himself or to a group of friends or family, so keeping close to the spoken element in the poem, but also, as a reader, having more time to savour its special quality. A more marked difference between the manuscript and the printed book appeared if the reader compared his copy with another. He would find slightly different spelling, which would not matter much. He would also find continuous minor and possibly even important major differences between the very wording of the various copies. Caxton discovered this from a displeased customer who compared his own manuscript of *The*

Canterbury Tales with Caxton's first edition set up direct from another manuscript, and found much wanting in Caxton's version, which, of course, being in print, would have varied hardly at all from copy to copy. A text in manuscript is much more 'fluid' than a text in print, and so nearer to oral delivery.

The balance between oral and written arises from the conditions of composition and publication. When Chaucer composed the poem he must first presumably have formed a general idea of what he wanted to do with Boccaccio's *Il Filostrato*, his main source, and then have worked with a copy of it on his desk before him. He translated the beginning of each stanza fairly closely, but tended to move away from his source as the stanza proceeded. Occasionally he broke away from the source for hundreds of lines (as at the beginning of Book II); more usually he continuously modified and added on a smaller scale. It is not likely that he knew the later French translation of Boccaccio's poem, but by this time he knew Italian well, and in the shelves under the desk he no doubt kept his *De Consolatione* (later with French crib) by Boethius, Boccaccio's *Teseida*, Dante's *Divina Commedia* (old favourites), and various Troy books, all of which he occasionally consulted, and from which he translated passages to insert into his poem. The same shelves perhaps held those other authors which so enriched his mind and his poem – French and Latin literature, historical and scientific (especially astronomical) works. (A reproduction of a fourteenth-century picture of a study with desk and bookshelves may be found in the first edition of my *Chaucer*, 1953, opposite p. 81.) This bookishness reminds us that Chaucer was no improvising minstrel, laying his hand on the nearest cliché to help himself out with a rhyme. The act of writing and the use of many written sources allow pause for thought and choice of words, care and precision of expression, 'loading every rift with ore', a progression towards uniqueness. Literacy fosters individualism just as oral culture fosters the group. Writing promotes that exactness which Chaucer reveals as one of his overriding concerns when he expresses his anxiety that no one should mis-write or mis-metre the poem 'for default of tongue', and that it should be understood (V, 1793–9). This is pre-eminently care for the *written* word. Besides all this, writing allows correction and second thoughts, denied to oral culture and the minstrel.

We know from Chaucer's sarcastic little poem to Adam Scriveyn that when he had written *Troilus* he sent the manuscript to Adam to be copied. Then he checked the copy, scraping out those errors he noticed and re-writing them while he cursed the scribe. Inevitably he would have missed some of the errors. Moreover, anyone who has copied out or corrected what he himself has written knows that it is almost impossible to do so without introducing further changes, and especially additions, as has happened with this very essay, though once with the printer such freedom is very much restricted. The manuscript copy, so much more laborious than print, is also so much freer, both in error and creation, though even modern poets constantly change their texts. The fluid and provisional nature of all language, the essentially *spoken* word, constantly asserts itself against the apparent fixity and finality of the written (even more, printed) word; the spoken word, as deed, asserts itself against the word as record in writing. So Chaucer continued to tinker with the poem after he had finished it, making minor corrections and changes, and adding a few substantial passages which emphasized the lyrical and philosophical element in the poem, as Troilus's Boethian hymn to love at the end of Book III (1744–71), his philosophical soliloquy in the temple (IV, 960–1078), even possibly the ending, based on *Teseida* (V, 1807–27). When Chaucer next sent the poem to Adam to be copied it would differ in such additions, apart from other minor changes, from earlier versions current among friends, etc., and unchanged. None of the manuscripts which have survived were written by Chaucer or Adam. We have copies of copies, though some, like the splendid one in Corpus Christi College Cambridge, are early fifteenth-century and carefully done. Some copies we have were made from early versions, others (like the Corpus text) from later versions, others (like the St. John's College Cambridge text), from a mixed version. All have their own errors. But the laborious comparison of manuscripts by Windeatt in his remarkable edition of *Troilus* in 1983, fortunately allows us to be fairly, if not completely, certain of the text of the poem as Chaucer left it.

The underlying 'fluidity' of the text within limits of certainty may remind us of the variety of interpretations of what the text says. They are similar phenomena. Literary creation and study can be only partially fixed, like language itself. The poets of the fourteenth century, poised so delicately between the spoken and written word, were in a particularly favourable situation to exploit the possibilities of their interaction. One of the poets' most frequent devices, as already suggested, was to '*write* up' a part for themselves as *speaking* the poem, as it were a dramatic imitation of a minstrel. The 'new' method of writing imitates the 'old' method of speaking a poem, as stone architecture when first invented imitated wooden structure and textures. Chaucer's contemporaries Langland and Gower both present their own selves in their poems, creating ambivalent, ironic and humorous effects, but the great master at this is Chaucer. In *Troilus and Criseyde* he does not deploy his own named character as he does in *The Canterbury Tales* but he makes us very conscious of the poet's imagined presence, the poet indeed as 'a man speaking to men'.

As we read, then, we are brought to imagine the poet before us, speaking to us. The first level of fiction in the poem, we may say, is the fiction of the presence of the poet himself, by himself, to 'act' in his own character. Recognition of this dramatic quality has been one of the most valuable advances in modern criticism. Some critics have even been led to speak of Chaucer the poet as 'narrator' of the poem 'inside' the poem, on the same dramatic level as Troilus and the other characters, just as Gulliver, the narrator of *Gulliver's Travels*, is a dramatic character inside the book and different from Swift, the true author, outside it. This is to put apart what God has joined together, a whole man; to impose the fictional illusionism of print culture, with its clear divisions, upon the fluid variability of manuscript culture. Chaucer the narrator, that is, the poet, cannot be thought of as clearly inside or clearly outside the work, but he is most certainly not inside it at all in the way that the dramatic characters are. He is telling a story.

We do not take everything Chaucer says in telling the story completely at its face value, or always in the same way. When a man is telling a story he is not upon oath, and we enter into the game or the conspiracy with him, as when a known raconteur among our friends tells us something amusing that he claims has actually happened to him. We may disbelieve him, yet enjoy the joke and know that he is not in any moral sense a liar. A formal story-teller sometimes leads you up the garden path, to give you a surprising view. He holds some things back. Some things he claims to know, and some he does not, without much consistency, just as we know and do not know things about people and events in real life. Sometimes he seems to be in real earnest. Sometimes he adopts a pose of uncomprehending simplicity. At all times he is dramatizing himself, to a greater or less extent, as the story-teller, both the instrument and the manipulator of his story, the servant and the master of his audience, like the old music-hall comedian, who both is, and is not, himself. Some radio and television stars, who act fictional situations under their own names, and partly in their own characters, carry on the tradition in which Chaucer is supreme, especially if they write their own scripts. The significant thing is that these are all directed towards oral delivery on stage or screen, though with a firm basis in the written word, in a mixture very like Chaucer's. It is also notable that they are all comics. The mixture of reality and fiction creates a flickering double image of the performer, a conjunction of the real and fictional, which seems essentially comic. Something of this comic quality, occasionally broadly humorous, often intensely refined, pervades *Troilus and Criseyde*, without denying an ultimate seriousness, (of which it is indeed the instrument) or the obvious meaning of some serious remarks. Yet one can rarely be *quite* certain of how to take many things that the poet tells us, or of what tone they are told in. Irony is the constant figure, and the dual meanings of irony have also something in them like metaphor. Many modern critics have equated the essence of poetry with irony. If this has any truth in it, Chaucer is indeed the supreme poet in English, a head and shoulders above almost everyone else, with his feet firmly set, so to speak, on the music-hall stage.

Chaucer's method, in a word, is only a specially interesting technique of *telling* a story, as opposed to *showing*. Modern critical theory, following the depersonalizing tendencies of modern scientific culture, has tended to favour 'showing', that is, a narrative which is presented 'anonymously', with the events telling themselves, untouched by human hand or mind: objective, realistic, illusionist, as near to life as possible. Novelists who make no bones about 'telling', like Fielding, Scott, Thackeray, have been condemned for it.

As we move through the opening stanza of *Troilus and Criseyde*, with the invocation to the 'goddess' Thesiphone, we also realize another characteristic of the music-hall, and of all popular oral entertainment, including Shakespeare and the medieval religious drama; the deliberate mixture of solemn and frivolous, sentimental and gay. The comic does not exclude the pathetic, as Dickens and Charlie Chaplin have shown. Music-hall was sometimes called 'variety', and no word is more applicable to Chaucer. The first stanza seems solemn and serious enough (and of course learned and intellectual in the way that the music-hall could never be). But already in the second stanza there is a lightening of tone modulated through the constant imagined presence of the poet himself, moving into a lighter mood. We have a long way to go, and cannot be burdened with the full weight of tragedy too early. We have a guarantee in the poet's self-deprecating lightness of tone, in the note even of mockery, that we shall have an amusing companion at times, even as he comments, apparently (I, 13–14), on the suitability of his gloomy face to his gloomy story. This comment is a very characteristic expression of the duality of narration, when the poet comments on his own mask, or rather, on one of the masks he puts on. The same poet, different masks; and we can never be sure if any, or which, is his own face, though all the masks have a family resemblance, and we remain convinced that a real man holds them up, even if he likes to puzzle us. But of course, the useful modern notion of 'masks' is not nearly fluid and delicate enough to do more than hint at what Chaucer is doing.

In the next fifty lines, having announced his story with sufficient gravity and impressiveness, Chaucer ingratiates himself with his audience, slightly mocks himself, flatters them a little, talks of lovers sympathetically, finally comes into a position of domination over the interest of his audience (where late-comers have now sat down and fidgets have settled themselves); then he turns to a fuller elaboration of his story. The story is set inside the poem, which is longer than the story. We are to be constantly reminded of the act of telling: the people and the events, pre-existing in known story, preserve their own autonomy.

II

The story of Troilus was fairly familiar in the English court, but Chaucer repeats necessary facts. He had mentioned Troilus in *The Parliament of Fowls*, and Froissart, Chaucer's exact contemporary, whose work was well known in the English court, had also mentioned him in a list of famous lovers. The chief account of him was only an incident in a long twelfth-century Anglo-French poem, probably still current in the English court, by Benoit de Ste.-Maure, *Le Roman de Troie*, which itself was based on earlier brief accounts by the Dares and Dictys referred to by Chaucer (I, 146). Benoit's poem had been translated and widely disseminated in Latin by Guido delle Colonne, and then Boccaccio in the middle of the fourteenth century had extracted and expanded the story of Troilus in his poem *Il Filostrato*. In essence it was a story of betrayal. Troilus's lady, Briseida, had been exchanged by the Trojans for Antenor, one of the Trojan leaders who had been captured by the Greeks, and who eventually betrayed Troy to the Greeks. When she came among the Greeks Briseida betrayed Troilus's love and took another lover, Diomede.

Betrayal was one of the great tragic themes in the Middle Ages. Men had an intensely personalized view of life. Nature was personalized, God was a Person, and the strongest ties were obligations between human beings, or between men and God, conceived in terms of personal loyalty, often sealed, as marriage still today often is, by solemn public ceremony. The compulsions of anonymous impersonal forces, external or inside the mind, of depersonalized science, or of deistic religion or atheism, were unrecognized. The highest good, and the deep structure of the universe, were thought of in terms of personal relationships, of love. Even the force of gravity was an aspect of the personal love of God. In such a personalized universe the greatest catastrophe takes the form of personal betrayal.

Boccaccio used the story of Troilus as an exemplum of betrayal, an image of how he himself had been abandoned by his beloved. To make the story more interesting and pathetic he expanded the preliminary love story, though careful to explain that he himself had never enjoyed those favours from *his* lady that he so warmly portrays his hero Troilo enjoying from Griseida, as he renamed Briseida. It seems unlikely that many, if anybody, apart from Chaucer, in Richard II's court, knew Boccaccio's poem, but it formed the basis of Chaucer's poem and he translated much of it literally, while further expanding and embroidering the preliminary love story, and – as will be seen – subtly changing the emphasis of betrayal.

It is true that Chaucer never mentions Boccaccio in this poem, or indeed anywhere else. He refers occasionally to ultimate authorities, for example Dares and Dictys, and also to 'Lollius'. He seems to have been under the mistaken impression, as others were, from a misreading of a line in one of Horace's *Epistles*, that Lollius was another ultimate authority on the Troy story. Reference to his 'author Lollius' is in fact another 'mask', not always a very serious one, held up by Chaucer when he wishes to distance himself somewhat from the subject-matter, isolating it, leaving it to work its own effect, deliberately leaving it to the reader to evaluate.

This effect of 'distance' is a special example of a more general characteristic of the poem, which we may call the autonomy of the story. The story is not merely the invention of one man; it is part of the true historical being of the world. Boccaccio diminishes the autonomy by employing the story as subjective relief and attempting to some extent to use it to further his own personal desires. Chaucer restores the autonomy by having no personal axe to grind, by treating the story more as an historian does, using and quoting different sources, and also, paradoxically, by his personalized narration. The poet's personal comments, his self-confessed limitations of knowledge and ability, his various poses (not all ironic) of sympathy, excessive enthusiasm, and bewilderment, de-limit his responsibility for, his control over, the story, and allow the story its own life. A personalized narration creates the opposite of a subjective narrative. Lacking an omniscient narrator the subject-matter appears to evade the simplifying consistencies of a single controlling mind and achieves a living autonomy. The poet does not attempt a completely rational, illusionist picture of life. There are gaps in knowledge and presentation; perhaps inconsistency; and the lack of overall realism allows the greater sense of reality. The story and the characters live, we feel, in their own right over-against the contemplation of the poet in which they live.

The balance between the poet and the subject-matter is well seen at the end of the fifty-line passage in which the poet has been addressing his audience direct. He resumes (I, 57–9):

Yt is wel wist how that the Grekes stronge
In armes, with a thousand shippes, wente
To Troiewardes . . .

Well known indeed, and Chaucer never lets us forget that Troilus's individual destiny has to be played out within the larger destiny of Troy, as that, in turn, is seen within larger issues again. Troilus may be said to be at the centre of a series of concentric 'circles', Troy, worldly destinies, divine ordinance; just as, in the Ptolemaic Universe of medieval science, the world was at the centre of a series of heavenly concentric spheres surrounded by the love of God.

When Chaucer refers to the larger story of Troy he invokes one of the great exemplary tragedies of the Middle Ages. That doomed ten-year siege, the total destruction of that splendid city, the slaughter of its inhabitants, was a mirror all too true of 'how the world goes'. This is what life is like; achievement lost in destruction and death. Such is the subject-matter of medieval tragedy, recog-nizable in the public events of our own lifetime, and inevitably to be enacted by each of us privately in his own life and death.

It sounds pessimistic, but it was not. For various reasons there was also an inexhaustible flow of self-confidence, that is, of faith, and an irreducible optimism. One man had escaped from burning Troy, carrying his father, and with a few followers. It was Aeneas, who thus salvaged his essential past and who founded Rome for the future. Rome had fallen in its turn, but Aeneas's grandson had settled and named Britain, establishing a line of kings, the greatest of whom was Arthur. Arthur's mighty empire had also fallen, betrayed from within, but the English counted themselves his legitimate successors, and Edward III, the English king whom Chaucer had served as a young man, not only developed an Arthurian cult in his court of which the Order of the Garter still remains, but was ruler over broad lands in France as well as in the British Isles. London is New Troy. Tragedy and suffering would always come, but there was also always hope of a personal saviour, of resurrection in a different manner of life, not negating tragedy, but justifying it. Even if disaster must come, one need not collaborate with it. If caught up in it, one must behave well and endure for the sake of the whole and in hope of the end, even against worldly 'sense' and profit. In the end we shall find that Chaucer has turned the story of betrayal into a poem about 'truth', loyalty, faith, 'moral virtue'.

But now that Chaucer has at last come to his story he proceeds briskly with the first step, small, but crucial and typical; the act of betrayal by Calkas, father of Criseyde, who as a soothsayer foreknows the defeat of Troy and deserts to the Greeks. A sensible man, doubtless, though what he is and all he is he owes to Troy, and he is a traitor. There is no time for comment. The people are enraged against his kin, of whom we are told only of his daughter, Criseyde, most beautiful of women, left defenceless, forced to appeal to the noble Hector, eldest son of king Priam, and chief support of Troy, who chivalrously assures her safety. The war casts its shadow, but Chaucer tells us it is not his subject, and we are brought immediately to the scene in the temple at the spring festival; we do not forget that Trojans are not Christians, but they are clearly decent, ordinary churchgoing pagans. All this has been told in a direct, unambiguous tone. The style is full, clear, translucent. The personal direct address never lapses, and enables Chaucer to take in his stride both his narration and a reference to his primary audience:

Among thise othere folk was Criseyda
In widewes habit blak; but natheles,
Right as oure firste lettre is now an A,
In beaute first so stood she, makeles. (I, 169–72)   *unequalled*

This must be a compliment to Queen Anne: at the same time it has that curious ambivalent quality that is often found in Chaucer's references to royalty; for after all, when has our first letter not been an A? The remark is graceful, polite, complimentary, true; and yet does not perhaps say as much as it seems to say; is less committed than it appears. It is not spoken of Criseyde, but in close association with her, and we may note now that Criseyde is hardly ever presented without some note of ambiguity, at least in the lines nearby. Here she is beautiful, with her golden hair set off so well by her black widow's dress, and with a mixture, familiar enough in young women, of shyness and haughtiness. She is the archetypal beloved: almost completely in the traditional beauty of the medieval heroine, whose blonde charms were first noted by the Greeks, and are not quite disregarded even now. Criseyde is a little different from the usual virginal heroine, being a widow and therefore more independent and yet more vulnerable, traditionally more wanton than a maiden. We are not told her age, here or anywhere else. She thinks of herself as 'right young' (II, 752), which in Chaucer's personal language can signify any age up to about 25, but Chaucer deliberately says later that he cannot tell her age (V, 826), and at what age does a woman cease to call herself young? Of course she could have been married at twelve, like the Wife of Bath, and been widowed soon after. On the other hand she could be about twenty-four, the age of the Black Knight in *The Book of the Duchess*, who is also described as 'right young' (454–5). Chaucer leaves the reader to make up his own mind.

Now enters 'this Troilus'; 'this' in Chaucer's language in the poem being usually a distancing, even half-mocking qualifier. He is a prince and walks up and down the temple with his followers, mocking at lovers, very characteristic of some kinds of shy boy in middle or late adolescence. Soldier as he is, he could be as young as sixteen. The Black Prince, son of Edward III, commanded his first battle when fourteen. In fact, there was a tradition, recorded by a ninth-century Latin writer, that Troilus was under twenty. Perhaps we should think of him as about nineteen. His battle prowess is therefore not impossible. In World War II Battle of Britain pilots and many army officers were no older.

The next couple of hundred lines are a beautiful example of medieval high narration, elaborate, varied, leisured, lyrical, subtle; a model of the conduct of the whole poem in little. One thing they do not offer; a narrative full of action and suspense. The events are there, but are there to be felt and thought about. They are known in broadest outline, and although there are plenty of interesting, even novel-like details, suspense is always sacrificed to a richer, longer-lasting effect, similar to dramatic irony, which may be called narrative irony. This is that device, of which the whole poem is an extended example, whereby the event in the immediate foreground is placed against the known background of the full story. We can see the event in the light of its consequences. The supreme example is Book V of this poem, and there the effect is peculiarly poignant and artistically satisfying. Conveyed through a mind as meditative and subtle as the mind of Henry James, written in a style sometimes as complex and obscure though rather more varied than that later master's, Chaucer's narrative irony strongly engages our feelings yet appeals especially to our passion for understanding. It tells us almost more than we want to know. We are forced to make that bitter-sweet act of cognition, recognizing and yet constantly re-evaluating, which is so markedly the characteristic of this poem above all others. We are constantly 'moved', though in no simply emotional disturbance. It is no good being impatient to get on with the story. The man who reads this poem for the story alone will find his patience so fretted that he will go hang himself: besides, we know the story.

Something of the basic structure of the narration at this point Chaucer owes to Boccaccio and to the tradition of medieval narrative (see Introduction), but he develops it far beyond precedent in his own characteristic way. He describes the god of love as angry at Troilus's speech (I, 206). The god of love 'suddenly, he hit him at the full' (I, 209). At this obscure note of action the poet (at a hint from Boccaccio) breaks into a rhetorical apostrophe.

O blynde world, O blynde entencioun! (I, 211)

The apostrophe heightens the feeling; the fine abstract word has intellectual and emotional power. The sentiment and style are high, perhaps deliberately a little pompous. Then the stanza finishes in sharp stylistic contrast:

But alday faileth thing that fooles wenden. (I, 217)   *believe*

The beginning has a touch of perhaps exaggerated alarm; the end of the stanza an amused sharpness. The poet, and so the audience or reader, do not *identify* closely with Troilus, though he is at the very centre of our interest, and nothing is told but what has relation to him. We remain sympathetic but detached. In the next stanza the proud prince is compared to proud 'Bayard' (a slightly mocking generic name for a horse in the fourteenth century) feeling his oats, to use the comparably undignified modern idiom, and getting a lash of the whip. Thus it was, says Chaucer, with this 'fierce and proud knight', although he was a worthy king's son; and such is the dominance of the poet that we accept both the praise and admiration and the amused deflating comments that preceded it.

Then the poet turns on *us*, though he kindly describes us as 'wise, proud and worthy': take example, he says with mocking sternness, and beware of Love, for

> Love is he that alle thing may bynde
> For may no man fordon the law of kynde. (I, 237–8)   *resist*

We smile uneasily, as members of the audience do when the comedian on the stage singles them out and addresses a truth to them. The poet goes on to say how even very clever, very good, very strong, very high-ranking persons (more so than us, we may understand) have been subdued by love. And indeed rightly, for love is sweet and comforting and virtuous. And so, since you can't resist it, you may as well give in to it. One is almost reminded of Fielding's heroine Letitia in *Jonathan Wild* who saved herself from being raped by a speedy compliance.

With such a series of propositions fired at us, all true, yet because of the way they are delivered, making us a little uneasy – in what way are they true? love of whom? – the poet turns back to his story of Troilus's joy and 'cold cares' (I, 264), while we may feel almost as bewildered as Troilus is *going* to be. For all this has gone on while Troilus is still 'playing' within the temple. Then the poet tells how Troilus sees Criseyde and says, with an exclamation, 'where have *you* been all my life?' or words to that effect. This is the event, tiny in itself, though rich in consequence; it has been underlined with social, historical, scientific, metaphysical commentary and implications, has been seen as half comic, noted as typical, related to ourselves, connected with the future. Such is the enrichment of narrative irony.

We now proceed in a world of realistic social comedy, and continue there, with little commentary, for the next twelve stanzas or so, which describe Criseyde a little more fully, tell us how Troilus disguised his feelings, give us a brief scientific account of how her image remained in his memory, and show us how when he got to his room and could be alone he sat on his bed, made a 'mirror of his mind', and determined to follow 'Love's craft' (I, 379). We are told how he made a song, which 'my authority Lollius', says the poet, records for us, and which we may find 'next this verse' (I, 399). Such references to the poet, to reading, and to Lollius set us at a little critical distance from Troilus, and we appreciate his passion with a little detachment; but in general this is full, steady narration. The poet rides us on an easy rein, and brings this first scene to a kind of pause with the song, which scholarship tells us is a translation from one of Petrarch's sonnets.

The song's plaint about the strange mixture of pain and joy that makes up love is interesting as one of the recurrent motifs of the whole poem, and true of life, though traditional enough. The song in itself is striking as a different form of narration; it is lyric more than dramatic speech. Throughout the poem the narration is lifted at significant points into warm expressiveness by such devices as the songs of Troilus, by lyrical formal speech, and also in his letters to Criseyde. In these songs and formal utterances the straightforward narration of events is deliberately abandoned for lyric meditation of a purely Chaucerian kind, that sweetens and warms the tone, and contributes important (though sometimes erroneous) ideas. Here we appreciate the lyric warmth (mediated through 'Lollius') without being swept away in an identity of passionate feeling.

The song is part of 'Love's craft', and such an expression may make us pause, the more so as there has been widespread critical misunderstanding about love in medieval literature. Since the purpose of this essay is to start with what Chaucer's own poem actually says, it is better to leave comparisons and broader issues aside for the moment.

Troilus sees a beautiful girl and 'falls in love'. No doubt the reactions of many young men might be less shy, but Troilus's response is natural enough. The naturalness and inevitability of love are several times emphasized by the poet (e.g. I, 225–59), with whatever ironic overtones. Since all natural activities are historically conditioned, the expression of and valuation put upon love naturally vary a good deal according to different times and societies. With our vastly increased sociological and anthropological sophistication today we are well aware of such relativity, and so is Chaucer himself, as he shows by a comment later noted (II, 22–35). The poet deliberately emphasizes the possible difference between the behaviour of Troilus and that of people in his own day. The character and feelings of Troilus are not presented as ordinary. Whatever degree of 'convention' Troilus may seem to illustrate, therefore, is, within the context of the poem, only the form that the 'natural' took for him. The poet never shows Troilus as deliberately adopting an artificial or hypocritical mode of behaviour. The whole drift of the poem emphasizes the involuntary aspect of Troilus's love.

The words *craft, art, science*, were almost completely interchangeable in Chaucer's day, and the fact may serve to remind us of the scope of the word *craft*. The 'craft of love' is what Chaucer calls elsewhere 'the craft of fine loving' (*Prologue to the Legend of Good Women*, F 544), translating the usual French term *fine amour*, 'refined love', and it would be better if we used this term rather than the modern invention 'courtly love', unless indeed we follow Chaucer's normal practice and call it simply 'love'. Love for Chaucer is always *fine amour*, but such terms as 'art' and 'craft' remind us of the willed element in all human behaviour but the most basic. Again, modern psychological study of the unconscious, and our knowledge of how the mind affects the body in psychosomatic illness, make it easy for us to accept the element of will in all behaviour, even as we accept the basic physical conditioning of the mind by the body. It is natural for Troilus to fall in love without his choice and equally natural for him to choose to follow love's craft, for they are two aspects of the same thing. The full subtleties of love are explored by the poem. It is based on physical desire, and aims at sexual fulfilment, but it is not mere lust. It makes Troilus more worthy, at any rate when he is successful in love, as Troilus's behaviour shows. He is modest, well-behaved, kindly, brave, 'flees every vice', as the poet later shows (III, 1772–1806), dresses well, is cheerful, and so forth. Any reading of the poem which denigrates the real beauty and joy of successful love, and of the fineness of Troilus's moral and social character, or sees the poem as a fundamentally cynical or satirical presentation of love, grossly oversimplifies it.

It is also an oversimplification to disregard other notes besides beauty and joy. Troilus's song tells us of its pain, as does the whole course of the story. Earthly love always causes pain. The word 'craft', too, also includes possible reference to a skill deliberately learned, even to what we might now call 'craftiness', implying slyness. The new moral sensibility conferred by love is also an instrument to win the lady's love, by making the lover more attractive to the lady, and so risks becoming a means, not an end, superficial manners rather than genuine worthiness. This does not happen with Troilus, but Diomede later will give a splendid demonstration of such hypocritical practice of the 'craft of love'.

Troilus's song, with its address to God, or rather, perhaps, the god of love, has a markedly religious note, and we shall find throughout the poem that Troilus frequently feels and expresses his love in religious language. Much of this appears as historical local colour, as here and in later invocations to the pagan goddess of love, the mother of Cupid, Venus. Some of this mythological colouring is used, as well as for historical realism, for poetical adornment and psychological symbol. But Venus is also a planet, and the stars were believed in the fourteenth century in sober scientific truth to influence the affairs of men, and thus to be part of the instruments of God's controlling love of the world. The way in which Troilus and indeed the poet suffuse the language of love with religious feeling and concept is not merely for the sake of dramatic emphasis, nor is it pagan, nor is it simple parody. One of the underlying questions posed by the poem is that of the puzzling relationship between natural love ('love of kynde'), and heavenly ('celestial') love (cf. I, 979). It is only Troilus, however, whose love is religiously coloured. Criseyde's is not. The real interest in love is as it proceeds from man to woman, or rather, knight to lady. The lady is the object, and one of the questions of the poem is whether the lady is a sufficient, or sufficiently worthy, object of such love. Troilus's religious fervour naturally arouses his own philosophical questioning, as in this same song, and in later formal song or speech. Our own questions follow.

The religious and philosophical interests re-inforce the deeply personal and individualistic way in which Troilus's love is presented. When Troilus falls in love society is agony to him and he avoids everybody, as far as he can to go and mope in solitude. One of the most striking and true things about the poem is the emphasis on the private quality of love and the refusal of a social context. Only Pandarus shares knowledge of the love-affair and as he says himself he is only a means to bring the lovers together, a pander (III, 253–5). In most other French and English love-stories the progress of private love culminates in the public statement and state of marriage, but in this poem the quintessentially private and personal quality of love is maintained to the bitter end. At first love is private merely by evading public life and values, but the progress of the story finally leads to a poignant conflict between private and public. Public necessity, in the form of political expediency, sends Criseyde to the Greeks as an exchange, and is hostile through ignorant indifference to Troilus's private world. The public world here comes out badly. It is both wrong and disastrous of the Trojan Parliament to exchange Criseyde for the ultimate betrayer Antenor. Yet one may also notice that if Troilus had connected his private love with normal public values, that is, if he had married Criseyde, he would have preserved her, as in the event he could not. This is not quite the same thing as condemning the unquestionable social immorality of Troilus's love. Such immorality seems relatively unimportant in the poem, largely because Troilus's total faithfulness needs no social validation, and the issues are deeper. (And of course Troilus and Criseyde cannot commit adultery, as far too many critics assume all medieval 'courtly lovers' do, because neither is married to anyone.)

It is a paradox of the essentially private quality of Troilus's love that it is also inevitably modelled on the only available pattern of human relationships, that of feudal society, as we see through what is now the somewhat strange language of love. To love is to 'serve'; a lover is a 'servant'; Troilus is Criseyde's 'man' (e.g. I, 468). Feudal relationships were intensely personal, often felt to be more binding even than marriage, and were essentially 'vertical' bonds of obligation, in which everyone was superior or inferior to other people. Only the masculine relationship of 'brotherhood' (as between Troilus and Pandarus) seems to have largely evaded the vertical pattern. So Troilus at this stage feels himself inferior to Criseyde, her servant and man, though in the climax of their relationship a genuine interchange is achieved when each obeys the other's will.

To conclude this digression on Troilus's love, then, it has been shown to be based on sexual desire but to be far more than mere lust, bringing the whole personality to a finer quality of sensibility and behaviour. It is modelled on religious and feudal ways of thought and feeling, but is essentially personal and private. Such love, both passionate and profound, may well be a man's deepest emotional, intellectual and imaginative experience and open up the greatest joys to him, make him vulnerable to the sharpest sorrows, lead him to the deepest questions.

III

For the rest of Book I Chaucer concentrates on the development of Troilus's feelings with the same narrative variety, impossible to follow in detail here. Poor Troilus whenever he can takes to his bed and groans. He conceals his feelings from everyone. Eventually his friend Pandarus comes in 'unaware'. What's wrong?

Han now thus soone Grekes maad yow leene?   *have/lean*
Or hastow som remors of conscience . . .? (I, 553–4)

Pandarus had no traditional character, though he acquired an un-enviable one later. In this poem he has no character in the way Troilus, Criseyde, even Diomede, have. They are each at some stage formally described, and fit obvious categories. Pandarus is never so described. We know nothing about him save what we learn indirectly from dialogue or his action as go-between. He has no independent existence. He is a function of the plot rather than a human character. He is needed because Troilus's character is what it is. Paradoxically this makes Pandarus all the more vivid to us, and he is a wonderful talker. Being what he does and says within this poem, he is much more like a person in a modern novel than are the other characters.

One small point should be noticed about his words just quoted. He first uses the polite second person plural *yow* to Troilus, who after all is a prince, Pandarus's 'most beloved lord' (cf. III, 239), then immediately switches to the intimate, warm, not respectful, second person singular, *hastow* (= hast thou), for Troilus is also his brother dear (III, 239). This is his normal practice with Troilus, who always (for after all, he is a prince) uses the second person singular, as to friends and servants (as well as enemies and children), to Pandarus. A nuance of their relationship is conveyed here; Troilus's acknowledged superiority, and possibly a touch of presumption by Pandarus. Troilus and Criseyde never use the familiar singular form to each other. The high quality of their devotion, its romance, its lack of ordinary, everyday familiarity and intimacy, is thereby suggested. If we neglect grammar we may miss a whole range of linguistic and therefore literary discriminations.

At this stage we may cast an eye forward on the whole rela-tionship of Troilus and Pandarus. The rest of Book I is concerned with the dialogue between Troilus and Pandarus, deadly serious for Troilus, rather amusing for us. How unwilling, how embarrassed, is Troilus to have his not very profound or unusual secret wheedled out of him! How relieved when Pandarus knows he loves Criseyde – then alarmed because he thinks Criseyde may be annoyed! What beautiful aristocratic young widow could be annoyed to hear that a prince, young and a fine soldier, good and modest, is in love with her? But Troilus genuinely thinks she may be. Pandarus by contrast is full of self-confidence and enthusiasm. He is an educated man, ready with proverbs and examples, much indeed to the irritation of Troilus, who is obviously not bookish as Pandarus is. Troilus is no milksop among men and he treats Pandarus pretty curtly, in pointing out that Pandarus is no good at managing his own love-affair. But Pandarus is unabashed. 'A fool may often guide a wise man' he says (cf. I, 630), though we have no evidence so far that however admirable Troilus may be, he is also wise. Pandarus mocks and even shakes Troilus, though the poet is careful to tell us early on that Pandarus knows that no man was braver, or more desired worthiness (I, 566–7) than Troilus. Pandarus passionately loves Troilus – he nearly melts for woe and pity to see him so cast down (I, 582). Pandarus is a wonderfully dramatic representation of a not unfamiliar type of person, lively, intelligent, emotional, generous, worldly and ingenious: he has no real interests of his own, so he is not selfish; but he has no ore, no ballast, no personal conviction. He is entirely conventional and superficial.

If we look at Troilus and Pandarus in a rather different way we can see that, granted the given plot, in which Troilus successfully seduces Criseyde, and granted the type of character Chaucer has created in Troilus (very different from his Italian counterpart), Pandarus is necessary because Troilus is far too good and modest to win Criseyde by his own efforts. Pandarus is complementary to Troilus: he provides the lover's necessary aggression. It is not that Troilus does not *want* Criseyde sexually, but that there is in himself a hindrance, almost as deep and enigmatic as that internal hindrance which prevents Hamlet sweeping to the revenge of his father. In each case in modern times we tend to see the difficulty in terms of the character's own temperament – Hamlet indecisive, Troilus feeble. In each case we are probably right as to the fact, but may be wrong in evaluation. In the case of Troilus as probably in Hamlet we may sense some underlying religious or moral preoccupation in the poet's mind. According to conventional morality seduction may be considered wrong. And as we know from the story it seriously damaged, and indeed destroyed, Troilus and Criseyde, as well as mightily rejoicing them. Because Troilus is a good and compassionate man he is not a cold-blooded seducer nor hot-blooded ravisher. But *somebody* has got to do the dirty work, and Pandarus is positively anxious to do it for the sake of friendship. We can put this another way. In Troilus Chaucer is attempting something difficult to appreciate. He is attempting to portray masculine sexual love entirely free from aggression. Perhaps this is impossible (even, to judge from the response of many feminine readers to Troilus, undesirable and undesired). Troilus will finally take possession of Criseyde like a sparrow-hawk killing a lark (III, 1191–2). But until that moment no lover could be less rapacious. With Troilus we are in the presence of one of those beautiful strained figures of Gothic art in which ordinary realism is sacrificed (within the bounds of recognition) to a daring attempt to present one fine high rare quality of human life. Gothic art is like modern art in not attempting the overall illusionist realism of nineteenth-century anecdotal painting. Chaucer, the supreme English Gothic writer, is not clumsily aiming at nineteenth-century naturalistic writing. If we accept this stylized portrayal of Troilus as a lover without aggression we may still find him on occasion realistically sympathetic or amusing. We must also accept Pandarus as representing the aggressive element in masculine sexuality (though he is not of course in any way allegorical).

We end Book I with Pandarus laying his plans in advance in accordance with the best precepts of the medieval rhetoricians, from the most famous of whom, Geoffrey of Vinsauf, Chaucer borrows the material for a stanza (I, 1065–71). Troilus is described as becoming ever better and better in a stanza of shining super-latives very characteristic of one aspect of Chaucer's style.

IV

The second book begins with a Prologue, directly addressing the audience or reader, promising us to sail out of these black waves and telling us not to judge the story by the superficial realism of a comparison with the manners of our own day – it all happened a long time ago, and there are many different ways of doing things. A tolerant recognition of human variety, a sympathetic acceptance of human difference, a sense of the validity of past experience, are characteristic of Chaucer.

The next eight hundred lines or so are perhaps the most simply delightful in the poem – a long passage of domestic high comedy not incomparable with Jane Austen, though with a vein of masculine harshness, and the further advantage of verse. It is the month of May and Pandarus, having spent a night as sleepless from unre-quited love as ever did Troilus, makes an astrological calculation that tells him it is a good day for journeys. Astrology was a valid and important science in the fourteenth century, and Pandarus is merely doing what any prudent man of affairs, or any doctor, would have done. The stars ruled worldly affairs. They themselves could be ruled by the wise man, it was well recognized, but only because he controlled and did not give in to his desires. And if we all did that, how would the world be served? Pandarus visits his niece, whom he finds sitting with two other ladies, having read to them the 'romance of Thebes'. Criseyde is mistress of a considerable establishment, for later we hear of her women 'a great route' (II, 818) and three nieces, who perhaps live with her. Pandarus, her uncle, can hardly be the brother of the traitor Calkas, one would think, so he is presumably brother of her mother, who must be dead. Criseyde must also have had either brother or sister, since she has nieces. So she has rather more of a family than one might have supposed from her appeal to Hector when her father absconded. Pandarus did not help her then. But none seems nearer to her than Pandarus, whom she asks to help her with her business affairs. Yet Pandarus might be little older than herself, even though he is her uncle, as sometimes happens in widely spaced families. These speculations may be interesting, and profitable, if we remember first that they are only speculations, and second, when we notice from the gaps in realistic detail, that we have to do with a Gothic poem, not a naturalistic novel. The realism is sharp and vital, but is part of a pattern of statement and symbol that does not need illusionism to achieve artistic – or real – truth.

Pandarus plays wonderfully with Criseyde's dependence on him, on her curiosity, timidity. She shows herself a fascinating woman, warm, gay, intelligent, responsive, sensitive, with a flattering yet sprightly deference to the male sex that is quite irresistible. Critics have emphasized her fearfulness, which is certainly there, and is not the least of her feminine charms. But she is also self-confident. It was this self-confidence which, in the form of haughtiness, Chaucer put side-by-side with her shrinking modesty in his first account of her. When Pandarus has sown the seed of love in her heart and departed she retires to her private room to think about what she has heard, going through the *pros* and *cons*, and saying to herself, in effect, 'After all, why not? I am one of the most beautiful women in Troy. I am my own woman, well off, right young, unconstrained by a husband' (II, 742–56). She continues to alternate between hope and fear, but it is her self-confidence, not her fearfulness, that triumphs and is fatal. It will lead her to Troilus. Above all, it will lead her to the folly of believing that she, a tender young woman, when sent to the Greeks, will have the nerve to find her way back to Troy, at night, through the enemy lines! She will even be ready to trust Diomede, an obvious ladykiller if ever there was one, on first acquaintance (V, 188).

To return to her dialogue with Pandarus, she is confident enough to think she can manipulate him to find out what he is really after (II, 387). But he, who has no high opinion of her intelligence – her 'tender wits' (II, 271) – easily manages her by a fascinating combination of jokes, hints, portentousness, gentle bullying, and downright lying. She is no match for him.

Pandarus in action reveals himself as intelligent, warm, responsive, calculating; an unscrupulous liar, with no moral ballast or structure. Friendly as he is, with no malice in the world, he is by no means on Criseyde's side. Indeed he later well recognizes, in a moment of misgiving that is perhaps his only moment of genuine independence as a person in the whole poem, that he has become, through his moral irresponsibility – 'Betwixen game and ernest' – what we now call after him a pander:

> for the am I bicomen,
> Bitwixen game and ernest, swich a meene
> As maken wommen unto men to comen. (III, 253–5)

Troilus very generously replies 'not so', and in order to demonstrate to Pandarus that he does not consider his service a shame, himself offers to procure Helen, or any of his sisters, or any other woman, for Pandarus's use in return, to show his gratitude; which shows Troilus characteristically missing the point. But Pandarus's catalytic action in bringing the lovers together need not blind us to Criseyde's real willingness. As she says to herself, she is 'not religious', not a nun, that is, and she stands untied in pleasant meadows (II, 752), being thereby caused by the poet to compare herself to a frisky young mare, just as he had compared Troilus to 'proud Bayard' (II, 218). They are a couple of healthy young animals. And in one of the most beautiful moments of love-literature she can later say, when first in Troilus's arms.

> Ne hadde I er now, my swete herte deere
> Ben yold, ywis, I were now nought heere, (III, 1210–1)   *yielded*

which is amusing as well as deeply touching – a characteristic and this time happy product of Criseyde's basic confidence that she knows where she is going. Even so, she needs to be persuaded. She is not a wanton, and therefore in the situational pattern Pandarus to some extent represents her sexual compliance as he represents Troilus's sexual aggression. In his hermaphrodite character he experiences his own queer kind of sexual pleasure in bringing the lovers together.

This is to anticipate. In the uneven battle of wits in Book II, the long rich passage of dramatic dialogue between Pandarus and Criseyde is deftly steered by the poet and we rely on his guidance. He is willing at times to show us even the inner depths of Criseyde's mind, though at other times he does not know even quite external facts.

Towards the end of the episode a lyric pause is created by the love song sung by Criseyde's niece in the garden to which they withdraw, and which is so precisely if briefly sketched in. Here a woman sings her love. The lyric note is prolonged by the beautiful stanza of the nightingale's song, a lovely, purely rhetorical, adornment. Yet it has been preceded by a joke against rhetoric by the poet (II, 904–5), and is followed by Criseyde's splendidly 'Freudian' dream of having her heart ripped out by an eagle who replaces it with his own. Such is the variety of narration.

We are now well launched on the upward turn of Fortune's wheel and must follow the broader movement. The plot describes Pandarus's contriving an exchange of letters between Troilus and Criseyde, in which Pandarus again reveals himself as a highly competent literary intellectual, and Troilus again as unbookish as a Rugger Blue, followed by a wonderfully contrived interview between Troilus and Criseyde. The situations are described with delightful touches of social realism. The interview has a touch of fabliau-like farce, for Troilus is in bed in the house of his brother Deiphebus, pretending to be ill, while Pandarus invents a cock-and-bull story to get Criseyde into him alone for a brief exchange of words. It is after this that Pandarus has the moment of misgiving already referred to. The social comedy extends over the end of Book II to Book III, which contains the topmost reach of Fortune's wheel, when the lovers are finally brought to bed together by Pandarus.

The narrative richly combines fabliau-like realism and comedy with the high sentiments of love and passion. Without Pandarus nothing would advance. He constantly feeds the fire (III, 484), carries letters, and carefully plans the outcome 'with great deliberation' (III, 519), sparing no cost. He persuades Criseyde to come to supper in his house, assuring her that Troilus will *not* be there, though what Criseyde thought about *that*, the poet remarks, his author does not make clear (III, 575). Troilus, however, has been cooped up in a little room (*stewe*, [III, 601] name for a little room with a fireplace, and for a brothel) in Pandarus's house since midnight the night before she comes. The point is that Pandarus has not only placed Troilus there, but foreseen that rare conjunction of planets – a conjunction which actually took place in May 1385 in England – which would bring about such a heavy rain that Criseyde would be forced to remain in the house overnight.

The poet here in a fine stanza invokes 'Fortune, executrice of wyrdes', and says that 'the goddes wil' was performed without Criseyde's leave (III, 617–23). There is a strong sense of destiny here. On the other hand, it was already raining, as Criseyde pointed out, that same morning when Pandarus asked her to supper for that evening (III, 562) – it sounds like a real English May – and the poet has been ostentatiously equivocal about Criseyde's belief in Troilus's absence.

Chaucer as usual balances the issues of choice and inevitability. Fortune is a mythological personification standing for 'what the world is like'. 'Wyrdes', Chaucer tells us elsewhere (*Legend of Good Women*, 2580) is what we call Destiny. Fortune, *wyrdes*, Destiny, all mean the same thing – the changeable universe of the world beneath the moon. Change meant imperfection, but it was thought to be operated by the influences of the stars, 'influences of thise hevenes hye' (III, 617). Fortune and her wheel are the poetic representation of this truth. None of this was anti-Christian. The problems then were to reconcile the ultimate controlling power and beneficence of God, operating through the stars, with the nature of existence. These are the perennial problems of man's freedom, of suffering and evil, of the mind's power to rise above material conditioning. Nowhere in the poem, however, is there any concept of a hostile and implacable Fate, except as far as Troilus's complaints, those of an unenlightened pagan, may interpret Fortune as such.

At this stage of the poem, however, Fortune is for a while on Troilus's side, and we move towards the consummation of his love. The sharp realism of the supper party, the impediment of the 'smoky rain' preventing Criseyde's return as Pandarus had foreseen, the details of the sleeping arrangements, Troilus's devout expectations, the secret passage to Criseyde's bed, Pandarus's bustling encouragement, Troilus's faint, Pandarus's tossing him into the bed, Pandarus's jokes, the rapturous love-making, make a fascinating narrative where the succession of events, deeply interesting in itself, is enriched but not hampered by the adornments of dialogue and description, by explicit and implicit commentary. No reader needs guidance to its understanding and enjoyment.

Chaucer is very explicit about their love, and if one thing is convincing in the poem it is the real joy and sweetness of consummated love. The poet emphasizes this without irony:

O blisful nyght, of hem so longe isought
How blithe unto hem bothe two thow weere. (III, 1317–8)

And after the long delays, culminating in Troilus's faint at the very bedside, the reader sympathizes with joyous relief. Yet perhaps there is even a touch of extravagance in the poet's next lines:

Why nad I swich oon with my soule ybought,   *had I not*
Ye, or the leeste joie that was theere? (III, 1319–20)

'To sell one's soul for something' is now merely a slightly old-fashioned and unserious cliché. Was it so for the poet? Is he being deliberately trivial here? Does he *really* mean he would sell his immortal soul, the eternity of heavenly bliss, for even the *least* of such joys? Surely that would be absurd? In other words, there is surely a calculated hint of excess in the narration here, that perhaps the gestures of personal delivery may have heightened if it was spoken before the court by the poet himself. By introducing himself here the poet frees our imagination to work on the implied events with what fervour it will: he also hands over some responsibility for our imagination and evaluation of the events, which he emphasizes in the next two stanzas by protesting his own inadequacy and putting it all in *our* discretion 'to increase or make diminution' of his language (III, 1335–6). The audience or reader is made a willing but uncertain accomplice. The event is certain, the interpretation fluid. Hence perhaps the variety of critical response.

When morning comes and Troilus must go he declaims at length against the 'cruel day'. It is of the essence of his situation that although he has chosen to follow the world, he is never one calmly to submit to the ordinary demands of worldly reality without passionate complaint. Troilus never really 'accepts the universe', as Pandarus and Criseyde do. This is his strength and weakness. By standards of worldly good sense there is a note of extravagance in his complaint which may even evoke a touch of that wry humour with which cool middle-age contemplates, not without envy, hot youth. Yet the very extremity of his passion, with its slightest hint of absurdity (for he will soon meet Criseyde again), may also be its validation; its unworldliness may in a sense overcome the world. Then Pandarus comes in with his waggish innuendoes, and worldly realism, that is, Fortune, asserts itself again.

And thus Fortune a *tyme* ledde in joie (III, 1714)

both Troilus and Criseyde. The account of their felicity is crowned with the beautiful lyric sung by Troilus in which he hymns the

Love, that of erthe and se hath governaunce. (III, 1744)   *sea*

It is philosophic in tone, and corresponds to a similarly placed song in the source, Boccaccio's *Filostrato*, but that song had been used by Chaucer as a basis for part of the Prologue of Book III, so here he turns to that philosophic work whose problems and solutions underlie the deeper concern that we are increasingly aware of as the poem proceeds. Boethius's *De Consolatione Philosophiae* was completed by its author, a noble Roman, when under sentence of death. From the height of power and felicity he was cast into prison by his barbarian master the Emperor Theodoricus and put to death in 524. In his book he represents himself complaining to the Lady Philosophy, who instructs him in the falseness of worldly felicity as governed by Fortune, and the true felicity to be attained by the steadfast mind which rises superior to the compulsions of the world by controlling the body's appetites. In so doing she discusses those perennial problems

Of Providence, Foreknowledge, Will and Fate –
Fixed fate, free will, foreknowledge absolute

which have so puzzled fallen angels and fallen men. The sections of prose discussion are followed by fine lyrics which sum up their conclusions. The book was immensely influential throughout Europe until the seventeenth century, and never more so than in fourteenth-century England. Chaucer translated it into elaborate prose about the same time as, or a little before, he composed *Troilus and Criseyde*. It was very much in his mind, and one might almost describe the genesis of his poem as out of *Il Filostrato* by the *De Consolatione*. Events are seen in the light of philosophy. Feelings arouse thoughts that modify feelings.

So it is with Troilus's Boethian song at the end of Book III. The song is not of course intended to give us an impression that Troilus has been so much improved by love that he has taken to reading and versifying philosophy. The philosophical expression, like the verse itself, is part of the medium, like the ability of a character in an opera to sing; it is not a stroke of realistic characterization. The lyric expresses Troilus's personal feelings, however, and the ability to sing a song of love, as the description of the Squire in *The Canterbury Tales* shows, was valued in a young soldier and courtier such as Troilus. In its high formal beauty the song follows Boethius in its expression of confidence and joy in the capacity of love – the love expressed by God – to maintain the order, beauty and goodness of the world. Love that of earth and sea has governance

Bynd this acord, that I have told and telle, (III, 1750)

sings Troilus. The accord is that between him and Criseyde. *Bynd* is subjunctive, or at most the kind of imperative used in prayer, expressing, that is to say, a wish or hope. The grammatical distinction, between subjunctive and indicative, slight in itself, is of the greatest importance for discrimination of literary meaning. The poet does not make Troilus sing that his love is certainly a part of the universal divine love as the indicative would indicate, only that he hopes it *may* be. Chaucer, as so often, is fertile in suggestion, but more precisely limited, and less committed, than a hasty reading may assume. Even if Troilus's love is indeed part of the divine love that moves the stars and the other planets (and we are told neither that it is or is not), yet it may be so in a way different from Troilus's and our own expectations, as with poignant knowledge of what is to come, we see how Troilus, inspired by successful love, excels even himself in the daily beauty of his life.

V

So has Book III ended, in joy, pleasure and quiet:

But al to litel, weylaway the whyle,
Lasteth swich joie, ythonked be Fortune. (IV, 1–2)

We begin the downward turn of Fortune's wheel as Book IV begins.

Political expediency demands the exchange of Criseyde for the Trojan leader Antenor, later the betrayer of Troy. Chaucer points out the irony of this (IV, 197–206). We know very little what we should desire; we cannot be sure that what we want will not harm us. We live in a 'cloud of error'. This could be said of more Trojans than the unprincipled people and politicians who overbear the honourable Hector and insist on exchanging Criseyde. The agonizing situation is discussed in every way by Troilus, Criseyde, and Pandarus. Troilus tells Pandarus he has even thought of asking his father for her, i.e. in marriage. But that would merely reveal that she was his mistress, and the king could not for that reason repeal the decision of parliament. Public necessity is totally alien to private desire. Criseyde's distress and grief, not so much for herself as for Troilus, are heavy. Pandarus himself, the universal fixer, cannot devise a plan. He appeals to Criseyde, of whose intelligence he had earlier cherished a low opinion (II, 271);

Women ben wise in short avysement (IV, 936)

he says, a flatterer to the last.

Troilus is in despair and is found in long, formal Boethian soliloquy in a temple. The grave meditations of the golden volume of the sixth-century Roman are again used to dilate on a crucial stage of the story: before it was love; here it is loss of love. In each case Troilus is the mouthpiece, and each passage is therefore to some extent a dramatic expression, appropriate to him, but not necessarily endorsed by the poet or reader. Troilus is without hope and Chaucer, in a way that is typical of his narrative technique, gives us Troilus's conclusion before he gives us the soliloquy; Troilus says

For al that comth, comth by necessitee:
Thus to ben lorn, it is my destinee. (IV, 958–9)   *lost*

Then in despair he goes through the *pros* and *cons* of some traditional arguments put forward by Boethius about man's freedom of action, and comes to the conclusion that we already know; that he is predestined to be 'lost'.

Although the meaning is dramatic, that is, the general idea is related to and arises from the specific situation and from Troilus's feelings, the *form* is not particularly so. Indeed, the state of the manuscripts of the poem strongly suggests that this passage from 1. 953 to 1. 1055, like the other Boethian passages, was added by Chaucer after the main body of the poem was completed, and there is little attempt at realistic characterization of speech appropriate to Troilus. The soliloquy arises out of Troilus's plight. Chaucer gives him the philosophical argument advanced by Boethius within the *De Consolatione* to the Lady Philosophy, in which Boethius argues that since God foreknows the outcome of all events, all are pre-ordained and man has no free will; no ability therefore to choose or to change events. The relevance of this to Troilus's despair is clear, but it also has general reference to the rest of the action. How free was Troilus to love or not to love Criseyde? Troilus himself, here and elsewhere, accepts a completely determinist position. For him his tragedy is one of necessity. But is it so for us? If we are complete determinists of course it will be. But almost always in practice, and very often in theory also, we believe in choice, though alternatives may be limited. As a matter of historical fact medieval Christianity normally believed in human free will. And the passage from the *De Consolatione* on which Troilus's soliloquy is based is conclusively answered by the Lady Philosophy. In the light of Boethius, of normal fourteenth-century thought, and of normal human belief, Troilus is wrong, and Chaucer's audience, which included, either as hearers or readers, learned middle-aged men like Gower and Strode to whom the poem is dedicated (V, 1856–7), knew he was wrong.

Nevertheless, Troilus is also right, and however illogical the paradox may be, we have to accept it as being one of the things the poem 'is about'. Troilus is right, as the course of the poem will show. Our foreknowledge of the outcome emphasizes the sense of destiny. And in ordinary life we often have a sense that some things 'are meant', are unavoidable, even apart from such certainties as death. Whether or not such impressions are philosophically justifiable is irrelevant here. Their existence gave life to the notion of Providence, that all is in the hand of God, and the emotional basis of the notion of Providence is close to that of predestination. We come back to one of the underlying concerns of the poem: the problem of the relation of divine values to worldly values; of the creative divine goodness to the created mixed good and evil of the world, which is Boethius's explicit concern.

We can collaborate with the way of the world, submit ourselves entirely to the revolutions of Fortune's wheel and be overwhelmed by it, as Troilus in his particular event is overwhelmed, and as men have been overwhelmed by concentration camps. But even in concentration camps some men and women, saints religious or secular, rose superior to their miseries by sheer moral force, by force of mind in its widest sense conquering matter, the mighty flesh, the world, the devil. Such an act of spiritual heroism is Boethius's answer to the compulsions of the world. In the medieval expression, 'the wise man rules the stars', that is, the mind can rise above the laws of matter. Troilus is not in this sense a wise man, and at this stage of the story he chooses to have no choice. Thus though his tragedy is for him a tragedy of necessity, for us it is a tragedy of choice. Troilus is of course a poor benighted pagan, and commits himself as all the time we knew he would to the ups-and-downs of the world governed by Fortune's wheel.

The course of events continues as we expect. The rest of the book describes the last painful meeting, with Pandarus cynically asking Troilus in private if Nature had made him only to please Criseyde (IV, 1096), and pointing out that there are 'mo sterres than a payre' as the duck in *The Parliament of Fowls*, 1. 595, would put it. The lovers weep and swoon. Criseyde rejects elopement. Instead, she says she will return through the enemy lines on the tenth day from her departure. They exchange vows. In a beautiful stanza Criseyde says that she has loved Troilus not at all for his royalty nor mere warlike bravery, nor wealth nor any outward circumstances, nor for 'vain delight' i.e. physical pleasure, but for his

moral vertu, grounded upon trouthe. (IV, 1672)

She goes on to characterize him in further noble terms. Yet in the previous stanza she has said that she has always found him so true that she will always behave

That ay honour to me-ward shal rebounde. (IV, 1666)

There is a narrative irony here. She genuinely loves Troilus, but she has also a vein of simple egotism. It is herself, and particularly her honour (which is mainly what the world thinks of one), that she considers, as so often in her speeches. Troilus himself suffers pains worse than hell (IV, 1679–88), and we must sympathize. Yet both Pandarus and Criseyde, easy worldlings, tell him in effect not to be so silly. He is not the only pebble on the beach. And we similarly must judge him to be extravagant in his grief. All the same we need not adopt the coarse blind optimism of Criseyde and Pandarus. For Troilus is right, just as he was (though by self-fulfilling prophecy) in his soliloquy in the temple. Criseyde will not come back. To anticipate what we all know, she will betray him. But from now on the bias of the poem shifts, or at least reveals more clearly what it has always been about: not Criseyde's falseness, but Troilus's 'trouthe'. Though Troilus has chosen completely to immerse himself in the ups-and-downs of the world, and so must suffer the sequence of woe and joy, and after joy, sadness, his 'trouthe' removes him from mere collaboration with the fickle universe. He goes so deep into it that he comes out the other side. His idealism, unworldliness, lack of practical sense, extravagant emotion, incapacity for compromise, that had their comic side earlier, reveal themselves also now as 'trouthe', as complete personal integrity. His obstinacy, as unwise and unprofitable as it is uncompromising, gives him a deeper insight into the inner reality of the situation than can be possessed by the more flexible, sensible, worldly, co-operative, compromising and morally superficial characters of Criseyde and Pandarus. It is surely this unremitting, unrewarded love for a finally unworthy person that ensures Troilus's transcendence of the world.

VI

Books IV and V tell of the pain that must pay for joy, recording the agony of hope deferred, of ultimate disappointment, irredeemable loss. Criseyde is easily seduced by the odious Diomede, though over a period of time. Chaucer shows us the process, and then uses the knowledge of it as a sombre backdrop for Troilus's waiting for Criseyde to return at the end of ten days. When she fails to come we read the exchange of letters (ironic counterpart to the earlier letter writing of Troilus at the beginning of the affair) in which Criseyde eventually even reproaches Troilus for his deceitfulness (V, 1615)! Troilus is brought to recognize the world's reality. Pandarus says he hates Criseyde (V, 1732). But Troilus cannot stop loving her 'a quarter of a day' (V, 1698). To use some words of Miss Iris Murdoch about art in general, such a situation shows us 'the absolute pointlessness of virtue while exhibiting its supreme importance'.

Though deeper knowledge of these last two books cannot lessen our sense of their painful truth, it brings us to recognize the truth of the artistry that modifies the pain and continually deepens the interest. The realism has both pity and justice, but not sentimentality.

The justice and lack of sentimentality abandon Troilus, once he has recognized the truth, to a casual death which is not even dignified by description, let alone glory.

Despitously hym slough the fierse Achille. (V, 1806)

Even before this, however, the poet has been steadily distancing events, and withdrawing himself and us from the story, with various personal comments, as elaborately as he performed the reverse process of slow immersion at the beginning of the poem. There are similar touches of flippancy. He calls his work a 'little tragedy' (characteristic phrase!), but even apart from his trivial flippancies in the process of withdrawal he now, at Troilus's death, springs a comic surprise on us, which, with the following stanzas, has enraged many critics. He sends Troilus 'blissfully' up to the eighth sphere, from where he looks down at this 'little spot of earth' and not only despises it and damns all our fuss (*werk*), but *laughs* at those who are weeping for his death (V, 1807–27).

To see this ending as Chaucer's feeble or craven capitulation to a joyless Christianity condemning a perfectly natural and therefore good love-affair, or to see the immortality of Troilus as a denial of his suffering and tragedy, is in either case to substitute a simplified modern notion of the story for the richness and variety of the poem as it is told. Of course the transcendental imagery can be a difficulty for a modern mind. We no longer believe in immortality, at least so simply, and we have no longer a Ptolemaic model of the universe. Most of us are not Christians. But Chaucer knew he was writing fiction, and this passage must be read fictionally and symbolically like all literature.

First the literal reading must be correct. Troilus himself seems happy after death, but Chaucer does not actually tell us *where* he is finally placed. It is not a question of importance. He despises and condemns worldly concerns, and the poet in a mask that seems totally unironic advises us to love God and to recognize the transience of the world. We should seek true, not feigned, love. Pagans were accursed. All this, including Troilus's apotheosis, is outside the story, but a reflection on it. To interpret we must translate the transcendental imagery.

Troilus's apotheosis represents his escape from the world governed by Fortune, this mutable world, beneath the moon. It is the culmination of his idealistic, unworldly devotion, but it is not part of his story nor of his character. The passage indeed may even be one of those added on revision and has the quality of a comment on the story, not an event added to it. The poem has never been mere story, never centred on character-study; it has continuously invoked and invited general reflection. The contrast between 'what the world is like' (a mixture of joy and sorrow) and a true evaluation of it which should lead us, for example, to reject the sentimentalities of mourning, is what is represented by Troilus's station among the stars as it contrasts with his life upon this little spot of earth.

That Troilus goes to heaven is not sure and not important. But in the light of the representation of ultimate truth it is straightforwardly logical for the poet, granted his premises, to commend the certainties of the love of Christ in contrast to the uncertainties and miseries of earthly love as suffered by Troilus. In this regard the transience of earthly love is necessarily false and feigned. And is it not sensible to prefer a permanent good to a transient one?

This is not particularly moralistic. Natural physical love is nowhere condemned as such in the poem. That Troilus's love was the highly refined, well-mannered, courtly *fine amour* does not make it less natural, less attractive or more deplorable in itself. Love then, as now, was sometimes adulterous, though the love of Troilus was not. His love was not sanctioned by marriage and had he married

Criseyde Troilus would have saved himself a lot of trouble, but that would not have been the story of Troilus as it existed. The immorality of the love-affair is inherent in the story, but Chaucer had no need to emphasize it in his poem. It was deplorable, but undoubtedly the way of the world. The *goodness* of Troilus is still important, however it should be qualified.

Nowhere does the poem totally condemn worldly love or worldly goodness. The paradoxical relationship between eternal values and 'the way of the world', between God and Fortune, is what haunts us throughout the poem, and there are no simple solutions, any more than there is agreement over the rich paradoxes evoked at the end of the poem. Chaucer asks his friends Gower and Strode to correct, 'where need is', avoiding finality to the last, and ends in a quietly magnificent prayer.

(iv) *THE CANTERBURY TALES*

D. A. Pearsall

Chaucer must have evolved the scheme of the *Canterbury Tales*, and written the *General Prologue*, about 1387, after he had completed the *Troilus* and abandoned the *Legend of Good Women*. One or two earlier pieces were subsequently incorporated into the design, but the bulk of the tales were written later, and the whole thus constitutes the work of Chaucer's later years. It does not read like the work of an old man: indeed there is a vigour and freedom of experimentation which is spectacular even for Chaucer, a sense almost that Chaucer had achieved his *magnum opus*, the *Troilus*, had laid his claim to enduring memory as a poet, and could now afford to explore less familiar terrain, to indulge his diverse and incomparable gifts as a narrative poet, to be truly himself. The air of relaxed ease in the *Tales* as a whole, the effortless insouciance which can stand the *Clerk's Tale* on its head without a tremor or change of tone, and find a happy issue even out of the Pardoner's afflictions, is partly the familiar illusion produced by perfect artistic control, but it is not untrue to the temper of the work, nor to the temper of the man whose maturer findings are that the chief problems of art are artistic ones. The *Tales* are always bound to suffer from comparison with the *Troilus* because of their unfinished state; they can never achieve total coherence in the mind of the reader, any more than they did in the mind of their creator. But their very open-endedness is part of their claim on us, for in them Chaucer pushes the art of narrative poetry far beyond the frontiers of the *Troilus*, into territories where we have only just begun to catch up with him.

The fictional framework is simple. The poet portrays himself meeting a group of pilgrims at the Tabard Inn in Southwark, where they are gathered ready to set out on their pilgrimage to the shrine of Thomas à Becket at Canterbury. They are to travel in a company, as was the custom, and the Host of the Tabard proposes that they should enliven the journey, which, taken at a leisurely pace, usually took about three days, by telling tales on the way. Each pilgrim should tell two tales on the way there and two on the way back, and the winner would receive a dinner 'at oure aller cost' when they return to the Tabard. The scheme is an ambitious one, and, with a possible 120 or so tales to tell, Chaucer was obviously intending to keep himself in business for the rest of his life. He came nowhere near completing this number, of course, and he himself must have realized how unlikely it was that he ever would, for the original plan for four each is never again mentioned. In the link preceding the *Franklin's Tale*, the Host speaks of everyone telling 'a tale or two' (V, 698), and in the Parson's Prologue he says to the Parson 'Every man, save thou, hath toold his tale', as if the Parson's one tale would complete the sequence. If this was the final plan, Chaucer comes near to fulfilling it, for there are in fact 24 tales, including three 'dramatically' unfinished, that is, interrupted (the *Squire's Tale*, *Thopas*, and the *Monk's Tale*), one fragmentary (the *Cook's Tale*), and one from a new character (the Canon's Yeoman). Chaucer the pilgrim tells two. The only pilgrims who do not get a word in are the five guildsmen, for whom only a composite portrait is provided in the *General Prologue*; two of the Prioress's four travelling companions, who again are not described in the *General Prologue*, and of whom three ('the preestes thre') were probably only introduced as an afterthought to provide one 'blank cheque' for the *Nun's Priest's Tale*; and the Yeoman and the Plowman, whose portraits are wholly idealized and who look to have been brought in as representatives of the secular lower orders simply to make the social range more comprehensive. Scribes copying the *Canterbury Tales* were much aware of these last two blanks, and provided spurious tales to fill the gaps, just as they often provided spurious links: the Robin Hood-like *Tale of Gamelyn* for the Yeoman, and a virulent piece of Lollard anti-clericalism for the *Plowman's Tale*.

It would have been easy, one may think, for Chaucer, having come so close to carrying out the shorter revised plan, to have tied up the loose ends and submitted the work to posterity in some semblance of order. He does not seem to have had time to do so. There are a good many signs of carelessness and inconsistency which would surely have been eliminated in even a cursory revision: the Shipman, whose tale was originally designed for the Wife of Bath, speaks of himself two or three times as a woman; and the Second Nun, who was allotted the already-written tale of St. Cecilia, refers to herself as an 'unworthy sone of Eve'. And the whole work has come down to us in a series of unrelated fragments, ten in some good manuscripts, nine in others, equally good, suggesting that Chaucer left the ordering of the *Tales* in some confusion. Later scribes had a merry time patching the fragments together. Modern editors have settled either for the order in the Ellesmere MS, the most famous of the 84 MSS of the *Tales*, or for the order proposed by Furnivall which includes the 'Bradshaw shift'. Briefly described, on the basis of Robinson's edition, which follows the Ellesmere and numbers the fragments I–IX, this involves moving fragment VII so that it follows fragment II, making up fragment B in the Furnivall sequence. The apparent advantage of this is that it places the reference to Rochester (VII, 1926) in its proper relation to the reference to Sittingbourne (III, 847), which is ten miles further on the way to Canterbury. The real advantage is that it offers some lead-up, in the *Melibeus* and the *Nun's Priest's Tale* in fragment VII, to the Wife of Bath's rather abrupt opening in fragment III:

Experience, though noon auctoritee   *no*
Were in this world, is right ynogh for me
To speke of wo that is in mariage. . . .

which reads as if it were alluding to some previous discussion of the subject. On the whole, opinion must favour the shift of fragment VII in this way, but the other change proposed by the Chaucer Society editors, that is, moving fragment VI so that it follows the newly-integrated B as fragment C, is not acceptable. Fragment VI is a floating fragment, that is, it is not tied by any reference to the physical sequence of the pilgrimage, and Furnivall, whose ordering is based on a theoretical diary-framework, therefore felt free to move it earlier to fill a 'space' on the morning of the third day. The objection to the move is that it places the Pardoner's interruption of the Wife of Bath's Prologue, which is in a light-hearted vein, *after* his tale, which is not.

It will have become clear in this discussion that the unrevised and fragmentary state of the *Canterbury Tales* has proved no obstacle to those who want to complete Chaucer's scheme for him. The illusion of reality that he creates in the *Prologue* and links is so convincing that there is constant temptation to take the illusion for reality, and to embark on naturalistic interpretations of the fictional framework. This approach, a further extension of which produces the 'dramatic' view of the *Canterbury Tales*, which will be dealt with in a moment, must be treated with caution, because it can only end in ludicrous speculations about the physical details of the pilgrimage – how long the stories took, how they all managed to hear, strung out as they were along the road, what the Prioress thought of the *Miller's Tale* or, more temptingly, the Wife of Bath of the *Clerk's Tale*, and so on – the ignoring of the reality of artistic illusion in pursuit of the illusory reality of 'life'. It may be that Chaucer knew what he was doing, and that his carelessness with the frame and ordering was meant to inhibit just this kind of interpretation, to allow the pilgrimage to be taken for what it was worth but not to distract attention from the main business of story-telling.

However, the dramatic framework of the pilgrimage is still of great importance, and gave to Chaucer a number of clear advantages. First, it enabled him to assemble together, in a plausible way, a great diversity of characters, and a great diversity, therefore, of possible narrative material. In particular, it opened the way for the exploitation of 'low' realism in the fabliaux – and Chaucer, though his apologia for these tales in the *General Prologue* (I,725) is more than a little disingenuous, must have felt the need, in view of his reputation as 'Love's servant' and 'our noble philosophical poet' (Thomas Usk, *ca*.1387), of some 'dramatic' justification for telling such tales. They figure quite prominently in the *Tales*, contribute proportionately to the general character of the work, and two of them at least, those of the Miller and the Merchant, are amongst his most brilliant achievements.

Secondly, the pilgrimage was much more flexible as a framework, and much more capable of evolving in its own dramatic way, than other methods of grouping stories. Mostly, these depended on the imposition of some external and abstract scheme, such as that of the Seven Deadly Sins in Gower's *Confessio Amantis*, and Chaucer had already tried and abandoned this kind of scheme in the *Legend of Good Women*, which he found desperately boring. Boccaccio's setting for the *Decameron* – a group of young noblemen and ladies gathered in a villa near Florence to pass the time while plague rages in the city – is potentially more lively, but Boccaccio makes little of it. Chaucer, however, allows the pilgrims their head almost from the start, and gives us the strongest impression that things are happening naturally. In the drawing of lots, by a happy coincidence, the Knight is chosen to tell the first story, but when he has finished, and the Host, with the natural bourgeois deference to rank, turns to the Monk for the next tale, the Miller erupts into the smooth ordered world of the professional master of ceremonies and insists, though drunk, on telling his story. His tale, in turn, causes offence to the Reeve (Millers and Reeves were traditionally at enmity), who caps it with a bitterly vindictive tale against a miller. The Cook is thrown into ecstasies by this,

For joye him thoughte he clawed him on the bak (1,4326),

and begins a tale in the same vein, which remains tantalizingly incomplete, though rich in suggestion: it ends,

And hadde a wyf that heeld for contenance	*appearance*
A shoppe, and swyved for hir sustenance (1,4421–2).	*fornicated*

Such is fragment I, and the impression of dramatic reality is overwhelming. It should be added, however, that the drama of the pilgrimage is not the sole, nor even the main point, for Chaucer achieves something more through the juxtaposition of the tales themselves: the *Miller's Tale*, in its low way, offers a shrewd parody of the *Knight's Tale*, with some deliberate echoes of style (e.g. 1870 in 3747, 2779 in 3204), and the sharp contrasts in tone of the Miller's and Reeve's tales help us to appreciate the uniqueness of each.

Fragment VII is another sequence in which the sense of evolving drama, of the natural but unexpected, is strong. The Shipman's fabliau is followed by the Host's exquisitely courteous address to the Prioress, subjunctive tumbling over subjunctive, and the Prioress's pathetic and sentimental tale of the 'litel clergeon' murdered by the Jews. The Host looks around for some likely butt to relieve the emotional tension and his eye lights on Chaucer,

And seyde thus: 'What man artow?' quod he;
'Thou lookest as thou woldest fynde an hare,
For evere upon the ground I se thee stare' (VII, 695–7).

He recommends him to the company with more of this patronizing raillery, and urges him to tell a story. Chaucer only knows one tale, he admits nervously, 'a rym I lerned longe agoon', but the Host is pleased with his own quips, and pats him encouragingly on the back, with a broad wink at the rest:

'Ye, that is good', quod he; 'now shul we heere	
Som deyntee thyng, me thynketh by his cheere' (VII, 710–11).	*expression*

The tale is *Sir Thopas*, a ludicrously brilliant parody of the worst kind of popular tail-rhyme romance, and by the beginning of the second 'Fit' even the Host has got the message, and he breaks in, spluttering with exasperation,

'Namoore of this, for Goddes dignitee!' (VII, 919).

Chaucer is indignant, demanding to know why he, and not others, should be interrupted,

'Syn that it is the beste rym I kan?' (VII, 928).   *since/know*

The Host plainly declares his tale to be 'nat worth a toord', but gives him another chance, a tale in prose, perhaps, and Chaucer eagerly obliges with 'a litel thyng in prose', the *Melibeus*. The joke is in 'litel', for the *Melibeus* is long, but the joke ends there: it is solid didacticism, and taken quite straight. Some relief, however, is needed afterwards, and the Host, after some rueful references to his married life, turns to the Monk. He compliments him on his handsome and virile appearance, and expresses elaborate and witty regret that such fine stud stock should be wasted in the cloister. The Monk waits for the flood to subside, 'took al in pacience', and replies with unexpected but very proper dignity. He ignores the Host's jocularity and blandly offers 'a tale, or two, or thre', the life of St. Edward,

Or ellis, first, tragedies wol I telle,
Of whiche I have an hundred in my celle (VII, 1971–2).

Tragedy is defined with academic precision, its various forms specified, and the Monk begins his tale of the falls of princes. It is fairly mechanical stuff except for the tale of Ugolino, and it may be presumed that Chaucer was again adapting some material that he had worked over earlier; when he comes to the end of what he has, the Knight interrupts – an important interruption, because the *Knight's Tale* offers the rationale for human suffering and tragedy which the *Monk's Tale*, with its monotonous catalogue of misfortune, so signally lacks. The Knight speaks, therefore, because he is the only one with the moral authority to say that the Monk is not telling the complete truth; he speaks also – Chaucer is careful about this – because he has the authority of rank (it is the Knight again, we remember, who smooths over the row between the Host and the Pardoner). The Host seizes on the Knight's remarks, exaggerates them, declares that only the clinking of the bells on the Monk's bridle has kept him awake – another 'turn' on the famous ironical line in the *General Prologue* – and asks the Monk to try again, 'somwhat of huntyng'. The Monk is not to be drawn, and the Host, who prides himself on his diplomacy, vents his frustration 'with rude speche and boold' on the humble Nun's Priest, so far an unknown quantity. The tale that follows is the biggest surprise of all, but we will leave it for a moment.

Examples could be multiplied, outside these two fragments, of the dramatic evolution of the *Canterbury Tales* through the links: the argument of the Friar and the Summoner, two more traditional enemies, prepared for at the end of the Wife of Bath's Prologue and materializing after her tale in virulent attacks on each other; the Wife of Bath flirting with the Friar, and beginning her tale with a sly allusion to the amorousness of the profession (III, 881) which we may compare, if we like, with the hard look she would have given the Pardoner when he interrupted her Prologue with news of his plans for marriage; the Franklin interrupting the *Squire's Tale* with a bland flow of compliment, as if the *Tale* were ended, when he realizes that the Squire's ambitions are blossoming to a tedious epic; the sensational debut of the Canon's Yeoman and his master, hot from their pursuit of the pilgrims –

But it was joye for to seen hym swete! (VIII, 579);   *sweat*

the revealing exchanges between the Cook and the Manciple, when the latter, after expressing his fastidious disgust at the Cook's drunken state, is suddenly reminded by the Host that the Cook may take powerful revenge

As for to pynchen at thy rekenynges (IX, 74),   *find fault*

and so, in a display of unctuous civility, offers the Cook, in recompense, his own hip-flask. All this – and there is much more – is sufficient to enable us to say that the links in the *Canterbury Tales* are the finest quasi-dramatic writing in English outside Shakespeare, satisfying every demand that we may make for realism, humour, richness of character, vividness of drama and sharpness of observation.

It is tempting to go on from this to a thorough-going 'dramatic' reading of the *Canterbury Tales*, in which every tale is taken primarily as a display of its teller's character. This is the view long ago plausibly argued by Kittredge and still very strongly held in some quarters. It is a view, however, that one must reject, with perhaps two examples of its dangerous consequences. One, unimportant enough in itself, is the *Melibeus*, which is taken on this reading as Chaucer's joke at the Host's expense, an interminably dull and dreary moralistic allegory which is intended to bore him beyond belief because he interrupted *Thopas*, or at least to show up the lack of discrimination which allowed him to reject a brilliant parody in favour of such tedious stuff. But such 'boredom' is artistically very expensive; if such a view were true, Chaucer would have made a small dramatic point at colossal cost, and we must recognize here, as often elsewhere, a total break in the dramatic continuity of the frame. Chaucer turns from his comic exchanges with the Host to an introduction to his tale, on the moral value of literature, which is perfectly serious and straight-forward, and the Host's response at the end is not to the Tale as such but to his own personal experience as prompted (in most unsophisticated fashion) by the Tale. We have lost the taste for straight didacticism in literature, but Chaucer's audience hadn't, and it is better to recognize this than to distort the realities in the interests of a spurious 'dramatic' interest.

The *Clerk's Tale* is a more serious case, for it is intrinsically of much greater value. Kittredge, recognizing the difficulties that Chaucer had in the narrative, and altogether out of sympathy with the explicitly allegorical and didactic form of the Tale, explains it away as the Clerk's 'reply' to the Wife of Bath. Having listened in patience to the Wife's heretical views on sovereignty in marriage, which strike at the root of all hierarchical order, and particularly to her sneers at clerks (III, 707–10), the Clerk retorts with a patently exaggerated tale of wifely submission, the absurdities of which (in terms of realism) are the balance to the Wife's own absurdities. Now it is true that the Clerk, in the Epilogue and Envoy to his Tale, does refer explicitly to the Wife of Bath, ironically encouraging her and her sect to take no notice of Griselda's patience, and there is a temptation to read this back into the Tale. But the cost is again desperately high: the whole of the *Clerk's Tale*, with its high austerity of style and fascinating clash of exemplary and mimetic techniques, is jettisoned in favour of a moment of character-drama for which the text of the Tale itself offers no clue. We must therefore take the Epilogue, which directly contradicts the interpretation of the Tale as allegory that has just (IV, 1142–62) been given, as an example of the 'Gothic' separability of tale and frame. Chaucer juxtaposes the two, but makes no attempt at organic continuity.

The *Clerk's Tale* is part of what Kittredge calls the 'Marriage-Group', a term so universally accepted in Chaucer criticism that it is worth examining for a moment. The Wife of Bath, according to this interpretation, initiates a discussion of sovereignty in marriage which provides the theme of fragments III, IV and V. After the interlude of the Friar and the Summoner, the Clerk replies, and his Envoy is taken up by the Merchant, who tells a tale of woman's deceitfulness in marriage. The *Squire's Tale* provides another interlude, and the discussion is resolved by the Franklin, who, in his opening description of the marriage of Arviragus and Dorigen, suggests that a compromise is possible, that Arviragus can be both

Servant in love, and lord in mariage (V, 793).

It is true that there are explicit references to the Wife of Bath in the Clerk's Epilogue and in the *Merchant's Tale* (from a character in the story, no less), and to the doctrine of marital sovereignty in the *Franklin's Tale*, and one can assume therefore that Chaucer wanted us to remember her. But to say more than this, to say that the four tales constitute the 'marriage-act of the human comedy' and focus on the question of 'maistrie', is to substitute accidentals for essentials. Both the *Merchant's Tale* and the *Franklin's Tale* are far more than episodes in a debate. There is linking allusion, therefore, but no theme.

However, these are the weakest links in the case for a dramatic reading of the *Tales*. There are other tales where the case is strong, indeed incontrovertible, namely those of the Wife of Bath, the Pardoner and the Canon's Yeoman, but it will readily be seen that these three constitute a distinct category, in that all have extended quasi-autobiographical prologues. In the Wife of Bath, for instance, dramatic realization of character is the dominant concern, and the Tale is almost completely absorbed into the richness of Chaucer's comic creation in the Prologue. Chaucer perhaps began with the notion of giving a new twist to the familiar anti-feminist material (of which the Prologue is an anthology) by placing it all in the mouth of a woman. The Prologue offers us a complexly-layered experience, in which we have not only the rich comedy of the Wife turning the Bible inside-out to prove her case for multiple marriages – which she soon abandons for the safer defensive position of marriage itself – but the richer prospect still of the Wife citing all the old anti-feminist arguments in a report of what she says her feeble old husbands would have said if they had had the nerve. New wine in old bottles indeed! But the many-faceted trickery gives way gradually, as she moves from polemics to reminiscence, to a deepening exploration of her nature. The crude combativeness, the desire to assert financial and sexual supremacy, comes to seem the weapon with which she fights the world on its own crude terms, and Chaucer suggests beneath it a touch of pathos, even of perverse fortitude:

The flour is goon, ther is namoore to telle;   *gone*
The bren, as I best kan, now moste I selle (III, 477–8).   *bran*

She has the infinite riches of a Hamlet or a Falstaff, not a 'character' exactly, but, as Robertson puts it, 'an elaborate iconographic figure designed to show the manifold implications of an attitude'. Her Tale is comparatively insignificant beside her Prologue, and bears to it the formal relation of exemplum to text. She proves her case for woman's sovereignty to her own satisfaction, and the Tale is skilfully manipulated to that end, but it lacks the tempting depths of the Prologue. It cannot be said to tell us much more about the Wife of Bath, and one would be wary of pseudo-psychological interpretations which see the transformation of the old hag into a beautiful young woman, for instance, as sublimated fantasy-fulfilment. It is, quite simply, a proof of her case.

With the Pardoner, again, Chaucer takes the opportunity for an extended display of character in verbal action. The stimulus once more is a literary one – the figure of Faux-Semblant, or Hypocrisy, in the *Roman de la Rose* – but Chaucer goes far beyond the traditional portrait. The Pardoner's egregious vanity and sensational skills are obvious: what is less obvious is the irony in which his exhibitionist ill-doing has trapped him, the fretful sense that he may be doing good against his own worser nature (VI, 430–4). His voice rises shrilly, and the homily which precedes his Tale has an edge of violence which reminds us who is speaking. The Tale itself is seemingly self-contained, and by the end of it Chaucer seems to have forgotten what preceded it, for the Pardoner addresses the pilgrims, and casts for their custom, in terms that suggest he has never opened his bag of tricks to them. Any number of 'psychological' explanations will do for this – he is covering up his supposed 'moment of truth' (915–18, the conventional benediction), he is carried away by his own Tale, and so on – but the real answer is probably a simple one, namely, that Chaucer is not worried by inconsistencies between tale and frame. The Tale itself is again formally related to the Pardoner as an exemplum of his main theme, *Radix malorum est cupiditas*, and as such it is brilliantly told, with such artful ease that it almost seems to be telling itself. The pressure of the Pardoner's character is felt behind it, though, in a way that the Wife of Bath's is not in her Tale; we can hardly forget the irony of the situation, which the Pardoner has himself underlined for us, and the contrast between the sinister inevitability of sin and retribution in the Tale and the total atrophy of moral sensibility in the teller. The sense of character is strong enough to make us think of the Old Man, cast out to wander the earth for ever,

Thus walke I, lyk a restelees kaityf,	*prisoner*
And on the ground, which is my moodres gate,	*mother's*
I knokke with my staf, bothe erly and late,	
And seye 'Leeve mooder, leet me in! . . .' (VI, 728–31)	*dear/let*

as the embodiment of the Pardoner's own outcast state.

The Canon's Yeoman is less well-known than the Wife of Bath or Pardoner, partly because the subject matter of his Prologue and Tale, alchemy, is dated, but Chaucer sustains a strong current of dramatic interest in the Yeoman's shifting attitudes to his profession. He begins in ambiguity, happy to trade on the glamour and mystery of alchemy and expressing ironically guarded admiration for his master. Gradually, under the stimulus of the Host's enquiries, he begins to unbutton, conveying as he does so both the frustrations of constant failure and some sense of the hope and optimism that drive men on:

As usage is, lat swepe the floor as swithe,   *quickly*
Plukke up youre hertes, and beeth glad and blithe (VIII, 936–7).

In the first part of his Tale, when he is describing his master's unsuccessful experiments, he is pathetically eager to show off his knowledge, but only succeeds in submerging himself in a chaos of names. In the second part, where he exposes some of the frauds of the profession, the high moral tone is suspect: he still sounds as if he is trying to convince himself. At the end, there is a characteristic switch of tone, and a more authoritative voice takes over to condemn, finally, the false alchemy which attempts to pervert God's purposes.

These three, then, come close to being dramatic monologues, with the Tale subordinated to our interest in the character of the teller. But it would be hard to go beyond this. It may be thought that the *General Prologue* itself is a good argument for a sustained 'dramatic' reading of the *Tales*, but the appropriateness of tale to teller, as described in the *Prologue*, is usually general, not specific. Sometimes, traits developed at length in the *General Prologue* are hardly referred to in the pilgrim's tale (such as the Wife of Bath's pilgrimages, or the Knight's crusading chivalry); sometimes, one feature of a quite complex portrait is picked out for exclusive emphasis in the tale (such as the Prioress's sentimentality over little, helpless things); sometimes, especially in the case of the sketchier portraits, such as those of the Man of Law and the Merchant, the relationship is more or less arbitrary. There are no contradictions, but on the other hand there are very few cases of complex organic continuity between portrait and tale: perhaps the Pardoner and the Reeve would be the best examples.

Attention to the *General Prologue* as a list of *dramatis personae* may distract us from its own self-contained artistic coherence as a type-analysis of society. Chaucer has here achieved the impossible: he sustains our interest in the pilgrims as individuals and at the same time works out through them a paradigm of moral evaluation. The realism is easy to respond to – some of the pilgrims, indeed, are real people (the Host and the Cook), though it is unprofitable to pursue Manly in his further speculations about the real identity of such as the Shipman and the Man of Law. It is the very authenticity of Chaucer's realistic art that tempts us to do so, the density of detail in portraits like those of the Pardoner and the Summoner, or the total conviction that is carried by precise detail of name and place. The only reason, it seems, for telling us that the Reeve came from Baldeswelle is that that is where he came from, and the only reason for withholding the Merchant's name must be that Chaucer didn't know it. Chaucer recognizes too the authenticating effect of arbitrary collocation of detail, such as the Cook's 'mormal'. But behind the vivid immediacy of realistic individuality there is at work a subtle and discriminating moral judgment. Often is it loaded into apparently innocent detail, like the Knight's 'bismotered habergeon' or the Reeve's 'dokked' top, like a tonsure; often too it is transmitted to us through irony – the Prioress's brooch, the Monk's bridle-bell. Chaucer makes particular use of the fallible narrator-*persona* to underline some of these ironies. He speaks, though not consistently, as if he were a naïve and simple-minded observer, meeting the pilgrims for the first time, full of 'wide-eyed wonder at the glamour of the great world', as Donaldson puts it. He is as impressed with the Monk as the Monk himself is, not sensing the complete condemnation that he is expressing through his enthusiastic agreement – 'And I seyde his opinion was good'. His joke about the Clerk,

But al be that he was a philosophre,
Yet hadde he but litel gold in cofre (I, 297–8),

is the usual complacent bourgeois joke about the 'unrealism' of scholarship. There are also other more pervasive techniques of moral commentary: three portraits of total moral idealizations, the Knight, the Parson and the Plowman, are strategically placed to present to us touchstones for each of the traditional three estates of society. The arrangement of the whole, though Chaucer does his best to make it look haphazard, is systematic, working from the landed gentry, through the upper clergy, upper professional classes, lower bourgeoisie, lower clergy and peasantry, to the last group, where Chaucer isolates the Miller, Reeve, Manciple, Summoner and Pardoner (and himself), as if aware that they represent in its most virulent form the parasitism of the new money-economy. Within this overall pattern, particular sequences are morally significant: Knight-Squire-Yeoman, for instance, sifting through the reality of chivalric idealism until only a handful of peacock-feathers is left; the steady descent from the Prioress, through the Monk, to the Friar; the sandwiching of the Clerk's austere integrity between those two wind-bags, the Merchant and the Man of Law; the secular recognition of the Parson's ideals in his brother, the Plowman. The *General Prologue* is a continual marvel, but a marvel in its own right.

What we may say about the tales and their dramatic relation is that Chaucer found in them the 'indirection' that he had always sought. His creation of a narrative *persona* in the love-visions and in the *Troilus* was a mark of his need for a flexible point of view in narrative, a stance or posture in which he was not committed in advance to particular attitudes. The characteristic of all his narratives is their multi-levelled complexity, the sense we have that Chaucer himself is always just beyond our grasp, and the *Canterbury Tales* provided the perfect vehicle for this dramatic indirection. Whoever is telling the tales, we can be sure that it is not Chaucer. In this way, Chaucer gained for himself the freedom of manoeuvre which he needed in order to experiment with confidence. One does not have to say, therefore, that a tale like that of the Miller has as its major function the illustration of the Miller's character. It is appropriate to him in a general way as a fabliau, and in a more specific way because of its gusto, but the sense of his character operates only on a limited level, and is transcended in the brilliance of the telling. He merely provides the opportunity for the exercise, a 'flawed frame' within which Chaucer can choose directions and manipulate response in a much more subtle and complex fashion than if he were writing from a 'fixed' point of view.

Variety, drama, indirection – these are three functions of the pilgrimage-frame as we have described it. There may be another, in the contribution that the pilgrimage makes to the overall unity of the *Canterbury Tales*. A pilgrimage, though it was often simply an excuse for a holiday, still retained its powerful spiritual significance. The profane and the sacred were inextricably mixed, as they are in Christmas now. Chaucer recognizes this in the very opening of the *General Prologue*, where the call of Nature, of spring's renewal, evokes the desire to go on pilgrimage, and the *Prologue* plays continually on our awareness of this duality of impulse. The theme of the pilgrimage is taken up again at the end, in the Parson's Prologue, where the Parson makes explicit the figural relation of the physical pilgrimage to the spiritual pilgrimage of man's life:

And Jhesu, for his grace, wit me sende	
To shewe yow the wey, in this viage,	*journey*
Of thilke parfit glorious pilgrymage	*that perfect*
That highte Jerusalem celestial (X, 48–51).	*is called*

The Parson deliberately displaces the Host as leader, and his proposal to 'telle a myrie tale in prose' introduces the sermon on Penitence and the Seven Deadly Sins with which the *Canterbury Tales* end. It is possible to see the *Parson's Tale* as a schematic moral commentary on all that has passed before – possible, for instance, to see 'individuated' detail of the Wife of Bath's behaviour at offertory or her views on 'maistrie' reappearing here in its more traditional context (X, 407,927). But if it is commentary, it is on a different level from that of the *Tales*, and the transition from the Parson's Prologue to his Tale is yet another abrupt discontinuity in the frame. The Tale in fact is perfectly isolated from the rest; its reference is to life not literature, and Chaucer's own personal act of penitence which follows it, the Retraction, in which he recants all his 'translacions and enditynges of worldly vanitees', is relevant only to the man, not his art. He was willing to see this stand at the end of the *Tales*, since life is, after all, a serious business, but there is no sense in which the *Parson's Tale* or the Retraction can work retrospectively on our reading of the *Tales* as a whole. As far as unity is concerned, it can be said that Chaucer, like Marlowe in Dr. Faustus, paid a good deal of attention to the beginning, and a good deal of attention, of a somewhat different kind, to the end, but the middle is mostly left to shift for itself.

If, then, Chaucer found in the framework of the *Canterbury Tales* a freedom which he had achieved only imperfectly elsewhere, we may legitimately ask, freedom to do what? The answer, I think, briefly, is freedom to explore the potentialities of narrative as a self-consistent and self-justifying literary form, and it is a freedom which makes of the *Canterbury Tales* a series of forays into the borderland of the exemplary and the mimetic. Chaucer had, handed down to him, a number of narrative types – fable, fabliau, exemplum, saint's legend, romance – which had one thing in common, that they all depended for their *sense* on some external and received values. Narrative is always therefore conceived of as illustration or demonstration of some truth already known to be true,

whether it be of an elevating or degrading kind. Chaucer's endeavour is to release narrative from this external pressure, and to
allow it a significance of its own which grows out of its own mimetic
nature as 'story'. Not all the Tales attempt to do this, and not all that
do, succeed, but it is the controlling pattern of his artistic development, and the bending of the material to this will is the fascination
of watching him at work.

If we take first the genre of pious tale and saint's legend, it is easy
to see that the external pressures are strong. In the *Second Nun's
Tale* of St. Cecilia and in the *Physician's Tale* of Appius and Virginia
he makes no attempt to resist them. The former is an orthodox
saint's life, distinguished only by its superior literary expression
from a thousand such legends, and the latter an exemplum of
virginity in which, as is usual in such tales, the moral imperative to
one kind of virtuous action deliberately defies all other kinds of
'natural' expectation: a father kills his daughter to preserve her
chastity. Chaucer exploits the predictable pathos, but no more, and
the allocation of the tale to the Physician is oddly arbitrary. Chaucer
could not long be content with such stereotyped patterns (the
Second Nun's Tale is in fact an earlier work), and two further tales,
those of the Man of Law and the Prioress, explore further possibilities in the genre. The *Man of Law's Tale* is preceded by an
exchange between the Host and the Man of Law, in which the latter
is made to appear a wonderfully obtuse and complacent critic of
literature. He speaks airily of Chaucer, complaining

> That Chaucer, thogh he kan but lewedly   *unlearnedly*
> On metres and on rymyng craftily (II, 47–8),

has used up all the best stories:

> And if he have noght seyd hem, leve brother,
> In o book, he hath seyd hem in another (II, 51–2).

He refers to the *Legend of Good Women*, mentioning some tales that
Chaucer did write, and some others that he didn't, as if his
knowledge of the work extended only to the proposals in the
Prologue – like a good reviewer, he knows how to make a little go a
long way ('And yet he semed bisier than he was') – and then
congratulates Chaucer at least on avoiding the incestuous filth of
stories like those of Canacee and Apollonius. It may be assumed
that he is referring to Gower, who told both stories in the *Confessio
Amantis*, though with a humanity and decorum which belies the
Man of Law's prurient outrage. The dramatic self-portrayal here is

quite superb, but this lively sense of character does not, and must not be allowed to, carry over into the Tale. The tone of the Tale is lofty and rhetorical. The misfortunes of the exiled Constance are surrounded with an elaborate apparatus of apostrophe, denunciation, prophecy, allusion and sententious digression which is so little to modern taste that some critics have assumed that it is meant to sound bombastic and strained, as if the Man of Law were shouting to disguise the hollowness of his feelings. This will not do; we must accept the taste for a highly coloured rhetorical style, and recognize the Tale for what it is, a superbly controlled and organized exercise in rhetorical amplification, and recognize too that it is rooted in a profound orthodoxy of belief. The 'digressions' return again and again to two points: the power of the stars, the inevitability of Fate, and in particular the ominous foreboding of Constance's horoscope; and against this the elaborate allusion to God's dark ways with His chosen. A powerful sense of surrounding darkness and impending doom is built up, in which Constance's faith is almost eclipsed, but not quite:

God liste to shewe his wonderful myracle   *is pleased*
In hire, for we sholde seen his myghty werkis (II, 477–8).

This is the central purpose of all hagiography, and the elaborately developed manner of the Tale should not disguise from us its essential simplicity of theme.

The *Prioress's Tale* has suffered a similar fate at the hands of 'dramatic' interpreters, who see behind the simple pathos of this tale of a little Christian boy murdered by the Jews and resurrected miraculously because of his faith in the Virgin, a bigoted anti-Semitic violence on the part of the teller which throws her charm and sentimentality into sharp relief. Again, this view is lamentably unhistorical, and totally ignores the nature of the genre, with its sharp distinction of black and white, good and bad, in which the Jews are inevitably cast in the role of villains. There is a promptness of judgment and condemnation in the *Prioress's Tale* which has little to do with 'tolerance', but it reflects on the genre, not on the Prioress's character, and it would destroy the Tale to suppose otherwise. There is a level of dramatic significance, but it has nothing to do with anti-Semitism. It is, fairly obviously, in the pathetic handling of the narrative, the repeated emphasis on 'litel', the pretty pathos in the detail of the 'litel clergeon' who learns the antiphon *Alma Redemptoris* even though he does not understand the words, and even though he will be beaten for not knowing his

Primer. This sentimental treatment, though, does not impose any limitations on the effectiveness of the legend, for infant martyrdoms are morally watertight.

Such is not the case with the *Clerk's Tale*, where two techniques of narrative, the allegorical and the naturalistic, collide, and provide us with a teasing problem in interpretation. The story of Griselda, of the patient wife who is tested by her husband by having her children torn from her and by then being cast out in favour of a younger bride, is from folk-tale, and it has the violent reversals and total neglect of human probability that we expect in the form. Chaucer took his version from Petrarch, who had re-embedded the folk-tale in an understandable moral context by making it an exemplum of one virtue, patience, carried to its ultimate inhuman extreme. The story was still meaningless in human terms, but meaningful in its allegorical enactment of a human situation, Griselda representing the patience that all must show in adversity. Petrarch made sense of the given *matiere*, therefore, by imposing upon it his own *sens*. Chaucer takes this over with the narrative, and preserves the allegorical frame, with especial care at the end to warn against a naturalistic interpretation:

This storie is seyd, nat for that wyves sholde
Folwen Grisilde as in humylitee,
For it were inportable, though they wolde;
But for that every wight, in his degree,
Sholde be constant in adversitee
As was Grisilde (IV, 1142–7).

But he tells the actual story in the way his imagination prompts him to, that is, by responding to it and interpreting it in terms of humane values, and in so doing sets up an irreconcilable opposition between the two levels of the narrative. If Griselda is an emblem of patience, then each touch of individuated human pathos in his sympathetic portrayal of Griselda – the poignant self-pity of

I have noght had no part of children tweyne
But first siknesse, and after, wo and peyne (IV, 650–1),

or the sudden bitterness of remembrance in

O goode God! how gentil and how kynde
Ye semed by youre speche and youre visage
The day that maked was oure mariage! (IV, 852–4),

or the wry self-awareness of her warning to Walter not to treat his new bride as he has treated her (1037) – will only remind us what she is suffering as a *person*, and that, as Chaucer says, is 'inportable'. These touches are all added by Chaucer to Petrarch, and though they come in a context which is heavy with scriptural allusion and in which for the most part Griselda behaves with an impeccably allegorical sense of what is expected of her, they have an effect in our reading out of all proportion to their bulk. Similarly, if Walter is allegorical of God, then each time Chaucer provides him with motives, as he does, frequently, he is undercutting the allegory and attributing to God precisely the wantonness in testing his creatures which he explicitly denies at the end (1153). The needs of the story are thus in conflict with Chaucer's imaginative needs as a writer, and the pressure of humanization seeks out the inhumanity of the story, so that one can neither take it on the level on which it would be understandable (Petrarch's) nor accept it in terms of its partial realization of other values.

At the same time, it must be said that there is genuine creative power at work here, as there is not in the other legends, a genuine struggle with intractable material, which leaves us in a state of fruitful imaginative disturbance. Chaucer makes us richly aware of *all* the possibilities of the narrative, and there is a possible reading, fragilely poised though it may be, in which one can accept Griselda's occasional quizzical self-awareness as being indicative of a real and profound self-awareness. In other words, she suffers because she knows that she is being improperly tested, because she chooses to suffer as the only way of fulfilling her vow of obedience. This voluntary offering up of the will is allegorically much more powerful than the dog-like submission of the analogues, and it also seals the poem's human integrity.

If we turn now to another genre, the romance, we find a similar process of experimentation and development. One tale, that of the Squire, is a complete misfire, being soon deflected from its grand ambitions into the trivia of Canacee's conversation with the love-sick falcon, and finally running into the sands. I suspect that Chaucer began it with the best will in the world, interested to see what he could make of the genre of high romance, with its remote courtly setting and magical paraphernalia, but soon tired of it. He found it offered no sustenance to his kind of imagination, and so he made the best of a bad job by intruding a sense of the Squire's incompetence, not his own, into the narrative, thus preparing for the Franklin's marvellously well-timed interruption. He took his revenge on the form in *Sir Thopas*, where he pins down with excruciating delicacy the inanities of minstrel-romance. Everything is here – the hero riding forth in search of adventures, his love for a faery mistress, his encounter with a giant, as well as a feast, an arming and a *locus amoenus* – but everything is *wrong*. Thopas is the wrong name (Topaz, a girl's name), and Poperynghe, in Flanders ('in fer contree'), certainly the wrong place to come from. The hero's white skin is compared to 'payndemayn', his beard to 'saffroun', as if all the author's imagery were drawn from the shelves of a grocer's store. All the girls love him and lie awake dreaming of him,

Whan hem were bet to slepe (VII, 744).   *it were better for them*

The landscape through which he rides is full of the wrong flora and fauna – parrots, liquorice, nutmeg – and when he gets to the 'contree of Fairye' no-one dares attack him,

Neither wyf ne childe (VII, 806).

It is only right that our hero, when he meets his giant adversary, Sir Olifaunt, should make off, with dire threats of what he will do tomorrow when he has his armour. Everything about this parody is perfect and precise, right down to the bad rhymes and the elaborately indecent play on the favourite romance-word, 'prikyng'.

Both these tales, the misfire and the squib, are original as far as narrative goes. Chaucer was prepared to take the form more seriously when it came to him through Boccaccio, as it does in the *Franklin's Tale* and the *Knight's Tale*, the former from the *Decameron*, the latter from the *Teseida*. The *Franklin's Tale* is beautifully contrived: developing towards much the same conflict of values as the *Clerk's Tale*, the direction of the Tale is deftly switched by Chaucer so that the poem ends in perfect poise. The problem is again that of investing a fairy-tale, that of the rash promise redeemed, with humane significance, and Chaucer does so by turning it into tragi-comedy. The first part is profoundly human and moving: the picture of the marriage of Arviragus and Dorigen, the questioning of providence and the purpose of evil in Dorigen's prayer, the delightful ambiguity of Dorigen's nature, as in her response to Aurelius's declaration of love, as well as many incidental felicities such as the portrayal of the 'magician' – are all serious dramatic realization in Chaucer's maturest manner. Somewhere, however, the seriousness evaporates, and the Tale ends in playful questioning as to who was the most generous – Arviragus, in allowing Dorigen to keep her promise, Aurelius, in giving up his claim to her, or the clerk, in cancelling the debt. The clue to the transition is in Dorigen's 'complaint', a long list of women unfortunate in love which, with its obvious formality and dramatic incongruity, it is easy to take as an excrescence on the Tale, a typical bit of medieval encyclopedism. It is better, however, to trust one's first response, which is that the complaint is faintly comic, for what it does, without destroying Dorigen as a character, is to detach us from her plight by playing upon our sense of her as an operatic or melodramatic heroine. It is impossible to take her completely seriously after this, and we are thus prepared for the change of tone. Arviragus has still to demonstrate for us the inviolability of principle, but once he has gritted his teeth on it,

Trouthe is the hyeste thyng that man may kepe (V, 1479),

the story moves into its own realm of truth, assisted by the narrator's sage winks to the audience:

Paraventure an heep of yow, ywis,
Wol holden hym a lewed man in this
That he wol putte his wyf in jupartie.
Herkneth the tale er ye upon hire crie.
She may have bettre fortune than yow semeth;
And whan that ye han herd the tale, demeth (V, 1493–8).

Henry James would not have liked this solution, but Henry James didn't have to face Chaucer's problem of shaping intractable *matiere*. What Chaucer manages to do is to detach us from the illusion of the story without destroying the truth at the heart of the story – that 'trouthe' or moral integrity is a man's whole being – and it is this delicacy of disengagement that makes the *Franklin's Tale* perfectly satisfying.

The *Knight's Tale* is more orthodox in approach, employing for its resolution of the story's human conflict and suffering the technique of transcendental shift. Theseus's speech at the end of the Tale rises above the misfortunes of the characters to the Boethian vision of God's controlling providence, and the wisdom of making 'vertu of necessitee'. It is possible to see the *Knight's Tale* as a fully Boethian poem, a story of men giving up their reason to passion and thus falling under the arbitrary sway of Fortune. Theseus, in this reading, plays the part of the man above Fortune, the arbiter of order, whose sarcasm at the lovers' expense (I, 1806) does not contradict his humane understanding of their condition, and who has an equal eye for justice and mercy. Chaucer, by his many changes in the story he has taken from Boccaccio's *Teseida*, shows a dominant interest in destinal influences and in concepts of cosmic order and justice. It is Chaucer who enriches the narrative with allusions to Providence and invocations to Fortune, who invests the pagan deities of Boccaccio – Mars, Venus, Diana, Saturn – with the real power of their planetary namesakes, and who gives therefore a strong philosophical content to the description of the oratories and to the prayers of Palamon, Arcite and Emelye before their patron-deities. In discarding Boccaccio's epic paraphernalia, he preserves the ceremony, formality and nobility of the high romantic mode, and infuses into it an undercurrent of philosophical questioning which demands and receives its answer in Theseus's final speech, and in his own person as the representative of hierarchical order.

This may explain what Chaucer was trying to do in the *Knight's Tale*, to write a 'Boethian romance', but it does not quite describe what he does. The Tale is inexhaustibly rich, but its riches are diverse, and there is an instability of tone which suggests that Chaucer's plans did not always meet with his own imaginative approval. There are moments of levity which are strangely at odds with their context and the flippancy of tone after Arcite's moving death-speech is maladroit. One can see that Chaucer is trying to readjust a balance, that Arcite's death, if it is handled with too generous a sympathy, will make a philosophical resolution impossible, but the method of adjustment is awkward. It is as if Chaucer were tuning an instrument, making a series of minute adjustments in tone to achieve the right balance – but allowing us to see him doing so. Later, the chequered complexity of events and our response to them was to be matched by an equal complexity of narrative technique in which all could be contained and controlled, but the *Knight's Tale* is an early work (about 1382), and Chaucer is still mastering the instrument. As a result, the images of disruption which the narrative contains, and must contain if the philosophical explanation is to be at all convincing, break out of their context and disturb us as realities. Palamon and Arcite may be 'wrong' to complain against Fortune, but a more compelling art is at the service of their wrongness than Theseus's rightness. The description of the planetary infortunes of Mars and Saturn,

The nayl ydryven in the shode a-nyght,   *head*
The colde deeth, with mouth gapyng upright (I, 2007–8),

is apt to the philosophical theme, but it violates literary decorum, and seems wantonly to extend the scale of suffering in the Tale. The temples of Venus, Mars, even of Diana, are dark with images of gloom and pain –

A wolf ther stood biforn hym at his feet
With eyen rede, and of a man he eet (I, 2047–8) –

so that we seem to see only the shadowed side of love and chivalry.
Theseus has an answer, but it cannot completely still the dis-
turbances aroused by the Tale. His scheme is good, but when he
comes down to cases, the consolation he offers to those who mourn
for Arcite is hollow beside the memory of Arcite's own words:

What is this world? what asketh men to have?
Now with his love, now in his colde grave
Allone, withouten any compaignye (I, 2777–9).

The *Knight's Tale* is imperfect, therefore, especially beside the
Troilus, where Chaucer was to grasp what here he can only reach
for, but its flawed structure does not disguise the lavish exuberance
of its parts. The grandeur of its set-piece writing, in description and
invocation particularly, was never to be equalled again by Chaucer.

The fable was another narrative genre to which Chaucer would
have come very naturally. Like any other schoolboy of his day, he
would have made his first halting steps in Latin with Aesop's *Fables*,
and there was no other type of tale in which the application of the
external 'moral' was so obvious and insistent. It was perhaps this
that persuaded him to make his work in the genre, the *Manciple's
Tale* and the *Nun's Priest's Tale*, so uncompromisingly critical of the
assumptions of exemplum-narrative. The *Manciple's Tale*, for which
we have already seen provided a very dubious dramatic context, is a
clear parody of the form. The tale of the crow who talked too much,
an old *pourquoi*, is made to illustrate a queasy kind of expediency
which seems to suit the Manciple very well, and the literary pre-
tences of the teller finally collapse in the barrage of commonplaces
with which the Tale ends. The advice itself is of unimpeachable
authority, much of it from the ever-popular *Distichs* of Cato, but it is
undercut by its dramatic placing and by the ludicrously insistent
repetition of 'My sone'. It is a good example of the economy of
Chaucer's satiric method; the material is entirely self-consistent,
like the traditional anti-feminist material of the Wife of Bath's
Prologue, and the comic ironies are released simply by new
juxtapositions and angles of view. It is an unfolding into narrative of
the technique of irony by collocation used in the description of the
General Prologue.

The *Nun Priest's Tale* is on a far grander scale, but it is similar in
the way it explodes fable into new and richer kinds of significance.
Some of the interest, in this elaborately digressive and allusive

handling of the fable of the Cock and the Fox, is simple burlesque – the sharp switch from the human to the animal, for instance, after Chauntecleer's lofty discourse on dreams:

And with that word he fley doun fro the beem (VII, 3172).

But there is more to it than that. Nearly half the Tale is taken up with the discussion of dreams, and this in itself is an epitome of the Tale in the way it is enveloped in an elaborate apparatus of moral and philosophical comment. Pertelot can speak on homely and womanly things like digestion and laxatives, but it is Chauntecleer who demonstrates the full range and power of the human mind in action – arguing, persuading, preaching, producing authority upon authority, quoting chapter and verse impromptu (3065), chuckling over an academic in-joke (3164), narrating exempla with superb panache – and then takes no notice at all of anything that he has said. The Tale itself is given the same treatment: Fortune is invoked at crucial moments, and the moral generalized with exquisite melancholy (3205). The narrator toys with the subject of predestination, and touches on the Fall,

Wommennes conseils been ful ofte colde;
Wommannes conseil broghte us first to wo,
And made Adam fro Paradys to go (VII, 3256–8),

but withdraws hastily, muttering in embarrassed fashion

Thise been the cokkes wordes, and nat myne (VII, 3265)

(which they are not). He annotates continually as he goes, referring his audience to the Latin bestiary, *Physiologus*, for a discussion of sirens (3271), and to the general law of contraries in nature (3279). Even the Fox has read Boethius, whose treatise on music he refers to, and the tale of Daun Burnel the Ass by Nigel Wireker. The catastrophe is introduced with a discourse on flatterers, and accompanied by elaborately mounting apostrophes to destiny, to Venus and to Gaufred for his elegy on Richard I (who also died on a Friday). Troy, Carthage and Rome are burnt in passing, and the hue and cry after the Fox produces an allusion even more remarkable for Chaucer – to Jack Straw and the Peasants' Revolt.

At the end the audience collects its scattered wits and prepares, dutifully, for the moral. But there is not *one*, but a whole handful of morals: the Cock has one, the Fox has one, the Nun's Priest has two or three, and finally he exhorts us:

But ye that holden this tale a folye,
As of a fox, or of a cok and hen,
Taketh the moralite, goode men (VII, 3438–40).

The multiplication of morals makes fun of the very idea that the bewildering riches of the Tale can be concentrated into any simple formula, and forces us back into the Tale itself, for it is there, and there only, in the texture of the narrative, that the *moralite* is embodied. It is not the content of the Tale that is so important, and interpretations which read it as an allegory of the Fall, or of the pernicious influence of the friars on the secular clergy, or of the temptations of the devil-heretic to the Christian, react to only part of its meaning. It is in some sense an allegory, an allegory of man in his condition – threatened, luckless, arrogant, absurd – but the literal level survives its own interpretation, partly in the portrayal of Chauntecleer, who is a splendid creature for all his ridiculousness, but more in the style, which enacts the workings of the trained mind for us to wonder at and deplore. The embodiment of the 'meaning' of the Tale in its manner is Chaucer's most sophisticated development from exemplum-type narrative, and he creates through it a kind of comedy so comprehensive as to make nonsense of accusations that he lacks 'seriousness'.

We come finally to the fabliaux, which contain some of Chaucer's maturest work. The basis of the form is simple: the middle-aged bourgeois husband is duped, and his wife 'swyved' by some young errant representative of the classless intellectual elite – a scholar, cleric, or perhaps a young squire. The setting is low, and so is the behaviour, but the appeal is obviously sophisticated, to the same audience, in fact, that would appreciate high romance: a bourgeois audience would swiftly tire of seeing themselves so consistently outwitted. Cleverness, smartness, cunning, is everything in the fabliaux: the hero is the one who knows most tricks, and ordinary morality is irrelevant. The form has its own conventions, one being that lust is universal and insatiable amongst young men, and is fixed in a stereotype of externally received values as firmly as the other genres we have been discussing. The difference is that the values here are reversed: romance proclaims the possibility that men can rise above themselves to individual acts of super-humanity; fabliau proclaims the certainty that men will always behave like animals. Both are 'ideals', and both have the satisfactorily tenuous connexion with real life which makes them suitable for the primary kind of 'externalized' narrative. The *Shipman's Tale* displays the form in its purest state. Merchant, wife and monk perform a brief series of manoeuvres in which monk outwits wife, wife outwits husband in turn, and in which the equation of sexual gratification with monetary reward is taken for granted by all. The marital pillow-scene at the end completes the equation with mathematical precision, where the wife offers herself to her husband on exactly the same terms as to the monk (it is the same sum of money involved), and the husband accepts,

For he was riche and cleerly out of dette (VII, 376).

There are several scenes of compelling authenticity, such as that between the wife and monk in the garden, but not a ripple disturbs the emotional surface, and the conduct of the narrative is brilliantly cold and detached. There is a fabliau-type 'moral' – be generous to your wife or she will be generous with herself – but the ending of the Tale really only asks for a *Quod erat demonstrandum*.

The *Miller's Tale* is more complex, both in structure and tone. Here there are two 'lovers', the student Nicholas and the parish-clerk Absolon, competing for the favours of the pretty *bourgeoise*, and two sub-plots which finally merge in Nicholas's climactic cry

'Help! water! water! help, for Goddes herte!' (I, 3815).

The interweaving of these sub-plots, and the anticipation of the needs of the story in the account of Nicholas's interest in astrology, or the carpenter's complacency, or tiny things like the height of the window in the bedroom (3696), are object-lessons in virtuoso narration. There is much more richness in the portraiture than in the *Shipman's Tale*, and a suggestion of crude morality in the Miller's argument that jealous old husbands deserve everything they get, and in the rough justice of his conclusion:

Thus swyved was this carpenteris wyf,
For al his kepyng and his jalousye;
And Absolon hath kist hir nether ye;   eye
And Nicholas is scalded in the towte (I, 3850–3).   buttocks

But it is the Miller's morality, and of a piece with his suggestion in the Prologue that husbands ought not to worry too much what their wives get up to in their spare time:

So he may fynde Goddes foyson there,   plenty
Of the remenant nedeth nat enquere (I, 3165–6).

These remarks give the Tale a rather more visible frame than the Shipman's, but it is only a frame, and our awareness of the teller does not carry over into the body of the narrative. The Miller's morality is a red herring, a mere aspect of the overall moral control exerted by the nature of the genre: it is as much a trap for the unwary as the open invitation to be seduced by the animal delight-fulness of the description of Alysoun. Chaucer enjoys these elusive games, but in all its essentials the *Miller's Tale* is an orthodox fabliau. It is the brilliance of the handling that makes it unfor-gettable, above all what Muscatine calls its 'overpowering sub-stantiality'. Every detail is precisely realized, whether it is necessary to the narrative, like the hole for the cat in Nicholas's door, or for the satire, like the 'Poules wyndow' carved in Absolon's shoes. The receding background of the narrative is sketched in in a few strokes – Gervase the blacksmith at work in his forge, the carpenter's commissions from the local abbey, the references to miracle-plays – so that we have the illusion of unbroken density, of life going on continuously behind the story. The narrative itself is full of subtle authenticity: nothing is taken for granted, not even the carpenter asleep in his tub:

And eft he routeth, for his heed myslay (I, 3647).   *snores*

Added to this is a constant play of allusion and irony around the characters – in the repeated use of the epithet 'hende' for Nicholas, or in Alysoun's visit to church,

Cristes owene werkes for to wirche (I, 3308) –

and what one can only describe as a kind of exuberant gaiety and gusto in the narration. The delight in plots superbly laid and ridiculously foiled, the delight that Nicholas takes, and we share, in his picture of the three of them afloat on the postdiluvian waters (3575), is all contained and transcended in the delight of sharing in the activity of a narrative imagination at the peak of its powers. The events of the story itself are both nasty and false: the art of the telling is everything.

The nastiness of the *Reeve's Tale* is of a different order. The Reeve is taking his revenge on the Miller, and there is about his character, as we saw in the *General Prologue*, a kind of warped moral rectitude (like Malvolio's) which makes his Tale narrowly purposive and vindictive, in contrast to the sense of largesse in the *Miller's Tale*. The slimily ingratiating Prologue is followed by a description of Symkyn the miller which is set up deliberately like a target, isolating the violence, avarice and pride which are each to be precisely punished in the dénouement. It comes at the same point in the narrative as the description of Alysoun in the *Miller's Tale*, and sets the tone in the same way. Everything is directed to destroying the Miller: even the Northern origin of the two students (as well as giving Chaucer the opportunity to exploit the comic possibilities of dialect – the first time in English) is intended to humiliate the Miller even further, by showing him outwitted by such bumpkins. The difference in tone from the *Miller's Tale* is sharply emphasized in the attitude to sex: in the *Miller's Tale* love-making does at least seem to be enjoyable –

Ther was the revel and the melodye (I, 3652) –

but in the *Reeve's Tale*, for the students at their business of revenge, it is all hard work and 'swynk'. The deliberate parody of the *aube*-scene,

Aleyn wax wery in the dawenynge,
For he had swonken al the longe nyght (I, 4234–5),   *worked*

and Aleyn's farewell to Malyne, the daughter, leaves a particularly unpleasant taste, and Chaucer trespasses here just near enough to personal feeling and sympathy to make us wince momentarily at the clinical vindictiveness of the narrator. But the Tale in the end recoils on the Reeve: the constant references to judgment and justice, and the cue in the Prologue,

He kan wel in myn eye seen a stalke,
But in his owene he kan nat seen a balke (I, 3919–20),

to the appropriate Biblical text ('With what measure ye mete,' &c.) remind us that the Reeve's morality is flawed, 'sclendre' and 'colerik' like the man, and rusty like his sword. The nastiness of the Tale is the Reeve's nastiness: by placing it in a flawed frame, Chaucer gives to fabliau here an added dramatic dimension.

The tales of the Friar and the Summoner explore something of this same dimension. They are not true fabliaux, but simply popular anecdotes redesigned and manipulated for the purposes of the *flyting* between these traditional enemies. The *Friar's Tale* is of how the devil seizes his own, in this case, of course, a Summoner, and it is told with infuriating blandness, with many sharp thrusts, as when the mysterious 'yeman' (the devil) meets the Summoner:

'Artow thanne a bailly?' 'Ye', quod he.
He dorste nat, for verray filthe and shame,
Seye that he was a somonour, for the name (III, 1392–4).

The real reductive comedy, though, is not in the description of the Summoner's office, nor in the many comparisons between summoners and devils, but in the impenetrable stupidity of the Summoner, who exasperates even the devil with his insistent questioning about the trivia of shape-changing, and who cannot understand the difference between the curses of the mouth and the curses of the heart. The disposal is neat, the tone equable, and the Friar heaps coals at the end with special prayers for summoners (they need them).

The *Summoner's Tale* is altogether richer. Like its Prologue with its allusion to the twenty thousand friars up the 'develes ers', it is anal-obsessive, depending for its point on the anecdote of the divided fart. It soars in the end to delicious comedy, where the insult offered to the Friar by Thomas is forgotten in the preoccupation of all present with the technical problem that he has posed. The core of the Tale, however, is in the portrayal of the Friar and his winning ways – smooth talk, a greasy sermon on anger, quickness of resource, which gives him an apt answer to the news of the dead child (III, 1854) as well as to Thomas's complaint that he is always giving money to different friars:

The frere answerde: 'O Thomas, dostow so?
What nedeth yow diverse freres seche? . . .   *seek*
Youre inconstance is youre confusioun' (III, 1954–5, 1958).

As he says, with unconscious anticipation of his own predicament later:

What is a ferthyng worth parted in twelve (III, 1967)?

In the end the figure of the friar is so completely filled out that we have quite forgotten the flyting.

The *Merchant's Tale*, the last of the fabliaux, is not funny at all. In it Chaucer does what he had always promised to do, explodes the fabliau into a new and complex kind of narrative of his own, in which he explores, among other things, the literary possibilities of cynicism and disgust. The abiding memories of the *Merchant's Tale* are of January sitting up in bed singing, the slack skin of his neck shaking, or of May casting Damyan's love-letter in the privy, or Damyan squatting like a toad under a bush in the garden. There is about the Tale a gratuitously repulsive quality: Chaucer probably saw the advantages of giving this a 'dramatic' reinforcement by assigning the Tale to the Merchant, and having him describe himself in the Prologue as bitterly disillusioned in marriage, but the Tale can stand on its own. It deals at length with what elsewhere would be called love and marriage, but here become lust and coupling. From the opening mock-encomium of marriage to the final playing out of the farce in the pear-tree,

And sodeynly anon this Damyan
Gan pullen up the smok, and in he throng (IV, 2352–3),   *thrust*

the telling of the Tale is dominated by a gross sexual disgust. Marriage is degraded to what January calls it, a licence 'to pleye us by the lawe', the ceremony being a piece of mumbo-jumbo in which the priest 'made al siker ynogh with hoolynesse'. When January says

For wedlok is so esy and so clene (IV, 1264),

he means what a simple solution it provides to the problems of rich and randy old men, and the attention that he lavishes on his choice of a bride is the same, explicitly, as that with which he would choose a tasty piece of meat. The sexual values of romance are reversed in fabliau, but the reference is recognizably to the same set of events; here they are perverted out of all recognition, and the lyricism of the wedding-scene is infected by the falseness of its rhetoric in just the same way that January's quotation of the Song of Solomon is undercut by the narrator's cynical comment:

Swiche olde lewed wordes used he (IV, 2149).

Chaucer seems to be exploring the same vein as Shakespeare in *Troilus and Cressida* and parts of *Hamlet*, and Chaucer pushes the supposed moral norm off-centre just as Shakespeare does with Thersites. Justinus, judging by his name, should provide us with some good sense, but all he has is the wisdom of a clear-eyed cynicism, as distinct from January's bleary self-delusion; he doesn't think of January's view of marriage as *wrong* – all he knows is that it is not true. Justinus, therefore, is peripheral. What is central to the *Merchant's Tale* is a powerful under-current of passion, chiefly repulsion, which is of course quite alien to the fabliau-form. The moment we feel anything about January, horror or disgust or, later, pity, the traditional form is burst open, and it is Chaucer's readiness to risk this that makes the *Merchant's Tale* such an extraordinary document. What it is in the end it is difficult to say. Such a diversity of materials have gone to its making that it cannot, seemingly, be squeezed back into the dramatic frame of the Merchant's character. It is perhaps a case where the sequence of the *Tales* has to be considered more carefully: the *Merchant's Tale* must stand in relation to the Franklin's. Where the one presses beyond fabliau to one kind of 'reality', the other presses beyond romance, like the *Troilus*, to another kind of reality, and the juxtapositon of the two gives us that complexly overlapping spectrum of attitudes which it was always Chaucer's aim to seek in narrative.

One should perhaps revert to the Pardoner and the Wife of Bath, finally, to complete the argument. If Chaucer's method was to work through various traditional genres of narrative until he had moulded them to his own vision and technique, or discarded them as useless for his purposes, then we could say that he found the final answer in the quasi-autobiographical monologue and in the free drama of the links. These are certainly the most specifically Chaucerian parts of the *Canterbury Tales*, and the ones which we are most likely to respond to immediately. However, immediate responses are not always the most enduring, and more of Chaucer's artistic struggle has gone into some of the other tales – the Clerk's, Franklin's, Knight's, Nun's Priest's and Merchant's. Easy answers – and the Pardoner, though he tempts speculation, is an easy answer – are less interesting than the grappling of the imagination with intractable forms and material, whether the result is perfect or not.

6

LATER POETRY: THE POPULAR TRADITION

Rosemary Woolf

The romances, lyrics, and mystery and morality plays, which are the subject-matter of this chapter, were the literature of the unlearned of all classes of society from roughly the thirteenth to the fifteenth century. The romances served the same purpose as the novel in later periods, namely recreational entertainment, and they similarly differ in seriousness of artistic purpose according to the skill of the author and the degree of literary sophistication to be expected in his intended audience. The romances may, indeed, be best defined as novels or short stories in verse, the chief difference being that, whereas the novelist has usually chosen to work out his theme of human relationships against a realistic and almost contemporary background, the romance-writer chose a setting that was temporally or geographically remote, in order that the idealization of conduct and the unquestioned presence of the marvellous might be met with a willing suspension of disbelief.

Whilst romances, such as *Athelston*, are occasionally rooted in the historically familiar, they are far more often set at a remote time in the distant past. Nowadays the past is so crowded with historical events that fantastic fictions have to be projected into the future, but in the Middle Ages only the small number of the learned thought of the past as being inflexibly bound by the same laws as the present: the writer of the romance, even of romances for the royal court, could therefore use it as an appropriate setting for the improbable or the impossible. The past had also the advantage that it could be endowed with the qualities of a chivalric Golden Age. Malory's chapter on the contrast between the faithful love of olden times and love *nowadays* is the most moving expression of this theme, but it is also the culmination of a long tradition. Chrétien de Troyes, a French court poet of the twelfth century and the first of the great French writers of romances, began the *Yvain* with a contrast between the present debasement of love, and the times of old when lovers were courteous, brave, faithful and honourable. In England the author of the *Ancrene Wisse*, in a very early allusion to romance convention, describes Christ as a noble lover who 'showed by knightly deeds that he was worthy of love ('luvewurthe') as knights at one time were accustomed to do'.

The landscape of the romances may be equally fictitious. Knights live in or visit castles, which are small interruptions in an endless forest, otherwise only broken by an occasional hill or river. Except for strange monsters or wild animals, the only natural inhabitants of the forest are hermits. According to medieval literary convention, a forest is always a place in which strange things may happen, but its naturalistic characteristic of being a bewildering place makes it an apt location for the surprise meetings and chance losses that are a common feature of the action of romances. The world of such romances is so convincingly self-contained that one forgets the possibility of the real countryside with villages and workers on the land. When in Chrétien's *Erec*, Erec in his journey comes across two men carrying cheese and wine to haymakers in a neighbouring field, this realistic detail does not confer solidity, but disturbs an otherwise imaginatively self-sufficient fiction.

The distant lands of the east also provided a setting for marvels. A large section of *King Alisaunder*, for instance, is given an account of the strange monsters that he and his army met and fought on their journey to India. These many strange creatures, which include the 'Anthropophagi, and men whose heads/Do grow beneath their shoulders' of whom Othello speaks, were also the subject of *Mandeville's Travels*, and Steel's comment upon this work, 'All is enchanted ground and fairy land', sums up evocatively the romance transformation of eastern Europe and Asia. It is unprofitable to speculate long on the extent to which a medieval audience believed in marvels of all kinds. Whilst authors obviously intended to arouse astonishment, people perhaps did not feel the immovable disbelief that is our modern reaction. The ambivalent response of more modern readers to the ghost story may provide an illuminating parallel, for the ghost story depends for its success upon the readers' disbelief tinctured by a nervous, titillating suspicion that ghosts may nevertheless exist. From a literary point of view the ideal response to the marvellous in the romances is at some point between total acceptance and total scepticism.

Though the landscape of romance is fanciful, the castles and social life within them are contemporary in style. Architecture, clothing, food, musical instruments, pastimes and conversation, all reflect the currently fashionable, though conceived to the highest degree of excellence. In the eighteenth century, antiquarian scholars supposed this imaginary translation of the contemporary to the past to be an example of ignorance and naïveté. Nowadays, however, we can see that this blending of the idealized but familiar with the remote and fanciful was a deliberately contrived and probably piquant effect. But though we can see, we cannot appreciate, for a Gothic castle now seems as remote and 'romantic' as the fictitious forest that surrounded it.

Love and chivalric adventure are the common subject-matter of romances. In what we think of as the most characteristic romances, and certainly in nearly all the finest of them, the two are related, and the knight engages in battles or tournaments to save his lady or to prove that he is 'luvewurthe'. There are, however, on the one hand, many poems, now classified as romances, which are akin to epic in their disregard for love and emphasis upon martial ethic, and on the other hand there are many poems, often having hagiographical affinities, in which fighting is incidental or plays no part at all: many of these latter are called Breton lays. The typical romance can best be discussed in terms of the English romances that take some part of the Arthurian legend as their subject, but before considering these, it is necessary to discuss the two extremes, the romantic epic and the Breton lay, and also some romances which overlap with other medieval narrative genres, the exemplum, the saint's life and the fabliau.

An exemplum is a story told to illustrate a theme or moral, and many preachers in the Middle Ages used them to enliven their sermons. All the stories in the *Confessio Amantis* purport to be exempla, and so also are the fifteen stories in the romance of the *Seven Sages of Rome*, a framed group of which the skeletal outline is a story of eastern origin, slightly resembling that of the *Arabian Nights*. Each day a wicked empress urges her husband by means of a story to kill his son, whom she falsely claims to be bent upon usurping the throne, and each day one of the sages counters with a story that illustrates the folly of heeding women's advice or rashly killing. This work bears a superficial resemblance to romance in the royal and Roman setting of the framework, but the stories, such as the still current one of the faithful hound, do not belong to the world of romance, and the narrative method is entirely different: for an exemplum story is economically told, with only sufficient detail included in order to bring the plot (which carries the moral) to life, whereas true romance lingers affectionately upon descriptive detail for its own rich and decorative effect.

More engaging than anything in the *Seven Sages* is the single story of King Robert of Sicily, an exemplum against pride, now better known from Longfellow's version. A comparison of the two is illuminating in that it shows up the subtlety and sureness of religious feeling in the Middle English work. The story is of an arrogant king, whose place is taken by an angel until he has learnt humility. Longfellow catches well the original haughtiness of the King with his contempt for the words of the *Magnificat*, 'He has put down the mighty from their seat', but the solution is expressed with sentimental religiosity: the humbled King has a semi-mystical experience on Easter morning and resolves to enter a monastery. In *Robert of Sicily*, however, the emphasis is upon the symbolical appropriateness of the King being reduced to the status of court fool, and it is this symbolic moral lesson that he learns. His understanding of this is expressed in a touching prayer of twenty-eight lines, in which the couplets fall into quatrains, with the refrain, 'Lord, on thi fool thou have pité'. The following is the fifth:

> Lord, i have igult the sore!   *sinned against*
> Merci, Lord: i nul no more;   *will*
> Ever thi fol, Lord, wol i be.
> Lord, on thi fol thou have pité.

This leads to the climax, in which, when the angel asks Robert who he is, he replies (in contrast to his earlier frantic protests that he is the King), 'Sire, a fol' and that as a fool he will continue to lead his life. Thus having accepted that he is a fool in the sight of God, he becomes once more the King of Sicily. The play upon the word fool gives the poem a very moving dramatic and religious pattern, and there is no straining for effect as there is in Longfellow's version. Unfortunately the very quietness of the Middle English has led to some critics not observing its merits.

Fabliau plots and motifs are to be found here and there in English and French romance. The earliest example in England is the Anglo-Norman *Lai du Cor*, which describes a chastity test at the court of King Arthur: both King and knights find that they are cuckolds, but the King's good spirits are restored when he finds that he has companionship in humiliation. This poem with its cynical comment on the invariable lasciviousness of women is typical of fabliau thought, detached of course from its low-life fabliau setting. Parallels in vernacular romance may be seen in the third part of the *Avowing of Arthur*, in which the King devises a way of testing the fidelity of Baldwin's wife, and in *Le bone Florence*, in which the heroine rejects an offer of marriage, not because, as elsewhere in romance, her would-be husband is a heathen or because she is in love with someone else, but because he is old, and indeed the poet has already described her suitor in terms that recall the traditional satiric description of old age upon which Chaucer drew for his account of January.

Far more important in number and substance are the romances that are related to hagiography. Saints' lives had initially drawn upon romance elements, and in the Middle Ages the wheel came full circle with hagiographic episodes appearing once again in romance. The maligned suffering heroines of many romances (Chaucer's Constance and Griselda belong to this type) often share the same ordeals as did the virgin martyrs in some of their more fabulous trials. Common to both are the false accusations (usually of adultery), and the attempts at rape foiled by miraculous intervention. *Le bone Florence*, despite its initial fabliau motif, is an example of this type of hagiographic story pattern. The companion portrait is of the patient suffering knight, who having at God's command been deprived of riches and family, endures his poverty and loneliness uncomplainingly, until at last everything is given back to him. The clearest example of this theme is *Sir Isumbras*, which has been shown to bear a close relationship to the Life of St. Eustace. The degree to which the religious affiliation of the plot is brought out in the method of narration varies from one romance to another: in both *Le bone Florence* and *Sir Isumbras* it is emphasized, for in them prayers for help do not belong solely to a surface piety, but are integrated to the action, and strange wonders, being of divine origin, are miraculous rather than marvellous.

Three of the romances which belong to this group of stories of 'trial and faith', *Emare*, the *Erl of Toulous* and *Sir Gowther*, are called Breton lays by their authors, and it is therefore worth considering whether the hagiographic affiliations of their story-patterns casts light on the English conception of the genre of the Breton lay. Though one of the seven surviving English Breton lays, *Sir Launfal*, is a translation from the French of Marie de France, as a group the English poems make a very different impression from Marie's collection. Attempts to define them have tended to concentrate on motifs that one or two of them share with Marie's poems, such as that of the supernatural parentage in *Sir Degare* and *Sir Gowther*, or the prominence of the land of fairy in *Sir Orfeo* and *Sir Launfal*. But the only substantial resemblance between the two groups of poems lies in their comparative brevity and the decisive outlines of their plots.

The plots of all the English lays – as in the hagiographic romances – involve the hero or heroine in a period of suffering. Sometimes this is brought about by a false accusation of adultery, as in *Sir Launfal*, the *Erl of Toulous* and *Emare*, sometimes by religious judgment as in *Sir Gowther* or by the inhumane intervention of the land of fairy as in *Sir Orfeo*. The suffering takes the form of exile and loneliness, and the stories thus become ones of loss and recovery, separation and recognition. Their basic pattern is therefore not that of the quest, typical of many romances, but rather that of a turn of Fortune's wheel, but a wheel presided over by a benign goddess, so that the movement is from happiness to misery to happiness. Some of the lays deal with suffering in a mechanical way, but the best achieve effects of pathos that are peculiar to the genre. The finest example is Sir Orfeo's sadness at the loss of Heurodis, as, for instance, in his lament when he hears that his wife will be snatched away from him:

Allas! quath he, 'Forlorn icham!	*I am lost*
Whider wiltow go, and to wham?	
Whider thou gost ichil with the,	*I will go*
And whider y go thou schalt with me.	

But they are found elsewhere, particularly in the treatment of solitary and helpless figures, such as the baby, Freine, left abandoned in the ash tree, or Emare, cast out to sea, with a young baby, cold and hungry, in her arms. It is noteworthy that two of the three stories in *The Canterbury Tales* that are much praised for their effects of pathos, the *Man of Law's Tale* and the *Clerk's Tale*, have analogues in the Breton lays.

The emphasis upon suffering is balanced by the emphasis upon the happy ending. Nearly all romances of course end happily, but the English Breton lays are remarkable in this, because their plots seem often to be potential tragedies, which the poet by ostentatious contrivance nevertheless brings to a fortunate issue: they are, as it were, *Cymbeline* as against *Othello*. This may be seen, for instance, in *Emare*, where the poet against all the natural odds reunites the twice-exiled heroine at the end with both husband and father. Yet more striking are *Sir Orfeo* and *Sir Degare*. *Sir Orfeo* is a charming medievalization of the Orpheus legend, in which Eurydice is set free and regained for ever. *Sir Degare*, at many farther removes, is the story of Oedipus, but Degare and his mother recognize each other in time to avoid the act of incest, and Degare's fight with his father has no fatal ending, because the father recognizes his son in time. The poets of course had traditional sources for these happy endings (though none is known for the incest theme), but their choice of potentially tragic material remains striking.

In the English Breton lays fighting either plays no part, as in *Emare*, *Sir Orfeo*, *Lai le Freine*, and *Sir Launfal* (the couplet not the coarser and expanded tail-rhyme version), or, as in the *Erl of Toulous* and *Sir Gowther*, it is strongly subordinated to the main theme. At the other end of the romance spectrum lies the romantic epic, in which fighting is all-important. The best example of this branch of romance is *King Alisaunder*, a long poem of 4,000 couplets, translated with additions and modifications from the twelfth-century Anglo-Norman poem, the *Roman de Toute Chevalerie*. This poem covers Alexander's youth, his many victorious wars, of which the battle with Darius is the most important, his search for marvels in his journey through the east, and his death when still young and at the height of his powers. The epic qualities lie partly in the geographical and the political solidity of the narrative. Whilst romances such as Chrétien's *Cligès* can unfold in the real Europe and not the fabulous Logres, these semi-historical elements serve only as a background for the story of love: in *Alisaunder* they are at the heart of the narrative. In typical romance knights fight for their ladies against villains and giants who seek to oppress those that travel through the forest. In *Alisaunder* the enemy are neighbouring nations, and the motive is the epic and politically-realistic one of the conquest of territory. At the same time the splendour of Alexander's victories and his indomitable bravery have, in the epic manner, a shadow cast across them in the form of recurring sententiae about the transience of happiness, and, at the end, in the emphasis upon the death of Alexander, magically and ominously foretold, and upon the break-up of his kingdom after his death. The poem achieves something of the epic equilibrium between the glorification of human achievement and the sense of futility in the ending of all human endeavour.

There is very little of the world of love in *Alisaunder*. The world of beautiful ladies and faithful knights is introduced chiefly through the lyrical headpieces, such as the following:

Mery tyme it is in Maij!
The foules syngeth her lay,
The knightes loveth the turnay;
Maydens so dauncen and thay play.

These headpieces have been shown by Professor Smithers to be characteristic of medieval epic style (Gavin Douglas was later to introduce them into his translation of the *Aeneid*), but no English poet uses them as refreshingly as does the author of *Alisaunder*. The only direct portrayal of love, the short episode of Queen Candace, is treated partly as a romantic interlude (the Queen, for instance, is singing of the love of Dido and Aeneas when Alexander arrives), but also as an example of the great man betrayed by the wiles of women, for Alexander sees himself in this plight as Sir Gawain in *Sir Gawain and the Green Knight* was later to do. Medieval vernacular epic does not aim at epic grandeur, and with its love of the marvellous, and the small scale of even its finest effects, *Alisaunder* now seems more like typical romance than like the *Aeneid*. Nevertheless within the romance genre its epic ancestry can be seen to guide the conduct of the narrative and to determine many of its devices of style.

In the typical romance, which is neither semi-hagiographic nor epic in its story-matter and assumptions, fighting in tournaments or in solitary adventures plays an important part, but its purpose is always a demonstration of love. Love can be said to be the chief subject of the romances. This love, however, is not courtly love. This artificial system is chiefly to be found in continental lyric poetry, being more suited to a form which presents a distillation of emotion, with the social background only lightly sketched in. The only romance of consequence to be fully founded upon it is the freakish *Chevalier de la Charette* of Chrétien de Troyes, and this poet's other three romances of love, *Yvain, Cligès* and *Erec* all treat of love in marriage. The *Franklin's Tale* is usually thought of as remarkable for its idealization of marriage, but the irrefutable reason for rejecting the courtly code expressed in Dorigen's words:

What deyntee sholde a man han in his lyf   *pleasure*
For to go love another mannes wyf,
That hath hir body whan so that hym liketh,

and the reconciliation of the two kinds of love in the famous passage:

Thus hath she take hir servant and hir lord,
Servant in love and lord in mariage.
Thanne was he bothe in lordshipe and servage.
Servage? nay, but in lordshipe above,
Sith he hath bothe his lady and his love;
His lady, certes, and his wyf also,

both have their ancestry in Chrétien's *Cligès*. C.S. Lewis in his remarkable book, *The Allegory of Love*, too readily believed that medieval writers found marriage and true love to be incompatible.

It is self-evident that there can be no story about the relationship of love unless there is some obstacle in the path of the lovers. The fact therefore that in the Middle Ages marriages were arranged was not, as Lewis supposed, an insuperable bar to the 'romantic' treatment of love in medieval narrative, but on the contrary a very convenient and ready-made obstacle for the story-teller to use. Occasionally it allowed the writer to use his skill to show the growth of love between a pair who have been married against their will. This is done very touchingly in *Havelok*, where the princess is compelled by a wicked usurper to marry Havelok, apparently a servant boy, though in fact of royal birth. At the end of the poem their love is praised as follows:

So mikel love was hem bitwene	
That all the werd spak of hem two.	*world*
He lovede hire and she him so,	
That neyther ower mighte be	*anywhere*
Fro other, ne no ioie se	
But-yf he were togidere bothe;	*they*
Nevere yete ne weren he wrothe,	
For here love was ay newe.	

More commonly, however, parental refusal to a marriage provides the substance of the plot, and is at last overcome to provide a happy ending. Romances of this kind stretch from the idyllic *Floris and Blancheflur* of the thirteenth century to the more formal and mannered *Squire of Low Degree* in the fifteenth: hero and heroine fall in love at the beginning, and after many trials and long adversity marry at the end. But even in other types of plot, marriage provides the happy ending. In *Libeaus Desconus*, for instance, the young knight sets out on a quest from Arthur's court to free a lady from two malignant enchanters, and when he has done so, marries her. Even *Ipomadon*, which displays more of the manners of courtly love (the hero falls in love without having seen the lady, endures many adventures to prove his worthiness, and, like Troilus, blushes, trembles and cannot sleep), ends in a happy marriage. In Breton lays, as we have seen, the happy ending can be the reunion of husband and wife who have been separated. The exception is *Sir Launfal*, where marriage cannot apply, since the knight's mistress belongs to the Land of Fairy.

The danger that marriage may seem too staid, two well-rooted in the every-day world, is sometimes averted by the authors bending a little the Christian moral law. Floris, for instance, having sought his beloved Blancheflur through many dangers and across half the world, and having at last by a ruse found a way to enter the high tower in which she is kept prisoner, does not refrain from the full contentment of love. There is a presupposition in many romances that true love cannot but be innocent and virtuous, that, as Chaucer says, every man 'That loveth well, meneth but gentillesse', and that it would be a churl or a villain (to use medieval terms) who would demand that lovers, when reunited, should await the marriage ceremony. But when Floris and Blancheflur, or the more famous corresponding pair in French romance, Aucassin and Nicolette, temporarily ignore the marriage bond, it is not because they despise it, but because a hostile, insensitive world has refused it to them. Invariably the stabilization of love in marriage provides the reason why the lovers are able to live happily ever after. Most romances deal with happy and requited love, for which marriage provided the only fitting framework. The famous love stories of Tristram and Isolde and Launcelot and Guinevere, where the love has to be adulterous, are moving because they are tragedies.

Of the romances so far discussed, only two had an Arthurian setting, *Sir Launfal* and *Libeaus Desconus*, and neither of these dealt with any of the famous Arthurian stories or any of the great knights, Launcelot, Gawain or Ywain. But the Arthurian legend is rightly thought of as being at the centre of the world of romance, and a discussion of the romance form naturally leads up to those that deal with it. There are nine non-alliterative romances that deal with important episodes of the Arthurian legend or important knights. Five of these, *Arthur, Arthour and Merlin*, Lovelich's *Merlin* and *Holy Grail*, and *Lancelot of the Laik*, do not merit individual discussion. The subject-matter of the first four, the early history of Arthur and the miraculous history of the Grail before it became the object of the chivalric quest, is unpromising in itself, and the authors make little of it. The fifth, which concerns the early history of Lancelot, has more attractive material, but the fifteenth century author has treated it mechanically. The other four, *Ywain and Gawain, Sir Tristrem, Sir Perceval de Galles*, and the stanzaic *Morte Arthur*, all repay investigation, for, in both their successes and their failures, they illustrate the methods and achievement of English romance.

Ywain and Gawain is the only extant translation of any of the romances of Chrétien de Troyes. It is unfortunately customary to belittle it by comparison with its source. Certainly the author has excised what is most characteristic of Chrétien's writing, namely the web of psychological generalization and paradoxical ratiocination in which he enmeshes his characters. Chrétien is interested in abstract questions and problematical relationships, in this poem the relationship between Yvain and Alundyne, for Yvain falls in love with Alundyne after having slain her husband, thus putting them both into the kind of moral and psychological dilemma that fascinated French writers and audience. The long passages of emotional and intellectual intricacy are much reduced by the English poet, who is only concerned to show that 'the course of true love never did run smooth'. Similarly he uses the later conflicting duties of husband to wife and knight to a life of chivalric adventure as a convenient obstacle to the tranquil happiness of marriage, not as a theme of intrinsic interest. What he seems to have liked in the poem was the tenderness of human relations, the world of the magical forest, and the nobility and hardihood of Ywain in his many dangerous and strange adventures. In particular he liked the faithful lion, who, like the lion of Androcles and St. Jerome, became a loving and devoted companion to the hero. It is interesting to compare the parallel accounts of Ywain's first succouring of the lion. In the French, Yvain sees a lion and a serpent fighting, and, having reflected that a serpent is a venomous and treacherous animal, Yvain decides to help the lion. After the serpent has been killed, the lion does homage to Yvain by standing on its hindfeet and bowing low to the ground. In the English poem Ywain engages on the lion's behalf for the more sentimental reason that it is the weaker of the combatants, and the lion's later gratitude is described as follows:

Grete fawnyng made he to the knyght.
Down on the grund he set hom oft,
His fortherfete he held oloft,   *front feet*
And thanked the knyght als he kowth,
Al if he myght noght speke with mowth;
So wele the lyon of him lete,   *took liking*
Ful law he lay and likked his fete.

And at the end of the work the poet makes a little addition to Chrétien's conclusion by telling us that the lion too lived happily ever after. The alterations that the English poet has made in this small episode are typical of his whole method: formality and intellectual reasoning vanish to be replaced by sweetness of tone and dramatic immediacy. *Ywain and Gawain* shows a different but not necessarily inferior taste. Chrétien's work is admittedly cleverer and more highly-wrought, but at the cost of some aridity; the English poem is simpler, but also more charming, light-hearted and tender.

   Sir Tristrem has as its subject one of the most famous love-stories of the Middle Ages. Amongst the finest versions of it is the *Tristram* of Thomas, an Anglo-Norman poem probably written for the court of Henry II, and it is this that is translated and paraphrased in the English work. It was, however, a perilous story. Put together from an amalgam of Celtic, Oriental, and French-fabliau themes, it contained many morally disconcerting episodes. Typical is the incident in which Tristram, disguised as a poor pilgrim, carries Isolde over a river, in order that the Queen, whose fidelity to King Mark has been challenged, may swear the deceptive oath that no-one but her husband and the pilgrim have ever touched her body. The story therefore has to be told as a tragedy in which the two lovers, constrained by the violence of love, are reduced to many unbecoming wiles and stratagems, until both love and dishonour are at last resolved in death. Thomas had made this pattern clear, but the English translator has tried to tell the story as though it were a simple one of young and faithful love and the sadness of separation. All the distasteful elements (which had led Chrétien to write a moral version in *Cligès*) lie exposed and unexplained. The difference may be illustrated from an early episode describing the begetting of Tristram, in which his mother visits her lover as he lies mortally wounded:

When she beheld him, she fell distract upon his bed, and rehearsed her woe and dolor. And when she had somewhat recovered her, she clipped him and kissed him oft, saying, 'Sweetest love', the tears wetting her face. And he in all his pain and anguish embraced her with such hot desire that this noble damozel conceived. She in grief and he in pain, they there begat a child, the which in his life brought woe to all his friends; and of him is this history made.

That Tristram should be born from the desperation of love, from pain and death, establishes the tone in the French. The English translator leaves out everything except the bare fact of the begetting.

The English poet was not without skill: some early lines on the sadness of things illustrate his style:

This semly somers day,
In winter it is nouht sen;
This greves wexen al gray,   *their*
That in her time were grene.
So dos this world, y say,
(Ywis and nouht at wene)
The gode ber al oway,
That our elders have bene.

He could have managed well a story such as that of Aucassin and Nicolette, but the tragedy of Tristram and Isolde is beyond his powers.

Sir Perceval de Galles is worth a brief mention, for it is the only surviving English romance to deal with the famous hero of the Grail quest, though here he is detached from the story of the Grail. It is not known whether the English poet made a divorce himself or whether he was working from a lost version that told only of the boyhood of the hero. The main motif of rustic ignorance had derived from stories of the youth of Celtic heroes, Cuchulainn and Finn, but, as far as is known, it entered French literature as a theme of Chrétien's *Perceval*, and as a theme much pointed by Chrétien in order to motivate on both a moral and psychological level the failure of Perceval to ask the life-giving question in the hall of the Fisher King, a failure that had some of the resonance of a Fall, and one for which atonement had to be made. The same emphasis is found in *Sir Perceval*, but in it the innocent but obstinate naïveté of Perceval exists for the sake of comedy and nothing more. The many episodes therefore that illustrate this theme, such as that in which he meets three of Arthur's knights in the woods, and on account of their unfamiliar splendour asks, 'Wilke of yow alle three/May the grete Godd be?', or the more savage one in which he burns a defeated knight because he does not know how otherwise to get possession of his armour, saying as he does so, 'Ly still therin now and roste!', entertain but have no farther significance. The English Perceval is in fact scarcely innocent, as is Wolfram's Parsifal, but rather, as Arthur is shown to think, a wild man of the woods:

The childe hadde wonnede in the wodde:
He knewe nother evyll ne gude;
The Kynge hymselfe understode
  He was a wilde man.

The story is told with zest and with a relish for farce, grotesque or brutal. The tail rhyme stanzas go with a swing, but it is a crude piece of work when compared with the French and German analogues.

The last Arthurian romance to be discussed, the stanzaic *Morte Arthur*, is also overshadowed by a greater work, Malory's *Morte Darthur* in its last books. But this is an undeserved misfortune, for the author has thoroughly understood his source, *La Mort le Roi Artu* (the last section of the Vulgate *Launcelot*), and relates with sympathy the tragic consequences of Launcelot's love for Guinevere. In this romance can be seen here and there the kind of imaginative re-arrangement of detail that Malory was later to practise so successfully, and for some of which he was actually indebted to this poem. One of the most moving and powerful scenes in Malory's work is that in which Launcelot, during his sad battle with Arthur, helps the King on to his horse again, and, Arthur, looking at Launcelot, thinks of his great courtesy and weeps. This is one of the great scenes of momentary forgiveness in any literature: though smaller in scale, it can stand comparison with the episode in *War and Peace*, in which Prince Andrew, seeing his ancient rival, Anatole Kuragin, in the operating tent, is moved by an ecstatic feeling for him of love and compassion. This scene is already in the *Morte Arthur*, and is only the less compelling for lack of the melancholic cadences of Malory's prose:

> Whan the kynge was horsyd there,
> Launcelot lokys he uppon,
> How corteise was in hym more
> Then evyr was in Any man;
> He thought on thyngis that had bene ore,
> The teres from hys eyen Ranne;
> He Sayde 'Allas!' with syghynge sore,
> 'That evyr yit thys werre began'.

This scene, however, is not in *La Mort le Roi Artu*, though the raw materials for it are there. In the French, Launcelot helps Arthur to remount, but it is in the evening, when the day's battle is over, that Arthur in reflective address to his councillors speaks of Launcelot's surpassing courtesy, and grieves that the war began. Thus by a simple transposition the author has created a scene of great imaginative power, one that dramatically and poignantly crystallizes the tragedy of Arthur being bound to fight his dearest and noblest knight.

The stanzaic *Morte* is the finest example of the English treatment of central Arthurian subject-matter before Malory's *Morte Darthur*. Very much earlier than this French and German writers had found in the use of the Arthurian legend a vehicle for serious and substantial literature: the romances of Chrétien de Troyes, the Vulgate *Launcelot*, the *Parsifal* of Wolfram von Eschenbach and the *Tristram* of Gottfried von Strassburg tower over the medieval literature of France and Germany. Malory's work comes almost two hundred years later, and unexpectedly, for when Chaucer had chosen as the source for *Troilus and Criseyde* the more realistic and urbane work of Boccaccio written for the Neapolitan court, English literature would appear to have embarked on another course.

Until the end of the fourteenth century, however, English romance was overshadowed by the French (since most of the aristocracy were French-speaking), and the best French romances circulated in English manuscripts. Despite or because of this a distinctive style developed in English romance, one that had greater sweetness and naturalism than its French counterpart. Therefore, though English romances must for a long time have seemed poor country cousins of the French, as in the fable of the town and country mouse the poor vernacular cousins showed qualities of simplicity, honesty, and directness of feeling, which to some tastes may prove more attractive than the poise and elegance of the higher-born French.

The English love-lyric shows a similar pattern in its development, except that, far from having a belated flowering, it degenerated into artificiality in the fifteenth century. But, before discussing the relationship between French and English lyrics, it is necessary to consider an equally important distinction, namely that between popular and courtly. It has long been the custom to make this distinction, though the surviving evidence that would enable this distinction to be safely applied is so scarce that it is hardly usable as a method of classification. In the Middle Ages lyrics composed by the common people for the common people will have had very little chance of surviving. In England at least the only popular lyrics that can be recognized beyond all doubt are the dance-songs; though of course most of these will have vanished, being ephemeral pieces, hardly worth recording when isolated from their music and social setting. One, however, has survived on a minstrel's sheet, which has been preserved through its casual use as a flyleaf of a learned manuscript (now MS Oxf. Rawl. D. 913); others survive as refrains to add a gay or lilting note to the more serious carols of the fifteenth century; most can be recognized by the invitation or encouragement to dancing that they express: 'Come and daunce wyt me' or 'Honnd by honnd we schulle ous take'. Perhaps the nonsense refrains of some of the carols (e.g. 'Trole, lole') also derive from dance song.

The other verses on this unique minstrel's sheet give the appearance of learned authorship, although they belonged to a minstrel's repertoire. Perhaps members of religious houses sometimes tried their hand at vernacular lyrics and then gave them to travelling minstrels, as it were for publication. The following is an example:

Al nist by the rose, rose –
  al nist bi the rose i lay;
darst ich noust the rose stele,
  ant yet i bar the flour awey.

These four lines have the economy of an epigram, not the un-designed brevity of some scrap of casually composed verse; the image of the rose derives directly from the learned and courtly tradition of love poetry, whilst the slightly cynical pun upon the word 'flour' suggests a style of wit formed by Latin education. The closest parallel lies in some Latin lines from an Italian manuscript, 'Flos in monte cernitur', in which a similar pun upon the word *flos* seems to lurk in the last line, and there is a similar tension between the delightfulness of the natural imagery and the hint of masculine self-congratulation at a successful seduction.

Many verses usually considered popular are of a later period than this. Most of them clearly belong to a convivial setting, and lose their vitality when coldly displayed on the printed page for the solitary reader. Some are drinking songs, more are bawdy anecdotes cast in the lyric form of the betrayed maiden's lament. They may be thought of as the medieval equivalent of recent music hall and cabaret songs, for which music, expressiveness in the performance, and the reaction of communal laughter are necessary accompaniments. In this way they may well have provided skilled and successful entertainment, though whether they were written and recited with zest it is impossible to tell. Perhaps even then there was a medieval Archie Rice who wearily moved from village to village, singing mechanically of the clerk, Jankin, or the knight, Sir John, who to her delight, but undoing, seduced the village maiden. Indecent songs, however, did not belong exclusively to tavern au-diences. In the Tudor song books, for instance, are some archery songs (set in the form of the old man's complaint), whose sole point lies in the ingenious and sly display of sexual symbolism. For the courtly audience this kind of song is more oblique and clever than the boisterously coarse songs provided for their rustic counterparts. But, as one would expect, obscenity in itself cannot be taken as criterion for distinguishing the popular from the courtly, if by courtly is meant the literature of the court.

The problems that arise from the use of these terms, popular and courtly, may be illustrated from a consideration of two famous lyrics, one early in date and one late. The late one is:

Western wind, when will thou blow,
  The small rain down can rain?
Christ, if my love were in my arms
  And I in my bed again.

This poem is preserved in an early sixteenth-century song-book, and this together with its accomplishment has suggested to some critics that it belongs with sophisticated and courtly pieces, but an elusive and almost numinous quality in its juxtaposition of natural imagery with direct passion has led others to call it popular. Undoubtedly the use of natural imagery here is different from the formal relationship of spring setting to the lover's mood in the conventional *reverdie*, and its felicity lies in the evasion of any traditional category. Nevertheless there is no evidence that so masterly a verse ever sprang from the untrained imagination of the common people, and it is therefore more likely to be the work of an educated poet who drew for his style and effects upon the traditions of folk poetry.

The other poem is probably the most famous of all medieval lyrics:

Sumer is icumen in,	
Lhude sing cuccu!	
Groweth sed and bloweth med	*the meadow flowers*
and springeth the wde nu.	*the wood is in leaf*
Sing cuccu!	
Awe bleteth after lomb,	*ewe*
lhouth after calve cu,	*lows*
Bulluc sterteth, bucke verteth.	*capers/farts*
Murie sing cuccu!	
Cuccu, cuccu,	
Wel singes thu cuccu.	
ne swik thu naver nu!	*cease*
Sing cuccu nu, Sing cuccu!	
Sing cuccu, Sing cuccu nu!	

The poem is preserved in a manuscript from Reading Abbey, and the music to which it is set has liturgical affinities and was therefore probably composed in the Abbey itself. The question therefore is whether the words too were written by a monk or whether the composer for jocular purposes set to serious music a popular verse learnt either from a travelling minstrel or perhaps from some lay worker on the estate. The lyric has been praised by Carleton Brown for its 'freshness and unstudied simplicity', and it has appealed to those who like to believe in a folk poetry of spontaneous charm, to which many of the finer passages in courtly lyrics are indebted. There is, however, a more cynical way of interpreting this lyric. As we read it, and even more as we listen to it sung, it becomes clear that the poem is dominated by the cry 'cuccu', and there is a definite possibility that already in the thirteenth century this was 'a word of fear, unpleasing to the married ear'. The possibility of mockery in this word is increased by the use of the word 'fart'. This base word does not reappear in English literature until its occurrence in Chaucer's *Miller's Tale*, and the belief that 'low' words, whether of a lavatorial or sexual meaning, were ever used with innocent seriousness is probably a romantic fantasy of the present century. On this interpretation there is the double joke in the poem, which lies partly in the setting of comic words to religious music (a still popular practice with hymns), and partly in a parody of the *reverdie*, in which spring is shown to be, not the season of romantic love and the song of the nightingale, but of deceived husbands and farmyard noises. In this case the religious Latin words that are set to the same music, but, according to musicologists, fit it less well, would be the attempt of a more solemn mind to patch over the profane work of a satiric predecessor.

There are various kinds of love lyrics in the Middle Ages which span the popular and the courtly traditions: one of their most noticeable characteristics is that they imply a dramatic context, which is far more particularized than is customary in the familiar lover's appeal to his mistress. The *aube*, for instance, presupposes a pair of lovers in bed, warned by a watchman or the rising sun that they must part. This form is found throughout nearly every literature of Europe and Asia, and must therefore have arisen outside the learned chain of source and derivative. In England, however, it first appears in *Troilus and Criseyde*, where Chaucer substantially amplifies the brief allusion in *Il Filostrato*:

And ek the sonne, Titan, gan he chide,	
And seyde, 'O fool, wel may men the dispise,	
That hast the dawyng al nyght by thi syde,	*daybreak*
And suffrest hire so soone up fro the rise,	
For to disese loveris in this wyse.	*vex*
What! holde youre bed ther, thow, and ek thi Morwe!	*Dawn*
I bidde God, so yeve yow bothe sorwe.	*to give*

This stylized chafing of the sun reminds one of Donne's 'Busie old foole, unruly sunne', and goes back to the parting of Leander from Hera in the *Heroides* of Ovid; an equally important classical source was one of Ovid's *Amores*, entirely set in the form of an *aube*, and containing the appeal to night, 'Lente currite, noctis equi!', now better known in its strikingly different context in *Doctor Faustus*. Simple examples of the *aube* are rare in English: there was a popular song, probably of fifteenth-century origin, which began something

like, 'Hay now the day dawis', but it is unfortunately lost; and a
refrain to a formal poem in honour of the white rose, Elizabeth of
York, must originally have been part or the whole of an *aube*:

This day day dawes,
This gentill day day dawes,
This gentill day dawes,
And I must home gone.

These fragments, read in isolation, now seem too gay to fit the
dramatic occasion.

The *aube* is precisely localized in time and place and its dramatic
context is fitting to either romance or ballad. By contrast the *chanson de
mal mariée* is individualized by the general dramatic situation, which is
one characteristic of fabliaux, a young wife married to an aged and
jealous husband. The lyric may be either the musings of the wife or an
address to the young lover whom she prefers. An Anglo-Norman scrap,
on the minstrel's sheet already referred to, consists of two lines: 'Amy
tenez vous ioyous/si moura lui gelous', a reassurance which, read on its
own, sounds either sinister or over-optimistic, but that epitomizes the
tone of this genre. Amongst the English verses prefixed to the Latin
cantilenae in the *Red Book of Ossory* is the following:

Alasx hou shold Y singe? Yloren is my playnge.　　　　*My happiness is lost*
Hou shold Y with that olde man
To leven, and let my leman,　　　　　　　　　　　　　*abandon my lover*
　Swettist of all thinge?

The theme here is more gently, even plangently, expressed. It
could be the lament of May in the *Merchant's Tale*, were she not
characterized as viciously as her repulsive husband. In English, at
least, the popular *chansons de mal mariées* combined with the
learned tradition of the evils of marriage (to her annoyance, the
Wife of Bath's fifth husband had a collection of Latin treatises on
this subject), and the fruit of this combination can be seen in
Dunbar's *Twa Mariit Wemen and the Wedo*.

Far commoner in English are the complaints of the betrayed
maiden, a dramatic situation that belongs to the ballads. In these
the maiden mourns a faithless lover, her grief often being
accentuated by the fact that she is about to bear a fatherless child.
The best known poem nowadays in this genre is the beautiful song
of uncertain date, 'Waly, waly', in which the sadness of enduring
love met by betrayal is poignantly expressed:

O waly, waly! but love be bony   *alas*
  A little time, while it is new;
But when't is auld, it waxeth cauld,
  And fades away like morning dew.

'Tis not the frost that freezes fell,
  Nor blawing snaw's inclemency;
'Tis not sic cauld that makes me cry,
  But my love's heart grown cauld to me.

In England the tradition extends from a simple fragment, which seems to allude to the maiden's shameful secret, 'Bryd on brere, y telle it to non other, y ne dar', to the more polished lyrics set to music for the Tudor court, such as 'In wyldernes/Ther founde I Besse'. This lyric, like many others of the genre, is set in the *chanson d'adventure* convention, that is the poet feigns that wandering in a wood or some other remote place he comes upon the maiden. This opening is especially appropriate to the complaints of the betrayed maiden, for the lonely place reflects the social isolation of the maiden brought about by her lover's abandonment of her and her child.

The most striking poem in this genre is an adaptation from the French probably written towards the end of the thirteenth century. In this poem, 'Nou sprinkes the sprai', the poet comes upon a little maiden who is regretting her lover in tones of extraordinary colloquial vindictiveness: 'the clot him clingge' (may he rot in his grave), she exclaims, and finally comes the threat, 'yiif i mai, it shal hime rewe,/bi this dai'. Very different from this is Besse's much later expression of constancy:

So fro my hert
Shall he not stert,
Thof he be gon.   *Though*

The vindictiveness of 'Nou sprinkes the sprai' is the invention of the English author: in the French the maiden only protests that she is too afflicted with grief to forget her lover. The French, however, has an ending that makes it closer in style to a pastourelle, for the poet offers his love to the maiden, and after three kisses she accepts this instantaneous consolation. It seems unlikely that the English poem had a fourth verse to correspond to this: if it did it would have been far more brutal than its French original, for the acceptance of the new lover would have come as the issue of the maiden's desire for vengeance on the old.

The pastourelles are the most dramatic of the lyric forms, drama-

tic in the sense that the drama is within the poems and not in the pre-
supposed context, and also in that they are almost entirely in dialogue
form: the reciter may well have modified his voice to mimic the
masculine pleading and the feminine coquettishness. The interest lies
entirely in the wit and spiritedness of the dialogue. Although the setting
of these poems is rural (a wood or field) and one of the participants is a
shepherdess (or, occasionally a milkmaid), the poems are not rustic in
tone, but urbane: they are as rustic as the paintings of Watteau or of the
desport of Marie Antoinette at the Petit Trianon. Beneath the pretty,
and vivacious, surface, the conception is cynical: men are deceivers, but
women are their match. The poems are usually a verbal game, in which
the man's protestations of true love and the maiden's protestations of
modesty are rightly believed by neither. They therefore bear the same
relationship to the formal love lyric as does the fabliau to the romance: in
the one women are unattainable, in the other a promise of a new dress is
enough to win them. But, whilst they share with the fabliaux the same
base view of human motives and passion, they are far more sophisticated
because in their expression of them there is no response to ugliness or
gross comedy.

The earliest known English pastourelle is that called by Brook in
his edition of the Harley lyrics, 'The Meeting in the Wood'. It
contains many of the typical features of the genre. The poet-narrator,
having come upon a maiden whose beauty is as radiant as gold, at first
addresses her formally, 'Yhere thou me nou, hendest in helde . . .',
but by the end gives a most colloquial invitation to love, 'the beste red
that y con to us bothe/that thou me take ant y the toward huppe',
whilst the maiden, who had begun with admirably moral sentiments,
'betere is were thunne boute laste/then syde robes ant synke into
synne' (it is better to wear poor clothes without shame than
sumptuous dress and fall into sin), has progressed to the unusually
frank admission 'ych am a maide, that me ofthuncheth'. It is this
abruptness, the sudden abandonment of the most strenuous verbal
resistance, that so often provides the punch at the end of a
pastourelle.

In another pastourelle of about the same date, however, the
maiden sends her would-be lover packing at the end: 'Wend fort ther
ye wenin better for to sped'. All her replies are in the same realistic
and colloquial style, whilst the lover's advances are on the verbal
surface irreproachably formal:

I sayd to that semly that Crist should hir save,
For the fairest may that I ever met . . .
That I mit becum her man, I began to crave.

The joke in this poem lies in the explosion of the courtly style, another common feature of the pastourelle form, but one not often so consistently and effectively carried through as it is here.

Two late examples of the pastourelle in English may be briefly mentioned. One, 'Hey, troly loly lo, maid, whither go yow', portrays a milk-maid who, unlike her usual counterparts, is not in her wit and imaginative resourcefulness a Shakespearean comic heroine in miniature, but a country bumpkin, and the joke lies in the fact that though the wooer's proposals grow more outrageously frank, she has but one answer, 'I pray you, sire, let me go milk my cow'. The other is the ballad of 'The Baffled Knight', which preserves an ancient theme of the pastourelle, that in which the maiden evades the unwanted wooer by some humiliating ruse. In this ballad the maiden meets the knight's offer of love by suggesting that he should take her to the comforts of her father's hall, but when they arrive she bars the gate to him, and mocks him for his faint-heartedness:

'You had me' quoth she, 'abroad in the field,
Among the corne, amidst the hay,
Where you might had your will of mee,
  For in good faith, sir, I never said nay.'

This ballad is more coarse-grained than the early French pastourelles with their delicate poise and irony, but it is a good example of a pastourelle in which the verbal sparring is matched by trickery in the action.

Allied to the pastourelles are the lyrics of the night visit. In these the meeting place is at the maiden's window (in German they are now called *Fensterlieder*), and the lover pleads for admission, which he usually gains after the maiden has pleaded excuses such as the wrath of her parents (also a recurrent argument in the pastourelles). The Harley lyric commonly called *De clerico et puella* seems to be of this type. The lover in this poem is, superficially at least, more courtly than is his usual counterpart in French and German. He does not call bluntly, 'ouvre ta porte', or, as in the ballad of 'Willie and Lady Maisry', 'Oh open, open, Lady Margerie,/Open and let me in', but begs in the language of *fine amour*, 'thou rewe on me, thy man'. But the maiden goes bluntly to the heart of the matter:

'Be stille, thou fol, y calle the riht; cost thou never blynne?   *can/stop*
thou art wayted day ant nyht with fader ant al my kynne.   *watched*
Be thou in mi bour ytake, lete they for no synne   *forbear*
me to holde ant the to slon, the deth so thou maht wynne!'   *kill*

This fear, incidentally, does not seem to be melodramatically feigned, if one measures it against the tragic action in the ballad of 'Clerk Saunders'. The ending of such lyrics is usually happy: neither wooer nor maiden is cynically conceived, and the maiden opens her door genuinely and rightly convinced of her wooer's love. Therefore the maiden's final submission in *De clerico et puella* is to be understood seriously, not ironically, and the clerk's protestations of love are not callous euphemisms as they would be in a pastourelle, but are in the fitting style for an educated man to use in the expression of his love.

Most of the other lyrics in the Harley manuscript are celebrations of the lady's beauty and virtue, which often culminate in an appeal for her love. As in most eulogies individuality fades in the periphrases for perfection: the lady is not conceived personally but as the archetype of womanhood. This may be expressed in a series of metaphors, as in the lists of jewels, flowers, birds and spices in 'Annot and John' or in a description of the lady's features and limbs in the correct rhetorical order from forehead to toe as in 'Blow, northerne wynde'. Sometimes, and most successfully, the two methods may be combined, as in 'The Fair Maid of Ribblesdale', in which the features are not simply praised in epithets of excellence or of conventional beauty (grey eyes, etc.), but in terms of sunbeams, rose-gardens, lilies and gold-thread. Though the imagery of these poems delights the imagination, it is almost entirely visual, rarely tactile: the line in which the side of the maiden is said to be 'softe ase sylk' stands out for its rare sensuousness. The general absence of sensuous imagery gives to the medieval love lyric, in contrast to the Elizabethan and Jacobean, a certain intellectual austerity. The only medieval lover to make an invitation to love in sensuous language is January in the *Merchant's Tale*.

Comparatively little of the Harley lyrics is given to analysis of the lover's feelings: tears, sighs, sleeplessness, longing for death with protestations of unending but hopeless service, never form the sole substance of the lyrics as they do in so many of their French counterparts and English successors. Moreover, when they do occur, they are not related introspectively, but with an external and unexpected zest, being offered as a fitting tribute to the lady's beauty. The subject of the lyrics is always the lady, not the lover's feelings. Indeed, despite some protestations of misery, these are poems of happy love, and the happiness irradiates both the formality of the praise and the conventional symptoms of the lover's distress. Though sometimes in literature it seems easier to convey unhappiness than happiness realistically, in the Harley lyrics the sense of happiness arises from a more naturalistic treatment of love than is found in comparable French poetry. The formal catalogues of 'Annot and John', for instance, are interrupted by the more colloquial couplets with which each stanza ends, and which culminate in the final lines that express the delight and gaiety of requited love:

He haveth me to hede, this hendy anon,	*this fair one has me to care for*
gentil ase Ionas, heo ioyeth with Ion.	

Whilst in 'Alysoun' the sadness of the poet's description of his cheeks wet with tears and his long weariness is belied by the gaiety of the (perhaps borrowed) refrain:

An hendy hap ichabbe yhent,	*A joyful fortune has befallen me*
ichot from hevene it is me sent;	*I know*
from alle wymmen mi love is lent,	*withdrawn*
ant lyht on Alysoun,	

a refrain that promises that the poet's last appeal, 'Geynest under gore,/herkne to my roun', will succeed. Similarly, a poem, 'Blow, northerne wynd', which appears to end in abstractions, is made more immediate and hopeful by its refrain, 'Blow, northerne wynd,/sent thou me my swetyng', which in its evocative inconsequence suggests an origin in popular song.

In other poems, the directness of the wish expressed in the last lines suggests an expectation of love returned. One, 'A wayle whyt ase whalles bon', for instance, uses in its final stanza an erotic conceit, deriving from a long tradition that stretches from Catullus's sparrow to Donne's flea:

Ich wolde ich were a threstelcok,	*song-thrush*
a bountyng other a lavercok,	*bunting/lark*
swete bryd!	
Bitwene hire curtel ant hire smok	*gown/shift*
y wolde ben hyd.	

Two others, 'The Lover's Complaint' and 'The Fair Maid of Ribblesdale', express the same thought in an extravagant but probably conventional hyperbole:

Hevene y tolde al his	*accounted*
that o niht were hire gest,	

an exclamation that seems to represent a Christianized and attenuated version of the magnification of sexual love found in some of the elegies of Propertius, particularly that (II, xv) in which such a night is said to confer a godlike immortality. Though these echoes of the robust yet subtle style of classical love poetry are faint, they add a note of strength of poetry that depends more upon the artificial manner of the French.

Two scholars, Audiau and Chaytor, and, more recently, Stemmler, who have written upon the relationship between French and English lyrics, have shown that the Harley lyrics are a tissue of borrowed formulae. But, as so often in medieval poetry, the borrowed details, through slight variations in emphasis, selection or juxtaposition, produce a quite different effect from that of their sources. The feeling in the French lyrics is that of the poems on the definitions for love (of which there is only one version in English), in which love is described in a series of paradoxes: it is a joyful pain, a health-giving sickness, a restless peace. But the world of the Harley lyrics is not one of tension and contradiction, an artificial world in which men resign themselves to perpetual despair, and women, if they respond to their pleas at all, are moved only by pity. As the author of the *Ancrene Wisse* says, 'Me sulleth wel love for love', love is a fair exchange for love, and this is the feeling of the Harley lyrics. Unlike narrative, the love lyric does not have to be concerned with moral laws, but the French lyrics seem so insistently related to the courtly love code that the lady's modesty and dignity have to be preserved by the appeal for pity. In the Harley lyrics the possibility of marriage is neither affirmed nor denied. Without any slur there-fore upon the virtue of the lady, it is a harmonious and optimistic world, in which, whilst lovers may have to wait, it is the natural law that love wins love and brings happiness.

One of the chief merits of the Harley lyrics is that, though they are filled with stereotyped thoughts and formulae, they nevertheless give an impression of freshness and spontaneity. These qualities are especially valuable in the love lyric for they give an effect of sincerity, an impression that the subject of the poem is an ex-perience and not a formal compliment. This of course does not mean that autobiographical truth should be sought in them: it is quite likely that their authors, like Lydgate, a later writer of love poetry, were in religious orders. But it is a fallacy to equate an impression of sincerity conveyed by style with personal revelation. Indeed some of the poems surviving from the fifteenth century may well have been genuinely addressed by the poet to his mistress, but by comparison with the earlier ones they appear insincere. Whilst the explanation may partly lie in the fact that by this time diction as well as convention had become stereotyped, it probably also lies in the fact that in the social context of the fifteenth century a love poem would have been an elegant gift in a situation whose emotional vitality existed outside the poem, whereas in a good love poem the relationship of the lovers must not simply provide the social framework, but must be constructed within the poem itself.

The cataloguing of feminine beauty continued in the fifteenth-century lyric; indeed the catalogue had become so recognized a form that for sport its content might be reversed: Hoccleve praises a lady for having a narrow (instead of broad) forehead, and eyes that shone like jet; his similes are comic, her shape is like a football, and her voice, when she sings, like that of a parrot. Though equally conventional, this kind of poem gives a welcome relief from the general monotony of the form. Metaphorical lists are extended from flowers and precious stones to the heroines of classical and medieval literature whom the lady is said to equal or surpass, Penelope, Griselda, Alcestis, Dido, Cleopatra, Isolde. The style is often aureate, and disagreeable clusters of words of ostentatiously Latin origin overload the line. Even in the simpler style, which was the direct ancestor of the sixteenth-century lyric style that C. S. Lewis nicknamed 'drab', abstract nouns predominate, and too often abstract suffixes in -esse or -aunce (e.g. Penaunce, remembraunce, grevaunce, displesaunce) provide the rhyme. Insofar as there is love poetry of this period to be praised it is the work of poets such as Charles d'Orléans, whose poetry will be discussed in another chapter. In general, convention which had for so long been the tool of many anonymous but masterly poets, at last in a period of decadence won the upper hand, and itself became the master.

The religious lyrics seem at first sight to resemble closely the love lyrics in both style and structure, though closer attention reveals radical differences, except in the lyrics addressed to the Virgin. These have the same development as the love lyrics. The early poems show a delight in the praise of the Virgin's beauty, and a serene yet intense joy in the duty of loving and serving her:

With al mi lif y love that may,   *maiden*
Heo is mi solas nyht and day,
my ioie and eke my beste play
    ant eke my lovelongynge;
al the betere me is that day
    that ich of hire synge.

But by the end of the fourteenth century the poems lose their freshness: the praise becomes less apparently spontaneous and more formal and rhetorical, the style more heavily ornate, and the conventions of secular poetry seem to be borrowed without any imaginative feeling for their propriety. In two poems, for instance, the individual beauty of the Virgin's features and limbs is praised in regular order from top to toe, in others she is said to surpass a long list of classical heroines, such a Cleopatra or Thisbe. The poems are dominated by a desire for correctness of verbal manners and by an ostentatious display of rhetorical conventions and aureate diction. Whilst it is possible to acquire a taste for these poems, it *is* an acquired one, and like their secular models, they would show poorly in quotation, for their merit lies in the artifice of the whole.

The more numerous and satisfying poems on the Passion, Nativity and Death in some ways resemble the dramatic genres of the love lyric such as the *aube* or complaint of the betrayed maiden, for many of these poems are speeches isolated from a dramatic scene which has to be understood, or like the pastourelles, they are self-contained dialogues: Crucifixion or Nativity scenes provide an understood framework for a speech from Christ on the Cross, for an address of the Virgin to the Christ-child, or for a dialogue between Christ and the Virgin; a churchyard setting may be assumed for a warning or lament of a dead body in its grave. These resemblances, however, are superficial in that they overlay a radical difference between secular and religious lyrics, that is the relationship between the 'I' character in the poem and the reader or hearer. In the secular lyric the narrator is an objective character within the poem, and the poem is a performance to which the audience is related almost as is an audience to a play. But in the religious lyric the 'I' character and the reader or hearer must become one; they are therefore more like prayers than poetry and are intended for memorizing or private reading. Moreover where a figure speaks, such as Christ or the Virgin, these speeches are not interior reflections nor (usually) words addressed to a character within the poem, but are addressed directly to the reader, who thus himself becomes a character within the poem. Poetry of this kind can best be described as meditative, for, as in traditional meditation upon the Gospel narratives, the reader has to visualize a whole dramatic scene, such as the Crucifixion, and to imagine himself present within it. The meditative purpose has two important effects upon the style. Firstly there is a strong emphasis upon visual detail in order to help the reader to form the scene in his imagination; secondly, the emotion expressed is deep (in order that the reader may be moved to make it his own) but restrained in order that the reader may not become alienated by excess.

The emotive use of visual detail may be illustrated from the following four lines from an early verse:

Wyt is thi nachede brest and blodi is thi side,	*naked*
Starke aren thine armes that strekede aren so wyde.	*stiff*
Falu is thi faire ler and dummes thi sithe,	*pale/cheek*
Drie es thin ende body on rode so ytycthe.	*lifeless/fair/fastened*

The dramatic and meditative context of this verse is that of the speaker standing or perhaps kneeling at the foot of the Cross (his position may be compared to that of the donor in many Italian paintings of the Crucifixion), and he speaks a description of what he sees, which is both a lament and a direct expression of compassion to the sufferer. There are six adjectives in these lines, four that are primarily descriptive, two ('faire' and 'ende') that are primarily loving. The two kinds, however, fade into one another, for to describe to a person the visible symptoms of his sufferings is an every-day and no doubt very ancient way of communicating sympathy and distress.

Often in expressions of personal lament the Virgin's sufferings are linked with those of Christ, for her grief provided an even more immediate and comprehensive stimulus to compassionate involvement. The little verse, sometimes called 'Sunset on Calvary', provides a moving example of this:

Nou goth sonne under wod, –	
me reweth, marie, thi faire rode.	*face*
Nou goth sonne under tre, –	
me reweth, marie, thi sone and the.	

Though it is possible to find logical and doctrinal explanations for the imagery of the setting sun (Christ, for instance, was traditionally called *sol justitiae*, the sun of righteousness, and 'wod' and 'tre' may be taken to apply to the Cross), nevertheless it seems to have an emotional and instinctive life of its own, so that the whole verse suggests the same kind of numinous quality that we noticed also in 'O western wind'.

'Nou goth sonne under wod' is addressed directly by the meditator to the Virgin; in another very beautiful poem the refrain is poetically addressed to the tear that lies upon the Virgin's cheek, whilst in the stanzas the meditator speaks to Christ:

Thu sikest sore,   *sighest*
Thi sorwe is more
Than mannis muth may telle;
Thu singest of sorwe,
Manken to borwe   *ransom*
Out of the pit of helle.
   Luveli ter of loveli eiye,
    Whi dostu me so wo?
   Sorfel ter of sorful eiye,
    Thu brekst myn herte a-to.
I prud and kene,   *violent*
Thu meke and clene,
With-outen wo or wile;   *sin or guile*
Thu art ded for me,
And I live thoru the,
So blissed be that wile.
   Luveli ter of loveli eiye, etc.

This poem has an elusive quality rare in the medieval lyric. The single tear upon the Virgin's cheek (so different from the sobbing and swooning that recur in fifteenth-century depictions of her) epitomizes the restraint of the whole, and is the symbol both of her grief and of the meditator's, becoming the still point of sorrow to which the meditator's address to Christ ever returns.

The antithetical contrasts briefly touched on at the beginning of the second stanza occur more commonly in the complaints of Christ where they are used to express reproach rather than contrition. The *Improperia* or Good Friday Reproaches, which Rosamund Tuve showed to lie behind Herbert's 'The Sacrifice', provided the rhetorical pattern, but this style of poised and witty antithesis, which is often achieved in medieval Latin poetry (and which was so subtly imitated in 'The Sacrifice'), did not usually fit well into the looser syntactical patterns of the Middle English lyric. There are, however, some striking exceptions, and the following is an excellent example of the style at its best:

Ihesus doth him bymene,   *makes his complaint*
and speketh to synful mon:
'Thi garland is of grene,
Of floures many on;
Myn of sharpe thornes,
myn hewe it maketh won.

Thyn hondes streite gloved,
white and clene kept;
Myne with nailes thorled,   *pierced*
on rode and eke my feet.

The visual parallels, ironically contrasted, between Christ
crucified and the fashionably dressed young man bent upon social
pleasure, were not the invention of the poet, but rather a commonplace of sermon literature. But with the aid of romance and
social satire the poet has brought them to life: Christ's nailed hands
are not simply contrasted with gloves as in the analogues, but with
gloves that are white, close-fitting and well-cared for, suffering
hands as against hands marked by absorption in the vanity of dress.
The poem is carefully contrived, for the satiric tone, which inevitably implies rejection, fades in the last stanza into an appeal for
love, 'Be thou kynde pur charite,/let thi synne and love thou me':
this stanza is less poetically ingenious than its predecessors but
smoothly returns the poem to the devotional tradition.

The complaints of Christ are, however, more often sustained
appeals for love, which are again filled with visual details, the
personal descriptions of suffering being manifest evidence of
Christ's love which can only fittingly be met by love returned. The
following two stanzas from a long fifteenth-century complaint are
typical of the later style:

Thow synfull man that by me gais,	*goest*
Ane whyle to me thou turne thi face!	
Behald my body, in everylk place,	
How it is dicht,	*treated*
All to-rent	*gashed*
And all to-schent	*destroyed*
Man, for thy plycht.	
....	
Behalde my schankis and my kneis,	*legs*
Body, heid, armes and theis;	*thighs*
Behald, on me na thing thou seis	
Bot sorrow and pyne –	*suffering*
Thus was I spylt,	*put to death*
Man for thi gylt	
And not for myne.	

As in many poems of this period the tone is more urgent and the
detail more dramatic than they had been in earlier lyrics. The
speaker is the figure of Christ on the Cross, made timeless by
representation in paint or stone, so that the narrative can stretch
from the scourging to the piercing of Christ's side after His death.
In one manuscript it is accompanied by an illustration, a stylized,
suffering figure of Christ on the Cross, whom one must imagine as
the speaker of the poem.

Just as the Virgin is sometimes the object of the meditator's compassionate address, so is she also the speaker of complaints. In the fourteenth century and earlier it is to Christ that she expresses her sorrow as she stands by the Cross:

Mi swete sone that art me dere,
Wat hast thu don, whi art thu here?
Thi swete bodi that in me rest,
That loveli mouth that i have kist, –
Nou is on rode mad thi nest.
Mi dere child, what is me best?

Love and distress shine out through the epithets of endearment, which are deliberately repeated, through the two questions, anguished in origin, but expressed with tenderness and restraint, and through the sadly ironic use of the word 'nest', which in the Middle Ages was used – probably as a conscious metaphor – for a small, snug, secure place.

In the fifteenth century the Virgin more commonly speaks her complaint to man: she is to be imagined sitting, with the dead body of Christ stretched across her lap, as in the famous statue of Michelangelo. Sometimes this leads to the type of ironic contrast, already noticed in the complaints of Christ:

O woman, a chaplet chosyn thu has	*garland*
Thy childe to were, hit dose the gret likyng,	*it gives you great pleasure*
Thu pynnes hit on with gret solas;	
And I sitte with my son sore wepyng,	
His chaplet is thornys sore prickyng,	
His mouth I kys with a carfull chere –	
I sitte wepyng and thu syngyng,	
for now liggus ded my dere son, dere.	*lies*

In this poem the appearance and gestures of the Virgin with the dead Christ are throughout contrasted with those of a mother who holds her child in her lap, playing with it, dancing it up and down, and fondling it. In this verse the mother is imagined to put on her child's head some little garland – presumably of the daisy-chain type – and to sing some song for its amusement: this contrasts bitterly with the crown of thorns and the Virgin's weeping.

Good medieval lyrics on the Passion (and, to a lesser extent, the Compassion) are abundant; in contrast, lyrics on the Nativity are fewer, late, and less interestingly varied. The nineteenth- and twentieth-century cult of the Christmas carol, with its supposed roots in the Middle Ages, has to some extent obscured the historical situation. *The Oxford Book of Carols* contains only a handful which are of medieval English origin, and only one or two that dwell in a meditative way upon the maternal tenderness of the Virgin, the sweetness and poverty of the Christ-child. The following is a verse from the finest:

A lovely lady sat and sange,
　And to her son thus gan she say:
'My Son, my Lord, my dere derlyng,
　Why liggus thou thus in hay?
　　Myn own dere Son,
　　How art thou cum?
　　　Art thou not God verey?
　　But neverthelesse
　　I will not sees
　　　To syng, 'By, by, lully lulley'.

There are, however, no English medieval lyrics amongst the carols now widely known and sung. *In dulci jubilo*, for instance, is a sixteenth-century translation from the German; whilst the very beautiful 'Tomorrow shall be my dancing day' has undergone stylistic alterations since the Middle Ages and perhaps some imaginative re-working, though its evocative combination of secular love-song and Passion narrative are undoubtedly of medieval origin.

Many Middle English carols are of a learned nature, being filled with types and prophecies of the Incarnation, whilst others are very simple narratives, which, divorced from their music, have little worth. The best are the lullaby carols, which, like the one quoted above, show the long shadow of the Crucifixion already dark upon the crib of the Christ-child. Many are dialogues between the Virgin and Child, in which the Child foretells the Passion; others are dialogues between the Virgin and St. Joseph, or perhaps between all three. The following is a particularly touching example:

This endurs nyght   *other*
I sawe a syght
　All in my slepe:
Mary, that may,   *maiden*
She sang lullay
　And sore did wepe.
To kepe she sought
Full fast aboute
　Her son from colde;

Joseph seyde, 'Wiff,
My joy, my lyff,
   Say what ye wolde.'
'Nothyng, my spowse,
Is in this howse
   Unto my pay;   *pleases me*
My Son, a Kyng
That made all thyng,
   Lyth in hay.'

This verse is characteristic of what is best in the medieval lyric: the expression of the tenderness of human relationships in a style of which the art lies in the total concealment of art.

Lyrics on the subject of death may be best approached through the graveyard scene in *Hamlet*. When Hamlet fancifully tells poor Yorick's skull, 'Now get you to my lady's chamber, and, tell her, let her paint an inch thick, to this favour she must come', he is urging the skull to deliver the macabre warning that had been the distinctive theme of many of the medieval death lyrics. One fifteenth-century lyric is actually described in its rubric as a mirror in which young ladies may look as they do their toilet, and it contains a warning from death personified:

Maist thou now be glade, with all thi fresshe aray,
One me to loke that wyll dystene thi face.   *deprive of beauty*
Rew one thy-self and all thi synne uprace!   *uproot*
Sone shalte thu flytte and seche another place,
Shorte is thy sesoun here, thogh thou go gay.

The speaker is the armed skeleton (the second stanza refers to his mace) who dominates late medieval literature and art, the figure who comes upon man unawares and when he is unprepared. Metaphorically he may be described as a thief, as in the *Pardoner's Tale* or in a little verse beginning, 'Behold man I come as thef', or as an officer of the law, 'that fell serjeant death', summoning his victims to judgment. Whilst he can sometimes frighten by appearing as a solemn and menacing figure, the Dance of Death, in which he flings up his skeleton arms and legs in a mockery of happiness, is especially appalling in its gruesome gaiety. Whilst some of the poems, such as the one quoted above, are direct addresses of Death to the reader, others are dramatically self-contained, and are designed to accompany artistic representations. The many wall-paintings of the Three Living and the Three Dead, in which time is broken down so that three young men meet their future skeletons, is often accompanied by short verses on scrolls that extend from their mouths like balloons in a modern strip cartoon. The only long English poem on this subject (there are quite a number in France) is written in the alliterative metre and diction, the romance associations being made apposite by the fact that the protagonists are three kings out hunting (in this poem exceptionally the dead are not their future selves but are their fathers). The warning given by the second skeleton sums up the theme:

Lokys on my bonus that blake bene and bare.
Fore wyle wondon in this word, at worchip we were,   *we lived/world*
Whe hadon oure wyfe at our wil well fore to ware.   *possess*
Thenkes ye no ferle bot frayns at me ferys,   *wonder/learn fear from me*
Thah ye be never so fayre thus schul ye fare.

The imaginative and didactic content of the Dance of Death is similar, but distinguished by its social inclusiveness and emphatic repetition. A figure of death could be a mirror to all, and medieval literature insisted upon the ancient theme of the levelling power of death, the equality of the grave; but this point was not made explicit in the Three Living and the Three Dead, whereas in the Dance of Death everyone might find his likeness both in the living (who are about to die) and in the dead. The introduction to Lydgate's poem emphasizes this:

In this myrrowre everi wight mai fynde
That him behoveth to go upon this daunce.

The poem consists of pairs of stanzas: Death's summons matched by the lament of the man about to die. Death, for instance, summons a high-born lady as follows:

Come forth anoon, my lady and Princesse,
ye moste also go up-on this daunce.
Nowt mai availe yowre grete straungenesse,   *aloofness*
Nowther yowre beaute ne yowre grete pleasaunce,
yowre riche a-rai ne yowre daliaunce
That somme-tyme cowde so many holde on honde *put off with false promises*
In luve: for al yowre dowble variaunce   *false inconstancy*
ye mote as now this foting understonde.   *the steps of this dance*

To the medieval imagination the mirror of death was provided not merely by a figure of death personified, but also by many non-allegorical figures, the old, the dying, and the dead themselves. Old age was described as a messenger of death, and the laments of the old man, such as 'Le regret de Maximian' or 'The Old Man's Prayer' (which led later into the obscene archery songs), originally conveyed a didactic warning. The dying were described in a list of signs, which had been formulated as medical symptoms by the famous ancient physician, Hippocrates, signs now more familiar from Mistress Quickly's description of the death of Falstaff. In an early lyric the dying man's appearance is described as follows:

When the hede quakyth	
And the lyppys blakyth	*grow pale*
And the nose sharpyth	
And the senow starkyth	*grow rigid*
And the brest pantyth	
And the brethe wantyth	*fails*
And the tethe ratelyth	*chatter*
And the throte roteleth	*make a rattling noise*
And the sowle is wente owte	
The body ne tyt but a clowte	*the body's lot is nothing*
Sone be it so stekene	*securely buried*
The sowle all clene ys forgetene.	

Most important of all, the dead warned the living from their graves. The narrative context of this is often the familiar preacher's injunction to the proud to visit the tomb and to learn from it the squalidness in which his own earthly life must end:

Wat so thu art that gost her be me
Witstand and behold and wel bethenk the
that swich as thu art i was wone to be
And swich as i am nou saltu sone be.

The crux of these verses is always the inexorable link made between the living and the dead, What I was you are, what I am you shall be. In the fifteenth century it became a common theme of epitaphs on tombs and brasses. A verse of this kind is stylistically at the opposite pole from the Dance of Death typified by the stanza quoted above. The Dance of Death with its reflective range and elevated diction has far more of the obvious qualities of poetry, but the bare, artless warning from the dead has an immediate dramatic impact, which could only be diminished by greater contrivance.

About two thousand religious lyrics survive from the Middle Ages, a quite considerable quantity even though the period spanned exceeds two hundred years. Furthermore many of them survive in a considerable number of manuscripts, which is sure evidence that they had a wide diffusion. In *Piers Plowman* one of the sins to which Sloth confesses is that he did not know any 'rymes' of Our Lord or Lady, and from the combined evidence of this and of the manuscripts it may be inferred that everyone was expected to know one or two religious lyrics and that many people in fact did so.

The mystery plays, which served the same devotional purpose, will probably have been almost as widely known, though the absence of actual theatre-buildings perhaps now conceals from us the fact that drama was a widespread literary form in the late fourteenth and fifteenth centuries. Though only four cycles of mystery plays survive, those of York, Chester, Coventry and Wakefield, documentary evidence shows that many other towns, such as Newcastle, Beverley, Norwich and Lincoln, performed cycles, whilst more than a hundred other towns and villages had individual religious plays of one kind or another. The surviving cycles show much individual variety, but within a pattern of broad resemblance: therefore, whilst much is lost, we may be reasonably confident that we know what medieval drama was like.

The plays were in all probability composed by men in religious orders, who, like the authors of the religious lyrics, drew on the wealth of doctrinal and devotional literature for their material and its interpretation, but presented it with a strong simplicity of outline, so that it would not baffle or bore the unlearned. The actors were usually the trade guilds, who, being already accustomed to put on elaborate pageants and tableaux for royal occasions, had the resources and expertise necessary for long and elaborate productions that had to please the eye as well as the ear. The audience was mixed, and, as in the Dance of Death, might extend from king to peasant. The Wife of Bath who went 'to pleyes of miracles' may perhaps be taken as typical of the inveterate play-goer in the late fourteenth century. The occasions were usually the feast of Corpus Christi or (less commonly) Whitsun: these were the festivals of the Church that could be fittingly celebrated with gaiety and rejoicing, and which fell in the season in which fine weather might reasonably be expected. For a massive performance that stretched from dawn to dusk long hours of daylight and rainless skies were essential conditions.

The English cycles differ from their continental counterparts in that their structure is the whole history of the world, beginning and ending in the heavens: the Creation of the Angels to the Last Judgment. Within this vast compass of time significant scenes were chosen: invariably the Creation and Fall, Cain and Abel, the Flood, the Sacrifice of Isaac, the Annunciation and Nativity, the Passion, Harrowing of Hell and the Resurrection, and the Last Judgment. Other scenes, which the custom of art and narrative had traditionally made important, could be added at will, their inclusion or exclusion perhaps depending to a large extent upon the number of guilds available. The scope of a play also depended upon the number of guilds. In the York cycle, for instance, the Creation and Fall is divided into five plays, in Chester it makes one. The need to provide for each of York's many guilds may be inferred here, for the divisions are as dramatically irrelevant as the 'natural breaks' in the plays on commercial television nowadays. Plays were allotted to guilds with an appropriateness that is often comic and sometimes brutally ironic: the watermen, for instance, might put on the Flood, the butchers the Crucifixion. The division into small units, however, is one of the chief characteristics of the form. Nowadays we expect large subjects to be executed in a bold and majestic plan; but the mystery cycles resemble the *Canterbury Tales* in that, whilst each small piece may be enjoyed for its own sake, the effect of the whole far exceeds in power the sum of the individual parts.

The mystery plays evade common critical assumptions about the kind of plot and characterization appropriate to drama. A mystery cycle may be said to have a theme rather than a plot: if one assumes with Aristotle that plots must be of reasonable length and present one action as a unified whole, then the narrative surface of the cycles looks more like that of a sprawling chronicle than a play; nevertheless their unwieldy length and episodic structure is held firmly and satisfyingly together by the doctrinal pattern of Fall and Redemption. Whilst some of the plays, such as those of the Fall of Man or of the Sacrifice of Isaac, contain plots that are potentially complete plays in themselves, others are undramatic incidents that have only didactic or doctrinal importance. But, in order that the pattern and proportions of the cycle may be preserved, promising plots are developed only within strictly measured bounds, and important episodes such as the Annunciation are built up so that they may carry equivalent weight. Throughout the cycles there is therefore a pleasing and restful alternation between the immediately dramatic and the more formal re-enaction of historical incident: a cycle that consisted solely of dramatically powerful subjects would be unbearable to watch.

Just as good plots are not allowed to outgrow their place in the whole, so also is the characterization developed only within limits. In the York cycle, there are, for instance, about a hundred and twenty characters, excluding attendant angels, devils, soldiers, etc. Such a crowd could only co-exist within one frame if none was allowed to dominate. The method of performance of course also precluded any psychological individuality in words or gesture: for, where a figure appeared in more than one play, he would have been acted by different people, and it must therefore have been dress, not physiognomy, that distinguished him. The authors dealt with these and other problems of characterization by creating an often animated surface which overlaid a doctrinal and aesthetic pattern, unrelated to psychological realism. Clear examples of this method of procedure are Noah's wife, who on one level is the obstinate, shrewish wife of the fabliaux, but on another repeats the self-willed disobedience of Eve, and Isaac, who on one level shows, like the 'litel clergeoun' of the *Prioress's Tale*, the pathos of innocent childhood, whilst on the deeper level he is a type of Christ, foreshadowing His willingness to die.

One of the largest patterns in the mystery plays is established in the opening of the Fall of Angels, in which there is an emphatic contrast between the stillness and harmony of God with the faithful angels and the noise and rowdy agitation of Lucifer with his companions after the Fall. In the written text this distinction is made through style and metre. The doxology of the unfallen angels is measured and dignified, and the weight of the eight-line stanzas is increased by the use of alliteration:

A! mercyfull maker, full mekill es thi mighte,
That all this warke at a worde worthely has wroghte,
Ay loved be that lufly lorde of his lighte,   *praised*
That us thus mighty has made, that nowe was righte noghte.

In contrast the devils speak in abusive and colloquial exclamations, and the stanza is broken up into scraps of speech so that its firm shapeliness is entirely obliterated:

Lucifer: Walaway! wa! es me now, nowe es it war thane it was.   *worse*
    Unthryvandely threpe ye, I sayde but a thoghte.   *quarrel with me uselessly*
2nd devil: We lurdane, thu lost us.   *ruffian/destroyed*
Lucifer: Ye ly, owte! allas!
    I wyste noghte this wo sculde be wroghte.
    Owte on yow! lurdans, ye smore me in smoke.   *smother*
2nd devil: This wo has thu wroghte us.
Lucifer: Ye ly, ye ly!
2nd devil: Thou lyes, and that sall thu by,   *pay for*
    We lurdans have at yowe, lat loke.

When the play is acted this contrast is repeated in appearance and action. In the York productions God the Father, with the angels posed symmetrically on either side, stands silent and motionless above, whilst beneath the devils writhe and scrabble in turmoil. It is likely that the medieval wagons on which the plays were acted had two levels, and that producers were then able to achieve the same effect.

This contrast between calm and silence and noise and agitation recurs throughout the cycles. From Cain to the executioners at the Crucifixion, the evil characters are marked by noise and stridency, the good by quietness and poise. This antithetical pattern is especially marked in the Passion sequence, where in play after play the evil boast and conspire, whilst Christ centrally on stage stands silent. So obtrusive is this silence that it can, as it were, even be heard from the printed page. The climax of the pattern comes in the Crucifixion scene, in which the executioners boisterously and callously nail Christ to the Cross. The Crucifixion play of the York Cycle consists of twenty-five twelve-line stanzas. All but two of these are divided up among the four soldiers who taunt Christ and keep up a running commentary on the action. Twice, however, a whole serene stanza is given to Christ. The following is the second of these with a little of the surrounding conversation:

3rd sold: Now will this crosse full stabely stande,
    All yf he rave thei will noght ryve.   *they [the wedges] will not split*
1st sold: Say, sir, howe likis thou nowe,
    this werke that we have wrought?   *work*
4th sold: We praye youe sais us howe,
    ye fele, or faynte ye ought?
Jesus: Al men that walkis by waye or strete,
    Takes tente ye schalle no travayle tyne,   *Take heed that you do*
                                      not lose sight of my suffering
By-holdes myn heede, myn handis, and my feete,
And fully feele nowe or ye fyne,
Yf any mournyng may be meete
Or myscheve mesured unto myne.
My Fadir, that alle bales may bete,
For-giffis thes men that dois my pyne.
What thai wirke wotte thai noght,
Therefore my Fadir I crave.
Latte nevere ther synnys be sought,   *may they not be condemned*
                                        for their sins
But see ther saules to save.
1st sold: We! harke! he jangelis like a jay.
2nd sold: Me thynke he pratis like a py.   *magpie*

There is irony in this jeering: it is the soldiers who throughout could be said to have jangled like a jay, to have jabbered like a magpie: indeed it is an excellent description of their ceaseless, brutal chattering; whilst Christ's magisterial appeal for compassion (based on the Lamentations of Jeremiah I, 12, 'Is it nothing to you, all ye that pass by? Behold and see if there be any sorrow like unto my sorrow', which was sung as the words of Christ in the Good Friday liturgy, and had given the opening lines of many lyric complaints of Christ) sounds serenely through the raucousness, and passes over the heads of the executioners to the audience.

This is one (though probably the best) of the many instances in which the audience are brought into the plays: it is they who pass by, not any actors on the stage. One can say either that, as in many lyrics, the audience must imagine themselves standing on Calvary, or that they must imagine that the Crucifixion takes place before their very eyes in their own local street: the traditions of meditation suggest the former, the deliberate use of anachronisms the latter. In the plays historical time is so carefully broken down that either or both of these interpretations is possible. Superficially the dramatic convention here used may seem to resemble the aside, familiar from classical and later English drama, but the medieval audience's role is substantially different. In Roman and Elizabethan plays the audience can at most be said to have the role of a confidant in the wings: but in the mystery cycles they take the part of characters central to the action, whom the dramatist has deliberately chosen not to represent on the stage. This is one of the many ways in which the cycles are dramatic in an entirely idiosyncratic way.

The mystery plays are rich in patterns and variations. Though at first sight they may seem simple to the point of naïveté, there are in fact few that will not repay detailed analysis. Their achievement, however, lies in a continuous series of small, subtle effects: the scale is never large, and it is as though one were looking at a huge landscape through the wrong end of a telescope.

Far more than the romances and lyrics, the reading of the mystery plays makes demands on the modern reader. Part of the difficulty is linguistic, for, being Northern texts, their language is not so comprehensible as Chaucer's London English, and no other literature will accustom one to their colloquialisms. But more serious is the fact that they were written for acting: on the printed page they lose some of their power. Fortunately the plays have recently become so popular that there is now hardly a year without an important production of them. Even then something may be lost. The play of the Creation of the World perhaps gained something from being performed at dawn with the first rising of the sun, and the Last Judgment from the background of falling night. But this is a small point. It has undoubtedly been the impression of modern critics and audiences that the mystery plays when watched are both compelling and moving.

The mystery cycles bear an evident relationship to the religious lyrics on the Passion and Nativity: the plays on these subjects sometimes incorporate earlier lyrics or, if not, make use of lyric themes; and behind both lies the same substantial sources, the Latin meditations (such as the *Meditationes vitae Christi*) which amplified the sparse Gospel narrative, filling it in with homely and realistic detail. The other main branch of medieval drama, the morality plays, bear the same kind of affinity to the lyrics on death and to their ultimate source in the sermons.

As early as 1215 a Lateran Council had decreed that all laymen must be thoroughly instructed in the nature of the seven deadly sins, and from the mid-twelfth-century onwards homiletic treatises on this subject multiplied: the *Parson's Tale* is a late example of this type of literature. By the end of the fourteenth century a play on the subject of the seven deadly sins in conflict with their opposite virtues was being performed at York and other towns. Unfortunately no version survives, though from what we can infer it seems that the plays would have been more interesting as a didactic spectacle than as drama. Certainly the apparently corresponding scene in the *Castle of Perseverance* (in which the Sins' attacks are repelled by the roses, symbolic of the Passion, which the Virtues throw at them) is the only dull part of the play. The early morality plays that survive are dramatically superior in that they do not present an abstract battle, but show man himself upon the stage, and often man at the moment of death. Even this type of allegorical drama may not sound promising: it would be difficult to make a good play out of the figure of a man who was an empty shell, with all his impulses towards good and evil scattered externally on the stage as abstract personifications. The allegory, however, does not work in such a clearcut way. The figure of man, though typical, is whole, retaining his natural impulses and capacities to respond to external situations; the personifications are only partially psychological (in the sense that Daungier or Belacueil in the *Romance of the Rose* externalize the lady's inward feelings), and are to a larger extent absolutes which become embodied in typical situations or characters that a man may literally meet in the course of his life. Temptation dialogues are already on the way to the genre scenes of the later interludes, in which the vices entice man to the tavern or the brothel. Moreover in the sense that the sins are abstractions, they have a malign energy and delight in manipulating man towards his downfall, and in this have plausibly been shown to be the remote ancestors of Iago.

The earliest of the known plays, *The Pride of Life*, survives only in an incomplete text, though fortunately a prologue gives the outline of the whole plot. Though the hero is called the 'King of Lyfe', he is not literally a king as in the later political moralities, but an everyman whose heedless self-confidence and disregard for death is indicated by his title and expressed in the supremely arrogant action of summoning Death to a battle, in order to determine who shall have the 'maistrye': He dies and is saved only through the mercy of God, symbolized in the intervention of the Blessed Virgin. The King of Life's challenge to death is reminiscent of the young revellers' search for death in the *Pardoner's Tale*. Both are guilty of an awe-inspiring blasphemy, for the only slayer of Death is Christ (occasionally in the iconography of the Dance of Death the previously dancing skeleton at last lies down, prostrate beneath the feet of Christ). The *Pardoner's Tale* of course deals with this theme far more subtly than does *The Pride of Life*, but in both the flamboyance of the action catches the imagination, and we, who, unlike the characters, understand the laws of the allegorical world in which they live, tensely await the allegory's inevitable end.

The pursuit of death seems to be peculiar to these two works. Usually in the morality plays man's forgetfulness of death is shown by the reverse, namely death's summons to him when he is least prepared. In the *Castle of Perseverance* this comes as the climax to the whole unfolding of man's life from birth to old age. In shape this play parallels the mystery cycles: whilst the latter give a history of mankind up to the Last Judgment, the *Castle* gives a history of the individual man up to the personal judgment (that is the judgment given at death). Both are without an artistically imposed design: their scope is determined by the nature of the material, not by artistic decision. Furthermore in the morality plays psychological verisimilitude contributes to an indecisiveness of outline: the plot, mirroring life, consists of moral fluctuations, from virtue to sin, back to virtue again, and then the final submission to love of material possessions as old age approaches. The seven deadly sins are divided under the leadership of the World, the Flesh and the Devil: to the flesh belong the three carnal deadly sins, sloth, lust and gluttony; to the devil the sins that were his own, pride, envy and wrath, and to the world, fittingly, avarice. Man, after succumbing to the wiles of avarice, and struck down by Death, is saved by the intervention of Mercy and Peace (two of the traditional four daughters of God), who plead the Passion on his behalf. The compelling power of the play lies in its buttonholing of the audience, who cannot fail to see a likeness to themselves in poor *Humanum Genus*, who hovers between virtue and sin, and at last, in a scene that must have resembled the illustrations of the *Ars Moriendi*, lies in his bed, emaciated and at the point of death. Attention to this long play is also won by the many passages of lively dialogue, the sins already showing the cold and dedicated energy to plotting that was to remain an important characteristic of the Tudor interludes.

Mankind is the most ebullient and least sombre of the early plays: man's lapse into sin is never brought into pointed focus by the approach of death, and there is therefore nothing in the action to counterbalance the zestful jocularity of the evil characters, Mischief, with his assistants, Nought, New-gyse and Now-a-days. It is probably this lack of a serious moral centre that has led some critics to believe it to be a morality play that fell into commercial hands (it was performed by travelling players) and thereby became debased. There seems, however, no reason to think that the occasional sexual obscenities and the more common lavatorial humour were money-getting concessions to the taste of village yokels. This kind of wit has a natural part in satire and invective, and in the Middle Ages it may be found in works that range from the plays of the Fall of the Angels to some of the satiric poems of Dunbar. It is admittedly more pronounced in *Mankind*, but the scatological and also the linguistic jokes are carefully woven into the structure. The play is primarily an ironic study in the conspiracy of evil, the vicious characters throughout enacting a parody of the good. The play is dramatically self-conscious. The aureate style, for instance, which in the fifteenth century was considered fitting to the virtuous, is mocked by the wicked, who mimic comically the learned abstract diction of Mercy, accusing her of speaking 'Englysch Laten'. When, for instance, at the beginning of the play Mercy solemnly announces that at the Day of Judgment the corn will be gathered in and the chaff burnt, Mischief replies:

For a wynter corn-threscher, ser, I have hyryde;   *hired*
And ye sayde the corn shulde be savyde, and the chaff shoulde be feryde;
                                                                    burnt
And he provyth nay, as yt schewth be this verse:

'Corn servit bredibus, chaffe horsibus, straw fyrybusque'.
Thys ys as moche to say to yowr leude undyrstondynge,
As the corn shall serve to brede at the nexte bakynge.
　'Chaff horsybus, et reliqua,'
The chaff to horse shall be goode produce;
When a man ys forcolde, the straw may be brent,   *chilled*
And so forth, et cetera.

This answer, with its pseudo-scholastic distinctions, has all the vitality of the best nonsense verse. The potential moral danger of the play is presumably that the good may seem dull, the wrong gay. But, whilst undoubtedly the imaginative life of the play lies in the treatment of the wicked characters, in the last resort our sympathy is given to the victim who escapes and not to the would-be machinators of his downfall.

By common consent *Everyman* is the most powerful of the morality plays. It lacks entirely the surface vitality of its predecessors: there are rare touches of irony as in Cosyn's excuse ('I have the crampe in my to') for not accompanying Everyman on his journey to death, and in Felawship's sententious farewell, 'For you I wyll remember that partyng is mournyng', but a search for such details would be a misreading of the text, in which the author has deliberately sought for an austerely dignified style. The pleasure to be gained from *Everyman* does not lie in the lively depiction of evil, but in a convincing representation of the plight of Everyman. In the other plays the hero has our sympathy because he is so plainly a mirror of us, what we are and what we shall be. But for a variety of reasons we are more dramatically involved in the fate of Everyman.

Everyman has the advantage of a definite plot. The substance is not the whole life of man, not a typical episode from it, but a shaped story, that of the man with four friends. The theme of faithless friends, whether in disaster, or, as later in *Timon*, in feigned disaster, was common in the Middle Ages, particularly in exempla. In a common version, a man condemned to die is abandoned by the friends that he first turned to and whom he cared for most, save the last, who signifies Christ. In *Everyman* the moral is different but equally orthodox: man can be shown as being saved through the mercy of God alone as in the *Pride of Life* and the *Castle of Perseverance* or through his good works as in the plays of the Last Judgment. In popular literature strands are disentangled which in strict theology are intricately involved.

Two novelties, that Everyman stands in a more complex allegorical relationship to the other characters and that he dies in a

state of grace, allow for more variation and subtlety in the characterization of Everyman. He can show a different range of emotions,
hope, hurt, and disappointment, as he seeks his friends and they
abandon him, emotions that arouse sympathy; and he can die with a
mixture of sadness and resignation. In the *Castle, Humanum Genus*
dies, uttering the warning to the living that is found in so many
lyrics:

Now, good men, takythe example at me.
  Do for youreself whyl ye han spase.
For many men thus servyd be
  Thorwe the werld in dyverse place.
I bolne and bleyke in blody ble,   *swell/grow pale/colour*
  And as a flour fadyth my face.

But as Everyman feels the approach of death he says:

Alas, I am so faynt I may not stande;
My lymmes under me do folde.
Frendes, let us not tourne agayne to this lande,
Not for all the worldes golde;
For in to this cave must I crepe,   *grave*
And tourne to erth, and there to slepe.

This touching speech has emotional reverberations foreign to and
far surpassing the normal morality style, and it is for this that
Everyman is to be admired, despite elsewhere a certain stiltedness in
dialogue. It is possible that *Everyman* was written to be read rather
than acted (it survives only in printed editions): if this were so, it
would account for the lack of verbal effervescence, which is far less
suited to private reading.

    The literature discussed in this chapter did not have one uniform
fate in the sixteenth century. The religious lyric is unique in
vanishing almost completely and without progeny. Love lyrics and
moralities influenced their Tudor successors, the poetry of Wyatt
and the many plays known as interludes. Mystery plays continued to
be acted for a long time until, against the will of the audiences, they
were suppressed on account of their 'Popish' strain. Romances
continued to be read and enjoyed: Marlowe and Spenser show
evidence of knowing them. There was therefore no sudden break in
the sixteenth century, but a gradual shift in emphasis, and the
emergence of new styles under continental influences.

7

LATER POETRY: THE COURTLY TRADITION

Douglas Gray

I

Most of the poetry which forms the subject of this chapter was
written, not by anonymous craftsmen, but by authors whose names
are known, who often display a marked individuality, and who take a
conscious interest in the art of writing. They are well-read and
sometimes learned men, and can draw easily on the traditions of
Latin and French literature. They are courtly poets. A few of them,
like Charles d'Orléans or William de la Pole, Duke of Suffolk, were
members of noble families; all of them either moved in courtly
circles or wrote poems for courtly patrons whose sophisticated and
fashionable tastes they shared.

The English courtly tradition was fostered in a splendid manner
by the generosity, indeed the extravagance, of the cultivated
Richard II, patron of Froissart, Chaucer, and Gower. His royal
successors could hardly compete with his display, nor could they
match the lavish patronage given to the arts by some of the French
kings or princes like Jean de Berry, but their record is not without
merit. Henry V was interested in books as well as in warfare, his
brother John, Duke of Bedford, was a notable connoisseur of
illuminated manuscripts and collected a fine library, while another
brother, Humfrey, Duke of Gloucester (1390–1447) was the outstanding English literary patron of the fifteenth century. By
bringing Italian scholars to England, communicating with Italian
humanists, and collecting newly discovered classical works and
Latin translations of Greek books, he played an important part in
the introduction of the 'new learning', and by his generous gifts to
the University of Oxford he established the basis of a great library.
Edward IV (1442–1483), a patron of Caxton, collected a number of
beautifully illuminated manuscripts from Bruges. And there were
many other noble patrons of lesser rank. The poet Lydgate produced works for such figures as Thomas Montacute, Earl of

Salisbury, and Richard Beauchamp, Earl of Warwick, and for noble ladies like Margaret Talbot, daughter of Beauchamp and wife of John Talbot, Earl of Shrewsbury. The most flamboyant of the literary nobility later in the century was John Tiptoft, Earl of Worcester (ca. 1427–1470), whose combination of cruelty and culture has been compared to that of some Italian Renaissance princes. He travelled to Italy, collected books, and was a friend and patron of humanists, but he was also known as 'the butcher of England'. The grim story of his end is told in *The Mirror for Magistrates* in the next century. We know, too, that some of the country gentry were active patrons of letters, and, as always, there was the traditional patronage of the Church, monasteries, and eminent clerics.

Courtly culture was still not defiantly national (anti-French sentiments, for instance, are usually found in more popular forms of literature), and still derived most of its inspiration from France. Chaucer's interest in Italian vernacular writing was not pursued by his followers, and although the influence of Italian humanism grew steadily throughout the period, in general the themes and interests of English courtly poetry remained those of the dominant 'international Gothic' literary culture. There were many personal and political contacts with France and Burgundy, and one suspects that Gower's facility in writing French verse was an achievement shared by more than one of his contemporaries. A few French writers visited England – Froissart was at the court of Richard II, and Charles d'Orléans was an eminent literary prisoner taken at Agincourt. One would like to be able to believe the story in Rabelais that the poet Villon came to England and entertained the court of Edward IV, but there seems to be no other evidence at all for it.

The most obvious literary influence on English poetry at this time, however, comes from a native source, the work of Chaucer. His poems were held in the highest esteem in the fifteenth century, and were carefully copied and preserved, sometimes in sumptuously produced presentation manuscripts. The poems of the period have many Chaucerian echoes or allusions, so that the poets, both English and Scottish, are sometimes given the title of 'Chaucerians'. This should not imply, as does the title 'Spenserian' given to some minor eighteenth-century poets, some sort of antiquarian revamping of a style which is felt to be pleasingly archaic. The late medieval poets are 'Chaucerian' in that they genuinely regard Chaucer as their acknowledged master, in whose steps they could, though unworthily, follow. It is true that in their treatment of

Chaucerian themes they are often cautious and limited – with proper humility they do not attempt to rival *Troilus and Criseyde* or *The Canterbury Tales* – but there are some lessons which they have learnt thoroughly.

The previous chapters of this book have shown that there was a great deal of good writing in England before Chaucer appeared. But in a real sense he was the first great poet of the language, a poet whose genius was acknowledged, and whose formative influence endured far beyond his own time. This, of course, is a commonplace of sixteenth-century criticism; Sidney, in the *Apology for Poetry*, lists the 'fathers of learning' – among the Romans Livius Andronicus and Ennius, among the Italians Dante, Boccaccio and Petrarch, and

so in our English were Gower and Chaucer, after whom, encouraged and delighted with their excellent fore-going, others have followed to beautify our mother-tongue, as well in the same kind as in other arts.

His remark about beautifying the mother-tongue echoes an important question in Renaissance criticism, the discussion of the status of the vernacular as against the classical languages, and of the ways in which it may be improved or 'illustrated' to become a fitting vehicle for literature. The theoretical discussion of this question in England belongs to the sixteenth century, but with the acknowledged greatness and dominance of Chaucer the conditions necessary for the discussion were already present in the fifteenth century, as they had been in Italy after the death of Dante. Some of the poets seem to be aware of this. In their many laudatory passages about Chaucer one common feature is the insistence on his eloquence, and the way in which this has 'illumined' 'our English'. Lydgate says that Chaucer

In his dayes hath so well him borne
Out of our tong t'avoyden al rudenes   *remove*
And to reforme it with colors of swetenes.

'Thy fresch anamalit (enamelled) termes celicall' (heavenly) says Dunbar of him at the end of *The Golden Targe* in his most ornamental and hyperbolical manner,

This mater coud illumynit have full brycht;
Was thou nocht of oure Inglisch all the lycht,
Surmounting eviry tong terrestriall,
Alls fer as Mayis morow dois mydnycht?

In fact the late medieval poets did learn from Chaucer a great deal about the art of writing well. Their verses may not be inspired, but they usually have an ease of movement and a confident handling of syntax, and the reader is aware of a constant striving for eloquence, a self-conscious attempt to write in a polished and distinguished manner. The passion for eloquence may sometimes be undiscriminating, but in the best poets it means more than prolixity and rhetorical display.

While the writers of the period prize eloquence (in the sense of 'the art of expressing thought with fluency, force and appropriateness' [*NED*]), the more refined literary virtue of elegance ('tasteful correctness, harmonious simplicity, in the choice and arrangement of words' [*NED*]) does not seem to have been sought for in the same self-conscious way, although it is from time to time achieved (notably in the work of Gower). It is interesting that the first use of the noun 'elegance' listed in the *NED* comes from the beginning of the sixteenth century. The quest for elegance in vernacular writing may well be a direct consequence of the growth of interest in polished and 'correct' Latin; a famous and influential manual by Lorenzo Valla was printed in 1471 under the significant title of *Elegantiae Linguae Latinae*.

One result of the widespread interest in style and rhetoric has often been exaggerated and misrepresented. This is the 'golden' or 'aureate' diction (the adjective *aureate* seems to have been introduced by Lydgate) found in some poems, the deliberate use of Latinate words like *celicall* ('heavenly') or *nebule* ('cloud'). This is not the normal manner of late medieval verse, nor is it necessarily bad 'poetic diction', 'rootless, without actuality' as one critic calls it. There are certainly cases where it is little more than 'half-changed Latin' (a contemporary criticism), but such experimental excesses, like those of the introducers of 'ink-horn terms' in the following century, were committed in the good cause of 'illuminating' the vernacular, and making it a fit vehicle for eloquent poetry. Moreover, the best fifteenth-century poets use 'aureate' diction with some tact and sense of decorum; it is found most characteristically in religious poetry, especially in poems of salutation to the Virgin Mary enthroned in majesty as Queen of Heaven, where it recalls the splendid, corruscated Latin of the Litany and the Marian hymns. And, as we shall see, it is not the only sort of stylistic experiment used by the poets; some make striking use of the rhythms and vocabulary of colloquial speech.

Our survey of the English courtly poets begins with a contemporary and friend of Chaucer, John Gower (*d.* 1408), a poet who,
like Chaucer, enjoyed the patronage of Richard II. The *Confessio
Amantis* was written at Richard's instigation; the original prologue
describes how the poet met the king in the royal barge on the Thames
and was requested to 'boke som newe thing'. Gower's poems are
preserved in beautiful manuscripts, some of which were illuminated
by the famous court painter Herman Scheere. They were read and
admired for two centuries, and Gower's name was traditionally
linked with that of Chaucer as one of the early masters of English
poetry. He wrote fluently in French and Latin as well as in English –
balades in the manner of Froissart, the *Mirour de l'Omme*, a long poem
on the vices of the age, and a learned political and satirical poem in
elegiacs, the *Vox Clamantis* – but it is his long poem in English, the
Confessio Amantis, which concerns us here. As its name suggests, it is
the confession of a lover, Amans, to his confessor Genius, the priest
of Nature, a combination of religious and love doctrine (as Thomas
Warton says, 'the ritual of religion is applied to the tender passion,
and Ovid's *Art of Love* is blended with the breviary') which the courtly
audience clearly found pleasing and sophisticated. The Confessor
illustrates the Deadly Sins which threaten the lover by a large
number of exemplary stories. Many of the best of them come from
Ovid, the 'clerk' of Venus. Gower was fascinated by classical myth
and legend, and he re-tells the pathetic and melodramatic stories of
the *Metamorphoses* with such sympathy that a recent editor, Professor
J. A. W. Bennett, has said that he 'stands at no great distance from the
later humanists and translators'.

The *Confessio Amantis* is now a neglected poem. The modern
reader may be repelled by its length, by the number of stories which
it contains, and by the encyclopedic material which he will encounter from time to time (like the account of the religions of the
world in Book V, or the disquisition on 'philosophy' in VII).
Moreover, Gower's manner of writing is remarkably unobtrusive. In
fact, his delicate simplicity is the result of deliberate and careful
artistry. His lines have a genuine polish, and a sense of verbal
melody which is rare in medieval English poetry. Typical are passages of simple description:

Bot whan the blake wynter nyht
Withoute mone or stere lyht
Bederked hath the water stronde,
Al prively thei gon to londe . . .   *secretly*

or of brisk vigorous narrative:

> The houndes weren in a throwe   *moment*
> Uncoupled and the hornes blowe:
> The grete hert anon was founde,   *immediately*
> Whiche swifte feet sette upon grounde,
> And he with spore in horse side
> Him hasteth faste forto ride,
> Til alle men be left behinde . . .

The rare descriptive detail often acts as a focus for the emotional atmosphere of a whole scene – thus, when Jason has won the Golden Fleece,

> On bothe his knes he gan doun falle,
> And yaf thonk to the goddes alle.   *gave*
> The flees he tok and goth to bote,
> The sonne schyneth bryhte and hote,
> The flees of gold schon forth withal,
> The water glistreth overal.

The simpler rhetorical devices such as anaphora or other forms of repetition are cleverly used in scenes of mental turmoil, and here the usually smooth rhythms and syntactic patterns are deliberately disrupted. Pygmalion has fallen in love with the statue he has made:

> And after, whan the nyht was come,
> He leide hire in his bed al nakid.
> He was forwept, he was forwakid,
> He keste hire colde lippes ofte,
> And wissheth that thei weren softe,
> And ofte he rouneth in hire ere,   *whispers*
> And ofte his arm now hier now there
> He leide, as he hir wolde embrace,
> And evere among he axeth grace
> As thogh sche wiste what he mente:
> And thus himself he gan tormente
> With such desese of loves peine,
> That noman mihte him more peine . . .

Against the usual plain and unassertive style, an unusual word stands out very strikingly (as Iris's 'reyny cope'), and the use of direct speech can give the impression of an outburst of unbearable emotion. In the story of Tereus and Philomena the account of the approach of the man intent on rape is given by the narrator until the climax, when Philomena calls out despairingly

'O fader, o mi moder diere
Nou help!'

Similes too, sparely used, can be given the same force. In the story of Jason and Medea, Medea goes out at midnight, 'with open hed and fot al bare', to practise her sorcery:

Al specheles and on the gras
Sche glod forth as an addre doth,   *glided*

and the very simple simile beautifully expresses the silent and sinister movement of the woman. Similes are used to increase the emotional atmosphere of the rape of Philomena. Tereus, the 'tirant raviner', advances on her

And in a rage on hire, he ran,
Riht as a wolf which takth his preie . . .

She is helpless and can only lie 'oppressed and desesed'

As if a goshauk hadde sesed
A brid, which dorste noght for fere
Remue . . .   *move*

There are a number of famous 'set pieces' of varying degrees of elaboration – the House of Sleep (from Ovid) in the story of Ceix and Alcyone (IV), the Loathly Lady in the story of Florent (I), Medea collecting the herbs for her magic (V), the eerie dream of Ulysses (VI) – and in every case the plain background increases the intensity. Sometimes the complaints of suffering characters have a more formal, 'higher' style. After the violent passion and action in the story of the rape of Philomena, the heroine utters a moving rhetorical lament:

. . . If I among the people duelle,
Unto the people I schal it telle;
And if I be withinne wall
Of stones closed, thanne I schal
Unto the stones clepe and crie,
And tellen hem thi felonie;
And if I to the wodes wende,
Ther schal I tellen tale and ende,
And crie it to the briddes oute,   *birds*
That thei schul hiere it al aboute.   *hear*
For I so loude it schal reherce,
That my vois schal to the hevene perce,
That it schal soune in goddes ere.

The *Confessio Amantis* is more than a collection of well-told stories. In its unobtrusive and undogmatic way, it is a deeply philosophical poem. In the stories and in the framework in which they are set, the nature of love is illustrated and explored. Gower is aware of the paradoxes and varieties of the 'tender passion'. Love is an overwhelming cosmic power. It may ennoble its servants or it may lead them to destruction. It may appear as madness, or as a sort of drunkenness. 'Honeste love', praised by the Confessor in the story of Apollonius, has its proper part in the realm of 'kinde' or Nature. As Amans says,

in the lawe a man mai finde
Hou God to man be weie of kinde   *by way of nature*
Hath set the world to multeplie.

In the story of Iphis, because

love hateth nothing more
Than thing which stant ayein the lore
Of that nature in kinde hath sett,

Cupid transforms Iphis into a man so that he may marry Iante. Love is vital for society; it is the principle of concord and of peace. In all, there emerges an attitude of gentle tolerance and mature wisdom.

A delicate and interesting relationship is built up between Amans and the complex figure of the Confessor. Their exchanges are invariably lively, and often amusing. Amans becomes a very engaging character. He tells the Confessor that he obeys his lady in almost everything, except when she orders him to stop talking of love:

And yit ful ofte I speke so
That sche is wroth and seith, 'Be stille!',

and describes the tricks he uses to avoid leaving her presence. But by the end of the poem, the Confessor has become, as C. S. Lewis says, 'the lover's deepest "heart", telling him bitter truths, now no longer avoidable.'

The conclusion, in which Amans is healed by Venus, and the fiery dart is removed by Cupid, is one of the most haunting pieces of writing in medieval English. When he hears the verdict of Venus, Amans is caught by a sudden cold and falls into a swoon. Lying there 'ne fully quick ne fully ded' he sees Cupid and his rout with their joyful music, surrounded by companies of the famous lovers whose stories, both fortunate and unfortunate, he has heard. It is a

passage full of nostalgia and gentle melancholy. Amans sees his face
'riveled' with age, and is told by Venus to go 'ther moral vertu
duelleth'. The goddess takes her leave –

    al sodeinly
Enclosid in a sterrid sky,
Venus which is the queene of love
Was take in to hire place above,

– while Amans goes 'homward a softe pas', and prays for the state
of England.

It is more difficult to claim that modern neglect of the poetry of
Thomas Hoccleve (?1368–1426), a younger contemporary of
Chaucer, who spent much of his life in the Privy Seal Office, is
altogether unjustified. His best known poem, *The Regement of Princes*
(1411), dedicated to Henry, Prince of Wales, soon to become
Henry V, is a work of moral instruction addressed to a ruler, a type
of literature which was popular throughout the Middle Ages.
Henry's son, the unfortunate Henry VI, was brought up on similar
material; his tutor, the Earl of Warwick, was to 'lay before him
mirrors and examples of times passed' of the grace and prosperity
which befell virtuous kings and their lands and subjects and of the
misfortune which befell wicked kings. The *Regement* is mostly
written in fluent but uninspired verse, and is heavily informative.
But Hoccleve has a genuine, if humble, talent, which is evident in
the introduction to the *Regement* and in some of his shorter poems.
His *Letter of Cupid*, adapted from a work of the French poetess
Christine de Pisan (1364–?1430), is done with verve and polish. It
presents for an English audience a contribution to a disputed
'question' of contemporary French courtly literature, the argument
over the anti-feminist views expressed in Jean de Meun's part of the
Roman de la Rose. Christine's *Epistre* is a passionate defence of
women against the remarks of their detractors and the 'sory bokes'
of clerks, and Hoccleve's lines preserve something of the impassioned tone of their original:

Malyce of wommen, what is it to drede?	
They slee no man, distroyen no citees;	
They not oppressen folke ne overlede,	*tyrannize*
Betraye empyres, remes, ne duchees,	*realms*
Ne men bereve hir landes ne hir mees,	*messuage*
Empoyson folk, ne houses sette on fyre,	
Ne false contractes maken for non hyre!	

Many of the great names of the age appear in Hoccleve's work – there are lines on Richard II's burial, poems addressed to Henry V, John, Duke of Bedford ('the riall egles excellence'), and a complimentary reference to Duke Humfrey – and sometimes we are almost alarmingly close to the life of the time. In the *Regement* the poet speaks feelingly about the plight of the veterans of the French wars, and refers to the fate of a Lollard, who was 'of heresye/ Convyct, and brent was unto ashen drye'. In the introduction to this poem, which is in the form of a dialogue between the poet and an old beggar, Hoccleve talks at length and in a very entertaining way about his life and problems. Being a scribe is much harder work than you might imagine; you have to concentrate and you can't talk or sing as other workmen can –

We stowpe and stare upon the shepes skyn,
And keepe muste our song and wordes in.

His perpetual worry about money is the theme of his one genuinely witty poem, a punning plea addressed to Master Somer, 'souztresourer' (sub-treasurer), to grant him his Michaelmas 'harvest'. In *La Male Regle* he tells us about his mis-spent life, describing with conventional exaggeration his rather feeble excesses and his (quite blameless) adventures at 'Poules heed' tavern with

Venus femel lusty children deere,
That so goodly so shaply were and fair.

In the *Complaint*, notable for its gravely eloquent opening:

After that hervest inned had his sheves,	*gathered/sheaves*
And that the broune season of Mykelmesse	
Was come, and gan the trees robbe of ther leves	
That grene had bene and in lusty fresshnesse,	
And them into colowre of yelownesse	
Hadd dyen and doune throwne under foote,	
That chaunge sank into myne herte roote,	

For freshely browght it to my remembraunce,
That stablenes in this world is there none,

he speaks about the 'savage sickness' of his mind:

Men seyden, I loked as a wilde steer	
. . . Another spake and of me seide also,	
My feete weren aye wavynge to and fro	
Whane that I stonde shulde and withe men talke,	
And that myne eyne sowghten every halke.	*corner*

The exchanges between Hoccleve and the old man at the beginning of the *Regement* and with his friend in the *Dialogus cum Amico* show a good command of the rhythms of speech. The latter opens briskly:

And, endyd my complaynt in this manere	
One knocked at my chambre dore sore,	
And cryed alowde, 'Howe, Hoccleve! Arte thow here?	
Open thy dore! Me thinkethe it full yore	*long*
Sythen I the se! What, man, for Goddes ore	*Since/mercy*
Come out, for this quarter I not the sy,	*saw*
By out I wot!', and out to hym cam I.	

But his most moving lines occur in his lament for his master Chaucer,

But weylaway! so is myn herte wo,
That the honour of englyssh tonge is deed . . .

Death knew well that this island could never again produce his equal, yet it could not destroy his fame:

. . . his hy vertu astertith	*escapes*
Unslayn fro the, which ay us lyfly hertyth,	*encourages*
With bookes of his ornat endyting,	
That is to al this land enlumynyng.	

The reputation of John Lydgate (*ca.* 1370–1450), a monk of the important Benedictine monastery at Bury St. Edmonds, has declined sensationally since his own time. His name, like that of Gower, was associated with Chaucer, and it seems to have been felt that he might fill the gap left by the death of Chaucer. It was a vain hope. Lydgate has almost nothing of Chaucer's complexity and creative imagination. But he does not deserve the abuse which is often heaped on him (of which Ritson's remark 'a voluminous, prosaick and drivelling monk' is the most extreme and famous example). In a competent if uninspired way he deals with the favourite forms and themes of late medieval poetry, and his enormous corpus of work was influential as well as popular. 'His muse was of universal access' says Thomas Warton, the great eighteenth-century literary historian and a judicious admirer of Lydgate,

And he was not only the poet of his monastery, but of the world in general. If a disguising was intended by the company of goldsmiths, a mask before his majesty at Eltham, a may-game for the sheriffs and aldermen of London, a mumming before the Lord Mayor, a procession of pageants from the creation for the festival of Corpus Christi, or a carol for the coronation, Lydgate was consulted, and gave the poetry.

Modern readers are likely to be alarmed by the sheer length of his more ambitious poems – the *Troy Book* runs to some 30,000 lines, *The Fall of Princes* to 36,000. Yet these poems – the early *Reson and Sensuallite* and *The Temple of Glass, The Siege of Thebes* (*ca.* 1420), the *Troy Book* (compiled for Henry V 1412–20), *The Fall of Princes* (based on a French version of Boccaccio's *De Casibus Virorum Illustrium* and written for Duke Humfrey *ca.* 1431–9) and *The Life of Our Lady* (*?ca.* 1434) – uneven though they are, contain some good writing. In *The Fall of Princes* (the direct ancestor of the sixteenth- century *Mirror for Magistrates*), for instance, can be found fine passages of passionate eloquence like the complaint of Canacee in Book I, or the solemn, elegiac 'Envoy to Rome' at the end of Book II:

Rome, remembre off thi fundacioun,	*of*
And off what peeple thou tooke thi gynnyng:	*beginning*
Thi bildyng gan off fals discensioun,	
Off slaughtre, moordre and outraious robbyng . . .	*violent*

Wher be thyn emperours, most sovereyn off renoun?	
Kynges exiled for outraious lyvyng?	*immoderate*
Thi senatours, with worthi Scipioun?	
Poetis olde thi tryumphes rehersyng,	
Thi lauriat knyhtis, most statli ther ridyng,	
Thyn aureat glories thy noblesse t'enlumyne,	
Is be long processe brouht onto ruyne . . .	

Wher is Tullius, cheeff lanterne off thi toun,	
In rethorik all other surmountyng?	
Moral Senek, or prudent sad Catoun,	
Thi comoun proffit alwei preferryng,	
Or rihtful Trajan, most just in his demyng,	*judgment*
Which on no parti list nat to declyne?	*wished*
But long processe hath brouht al to ruyne . . .	

But for most readers who have penetrated into the depths of the *Fall of Princes*, the narrative style becomes monotonous, and the handling of moral and political themes – the mutability of men's lives, the dangers of discord in the realm, the need for obedience, etc. – seems very ordinary.

Lydgate's poetic virtues are more immediately apparent in some of his shorter occasional poems. The *Letter to Gloucester* is addressed to Duke Humfrey while the poet is engaged on *The Fall of Princes*. The Duke seems to have given Lydgate advice rather than money. So, in the manner of Chaucer and Hoccleve, the poet gives a witty account of the plight of his purse. Dreadful diseases afflict it, for which he cannot find either apothecary or drugs in

Bury. He continues with some nice punning on the alchemical terms *sol* and *luna* (sun and moon, gold and silver), imagery which is carefully directed at the duke's interest in alchemy:

Gold is a cordial, gladdest confeccioun,
Ageyn etiques of cold consumpcion,   *wasting fevers*
Aurum potabile for folk ferre ronne in age   *drinkable gold*
In quyntessence best restauracioun
With silver plate enprentyd with coignage,

and the poem ends with an envoy which affects a shocked surprise at the impertinence of the preceding lines. Only dire need could possibly excuse them. Or there is the lively *Churl and the Bird*, a fable which describes how a captive bird escapes by its wits from a dull and envious churl, or the satirical *Bycorne and Chichevache* (the legendary monsters mentioned in the envoy to Chaucer's *Clerk's Tale* – the first stout and fat because she feeds on henpecked husbands, the second thin and starved because she feeds on obedient wives), which was to be accompanied by illustrations. Or some of the mummings – like the *Mumming at Hertford* in which six peasants complain of the tyranny of their wives. In this sort of subject Lydgate cannot compete with the later poets Skelton or Dunbar, but he makes a passable attempt at a lower style:

... Obbe the Reeve, that goothe heere al toforne,
He pleynethe sore his mariage is not meete,
For his wyff, Beautryce Bittersweete,
Cast upon him an hougly cheer ful rowhe,   *expression*
Whane he komethe home ful wery frome the ploughe,
With hungry stomake, deed and paale of cheere,
In hope to fynde redy his dynier;
Thanne sittethe Beautryce bolling at the nale,   *boozing/ale*
And she gyvethe of him no maner tale;
For she al day, with hir jowsy nolle,   *'juicy' head*
Hath for the collyk pouped in the bolle,   *gulped/Bull Inn*
And for heed aache with pepir and gynger
Dronk dolled ale to make hir throte cleer;   *warmed*
And komethe hir hoome, whane hit drawethe to eve,
And thanne Robyn, the cely poure Reeve,   *innocent*
Fyndeth noone amendes of harme ne damage,
But leene growell, and sowpethe colde potage ...

Lydgate shows a constant interest in style. He experiments with aureate diction and, in his late poems, with cryptic syntax. At his best he can produce 'strong lines' such as these, from *The Dolerous Pyte of Crystes Passioun*:

My deth of deth hadde the victorye
Fauht with Sathan a myhty strong batayle . . .

. . . crownyd with thornys through Jewis cruelte . . .

. . . In Borsa steyned of purpil al my weede . . .

which would have pleased later poets, and did please Thomas
Warton: 'he is the first of our writers whose style is clothed with that
perspicuity, in which the English phraseology appears at this day to
an English reader'.

Some of the most attractive and delightful poems of the period
are those which were thought by scribes or early editors to be the
work of Chaucer. These – the best-known are *The Cuckoo and the
Nightingale* (or *The Book of Cupid*), *The Floure and the Leafe*, *The
Assembly of Ladies, La Belle Dame Sans Merci, The Court of Love* – are
in fact by a number of authors, and vary considerably in date and
style. Before they were removed from the canon in the nineteenth
century, they enjoyed a wide esteem. Dryden, Wordsworth, and
Hazlitt praised *The Floure and the Leafe*, and Keats took the title of a
famous poem from another of the group. Their indebtedness to
Chaucer is never in doubt. *The Cuckoo and the Nightingale* (possibly
written by Sir John Clanvowe, *d.* 1391) opened with a direct
quotation from *The Knight's Tale*:

The god of love, a! benedicite!
How mighty and how greet a lord is he!
For he can make of lowe hertes hye,
And of hye lowe, and lyke for to dye,
And harde hertes he can maken free.

Equally obvious is their indebtedness to the courtly tradition. They
are love poems, and the love they celebrate is exquisite, refined and
ennobling. Thus the Nightingale upbraids the mocking Cuckoo:

'What?' quod she, 'thou art out of thy minde!
How might thou in thy cherles herte finde
To speke of Loves servaunts in this wyse?
For in this world is noon so good servyse
To every wight that gentil is of kinde.

For therof, trewly, cometh al goodnesse,
Al honour, and eke al gentilnesse,
Worship, ese, and al hertes lust,
Parfit joye, and ful assured trust,
Jolitee, plesaunce, and freshnesse,

Lowliheed, and trewe companye,   *humility*
Seemliheed, largesse, and curtesye,   *generosity*
Drede of shame for to doon amis;
For he that trewly Loves servaunt is
Were lother to be shamed than to dye ...

    La Belle Dame Sans Merci is a translation of a French poem by
Alain Chartier, made by Sir Richard Ros, perhaps at the beginning
of the second half of the fifteenth century. The poet overhears a
dialogue between a lover and his implacable mistress, who scorns
his pleas so mercilessly that in the end he dies of unrequited love.
The English is polished and fluent, and is a most impressive
example of the ease in writing which polite authors of the time
could achieve. The flexible style easily captures the ring of the
speaking voice, and the dialectic of the debate is maintained by
delicate variations of conversational tone – the passionate, almost
frenetic tone of the lover, whose 'desyr fer passed his resoun':

... If I purpose your honour to deface,
Or ever did, God and Fortune me shende!   *injure*

... I can no skil of song; by God aloon,
I have more cause to wepe in your presence ...,

and the forthright, reasonable, and unromantic speech of the lady:

'To live in wo he hath gret fantasy
And of his hert also hath slipper holde,
That, only for beholdyng of an y,   *eye*
Can nat abyde in pees, as resoun wolde!
Other or me if ye list to beholde,
Our eyen are made to loke; why shuld we spare?
I take no kepe, neither of yong nor olde;
Who feleth smert, I counsayle him be ware!'

    The lady, who makes much of her 'mesure' (moderation), de-
fiantly defends her freedom:

Free am I now, and free wil I endure:
To be ruled by mannes governaunce
For erthely good, nay! that I you ensure,

and is severe on the perils and treacheries of love:

Love is subtel, and hath a greet awayt,   *snare*
Sharp in worching, in gabbing great plesaunce,
And can him venge of suche as by desceyt
Wold fele and knowe his secret governaunce. ...

It would be rash to call her, as one critic has, a 'bourgoise, concerned solely with her reputation', for the courtly tradition had always allowed plenty of scope for the expression of unidealistic, even cynical and bawdy sentiments, and no doubt many courtly ladies of the time, like her, preferred sense to sensibility. Her attitude, however, certainly caused a scandal in French literary circles. Her railing remark 'Amours est cruel losengier' was condemned as a sin against the God of Love, and her unreasonable cruelty to her lover was stigmatized in a whole series of poetic replies, refutations, and pleadings before the God of Love. It is likely that interest in a disputed 'question' of courtly literature, as in the case of Hoccleve's version of Christine de Pisan's *Epistre*, was responsible for the charge to a knightly author to produce a version in English for ladies ('for hem to whom I durst nat disobey').

In *The Floure and the Leafe* (which seems to have been written by a lady, perhaps in the third quarter of the fifteenth century) we are close to the splendid surface, the pageantry and pastime of courtly life. It is a simple, pleasant allegory. The poetess sees two companies of knights and ladies, the first, dressed in white, with chaplets and branches of laurel, woodbine, and hawthorn, the second dressed in green, with chaplets of flowers. After singing, dancing, and jousting, the first company goes beneath a huge laurel tree. The knights and ladies of the second company sing in praise of the daisy a French *bergerette* or pastoral song. But the sun becomes hot, and they faint; the wind blows, the flowers fall, a storm of hail and rain comes, and they are drenched. Meanwhile the first group is safe under its laurel tree. One of the ladies explains the meaning to the narrator: the company of the Leaf consists of the chaste, the faithful, and the noble, with their queen Diana, the others are the servants of Flora, who loved idleness, and

For to hunt and hauke, and play in medes,
And many other such idle dedes.

References in Chaucer, Deschamps, and Charles d'Orléans suggest that the cult of the flower and the leaf was an actual courtly game, in which everyone, at a May festival, was to choose to serve either the Flower or the Leaf for a year.

Like the other poems of the 'Chauceriana', *The Floure and the Leafe* is written with simplicity and clarity. The delightfully direct account of the effect of the nightingale's song (one wonders if Keats knew this passage) –

The nightingale with so merry a note
Answered him that all the wood rong
So sodainly that, as it were a sote,   *fool*
I stood astonied, so was I with the song
Thorow ravished, that till late and long,
I ne wist in what place I was, ne where,
And ayen, me thought, she song even by mine ere –   *dose*

makes Dryden's modernization sound very verbose:

When she I sought, the nightingale replied:
So sweet, so shrill, so variously she sung,
That the grove echo'd, and the valleys rung;
And I so ravish'd with her heav'nly note,
I stood intranc'd, and had no room for thought,
But all o'erpower'd with ecstacy of bliss,
Was in a pleasing state of Paradise.

The Court of Love (possibly written in the early sixteenth century)
is also close to this social *milieu*. We know of an actual *cour
amoureuse* at the French court at the beginning of the fifteenth
century, which had its ministers and officers, and included the
name of the king, Charles VI, in its register of members. A mass
was directed to be said on St. Valentine's Day, to be followed by a
meal, and 'joieuse recreation et amoureuse conversacion'. Poems
were to be read to the ladies, and to be judged by them. Penalties
too could be imposed: any one who made a *complainte, balade,* or
rondeau 'au deshonneur, reproche, amenrissement ou blame' of
ladies would be driven from 'toutes gracieuses assemblees et com-
paignies de dames et demoiselles'. This is very much the world of
the debates on the *Roman de la Rose* and *La Belle Dame Sans Merci*.
The English *Court of Love* is a very entertaining work. The narrator,
Philogenet, a clerk of Cambridge, is a lively and witty figure, with a
touching devotion to his 'litel Pilobone'. There is much vivid descriptive writing and 'joieuse recreation'; the anguish of the friars,
monks and nuns in the court of Love is recounted with some zest:

Se how they cry and wring their handes whyte,
For they so sone went to religion!
And eke the nonnes, with vaile and wimple plight,
There thought that they ben in confusion . . .,

and there is a fine passage when the birds sing the Matins of Love:

On May day, whan the lark began to ryse,
To matens went the lusty nightingale
Within a temple shapen hawthorn-wise;

He might not slepe in all the nightertale,
But *'Domine labia'* gan he crye and gale,
'My lippes open, Lord of Love, I crye,
And let my mouth thy preising now bewrye.'   *utter*
The eagle sang, *'Venite*, bodies all,
And let us joye to Love that is our helth.'
And to the deske anon they gan to fall,
And who com late, he pressed in by stelth:
Than seid the fawcon, our own hartis welth,
'Domine, Dominus noster, I wot,
Ye be the god that don us bren thus hot.'   *causes us to burn*

'Celi enarrant' said the popingay,   *parrot*
'Your might is told in heven and firmament.'
And than came in the goldfinch fresh and gay,
And said this psalm with hertly glad intent,
'Domini est terra; this Laten intent,
The God of Love hath erth in governaunce';
And than the wren gan skippen and to daunce....

Most of the great mass of minor verse on miscellaneous subjects
which was produced in England during the fifteenth century is of
interest only to the specialist. Saints' lives were written by Lydgate
and by Osbern Bokenham (*ca.* 1392–*ca.* 1447) and John Capgrave
(1393–1464). There is a great deal of practical verse of instruction
– books of courtesy, advice on social behaviour, on diet, on the
practice of alchemy, etc. The *Assembly of Gods* is evidence of the
continued interest in mythology, and *The Court of Sapience* is an
encyclopedic poem which shows some real talent. Walton's verse
translation of Boethius was much admired in its day. The *Metrical
Chronicle* of John Hardyng (1378–*ca.* 1465) drew from Warton,
usually so generous to late medieval writing, the harsh but just
comment 'this work is almost beneath criticism and fit only for the
attention of an antiquary'. Its poetic value can be judged from its
handling of the famous reply of King Lear's youngest daughter:

Cordell the youngest then saied full soberly,
'Father, as muche as ye been in value,
So muche I love you, and shall, sikirly,
At all my might and all my herte full trewe'.
With that he grevid at hir and chaunged hewe,
'Senne thou me loves lesse than thy sisters twain,
The leest porcion shalt thou have of Brytaine'.

At the end of the period, however, there were again poets of merit,
if not of genius, writing in England. The work of three men –
Hawes, Barclay and Skelton – deserves remark. Each spent his

formative years in the reign, and in the case of Hawes and Skelton, at the court, of Henry VII, a monarch who is perhaps remembered for his success as a statesman, and as a patron of discoverers like the Cabots, rather than as a patron of the arts. But we should remember not only his splendid chapel at Westminster, but also the remarkable growth of humanist influence at his court. Interest in the new learning was fostered by foreign scholars, and by diplomatic necessity, and it is in this period that the unfamiliar names of the English humanists of the earlier fifteenth century begin to give way to names like Linacre, Grocyn, and Colet. Something of the new interest is reflected in vernacular poetry.

Stephen Hawes (*ca.* 1475–1530) was a groom of the chamber of Henry VII; tradition has it that he was educated at Oxford, and 'sought the muses in England, Scotland and France'. Even specialists rarely open his minor works – *Comforte of Lovers, The Example of Virtue,* or *The Convercyon of Swerers* (the first 'pattern poem' [1509] in English); his reputation, such as it is, rests on *The Passetyme of Pleasure* (printed 1509). This is a long didactic allegorical romance, which may have been known to Spenser. Like *The Faerie Queene* it unites the form of romance with the mode of allegory; the hero, Graunde Amoure, after instruction in the Seven Arts, and after undergoing tests of valour and fidelity, wins his love, La Bell Pucell. Unfortunately, Hawes did not have the imaginative power to make a success of this demanding and novel type of poem. From time to time, though often dimly or clumsily, something of the spirit of romance emerges:

So longe we rode over hyll and valey
Tyll that we came into a wyldernes;
On every syde there wylde bestes lay,
Ryght straunge and fyerse in sundry lykenes –
It was a place of dyssolate derkenes,

and there are a number of lively scenes and incidents – the meeting with Fame, 'a goodly lady envyronned aboute/With tongues of fyre as bryght as ony sterre' with two white greyhounds and a palfray 'swyfte rennynge as the wynde', or with Godfrey Gobylyve, a foolish and ugly, but very entertaining dwarf – and some good descriptions of the elaborate ornaments on the Tower of Doctryne, especially of the various automata that seem to have fascinated Hawes – images with pipes that, moved by the wind, 'pyped a daunce/Ycleped amour de la hault pleasaunce', and a group of figures on horseback that could perform a mechanical joust. But there are grimly didactic stretches that make desperate reading, and generally the allegorical 'sentence' and the romance adventures seem too easily separable. Sometimes the trouble is that Hawes, like other poets of the time, strives too hard to be eloquent, and strives to be eloquent in the wrong way. He seems to regard rhetoric as a sort of smokescreen (an 'aromatyke fume' is his own unfortunate phrase) with the result that his set descriptions are often incredibly verbose. This one, for instance, compares disastrously with the opening of Chaucer's *General Prologue*:

Into a medowe bothe gaye and gloryous
Whiche Flora depaynted with many a colour
Lyke a place of pleasure most solacyous
Encensynge out the aromatyke odoure
Of Zepherus brethe whiche that every floure
Throughe his fume dothe alwaye engendre. . . .

Yet when he abandons such unfortunate attempts at fine writing, his style often has a pleasing simplicity, and, fitfully, even a curious haunting beauty. At the end of the poem, in the epitaph over the grave of Graunde Amoure, come his most famous lines, which echo the simple, proverbial style of the medieval vernacular epitaphs, and have the clarity and the solemnity of the best religious verse:

O mortall folke, you may beholde and se
How I lye here, somtyme a myghty knyght.
The ende of joie and all prosperyte
Is dethe at laste, through his course and myght;
After the day there cometh the derke nyght –
For though the day be never so longe
At last the belles ryngeth to evensonge.

The poetry of Alexander Barclay (*ca.* 1475–1552) shows the same fitful glimpses of talent as that of Hawes. He was a well-known poet in his own time – a letter concerning the preparations for the Field of the Cloth of Gold asks for 'maistre Barkleye, the blacke monke and poete' to be sent 'to devise histoires and convenient raisons to florisshe the buildings and banquet house withal' – and in the course of his long life, he produced a large number of works, ranging from a translation of Sallust's *Bellum Jugurthinum* to an elementary French grammar. The only two which are remembered are his *The Shyp of Folys of the Worlde* (printed 1509) and his *Egloges* (I–III printed *ca.* 1515, IV–V *ca.* 1521). He first presented to English readers a version of a contemporary best-seller, *Das Narren Schyff* (printed in 1494 at Basel), a satirical work by Sebastian Brant, a native (and later chancellor) of Strasbourg.

Its jaunty and quotable verse, vivid language, rough humour, and display of learning made it immediately popular. Its joyous enumeration of the infinite types of folly was illustrated by a series of brilliant wood-cuts; it is both the last great example of the medieval illustrated poem and a distant precursor of the emblem-books of the sixteenth century. Thanks to a rather dull Latin translation by Brant's pupil, Locher, it was disseminated throughout Northern Europe, and became, in the words of a German scholar, a 'secular Bible which nourished an entire age'. It was translated into Low German, French, Dutch, Flemish and English (in the year in which Barclay's version, based primarily on Locher, was printed, there also appeared a prose version by Watson). The central image of the work, the ship filled with different types of fools, became very popular – Bosch has a finely grotesque and crazy shipload of fools, Skelton uses the idea in *The Bowge of Court*, and about 1510 Pynson printed an anonymous poem called *Cocke Lorelles Bote*, which tells of a boatload of rogues who revel and riot (in one of its lists appear such splendid figures as 'Slygethryfte fleshemonger', 'Mathewe tothe-drawer of London', and 'gogle-eyed Tomson, shepster of Lyn').

Barclay's version is disappointing. It is readable, but often stiff and undistinguished. This is due partly, but by no means entirely, to the comparative flatness of Locher's intermediate version. Barclay's poem is the first work in English to apply the name *satire* to itself, but its satirical power is limited. The writing is too remote and general, and lacks the vital crudity and sharpness of Skelton, and too often the words compare poorly with the inherited woodcuts which accompany them. But there are enough lively passages to make us wish that Barclay's talent had been more sustained. He makes fairly substantial additions, including some interesting local references (he was at one time priest of the college of Ottery St. Mary):

Mansell of Ottery, for powlynge of the pore   *plundering*
Were nat his great wombe, here sholde have an ore. . . .

For if one can flater, and beare a hauke on his fist
He shalbe made parson of Honington or Clist. . . .

and sometimes his indignation is aroused. He describes rowdy scenes in church which make us think of Skelton's *Ware the Hawk*:

One tyme the hawkys bellys jenglyth hye,
Another tyme they flutter with theyr wynges,
And nowe the houndes barkynge strykes the skye,

Nowe sounds theyr fete, and nowe the chaynes rynges,
They clap with theyr handes – by suche maner thynges
They make of the churches for theyr hawkes a mewe,
And canell to theyr dogges, whiche they shall after rewe.

The Shyp of Folys ends with a slighting reference to Skelton and
Phyllyp Sparowe (it is evident that Barclay thought little of either),
but one cannot help feeling that Skelton would have been an
adapter more worthy of Brant's original.

The *Egloges* (the first occurrence, it seems, both of the word
eclogue and of the kind in English) transfer into the vernacular a
popular Latin form; the 'matter' of the first three is taken from
a work on the miserable life of courtiers by the fifteenth century
Pope Pius II (Aeneas Silvius Piccolomini), the last two (on the
behaviour of rich men to poets and on the relative merits of town
and country life) are adaptations of eclogues by the influential
Mantuan (1448–1516). Barclay's *Egloges*, like Mantuan's, are
satirical, and on the whole his writing here is less diffuse than in
The Shyp of Folys. In *Egloge* II Cornix lectures Coridon on the
abominable food of courtiers and rises to a fine pitch of invective:

Seldome at chese hast thou a little licke,
And if thou ought have within it shall be quicke,
All full of magots and like to the raynebowe,
Of divers colours as red, grene and yelowe,
On eache side gnawen with mise or with rattes,
Or with vile wormes, with dogges or with cattes,
Uncleane and scorvy, and harde as the stone . . .

Barclay's *Egloges* do not seem to have had much direct influence on
later English pastoral, but they do from time to time make us think
of later works. Just as, under the pseudonym of Algrin, Bishop
Grindall is praised in *The Shepheardes Calendar*, so here there is a
compliment in homely shepherd's style to the dead Bishop Alcock
of Ely (*d.* 1500), the founder of Jesus College, Cambridge:

Yes, since his dayes a cocke was in the fen,
I knowe his voyce among a thousand men,
He taught, he preached, he mended every wrong,
But, Coridon, alas, no good thing bideth long.
He all was a cocke, he wakened us from slepe,
And while we slumbred he did our foldes kepe,
No cur, no foxes, nor butchers dogges wood   *mad*
Could hurte our fouldes, his watching was so good,
The hungry wolves which that time did abounde
What time he crowed abashed at the sounde. . . .

By far the most important and the most interesting of the poets writing in England at the end of this period is John Skelton (*ca.* 1460–1529). His reputation has swung violently between extremes. Esteemed in his own day, given the title of *orator regius*, and praised by Erasmus, he was generally regarded by the Elizabethans, although they continued to read him, as a buffoon. Puttenham calls him a 'sharpe satirist, but with more rayling and scoffery then became a Poet Lawreat, such among the Greekes were called *Pantomimi*, with us Buffons, altogether applying their wits to scurrilities and other ridiculous matters'. It is not far from this to the 'beastly Skelton' of Pope. But in the twentieth century there has been a remarkable renewal of interest in him, led mostly by poets like Robert Graves and W. H. Auden who admired and found a model in his helter-skelter verse and brilliant colloquial rhythms.

Skelton writes a lot about himself. He is a learned man, and conservative in taste. He is scornful of the quality of some of the new Greek:

> But our Grekis theyr Greke so well have applyed,
> That they cannot say in Greke, rydynge by the way,
> 'How, hosteler, fetche my hors a botell of hay!',   *bundle*

and as a good 'Trojan' he deplores the effects of such newfangled studies on traditional Latin learning. He is inordinately proud of his title of 'poet laureate' but he feels deeply not only about the excellence of his own writing but about the high and serious calling of *vates*. He was a cleric, with experience both of court and country. He was for a time tutor to the Duke of York, later to become Henry VIII. This office ended in 1502 when Henry became heir to the throne, and Skelton was rewarded with the living of Diss, in Norfolk, a town of appropriately curious shape. But he returned to London to become *orator regius* and, for a time, a literary opponent of Wolsey.

An early poem on the death of the Earl of Northumberland (1489) shows an easy fluency and command of rhetoric. The poet makes the traditional and courtly apology for the inadequacy of his words, and encourages and advises the heir without sounding solemnly didactic:

> If the whole quere of the Musis nyne   *choir*
> In me all onely wer set and comprysed,
> Enbrethed with the blast of influence devyne   *inspired*
> As perfytly as could be thought or devised,
> To me also allthough it were promised
> Of laureat Phebus holy the eloquence,
> All were to lytell for his magnificence.

O yonge lyon, but tender yet of age,
Grow and encrease, remembre thyn estate;
God the assyst unto thyn herytage,   *thee*
And geve the grace to be more fortunate!
Agayn rebellyones arme the to make debate;
And as the lyone, whiche is of bestes kynge,
Unto thy subjectes be curteis and benygne,

In *The Bowge of Court* (bowge, 'reward'), a satirical poem on the
vices of courtiers, Skelton takes up the traditional theme of the
dangers of life at court, and the even more traditional form of the
dream allegory, and uses them with startling freshness and sublety.
He cleverly makes the narrator one of the allegorical characters in
the narrative, and uses the image of the ship of fools economically
and vividly. One of the characters that the unfortunate narrator
Drede meets is particularly lively. This is Harvey Hafter, an expert
at 'picking': 'when I looked on him my purse was half afeard'. His
speach is full of echoes of popular songs:

Holde up the helme, loke up, and lete God stere:
I wolde be mery, what wynde that ever blowe,
Heve and how, rombelow, row the bote, Norman, rowe!,

and of colloquial phrases like 'bob me on the noll'. For the first time
since Chaucer we are in the presence of a poet who can exploit
boldly and at length the resources of colloquial speech.

Skelton's time at Diss produced a group of highly entertaining
and talented poems. Whether the scandalous reputation which
tradition ascribes to him there is justified or not, it seems that he
had some difficult parishioners. He writes comic mock-epitaphs for
Adam Udersall and old John Clarke, bestowing on them a kind of
fame ('their names shall never die'). In the *Clarke Trental*, the
insistent drive of the Latin lines is suddenly and comically brought
to rest by a few English words:

. . . In parochia de Dis	*In the parish of Diss*
Non erat sibi similis;	*There was none his like;*
In malitia vir insignis,	*A man outstanding for malice,*
Duplex corde et bilinguis;	*Doubled-hearted and forked-tongued;*
Senio confectus,	*Old and worn out*
Omnibus suspectus,	*Suspected by all,*
Nemini dilectus;	*Beloved to none;*
Sepultus est amonge the wedes	*He is buried . . .*
God forgeve hym his mysdedes!	

In *Ware the Hawk* (?1508) he attacks a parson who was bold enough
to fly a hawk 'in my church of Diss' (such an event is not un-

thinkable at the time). The description of the brouhaha caused by
this 'fond frantic falconer' and the poet's vituperation rise to a
comic crescendo. With a wild display of learning, the offending
parson is compared to a long list of tyrannical oppressors. It is all
done in the breathless, galloping short lines which become characteristic of his later satirical poems, and which bear his name –
Skeltonics.

From this period come a pair of opposites – *The Tunning of
Elynour Rummyng* and *Phyllyp Sparowe*. The first handles the
traditional subject of drinking ale-wives with brilliant and controlled dramatic skill. 'The geste of this worthy feast' describes the
mad rush of wives to try Elynour's unsavoury brew, and the
gruesome scenes that follow. At first one thinks of peasant scenes in
Flemish painting, but the scenes of the poem are never still as the
'mad mummynge' pursues its coarse and crazy way. Like the other
poems it is full of extraordinary diction – 'jawed like a jelly', 'a
tonnysh gyb', 'lampatram', 'bullyphant', 'fysgygge', etc. And in one
memorable passage the verse is punctuated by Elynour's shouts:

Some have no mony	
That thyder comy	*come*
For theyr ale to pay.	
That is a shrewd aray!	
Elynour swered, 'Nay,	*swore*
Ye shall not beare away	
My ale for nought,	
By Him that me bought!'	
With 'Hey, dogge, hey!'	
Have these hogges away!'	
With 'Get me a staffe,	
The swyne eate my draffe!	
Stryke the hogges with a clubbe,	
They have dronke up my swyllyng tubbe!'	
For, be there never so much prese,	*crowding*
These swyne go to the hye dese,	*dais*
The sowe with her pigges,	
The bore his tayle wrygges,	
His rumpe also he frygges,	
Agaynst the hye benche!	
With 'Fo, ther is a stenche!	
Gather up thou wenche;	
Seest thou not what is fall? . . .	

Where *Elynour Rummyng* is crude and rumbustious, *Phyllyp Sparowe*
is subtle and tender, and preserves a remarkable variety of tone.

The first part is a lament spoken by a girl, Jane Scrope, over her dead pet sparrow. This is followed by a section (the 'Commendations') spoken by the poet himself, praising Jane's beauty (even the wart with which Nature has 'augmented' her cheek) with controlled hyperbole and wry affection. Jane's lament is a remarkable piece of writing, which balances half-comic hyperbole with genuine emotion, and is full of dramatic switches of feeling. An operatic curse on the malevolent cat:

O cat of carlyshe kynde . . .   *churlish*
The leoparde savage,
The lyons in theyr rage
Myght catche the in theyr pawes,   *thee*
And gnawe the in theyr jawes!
The serpentes of Lybany
Myght styng the venymously!,

is succeeded by a great list of birds who are called to sing the sparrow's requiem (about seventy sorts, including a few exotica, and some typically bizarre details – 'the mad coot/with balde face to toot'), and by some clear and moving lyrical writing:

And now the darke cloudy nyght
Chaseth away Phebus bryght,
Taking his course toward the west,
God sende my sparroes sole good rest.

The remarkable balance of tones – tender, playfully erotic, affectionately mock-heroic, with a hint of a naughty parody of religious offices and images – makes *Phyllyp Sparowe* a unique and delightful poem.

Skelton is perhaps best known for the group of political and satirical poems written between 1513 and 1523. One or two of these are examples of common types – e.g. the poem against the Scots – or of courtly entertainments – e.g. the 'flyting' against Garnesche. *Speke Parrot* (1521), however, is a poem of a very different sort, indeed it is the most boldly experimental poem in this whole period. As in all his best poems, Skelton invents a figure to speak for him, in this case a peculiarly interesting one:

My name is Parrot, a byrd of Paradyse,
By nature devysed of a wonderous kynde,
Dyentely dyeted with dyvers dylycate spyce
Tyl Euphrates that flode dryveth me into Inde,
Where men of that countrey by fortune me fynd
And send me to greate ladyes of estate:
Then Parot must have an almon or a date . . .

Speke Parrot is not an easy poem. It is full of cryptic allusions, and much of it is baffling and apparent nonsense. C. S. Lewis went as far as to call it 'a cryptogram of which we have lost the key'. But it is by no means completely baffling. Parrot has celestial origins – he is 'a bird of paradise' – and is endowed with supra-human wisdom: there is an allusion to the story of Pittacus (from whom the Latin word for parrot, *psittacus*, is said to be derived), a son of Deucalion, who after the flood lived among the Ethiopians, was renowned for wisdom, and was eventually transformed into a parrot – and longevity. He has also become a lady's toy, a minion, a 'little pretty fool', and he is by repute wanton, bibulous, and a chatterer. And he chatters on, dropping phrases in several languages (including 'Chaldean'), speaking in riddles, mingling apparent foolishness with sharp 'sentence'. He attacks the wickedness and folly of the times – the power and influence of *parvenus* (it is not hard to see a reference to Wolsey, though the satire is not by any means entirely personal and particular), the weakness of those destined by tradition to exercise authority; he alludes to contemporary politics (the conference at Calais) and academic fashions (the learning of Greek). It is a crazy and complex and curiously impressive performance, which exhibits extraordinary stylistic variety and Skelton's usual fantastic and startling diction ('Let Sir Wrigwrag wrestle with Sir Dalyrag', 'nodipols and gramatolls of smalle intelligence' etc., etc.).

In *Colyn Cloute* (?1522), Skelton adopts the figure of a 'simple' man, who speaks roughly and raggedly, and can do nothing but record what he sees and hears (the figure is revived by Spenser). He exposes the vices of the secular clergy and the laity. There are some biting satirical passages – Colyn says of the great prelates

Theyr moyles golde dothe eate,
Theyr neyghbours dye for meate –

mules

but the poem as a whole lacks the complexity and the form of the early satires. This is true also of *Why come ye nat to Court?*, an invective against Wolsey. This rushes on in a breathless way, and is crude, violent, and ranting. The flood of abuse is often over-whelming, but it is rarely artful, except where Skelton's sense of comic fantasy and bizarre games with the language appear:

And hathe his pasport to pas
Ultra Sauromatas
To the devyl, Syr Sathanas,
To Pluto, and Syr Bellyall,
The Devyls vycare generall,

And to his college conventuall,
As well to calodemonyall
As to cacodemonyall,
To purvey for our cardynall
A palace pontifycall
To kepe his court provyncyall,
Upon artycles judicyall,
To contende and to stryve
For his prerogatyve,
Within that consystory
To make sommons peremptory
Before some prothonotary
Imperyall or papall . . .

. . . Balthasor, that helyd Domingos nose
From the puskylde poksy pose,
Now with his gummys of Araby
Hath promised to hele our cardinals eye.

In *The Garland of Laurel* (1523) Skelton returns to the dream-vision. It is a rather traditional poem, and is under-estimated by critics. Like Chaucer's *House of Fame*, its remote progenitor, it shows an intelligent and self-conscious interest in the craft of poetry and in the nature of literary fame. And it contains some very lively writing. As one might expect there are some chaotic crowd scenes, and the poet shows a nice fancy when he describes the gentlewomen of the countess of Surrey at work making a garland of laurel for him; he graciously responds with lyrics addressed to each of them. Skelton's works are recorded in a book of remembrance, and at the end all orators and poets rise to him:

A thowsande thowsande, I trow, to my dome,
Triumpha! triumpha! they cryid all aboute;
Of trumpettis and clariouns the noyse went to Rome;
The starry hevyn, me thought, shoke with the showte;
The grounde gronid and tremblid, the noyse was so stowte.
The Quene of Fame commaundid shett fast the boke,
And therewith sodenly out of my dreme I woke.

Probably Skelton's muse did not quite deserve this universal acclamation. He can be tedious and crude; his satire often is neither polished nor carefully directed (one can see why a great master in the kind, Pope, found his poems 'low and bad'). No doubt he would have said that the objects were themselves gross and crude and vulgar, and that it was necessary for the satirist to adopt the role of the learned buffoon. And he is capable of surprisingly sophisticated and complex writing and of daring experimentation; everything he does is the product of a restless and fertile imagination. Above all, he can use 'our English' in a way which none of his contemporaries can equal – it is, in Elizabeth Barrett Browning's phrase, 'the very sansculottism of eloquence'.

II

Lyric verse continued to flourish in the fifteenth century. Besides the religious lyrics and carols (see chapter 6), secular lyrics are found in much larger numbers than in the preceding centuries. The most numerous and the most distinctive are the 'courtly' lyrics. Here we find ourselves back in the world of *La Belle Dame Sans Merci*, with its languishing suitor and hard-hearted lady. And to a certain extent we are back in the actual world of courts, noble ladies and the 'game of love', for it is possible that some of these lyrics were put to a quite practical social use. Some may have been presented to ladies as expressions of devotion; some may have been given with gifts or emblems (a heart, perhaps, or a 'truelove'). Many of them achieve a smooth and easy eloquence, a style which is polished if unexciting. This poem, for instance, has a certain solemn fervour:

This ys no lyf, alas, that y do lede;
  It is but deth as yn lyves lyckenesse,
Endeles sorow assured owte of drede,
  Past all despayre and owte of all gladenesse,
  Thus well y wote y am remedylesse,
    For me nothyng may comforte nor amende
    Tyl deith come forthe and make of me an ende,

and this song (of which the music survives) moves with a genuine lightness:

Go hert, hurt with adversite,
And let my lady thi wondis see;
And sey hir this, as y say the: *thee*
Farewel my joy, and welcom peyne,
Tyl y se my lady agayne.

But this way of writing too easily becomes lifeless and flat, and all too many of these lyrics are nothing but dull compilations of conventional themes and hackneyed phrases. The oppressive sense of sameness is emphasized by the limited number of themes which are treated (most notably the formal description of the lady's beauty, the plea for love, the grief of love, and the lover's farewell). But there is some variety. Occasionally a rather undistinguished context will be suddenly illuminated by one striking line:

Full sore hit greveth me when I by yow sate
   And say other better belovyd than I,
And ye in your armes so truly hym knyt,
   And I lyke a syphyr syt yow by.

Sometimes the variety comes from within the tradition of courtly lyric itself, which allowed a playful exploitation of the contradictions in attitudes to love and ladies, ranging from a gentle mockery to cynical abuse. In one lyric the poet sees his lady come into church with a 'gentilwoman'; the lines have an almost Skeltonic movement:

Even byhynd the kirk dore
They kneled bothe on the flore
And fast they did piter-pater –
I hope thay said matens togeder!   *believe*
Yet ones or twyes at the lest,
Sho did on me her ee kest . . .   *eye cast*

There is also a pair of mock-verse-letters supposed to be exchanged by a 'lady' and her 'lover'. The lady addresses hers to

My trewe love and able –
As the wedyr cok he is stable . . .   *weather*

and soon shows a fine command of abusive language:

. . . Your garmentes upon you ful gayly they hynge
As it were an olde gose had a broken wynge.

Her lover's reply is slightly more literary ('the ynglysch of Chaucere was nat in youre mynd') and it deliberately parodies the set 'praise of the lady's beauty':

O fresch floure, most plesant of pryse,
Fragrant as fedyrfoy to mannys inspeccion . . .   *feverfew*

He strives to match her in abuse:

Youre camusyd nose, with nose-thryllys brode   *snub*
Unto the chyrch a noble instrument
To quenche tapers brennyng afore the roode . . .
. . . Your babyr lyppys of colour ded and wan,   *thick*
Wyth suche mouth lyke to Jacobys brother,
And yelow tethe not lyk to the swan –
Set wyde asondyr as yche cursed other.   *each*

These lyrics are sometimes written by well-known poets: a mock 'Praise of his Lady' is attributed to Hoccleve, another lyric is described as a 'balade that Lydgate wrote at the request of a squire that served in Love's court'. Others are the work of 'amateurs', either members of the great nobility like the Duke of Suffolk, or humbler gentry like Humfrey Newton. One group is associated with the name of Charles d'Orléans, one of the most distinguished French poets of the century, who remained in England after his capture at Agincourt until 1440. It cannot be said with absolute certainty that he is the author of these English lyrics, but it is more than likely. It is the first example of an organized sequence of love poems in English. In fact, there are really two sequences. The first consists of a series of baladoes addressed to a 'Lady Beauty'; at the end of it the lady dies, and the lover renounces love. It is followed by an interlude, a series of songs and rondeaux called a 'Jubilee'. In the sequence which follows this, Venus and Fortune appear, and the poet is introduced to a second lady. But this romance is cut short by the enforced departure of Charles for France. The poems vary in quality. Some are rough, some dull; some begin well but collapse into flatness. But in them can very often be heard the voice of a real poet. The vigorous colloquial openings of some of the lyrics make the reader think of Wyatt:

How, how, myn hert! Opyn the gate of thought . . .
A! Daunger, here y cast to thee my glove,
And thee appele, O traytoure of tresoun . . .

What menyst thou, hope? Dost thou me skoffe and skorne?

Hadde y hertis a thousand thousand score
Alle shulde thei thanke you myn owen ladi dere . . .

Sometimes a rather tortured and jerky style and a broken rhythm are used to heighten the emotion:

Retorne, for shame, retorne, retorne ageyne.
Hye not to fast – parde ye gon amys.
Leve wayes twart, and take the pathis playne . . .   *oblique*

In other poems the style is consciously rhetorical and 'enamelled'. Others evoke the mysterious and romantic world of love allegory – cf. the haunting opening of *Balade* 70:

In the forest of Noyous Hevynes
As y went wandryng in the moneth of May,
I mette of Love the mighti gret goddes,
Which axid me whithir y was away . . .

And the poet can use with delicate wit the tradition of the 'religion of love':

My gostly fadir, y me confesse,   *spiritual father*
First to God and then to yow
That at a wyndow (wot ye how)   *you know how*
I stale a cosse of gret swetnes,   *stole kiss*
Which don was out avisynes;
    But hit is doon, not undoon, now –
My gostly fadir, y me confesse,
    First to God and than to you.
But y restore it shall dowtles
    Ageyn, if so be that y mow;   *may*
    And that, God, y make a vow,
And ellis y axe foryefnes –
My gostly fadir y me confesse,
First to God and then to yow.

The exquisite melancholy and the formalized anguish of *fine amour* is not the only subject of the secular lyrics. A number are inspired by contemporary political events, ranging from the victory of Agincourt (e.g. the 'Agincourt Carol') to the death of Archbishop Scrope. Most of these verses have greater interest for the social historian than for the student of literature. At best they manage a rough vigour or a venomous invective. A poem on the arrest of the Duke of Suffolk (1450) begins with crowing exultation:

Now is the fox drevin to hole! hoo to hym, hoo hoo!

Another puns on the name of Lord Scales, who was murdered by boatmen when he tried to escape from the Tower:

All thei had scaped upon a nyght,
    Save theire skales were plucked away!
Than had the fissh lost all here might,
    And litel joy in watyr to play.

And there are a few which would now be called 'protest songs', the expression (rarely found in medieval literature) of the rebels and the oppressed. One such is the verse associated with the ill-fated Kentish insurrection of 1450 led by Jack Cade:

God be oure gyde,
And then schull we spede.
Whosoevur say nay,
Ffalse for ther money reuleth!
Trweth for his tales spolleth!
God seend us a ffayre day!
Awey, traytoure, away!

A fair number of satirical short poems attack contemporary abuses. Of these the best known is the anonymous *London Lickpenny*. The poet says that he has come to London to 'make complaynt' to a 'man of law'; the recurring refrain 'for lack of money I could not spede' (succeed) indicates the reason for his lack of success in the big city. Some stanzas give a lively sense of the bustle of London streets:

> . . . 'hot pescodes!' one began to crye, . . .
> . . . Drapers mutch cloth me offred anone.
>   Then come me one, cryed 'hot shepes feete!'
>   One cryed 'makerell!' 'ryshes grene!' another gan greete.
> . . . Then I hyed me into Estchepe.
>   One cryes 'rybbes of befe, and many a pye!'
> Pewter pottes they clattered on an heape;
>   There was harpe, pype, and mynstrelsye.
>   'Yea by cock!' 'Nay, by cock!' some began crye;
>   Some songe of 'Jenken and Julyan' for three mede –
>   But for lack of mony I myght not spede.

A rather more interesting group consists of the drinking songs and the lyrics which celebrate the amorous encounters of 'Jenkens and Julyans'. These often reach a high level of technical achievement. The opening of 'Old Hogyn's Adventure', for instance, has the confident vigour of the best Elizabethan songs:

> Hogyn cam to bowers dore,
> Hogyn cam to bowers dore;
>   He tryld upon the pyn for love,
>   Hum, ha, trill go bell –
>   He tryld upon the pyn for love,
>   Hum, ha, trill go bell.
>
> Up she rose and lett hym yn. . . .

(old Hogyn, unfortunately, is no longer up to it). The drinking songs are worthy antecedents of the song in *Gammer Gurton's Needle*, 'Backe and syde goo bare', which Warton said was the 'first *chanson à boire* or drinking-ballad, of any merit, in our language'. The best of them is the carol 'Bryng us in good ale', which cleverly uses the cumulative possibilities of a repetitive structure:

> Bryng us in no browne bred, fore that is mad of brane;
> Nor bryng us in no whyt bred fore therin is no game,
>   But bryng us in good ale.
>
> Bryng us in no befe, for ther is many bonys;
> But bryng us in good ale, for that goth downe at onys,
>   And bryng us in good ale . . .

. . . Bryng us in no capons flesch, for that is ofte der,
Nor bryng us in no dokes flesch, for thei slober in the mer,
    But bryng us in good ale.

The amorous songs, with their wily clerks and too-generous maidens, are often very close to the world of the fabliaux. Many of them create a dramatic situation, and exploit the possibilities of *double entendre* and of colloquial speech. When one unfortunate girl returns after spending 'the merriest night that ever I came in' with 'Jack our holy water clerk', she is met by her angry mistress:

'Sey, thou stronge strumpeth, ware hastu bene?
Thy trippyng and thy dauncyng wel it wol be sene!'

One of the best is 'Jolly Jankin', which with remarkable economy creates and uses a situation not unlike the scene in the *Miller's Tale* where Absolon

Gooth with a sencer on the haliday,
Sensynge the wyves of the parisshe faste.

There is a gentle liturgical parody; the burden, which is repeated after each stanza, *kyrie eleison* ('Lord, have mercy') plays on the girl's name, Alison. We see the scene through the girl's eyes. Her comments record her reactions to Jankin at various stages of the service – his vocal dexterity at the *sanctus* provokes the rather earthly mental ejaculation 'I payid for his cote', and when he gloriously 'cracks' his notes in the following stanza there is an appropriately rustic ring to her smile – 'smaller than wortes to the pot'. In the final stanza the two sides of the situation – the religious procession and the love relationship – are neatly connected, and the girl's final cry 'Alas, I go with chylde!' puts everything which has preceded it into a new perspective. The final *kyrie* burden becomes finely ambiguous and ironic.

Another small group of lyrics sometimes reminds us either of modern nursery rhymes (e.g. 'I have a yong suster/Fer beyonden the se') or of modern folk-songs. A couple of poems about the Fox and the Goose are examples of a folk-song which survived into modern tradition, becoming a nursery song in eighteenth-century England and a Negro song in nineteenth-century America. One of them exploits the traditionally shifting and deceptive character of Reynard. First the Fox appears with an ironic ecclesiastical greeting 'Pax vobis'. When he has the Goose, he looks forward to her fate with an almost sexual enjoyment:

Sche shall goo unto the wode with me;
Sche and I unther a tre,
  Emange the beryis browne.

Then his tone immediately changes to the wheedling wail of a
beggar, with a final touch of gleeful sadism;

I have a wyf, and sche lyeth seke;
Many smale whelppis sche haveth eke –
Many bonys they muste pike
  Will they ley adowne.   *until*

Burlesque and nonsense verse is also found. One poem, on the
danger of trusting women, makes use of a long list of impossibilities.
It belongs to a type which is widespread in later folk-song and
literary tradition (the most famous example is Donne's 'Goe and
catch a falling star'). This medieval lyric strings together a
wonderful series of brilliant, absurd, almost surrealist images of
impossible reversals of the natural order. The reader's imagination
is playfully pulled and twisted, and the refrain concludes each
dazzling stanza with an air of triumph:

Whan netilles in wynter bere rosis rede,
And thornys bere figges naturally,
And bromes bere appylles in every mede,
And lorelles bere cheris in the croppis so hie,   *laurels*
And okys bere dates so plentuosly,
And lekes geve hony in ther superfluens –
Than put in a woman your trust and confidens.

Whan whityng walk in forestes hartes for to chase,
And herynges in parkys hornys boldly blowe,
And flownders more-hennes in fennes embrace,
And gornardes shote rolyons out of a crosse bowe,   *?rough shoes*
And grengese ride in huntyng the wolf to overthrowe,   *goslings*
And sperlynges rone with speris in harnes to defence –   *smelts*
Than put in a woman your trust and confidence.

. . . Whan crabbis tak wodcokes in forestes and parkes,
And haris ben taken with swetnes of snaylis,
And camelles with ther here tak swalowes and perchis,
And myse mowe corn with wafeyyng of ther taylis,
Whan dukkes of the dunghill sek the blod of Haylis,
Whan shrewd wyffes to ther husbonds do non offens –   *shrewish*
Than put in a woman your trust and confidence.

The type of folk-song which has the most distinguished place in English literature is the ballad, and it is usually assumed that it began in the Middle Ages. The earliest English poem which is remotely like a ballad is a piece on Judas which is found in a late thirteenth-century manuscript. A number of ballads can certainly be assigned to the later Middle Ages, and it is likely that others which we know only in later versions originated in this period. Some are patently related to medieval romances and tales. For this reason it is appropriate to say something here about the ballads in general. It must, however, be remembered that many of the examples which are quoted come from later versions or later times. The ballad continues in oral tradition until the twentieth century. Many are associated with the turbulent history of the Borders; some migrated to America and began a new and fertile tradition there.

The ballad is defined by G. H. Gerould as 'a folk-song that tells a story with stress on the crucial situation, tells it by letting the action unfold itself in event and speech, and tells it objectively with little comment or intrusion or personal bias'. It is, first, a folk-song – a poem which is not regarded as the 'property' of a known poet. It was transmitted orally, from singer to singer, continually changed and adapted, by a process which was probably more like a constant re-creation than the careful recitation of a text learned by heart. As we struggle with the tags and weak lines which disfigure some ballads we need to remember that it was in *performance* that the ballads were born and developed; they were never intended to be 'literary' works read and re-read on the page. Sir Philip Sidney, in one of the earliest references to a traditional ballad, reminds us of this:

I never heard the old song of Percy and Douglas that I found not my heart moved more than with a trumpet; and yet it is sung by some blind crowder, with no rougher voice than rude style.

The crucial situation is very often, though not invariably, a tragic one. Comedy is not unknown, as in *King Edward and the Tanner* and some of the Robin Hood ballads, or (of a rather more grim sort) in *Queen Eleanor's Confession*. Here the king and Earl Martial, disguised as friars, persuade the queen to make her confession to them:

'The first vile thing that ere I did
    I will to you unfold;
Earl Martial had my maidenhead,
    Underneath this cloath of gold.'

'That is a vile sin,' then said the king,
  'God may forgive it thee!'
'Amen! Amen!' quoth Earl Martial,
  With a heavy heart then spoke he . . .

Many ballads treat, with intensity if not with subtlety, the great simple themes – passion, treachery, death. Some seem to spring directly from a 'heroic' society in which personal honour and loyalty to one's chief and to one's kin are the positive virtues, and in which the duty of vengeance through private slaying or through blood-feud is taken for granted. It has been suggested that the figure of Robin Hood gives expression to the disaffection of the yeoman class in the late Middle Ages. He certainly seems a more 'popular' figure than most of the noble outlaws of medieval romance and legend, yet there is no sense of outrage or violent protest in the Robin Hood ballads – the characteristic tone is rather one of rowdy comedy and clever japes. Other ballads preserve popular beliefs, notably or fairyland, a place which is at once mysteriously close to the world of men and immensely remote, at once beautiful and perilous.

    The ballad narrative characteristically moves with great swiftness, almost as if in a series of flashes. It often omits obvious narrative links, and relies heavily on exchange of direct speech. The typical abruptness of movement can be seen in miniature in a quatrain of *Sir Patrick Spens*:

The king has written a braid letter,
  And signd it wi his hand
And sent it to Sir Patrick Spense
  Was walking on the sand.

    The Border ballad usually begins just before the climax of the action; as Thomas Gray says of *Child Maurice*, 'it begins in the fifth act of the play'.

    But it is not all rapid forward movement; the characteristic movement of the ballads has been described as 'leaping and lingering'. Ballads are often curiously stylized, and have their own sort of conventional rhetoric with which they can emphasize moments or details. One very distinctive technique is that of 'in-cremental repetition', which, if well used, can give an almost lyrical intensity of emotion and can succinctly give the sense of an in-evitable movement of events. In *Lord Randall*, for instance, the tragic story is obliquely presented through a highly formalized series of questions and answers, with the insistent refrain

For I'm wearied wi hunting and fain wad lie down

which later changes, slightly but significantly, to

For I'm sick at the heart and I fain wad lie down.

The curious tempo is well illustrated in *Babylon*, where an abrupt, almost melodramatic action alternates with a stylized, ceremonious movement. The ladies pull a flower, and are confronted by a sudden apparition:

They hadna pu'ed a flower but ane   *one*
When up started to them a banisht man.

The description of how he kills each of them in turn is done with elaborate formality, with set repetitions and questions and answers. Then this is followed by the sudden revelation that he is their brother.

In the bare style of narration usually adopted in the ballad, the details which are singled out for mention often take on a special emotional significance. *Fair Annie* is a version of a medieval story of sentiment of the type found in Marie de France's *Lai le Freine*. At one point the faithful woman who has lived for years with the man and borne him children sees the ship of his new bride coming to land:

And she's gane down, and farther down,
    The bride's ship to behold
And the topmast and the mainmast
    They shone just like the gold,

where the hyperbole is conventional enough, yet in the context the descriptive detail becomes almost the symbol of the splendour and pathos of the moment. In *Sir Patrick Spens* a detail picked out can give a haunting and foreboding effect:

Late, late yestreen I saw the new moone   *yesterday evening*
    Wi the auld moone in hir arme,

or can effortlessly 'point' the tragic and ironic reversal of fortune which came upon the fastidious and elegant nobles:

O our Scots nobles wer richt laith
    To weet their cork-heild schoone   *wet/heeled shoes*
Bot long owre a' the play wer playd,   *before ever*
    Their hats they swam aboone.   *above*

In diction the ballads are conventional and formulaic. They are fond of certain favourite adjectives. Some of the finest lines, like these in *Tam Lin*,

```
. . . the steed that my true-love rides on
  Is lighter than the wind;
Wi siller he is shod before
  Wi burning gowd behind,                              gold
```

are found in a number of ballads. But the best ballads use the connotations and emotional resonance of these simple traditional words to achieve a remarkable imaginative power and eloquence. In *Thomas Rhymer* (Jameson version) the Queen of Elfland takes Thomas to her realm:

```
She turned about her milk-white steed
  And took true Thomas up behind
And aye wheneer her bridle rang,
  The steed flew swifter than the wind.

For forty days and forty nights
  He wade thro red blude to the knee               blood
And he saw neither sun nor moon
  But heard the roaring of the sea.
```

Of such passages we could rightly use the words of Addison, whose enthusiasm did so much to revive interest in the traditional ballads, that they 'are full of that majestick simplicity which we admire in the greatest of the ancient poets'.

III

The traditional ballads have already led us to the Borders, and in the remainder of this chapter we must go on to discuss the more literary poetry of Scotland, which is the most consistently imaginative and creative of the period. Scotland was of course at this time a separate kingdom, but it shared with England a common language (its version of the Northern dialect is regularly called 'Inglis') and a common literary tradition – French poetry, and the work of Chaucer and Lydgate – except that the influence of alliterative poetry, which long survived in Scotland, is much more apparent in courtly writers. In spite of a turbulent political scene, there was, as in England, a great interest in education and learning. Three of the four oldest Scottish universities – St. Andrews, Glasgow, and Aberdeen – are fifteenth-century foundations. And, as in England, there was a gradual growth of interest in the 'new learning'. The humanist Hector Boece, the first principal of Aberdeen, flourished at the beginning of the sixteenth century, but he was preceded by distinguished scholars like Bishop William

Turnbull, Archibald Whitelaw, and promising men like Alexander Stewart, the natural son of James IV, and bishop of St. Andrews, who perished in the disaster of Flodden (1513), of whom Erasmus, once his tutor, said 'What hadst thou to do with fierce Mars . . . thou that wert destined for the muses and for Christ?'

The tradition of Scottish vernacular poetry had begun in the fourteenth century with the work of John Barbour (?1320–1395). His long poem *The Bruce* is an example of what now seems to us to be a very curious form of literature – a verse chronicle – and does not really succeed in overcoming the difficulties which the form presents. Barbour does not handle his material boldly enough, and does not give to the work the epic scope which the subject demands, but seems to remain too much the servant of the episodes he chronicles. After the battle of Bannockburn, the climax of the war of independence, there is a distinct falling off in interest, and that the battle is the climax of the poem seems due to history rather than to Barbour's art. But *The Bruce* has distinct virtues. It is a fine simple heroic narrative, celebrating the qualities of loyalty and fortitude, and the desire for freedom. It moves rapidly – sometimes too rapidly and with insufficient variation – and makes good use of direct speech and descriptive detail. Barbour is not much interested in psychology or in abstract ideas, but he has a fine eye for the surface of things, and some of his best writing is to be found in descriptions of the pomp and splendour of the English host before Bannockburn.

Verse chronicles continued to be written in the fifteenth century. Wyntoun's *Orygynale Cronykil* (*ca.* 1430) is almost unreadable, but *Schir William Wallace*, attributed to 'Blind Harry' (*ca.* 1450–60) has some degree of merit, and enjoyed an enormous popularity. It was often reprinted, and an eighteenth-century paraphrase by William Hamilton inspired Burns ('the story of Wallace poured a Scottish prejudice into my veins which will boil along them till the floodgates of life shut in eternal rest'). It is much more aggressively patriotic than *The Bruce*, and describes some violent and swashbuckling episodes with a glee which is reminiscent of *Havelok*. Harry's attempts at elaborate and rhetorical writing are hardly ever successful, and generally he has not the narrative skill to do justice to the genuinely exciting nature of his material. Again and again we are left wishing that an adventure had been told by Scott. But there are good passages – that in Book V where Wallace sees the ghost of Fawdoun, a man whom he has just slain, and the description of the sea-battle with the 'Red Revar' are memorable – and occasionally

Harry gives moving expression to one of the great simple themes. In Book VII Wallace asks a woman if his uncle is dead. She replies

'Out off yon bern,' scho said, 'I saw him born,	*barn*
Nakit, laid law on cald erd, me beforn.	*earth*
His frosty mouth I kissit in that sted:	*place*
Rycht now manlik, now bar, and brocht to ded.	
And with a claith I coverit his licaym. . . .'	*body*

The first Scots poem of any merit in the courtly tradition is *The Kingis Quhair* ('The King's Book'), which is usually ascribed to King James I (*d.* 1437), who was captured by the English in 1406, and remained in England until he was ransomed, and married Joan Beaufort, the daughter of the Earl of Somerset, in 1424. The authorship of the poem has been discussed at great length; it is sufficient here to say that there seems to be no compelling argument against the attribution to the Scottish king. Whoever the author was, *The Kingis Quhair* is a fine poem. It is very like the English Chauceriana but far surpasses them in poetic skill and imaginative freshness. It is a love poem. The narrator recalls how Fortune caused his shipwreck and captivity, and how from his prison cell, like Palamon and Arcite, he caught his first sight of his lady as she walked in a garden.

For quhich sodayn abate, anon astert	*which sudden discomfiture/rushed*
The blude of all my body to my hert.	

The overwhelming suddenness of love and the agony and passion of his situation are recalled in urgent and lyrical verse. He looks down and envies the lady's

lytill hound
That with his bellis playit on the ground,

and desperately appeals to the nightingale in the garden to sing in her honour:

O lytill wrecch, allace! maist thou noght se	
Quho commyth yond? Is it now tyme to wryng?	*Who/lament*
Quhat sory thoght is fallin upon the?	*What*
Opyn thy throte; hastow no lest to sing?	*desire*
Allace! sen thou of resoun had felyng,	*since*
Now suete bird, say ones to me 'pepe',	
I dee for wo; me think thou gynnis slepe.	*begin to*

Illumination is given to him in a dream. He visits the house of Venus, where he sees the companies of Love's servants – the 'gude folkis', both old and young, who served love faithfully, and the 'folk

of religioun' with their 'capis wide' who served him secretly – and
the multitude who bring their plaints to Love's court. Venus sends
her new servant to Minerva, 'the pacient goddess', who tells him
that his love should be steadfast and founded upon virtue. Lastly, he
is taken to Fortune, who looks favourably upon him. Without ever
becoming heavily didactic, the poem discusses the nature of love,
and the place which it has in the universe, and celebrates its great
power and nobility. At the end, when all is resolved and he looks
back on the happy culmination of his love, the narrator is moved to
pour out his heart in thankfulness and gratitude, and to pray for all
Love's servants, and even for those dull hearts

That lyven here in sleuth and ignorance
And has no curage at the ros to pull.

He blesses the gods, 'fortunys exiltree', the nightingale, and even
his prison wall, and the 'sanctis martiall' that first brought about his
captivity. The golden chain of Love is an easy thraldom, and binds
all creatures together in concord. The emotional and intellectual
movement of the poem, from complaint to illumination and to
grace, is complete. It is a work which needs no apology; it is written
with beautiful simplicity and exhibits a shaping imagination of a
high order.

At the end of this period, during the reigns of James III and
James IV (*d.* 1513), Scottish vernacular poetry reached heights
which it was not to approach again before the time of Burns.
Besides some talented minor verse, like *The Freiris of Berwik, The
Three Preistis of Peblis* or the poems of Walter Kennedy, Scotland
produced three of the best poets of the late Middle Ages – Robert
Henryson, William Dunbar, and Gavin Douglas.

Of the life of Robert Henryson, the earliest and probably the
most distinguished of the three, we know almost nothing, except
that a reference in Dunbar's *Lament for the Makaris* shows that he
was dead by about 1505, that he was a university graduate, and
possibly a notary, and, according to tradition, schoolmaster at
Dunfermline. It should be pointed out that Dunfermline was not an
obscure country town but an important centre favoured by the royal
court, and that there is no evidence at all in Henryson's work for the
view which is still sometimes expressed that he was a sort of rustic,
unlettered poet; in every way his poetry belongs to the learned and
courtly tradition.

Henryson is the author of a number of competent short poems –
moral and religious lyrics like *The Thre Deid Pollis* or *The Ressoning*

betwixt Death and Man, a burlesque alliterative piece, *Sum Practysis of Medecyne*, and others. His version of the story of Orpheus and Eurydice is uneven, but contains passages which remind us of the mature narrative poet of the *Fables* and *The Testament of Cresseid*. It is a *conte moralisé* in the manner of the stories in the popular medieval 'moralized Ovid': in the body of the tale the philosophical ideas are handled with ease, but the *moralitas* which concludes it is overlong. *Robene and Makene* is an altogether delightful pastoral dialogue. It is done with genuine simplicity and wit, and has no trace of the condescension which sometimes mars this sort of poem. It is very brief, and is conducted almost entirely in dialogue, but, as in the *Fables*, Henryson relishes the challenge of a restricted form. As 'mirry' Makene pleads with the recalcitrant Robene, we quickly become aware of his personality – his innocence, his slowness, his comic devotion to his sheep, and his totally unconscious cruelty. The sudden reversal of roles is both comic and touching; the poor passive Robene deserves his rebuke

'Robene, that warld is all away	
And quhyt brocht till ane end,	*quite brought to an*
And nevir agane thairto perfay	*indeed*
Sall it be as thow wend;	*believe*
For of my pane thow maid it play,	
And all in vane I spend;	
As thow hes done, sa sall I say,	
Murne on, I think to mend',	

and the proverbial moral which is deftly loosed at him:

'Robene, thow hes hard soung and say,	*heard*
In gestis and storeis auld,	
The man that will nocht quhen he may	
Sall haif nocht quhen he wald'.	

It was natural that a poet who so prized the stylistic virtue of concision, and who could, like the god Mercury in *The Testament of Cresseid*,

in breif sermone ane pregnant sentence wryte,

should be attracted to the very limited and demanding form of the literary fable. The traditional Aesopic fable (Henryson's fables come both from these and from the beast-epic of Reynard the Fox) is often no longer than a paragraph. Henryson's fables are longer than this, but are still short stories in verse. They are tightly related, with a fine control of tone and pace. Irony is rarely absent, and he is fond of grim, abrupt endings. In *The Wolf and the Wedder*, for instance, we are given the story of the sheep which wore a dog's skin to frighten away the wolf from the rest of the sheep. It opens slowly, and carefully suggests the way in which the sheep assumes, not only the skin and duties of the deceased dog, but its character as well. The deception is hilariously successful, it seems. But events move rapidly when the wolf in desperation decides to risk the wrath of the 'dog'. His headlong flight from the 'dog' is described with enormous comic zest, carefully chosen details giving point and emphasis to the scene ('with that the wolff let out his taill on lenth', etc.). The wolf is so terrified that he even throws away the lamb he has stolen, but this will not satisfy the sheep's assumed personality; in a moment of acute psychological observation he is shown to have been deceived by his own deceit:

> 'Na' (quod the wedder), in faith we part not swa:
> It is not the lamb, bot the, that I desyre,   *thee*
> I sall cum neir, ffor now I se the tyre.'   *nearer*

The 'game' now really becomes 'earnest'. Suddenly a briar bush whips off the sheep's skin. In a vivid scene we are shown the suppressed wrath of the wolf: 'To God I vow that ye sall rew this rais' (attack), and the rather feeble true character of the sheep, who can only offer the weak excuse that he really meant it to be a game. The ironic pattern suddenly becomes sinister, and culminates in a typically violent and abrupt end. 'Sikkerlie' says the wolf 'now sall we not dissever' (part).

> Than be crag bane smertlie he him tuke,   *bone*
> Or ever he seisit, and it in schunder schuke.   *ceased/asunder*

From the fables and their moralities there emerges a series of traditional moral themes, a sort of loosely-organized 'mirror of human life'. Man's life is frail and 'brukkil'; fortune is unreliable, death comes suddenly. What 'sikernes' there is lies in virtue, good works, wisdom and self-knowledge. There is a very clear-sighted view of the world as it actually is. Justice is not always done, and the innocent suffer: in *The Sheep and the Dog*, a bitter tale of legal injustice, the innocent sheep (the 'pure commounis' in the morality) is ruthlessly defrauded by its brutal adversaries.

The Testament of Cresseid is one of the most complex and interesting poems of the late Middle Ages. The dominant mood is established at the beginning by the formal setting in a 'doolie sesoun' – it is spring, but not the usual spring of the poets. The weather is cold, and 'schouris of haill' are falling from the North. The poet presents himself as a weary old man, vainly hoping that Venus will 'make green' his 'faded heart of love'. He takes Chaucer's *Troilus and Criseyde*, which tells him of the woes of Troilus, and then 'another book' which tells

> the fatall destenie
Of fair Cresseid, that endit wretchitlie,

and this is the grim subject of his poem. Cresseid, forsaken by her Greek lover Diomeid, returns to the house of her father Calchas. Overwhelmed by her ill-fortune, she curses Venus and Cupid for betraying her. The gods take cruel vengeance: for her blasphemy she is afflicted with leprosy, and dies among the 'lipper folk'. Henryson is not the poet to spare us harsh and macabre detail. The sombre imagery of the beginning of the poem recurs in the grotesque and terrifying portrait of Saturn:

And first of all Saturne gave his sentence,	
Quhilk gave to Cupide litill reverence,	*Which*
Bot, as ane busteous Churle on his maneir,	
Come crabitlie with auster luik and cheir.	*severe look and expression*
His face fronsit, his lyre was lyke the leid,	
His teith chatterit, and cheverit with the chin,	
His ene drowpit, how sonkin in his heid,	*eyes*
Out of his nois the meldrop fast can rin,	*drop of mucus*
With lippis bla and cheikis leine and thin;	*livid*
The iseschoklis that fra his hair doun hang	
Was wonder greit, and as ane speir als lang.	
Atouir his belt his lyart lokkis lay	*About/silvery grey*
Felterit unfair, ovirfret with froistis hoir,	*matted; covered*
His garmound and his gyis full gay of gray,	*?attire*
His widderit weid fra him the wind out woir;	*blew*
Ane busteous bow within his hand he boir,	
Under his girdill ane flasche of felloun flanis,	
Fedderit with ice, and heidit with hailstanis	

– it is with a 'frosty wand' that he touches Cresseid's head when he curses her with leprosy. The effect of the terrible sentence is pointed with the concision and irony which we have seen in the *Fables*. The 'ugly vision' of the planetary deities and their curse is immediately succeeded by a simple and moving little domestic scene – a child comes in to Cresseid to warn her that supper is ready:

'Madame your father biddis you cum in hy.
He hes mervell sa lang on grouf ye ly,
And sayis your prayers bene to lang sum deill:
The goddis wait all your intent full weill.'

But the poem is not totally bleak and wretched. The narrator
shows a strong and Chaucerian compassion for his unfortunate
heroine. He echoes Chaucer in excusing her for her reputed
'brukkilnes' –

I sall excuse, als far furth as I may,
Thy womanheid, thy wisdome and fairnes
The quhilk Fortoun hes put to sic distres
As hir pleisit . . .

– and he goes out of his way to criticize Saturn's sentence as 'hard',
'to malitious' and 'wraikfull'. And Cresseid's death, although it
takes place in the most wretched circumstances, has a certain
dignity and nobility. There is a distinct emotional change in her
after the scene in which she and Troilus meet again for the last
time. This moving episode is correctly called a 'recognition scene'
even though apparently there is no recognition – Cresseid has been
treated so hardly by Fortune that she does not recognize Troilus as
he rides by in his splendour, while he, when the leper woman casts
up her eyes

with ane blenk it come into his thocht,	*glance*
That he sumtime hir face befoir had sene.	
But scho was in sic plye he knew hir nocht,	*plight*
Yit than hir luik into his mynd it brocht	
The sweit visage and amorous blenking	
Of fair Cresseid sumtyme his awin darling.	

Her 'recognition' comes after he has gone, when the other lepers
tell her who it was, and it is profound in its effect. She no longer
chides her 'dreary destiny', but her final 'complaint' has as its
refrain the words 'O fals Cresseid and trew knicht Troilus'; 'nane
but myself as now I will accuse', she says. There is no false
optimism in the ending, and it is probably wrong to speak, as some
critics have, of 'redemption' or 'healing', but she has, finally and
painfully, come to a sort of self-knowledge. Although she dies a
leper and in misery, the victim of the cruel verdict of the gods, we
feel that human love and values have not been crushed. It is the
memory of a human love, the 'trew lufe' of Troilus, which has
changed her.

The poetry of William Dunbar (*ca.* 1456–*ca.* 1513) is closely connected with the court of James IV. One of his more successful public poems, *The Thrissill and the Rois*, celebrates the marriage of James to the English princess Margaret in 1503. It is formal and ceremonial, and uses, appropriately, the 'luminous language of Lydgate' (Warton) and extended heraldic imagery:

The purpour sone, with tendir bemys reid,
In orient bricht as angell did appeir,
Throw goldin skyis putting up his heid,
Quhois gilt tressis schone so wondir cleir,
That all the world tuke confort, fer and neir,
To luke upone his fresche and blisful face,
Doing all sable fro the hevynnis chace.

It contrives to praise without extravagant flattery. At the end the birds' song of honour suggests the blessing of nature on the union:

The merle scho sang, 'Haill, Rois of most delyt,   *she*
Haill, of all flouris quene and soverane'.
The lark scho song, 'Haill, Rois, both reid and quhyt,
Most plesand flour, of michty cullouris twane'.
The nychtingaill song, 'Haill, naturis suffragene,
In bewty, nurtour, and every nobilnes,
In riche array, renown, and gentilnes.'

Dunbar writes poems to celebrate the arrival on a visit (1508) of a famous Scottish captain in the service of the French king, Lord Bernard Stewart, and to lament his death in Edinburgh about a month later. Others give comic, grotesque, and scurrilous views of court life. Like Hoccleve and Lydgate, he writes verse petitions for money.

Critics have sometimes been troubled by the violent contrasts in Dunbar's poetry. He ranges from elaborate courtly allegory to bawdy song, from religious parody to pious lyric. Neither human nature nor human society, however, has ever been notable for its simplicity or consistency, and, of all historical epochs perhaps, the late middle ages made the least attempt to conceal its violent and extreme contrasts. King James IV himself indulged both in pious and penitential practices and in a number of mistresses. The variety of Dunbar's work is not a sign of any insincerity; it is rather the mark of the craftsman-poet. His superb stylistic skill is rigorously applied to the requirements of traditional types of verse. He does not usually exhibit the taste for innovation and experiment which we find in Skelton, but his exactly calculated effects are infused with a characteristic energy and zest, in Edwin Morgan's happy phrase 'the display of poetic energy'. In the manner of the consummate craftsmen he can produce a dazzling display of technical brilliance. Nothing in the aureate language of the English poets can match the splendid virtuosity of *Ane Ballat of Our Lady*:

Hale, sterne superne! Hale, in eterne,
  In Godis sicht to schyne!
Lucerne in derne for to discerne   *light/darkness*
  Be glory and grace devyne;
Hodiern, modern, sempitern,   *Of today/now existing/everlasting*
  Angelicall regyne!

and, at the other extreme of the stylistic spectrum, he can produce an equally dazzling, and equally mannered display of abuse in *The Flyting of Dunbar and Kennedie*:

Loun lyk Mahoun, be boun me till obey,   *rogue/ready*
  Theif, or in grief mischeif sall the betyd;
Cry grace, tykis face, or I the chece and sley;
  Oule, rare and yowle, I sall defowll thy pryd . . . etc., etc.   *roar*

But such passages represent extremes. Dunbar's characteristic style is simple and tough, quite without flabbiness. No amount of talk about 'aureate' or 'eldritch' styles is at all relevant to the remarkable couplet

My deathe chasis my lyfe so besalie
That wery is my goist to fle so fast,

whose compressed vigour and simple expressiveness satisfies both intellect and feeling.

The more subtle and complex subjects of literature are not usually handled very happily by Dunbar. He is not a 'philosophical' or even a particularly thoughtful poet. Significantly, his love poetry is rather disappointing. He can produce a pleasingly turned courtly lyric, as 'Sweit rois of vertew', and his extended love-allegories, *Bewty and the Presoneir* and *The Goldyn Targe*, are beautifully decorative, but their central allegorical events are less exciting than the splendid settings. Dunbar's love poetry totally lacks the anguished grappling with the contrarieties of love, or the philosophical attempts to relate it to divine love, to principles of order and concord or to noble behaviour, which are so characteristic of the best medieval poets.

Much has been claimed for the satirical *Twa Mariit Wemen and the Wedo*, but if it is compared with Chaucer's *Wife of Bath's*

Prologue, to which it owes a good deal, it seems rather simple. The two married women's experiences are related with directness and gusto, but the excitement, as often in Dunbar, comes from the language, which is wonderfully exaggerated and bizarre – one of the women describes her old husband's looks

The luf-blenkis of that bogill, fra his blerde ene   *looked/cast down*
As Belzebub had on me blent, abasit my spreit. . . .

The texture of the poem becomes more complex with the widow's speech, or as she playfully calls it, her 'preaching' (rather nicely, a faintly ecclesiastical air is given to it – it is the 'legend' of her life, and she tells the stories of her two husbands as if they were *exempla*). It culminates in an excellent passage of sustained hypocrisy, as she describes herself at church:

Quhen that I go to the kirk, cled in cair weid,
As foxe in a lambis fleise fenye I my cheir;
Than lay I furght my bright buke breid one my knee,
With mony lusty letter ellummynit with gold;
And drawis my clok forthwart our my face quhit,   *over*
That I may spy, unaspyit, a space me beside:
Full oft I blenk by my buke, and blynis of devotioun,   *cease*
To se quhat berne is best brand or bredest in schulderis,   *man/brawned*
Or forgeit is maist forcely to furnyse a bancat   *moulded*
In Venus chalmer, valyeandly, withoutin vane ruse:
And, as the new mone all pale, oppressit with change,
Kythis quhilis her cleir face through cluddis of sable,   *Shows at times*
So keik I through my clokis, and castis kynd lukis   *peep*
To knychtis, and to cleirkis, and cortly personis . . .

In satirical writing Dunbar's talent is for the simpler forms. His favourite device is the cumulative catalogue which can often make the satire over-generalized or monotonous unless it is infused with his wild energy or fantastic imagination. A successful example occurs at the end of *Tydingis fra the Sessioun*:

Sum sweiris and forsaikis God,
Sum in ane lambskin is ane tod;
Sum in his toung his kyndnes tursis;   *carries*
Sum cuttis throttis, and sum pykis pursis;
Sum gois to gallous with processioun;
Sum sanis the Sait, and sum thame cursis: *blesses the Court of Session*
Sic tydingis hard I at the Sessioun.

Religious men of divers placis
Cumis thair to wow and se fair facis;

Baith Carmeleitis and Cordilleris   *Franciscans*
Cumis thair to genner and get ma freiris,   *engender*
And ar unmyndfull of thair professioun;
The yungar at the eldar leiris:
Sic tydingis hard I at the Sessioun . . .

An even more spirited example is *The Fenyeit Freir of Tungland*, which is based on an actual occurrence of a sort which was bound to appeal to Dunbar's taste for the bizarre. An Italian alchemist, one Damian, made an attempt to fly through the air by means of wings. His attempt was unsuccessful; a later chronicler (Leslie) writes

al rinis (runs) to visit him, tha ask the Abbot with his wings how he did. He answers that his thich bane is brokne, and he hopet never to gang agane; al war lyk to cleive of lauchter.

He is said to have produced the ingenious excuse that his wings were not made entirely of eagle's feathers but contained some cock and capon feathers! People in Dunbar's time, of course, rarely shared our sympathy for the very first daring young men in flying machines, but generally regarded them as proud and unnatural. Dunbar's poem on the incident makes a rather slow start, but works up to a tremendous climax in which all the birds of the air unite in attacking the unfortunate flyer as an unnatural intruder (they first take him to be a monster, then decide that he is a 'hornit howle'), and he falls up to his eyes in a 'mire' while

The air was dirkit with the fowlis,   *darkened*
That come with yawmeris and with yowlis,   *shrieks*
With skryking, skrymming, and with scowlis,   *screeching/darting*
     To tak him in the tyde.

Dunbar's total poetic achievement is not adequately represented by any single poem, or even group of poems, but he is probably most often seen at his best in his religious lyrics. His poem on the Resurrection opens triumphantly and dramatically:

Done is a battell on the dragon blak,
Our campioun Chryst confountet hes his force;
The yettis of hell ar brokin with a crak,   *gates*
The signe triumphall rasit is of the croce,
The divillis trymmillis with hiddous voce,
The saulis ar borrowit and to the blis can go;
Chryst with his blud our ransonis dois indoce: *endorse*
Surrexit Dominus de sepulchro.   *The Lord has arisen from the grave.*

This poem owes its success to its simplicity and energy of style, but two of his poems on death – the *Meditatioun in Wyntir* and *The Lament for the Makaris* – are more personal and complex. The first ends with the thought of summer's approach bringing an unusually ambiguous and tentative comfort for the cares of mortality:

Yit, quhone the nycht begynnis to schort,	*when/grow short*
It dois my spreit sum pairt confort,	
Off thocht oppressit with the schowris.	*Although*
Cum, lustie symmer! with thi flowris,	
That I may leif in sum disport.	

The Lament for the Makaris begins with a note of ominous threat. The poet's own sickness leads him to consider the fate of all men:

I that in heill wes and gladnes,	*health*
Am trublit now with gret seiknes,	
And feblit with infermite;	
Timor mortis conturbat me.	*The fear of death afflicts me.*

Our plesance heir is all vane glory,	
This fals warld is bot transitory,	
Tha flesche is brukle, the Fend is sle;	*sly*
Timor mortis conturbat me.	

The stait of man dois change and vary,	
Now sound, now seik, now blith, now sary,	
Now dansand mery, now like to dee;	*dancing/die*
Timor mortis conturbat me.	

It rehearses the great commonplaces of the literature of death with a sombre eloquence which is reinforced by the haunting, inevitable refrain. A long list of the names of Dunbar's 'brothers', the poets whom death has taken off, is evidence of its overwhelming and ineluctable power:

... He hes Blind Hary and Sandy Traill	
Slaine with his schour of mortall naill,	*shower*
Quhilk Patrik Johnestoun mycht nocht fle.	*which*
Timor mortis conturbat me.	

... In Dunfermelyne he hes done roune	
With Maister Robert Henrysoun;	
Schir Johne the Ros enbrast hes he;	*embraced*
Timor mortis conturbat me.	

As the list continues, the reader begins to feel in a curious under-hand way that the very recording of their names suggests a limit to the power of death, but the ending of the poem is simple and devotional:

Sen he hes al my brether tane,	*Since/taken*
He will nocht lat me lif alane,	
On forse I man his nyxt pray be;	*Necessarily I must*
Timor mortis conturbat me.	

Sen for the deid remeid is none,	*remedy*
Best is that we for dede dispone,	*prepare*
Eftir our deid that lif may we;	
Timor mortis conturbat me.	

Gavin Douglas (1474/5–1522) was a member of one of the most powerful families in Scotland. He was educated at St. Andrews and probably at Paris. He became Provost of St. Giles, and after much ecclesiastical intrigue Bishop of Dunkeld in 1515, but he was soon imprisoned, and though the see was regained on his release, he died an exile in London. Fortunately, a turbulent political life did not prevent a distinguished contribution to literature. The allegorical poem *King Hart* was formerly ascribed to him, but seems almost certainly not to be from his hand. His early poem *The Palice of Honour* (written in 1501 when he was about 26) is a self-consciously learned work, remotely based on the *House of Fame*, and exhibits a remarkable intellectual power and scope. But his literary reputation rests mainly on the translation of the *Aeneid* which he completed in 1513. It is in thirteen books (the last being the addition made by the fifteenth-century humanist Maffeo Vegio), each preceded by a prologue. In these Douglas discusses the subject-matter, the circumstances of his composition, or questions of style. They are full of his scholarly personality and sharp observation, and sometimes become poems in their own right. Indeed the descriptions of Winter (Prologue to Book VII) and Spring (XII) were modernized and published separately in the eighteenth century, when the taste for this sort of writing returned. Douglas' Northern winter is even bleaker than that of *Sir Gawain and the Green Knight*:

... The ground fadyt, and fauch wolx all the feildis,	*'fallow'/withered grew*
Montayne toppis sleikit with snaw ourheildis,	*smooth/covers*
On raggit rolkis of hard harsk quhyne stane,	*rocks/whinstone*
With frosyne frontis cauld clynty clewis schane;	*with 'clints', rocky ravines*
Bewtie wes lost, and barrand schew the landis,	
With frostis haire ourfret the feildis standis.	
Soure bittir bubbis, and the schowris snell,	*blasts/sharp*
Semyt on the sward ane similitude of hell. ...	

In his Prologue to the first Book he launches a scathing and amusing attack on Caxton's translation of a French re-telling of the

story of the *Aeneid*. Douglas speaks with genuine scholarly horror –
'this Caxton' has committed howlers, he has produced a work
without 'sentence or engyne', he has perverted the story of Dido,
the fifth Book 'is ourhippit quyte', etc. etc. The whole thing is

... na mair lyke Virgill, dar I lay,
Na the owle resemblis the papyngay.

Douglas produces what is arguably the best version of Virgil in
English poetry, and certainly is the most readable. Quite unmarred
by pedantry or stiff 'classicism', it moves with enormous verve and
vigour, and does full justice to the excitement of the narrative. It is
true that Douglas rarely catches the verbal melody, the sweet and
flowing elegance of Virgil, but his Scottish verse has its own virtues.
He achieved triumphantly what Dryden later set out to do – 'to
make Virgil speak such English as he would himself have spoken if
he had been born in England, and in the present age'. Virgil here is
made to speak with the tough and energetic diction of Middle
Scots:

               insequitur
cumulo praeruptus aquae mons

becomes

Heich as ane hill the jaw of watter brak   *wave*
And in ane heip come on thame with ane swak,

and the whirlpool in Book VI which seethed and belched its sand
into Cocytus is described as

Popland and bullerand furth on athir hand   *Boiling and foaming*
Onto Cochitus all his slik and sand.

His homely expressions are always vivid, and sometimes moving –
Priam, when he is surrounded by his enemies in the palace and puts
on his long-disused armour, is called the 'auld gray'. Douglas is
faithful to his original, but not subservient; he will allow himself to
expand a line or a passage, for stylistic reasons, for explanation, for
material from a commentary, or simply because he likes the subject.
Sometimes Virgil's concision is painfully lost – *timeo Danaos et dona
ferentes* becomes the clumsily turned

How ever it be, I dreid the Grekis fors
And thame that sendis this gift alwais I feir –

– but sometimes, as C. S. Lewis, the best critic of Douglas, has
pointed out, his additions have a curiously Virgilian ring.

With his taste for expansive translations, like 'schowting, gowling and clamour' for *gemitus*, for doublets like 'braid and large', 'oppin and patent', etc., Douglas is attempting an ample and copious eloquence. In his Prologue to Book IX he talks interestingly about his theories of style. Although he seems very happy in practice with his 'hamely playn termys', he apologizes for his 'harsk spech and lewit barbour tong'. He describes the 'heroic style' ('the ryall style clepyt heroycall') which is proper for the subject: it will have no 'low' language, and will be fitted for the ear of a noble patron –

Full litill it wald delite	
To write of scroggis, broym, haddir or remale	*shrubs/small branches*
The lawrer, cedir, or the palm triumphale	
Ar mayr ganand for nobillis of estait.	*proper*

In the interests of the 'ryall style clepyt heroycall' Douglas will often use a Virgilian rhetorical figure, sometimes making it more obviously emphatic and less subtle – *quo lati ducunt aditus centum, ostia centum* is spread over two lines:

Ane hundreith entreis had it, large and wyde
Ane hundreth durris tharon stekit clos.

Sometimes he will echo a Latin word – 'thair labour is besy and fervent for to se' (*fervet opus*); occasionally the syntax – 'an active bow apon hir schulder bar' (*habilem suspenderat arcum*). Sometimes he will adapt normal word-order – 'quhair profound nycht perpetuall doith repair'. But generally these devices are much rarer than in his successor Surrey, a more obviously 'neo-classical' poet. Douglas, however, is sensitive to the tone of the original. He catches the joyful excitement of the first sight of Italy (Book III), and he sometimes makes a good attempt at the lighter movement of some Virgilian lines – in Book IV Mercury is compared to a bird that

fleis by the watir, scummand the fludis law
(*humilis volat aequora iuxta*).

But the best lines in Douglas are usually good literal translations of the Latin, with the toughness and spare concision characteristic of the 'makars':

The cald dreid ran in throw ther banis. . . .

. . . And under the fluide Simois mony ane
With scheild and helme, stalwart bodyis lyis warpit . . .

... We war Troianis; wmquhill was Ilion;   *formerly, past*
The schynyng gloir of Phrygianis now is gone.
Ferce Jupiter to Greice all has translait;
Our all the citie, kendlit in flambis hait,
The Grekis now are lordis ...

With Douglas we take leave of the tradition of learned poetry in Scotland. Courtly literature continued in the work of Sir David Lyndsay (now best known for his morality play *Ane Satyr of the Thrie Estaits*) and in later minor sixteenth-century poets, but never reached the heights of the 'makars' of the time of James IV.

It is significant perhaps that this chapter which began with an English admirer of Ovid should end with a Scottish enthusiast for Virgil. The example of the classical authors was often in the minds of those medieval poets who strove to write with eloquence. Possibly the fact that Gower was content to re-tell Ovid's stories while Douglas was led to a scholarly translation of Virgil's lines is an indication of a general change in attitude. The newer fashion for the imitation of classical elegance and correct usage was to have a varied and creative influence on the diction and style of later poets. But it was not without its dangers for vernacular poetry. Adulation of classical writing could reinforce the traditional view that the vernacular was inferior (a 'lewit barbour tong'), and bring it to the extreme position – that a poet should not attempt to write serious literature in the sand of the vernacular, but should carve only in the lasting marble of the classical languages. Indeed in Scotland after Douglas, it seems that classical learning became rather the province of scholars and antiquarians, who were learned men but not learned poets. In England, fortunately, the new learning never quite lost touch with the courtly tradition of verse, and the poets were able to use it to beautify and 'illumine' the language of native poetry.

8

LATE MEDIEVAL PROSE

N. F. Blake

Prose may be considered a more delicate growth than poetry since it will flourish only under conditions in which culture, learning and peace are present. It developed in England later than poetry, for it had to await the impetus provided by the Latinate civilization of the Church and throughout most of its development in medieval times it drew constant inspiration from Latin works of ecclesiastical authors, both English and foreign. This dependence meant that English prose developed from translation, which remained an important factor in its later history. A Latin style and a Latinate vocabulary are found frequently in English prose works, partly because the English writers used Latin works as their models and partly because the English language was not sufficiently developed to provide writers with the syntactical constructions or the technical language they required. On the other hand, since the alliterative style in poetry was the only indigenous one in England, it was natural that those prose-writers who wanted to give their writing a more native colouring should have adopted many of the techniques characteristic of that style. As early as Ælfric and Wulfstan we find English writers using an alliterative framework for their prose; and alliteration became a feature of the more sophisticated writers, of those who wanted to give their work a style of its own instead of blindly following their Latin originals. It will be one of our tasks in this chapter to see how that style fared in the late medieval period.

The association of prose with learning and Latin meant that it was fostered by the Church in England. As the Church had monasteries and bishoprics scattered over the country, prose developed quite freely in different regions except at such times as the age of the viking raids when political catastrophe intervened. It is true that a king like Alfred tried to encourage the growth of prose at his court; yet not only was he unusual in this respect, but also he was forced to rely upon the Church to provide him with helpers.

And even if the *Anglo-Saxon Chronicle* was initiated by Alfred, it was kept up to date at certain monasteries. The patronage of the Church is reflected in the contents of the extant prose works: homilies, sermons, lives of saints and commentaries on religious texts are normal. This state of affairs prevailed at the opening of the period dealt with in this chapter. But during the fourteenth century, with the growth of a richer and more enlightened aristocracy, prose works, which had hitherto been sponsored only infrequently by secular patrons, began to be made at the request of or for the approval of the nobility. As the king was the richest and most influential member of that nobility, his court tended to become the most important centre of patronage. Authors who wanted to gain preferment were attracted there. Hence we shall see that during our period the court increasingly set the pace in literary affairs. This resulted in both a change in the types of work produced, since the king and his nobles preferred romances of chivalry and adventure, and the increasing domination of London in cultural matters. The Church continued to produce English works of one sort or another, but since it had to contend with troubles within its own body, such as heresy, its influence waned. This was unfortunate as the Church might have been able to continue encouraging regional prose-writing; for when the court became the arbiter of fashion, those who wrote in a style or language not approved by the courtiers were dubbed provincial. This division of the country into the fashionable court and the unfashionable provinces was accelerated by the growth of a standard language based on London speech. For most of the Middle English period one dialect was considered as good as another as a vehicle for prose; but as the language became standardized, it was accepted that all works should conform to that standard.

In order to understand the problems involved in tracing the development of late medieval prose, it is necessary to have some acquaintance with the different varieties of English prose then being produced. So we shall start our investigation with a brief survey of the major writers and styles of the fourteenth century. It is an interesting century because one can glimpse the beginnings of new trends in English prose. At the same time, it must be emphasized that many older works were popular in the fourteenth century. Our survey will include only those works produced in that century; but the *Ancrene Wisse*, written about 1200, may well have been one of the more popular books of the century. We should bear in mind in what follows that the older books were still circulating and were still being modernized and adapted. It will be convenient to begin the survey with Richard Rolle, as his poetry has already been mentioned. Born in Yorkshire about 1300, he went to Oxford University through the patronage of the Archdeacon of Durham. Either his disgust at his dependence upon a worldly clergyman or his scorn for the aridity of theological disputation caused him to leave Oxford abruptly to become a hermit. In due course he settled at Hampole, where he died in 1349. Rolle was an educated man who composed works in Latin and English. Of the latter his *Meditations on the Passion* are among the earliest, while his best-known and later pieces are *Ego Dormio*, *The Commandment of Love* and *The Form of Living*. Many of his English works were written for his women disciples; their ignorance of Latin may have been the cause of his writing in English. Rolle's writings, with the exception of the *Meditations*, are intensely personal: they form a kind of spiritual autobiography. From them we can trace the development of his mystical experiences. It is impossible to give any idea of his mysticism here, but themes which recur in his work are the importance of solitude, his devotion to the Holy Name of Jesus, his love-longing, and the manifestation of grace in heat, sweetness and song.

Like previous writers in English, Rolle wrote in his own dialect, in his case the Northern dialect. Rolle shows other similarities with earlier writers. His two *Meditations* form part of the Middle English tradition of lyrical prayer addressed to Christ and the Virgin Mary, which in the thirteenth century had been exemplified in such works as *On Ureisun of Ure Louerde* and *þe Wohunge of Ure Lauerd*. Apart from Rolle, it is also found in the fourteenth century in *A Talking of the Love of God*. The *Meditations* echo the content and language of these works, though Rolle's style may have been influenced by Latin works on the same theme. All these works give expression to the sweetness of Christ and his name, and all employ a highly rhetorical style. This is an example from the *Meditations*.

I se in my soule how reufully thou gost: thi body is	*pitifully*
so blody, so rowed and so bledderyd; thi crowne is	*made raw/blistered*
so kene, that sytteth on thi hed; thi heere mevyth	
with the wynde, clemyd with the blood; thi lovely	*clotted*
face so wan and so bolynd with bofetynge and with	*swollen*
betynge, with spyttynge, with spowtynge; the blood	
ran therewith, that grysyth in my syght; so lothly and	*makes me shudder*
so wlatsome the Jues han the mad, that a mysel art	*leper*
thou lyckere than a clene man. The cros is so hevy,	
so hye and so stark, that thei hangyd on thi bare bac	
trossyd so harde. (I, 59–69)	

The heightened tone is achieved by use of rhetorical devices, among which may be mentioned alliteration (often in doublets), anaphora (repetition), isoscolon (balance), doublets, three parallel adjectives, and rhyme or homoeoteleuton, as in the repetition of the *-ynge, -yd* and *-ly* suffixes. Rolle shares these devices with other English works written in this tradition. To what extent he based his style on such English works is uncertain, for he wrote Latin prose in much the same style, except that his Latin writings are even more artificial. Since the style of his Latin texts is based on Latin models, and since they are among his earlier compositions, it is possible that he worked out his rhetorical English style for himself from his Latin one. But as there are resemblances of approach and verbal usage between Rolle's and the other English treatises, he was no doubt aware of this English prose tradition and followed it at least to some extent.

Later in life when he turned to writing more personally of his mystical experiences, he used rhetorical devices more sparingly. Yet even here they reappear, as this passage from the *Commandment* shows.

Tharfore, if the lyst lufe any thyng, lufe Jhesu Criste, that es *you/is* fayrest, richest, and wysest, whas lufe lastes in joy endles. For *whose* al erthly lufe es passand, and wytes sone away. If thou be *fades* covetose after gode, luf hym, and thou sal have al gode. *shall* Desyre hym trewly, and the sal wante na thyng. If delites like the, lufe hym, for he gyfes delites til hys lovers, that never may *to* perisch. Bot al the delytes of this world er faynt and fals and *are* fayland in maste nede; thai begyn in swettnes, and thair *failing* endyng es bitterer than the gall. (55–64)

Here the tone is less strident; the rhetorical embellishments are worked into his style more appropriately. They contribute to the general effect instead of calling attention to themselves. With this style he laid the foundations of English mystical prose. The intensity of his emotional condition, however, was such that even in these works he could not refrain from breaking into verse, both rhymed and alliterative. One example of this alliterative poetry (*Ego Dormio* 104–13) reveals that he knew of the English homiletic tradition in which the decay of the world is expressed in a loose alliterative style. It suggests that Rolle may on occasions have modelled his prose style on the alliterative poetry available at the time; it may have been from this poetry that he developed his feeling for the rhythm of alliterative prose. But Rolle can also be moderate in his advice and its expression, relying upon aphorism and colloquialism to drive his message home. This is more often true of his later writings than of his earlier ones.

With the works of John Wyclif we are presented with a different side of English medieval prose. He has much in common with Rolle, though there are also some important differences. He was born in the same county about twenty years after Rolle. He also studied at Oxford University, eventually becoming Master of Balliol College. He took orders and received advancement within the Church, though he probably continued to pass much of his time at Oxford where he took his doctorate in theology in 1372. By then he had achieved a reputation as a man of learning and he had several academic works in Latin to his credit. Like Rolle, he was offended by some of the malpractices in the Church, though he followed the traditional method of commenting upon them in Latin theological works. Objects of his concern were the endowments of the Church and its secularization, particularly by means of the employment of its officers in secular affairs of state. These views brought him to the attention of the politicians and he was taken up by John of Gaunt. The result was an investigation into those views by his ecclesiastical superiors, though initially the proceedings were inconclusive. When the papal schism started in 1378, Wyclif's antagonism towards papal abuses became pronounced. Possibly at this time he embarked on English works, such as the translation of the Bible, and encouraged the dissemination of his views by the poor preachers. In 1382 a court convened by the Archbishop of Canterbury condemned his writings and he was suspended from his appointment at Oxford. The remaining two years of his life were spent at Lutterworth, where many of his English works were written.

Today Wyclif is remembered principally as a translator of the Bible; but here we are concerned more with his English sermons. It is remarkable that a scholar of his stature used to writing and lecturing in Latin should have written anything in English. But just as Rolle was forced to write in English for his female disciples, so Wyclif's involvement in fourteenth-century political issues led him to compose tracts in English, for even the views he propounded on theological matters such as transubstantiation became used by some in the wider attack on the Church. Wyclif was thus forced to appeal to the general public for support against the Church. Perhaps because he was aiming at an unlettered audience he preferred a simple style, though Rolle had used rhetorical embellishments when writing for his disciples. Wyclif's views on preaching are

contained in his Latin sermons. From these we see that he objected
to the use of an elevated style with its rhythmical ornaments, its
logical subtleties and its employment of exempla, snatches of poetry
and points of natural history. Style should be adapted to the audience, but simplicity and straightforward plainness were the
essentials of any sermon. He followed these precepts when he wrote
his English works which are notable for their plain style. Compared
with his contemporaries, he used fewer descriptive adjectives, his
sentences are shorter and his word order is more modern. His
vocabulary often contains words of Latin or French origin, since
there were no corresponding English words for some of the concepts he employed, but his style is otherwise striking for its absence
of rhetorical refinements. There is no alliteration or rhyme, no
parallelism or verbal artistry, and only a few examples of anaphora.
The main stylistic trick he allowed himself was the rhetorical
question. The following attack on the Pope and cardinals may stand
as an example of his style.

For ypocrisie makith hem not good, but more stynke	*them*
bifore treuthe. And thei ben not porest here, making	*are*
hem tresour in hevene, for al ther breeth and ther liif	
is about worldli goodis; and thus thei lasten not in this	
boot, but ben drenchid in this see. And thus thei axen	*boat/drowned/*
not Crist helpe, as dide Petre, whanne he sank; but al	*ask*
ther hope and desire is in thingis that ben binethe. For	
yif their lyven contrarie to Crist, in this world ben no	*if*
falser men. And neither kynrede ne place maken men	*kindred*
Cristis vikeris, but suying in weie of vertues, what man-	*following*
ere men that ever their ben. Errour in sich wittis makith	
many dremeris to faile, for thei taken noon hede to	
good liif, but to fals opynyouns here. (*Sermon* cx)	

The impression this passage creates is that the message is forcibly
and plainly expressed, though occasionally one feels that the writer
could not express himself adequately with the language he was
using. The sentences are brief and make the style somewhat
breathless; but the whole is transfused with vigour. There is a
notable lack of embellishment, though there is an occasional
doublet as well as some antithesis.

Unlike Rolle, Wyclif did not use his native Northern dialect for
his writings, but a Midland one. This may be the result of his
lengthy stay in Oxford, though it is possible that he thought it was
the better form of English to use. To what extent he influenced
later writers has yet to be settled. Like Rolle, he had many imitators

and disciples, who popularized his teaching and style. It is difficult
to be sure which works were by Wyclif and which by his
supporters. The division has often been made on stylistic grounds,
for some of the imitative works contain more decoration than
Wyclif's own writings. Yet it is conceivable that he himself may
have written in more than one style. However that may be, his
views became very popular and his followers adapted earlier texts
to conform to his opinions. One of these, *The Recluse*, is a
fourteenth-century Lollard adaptation of the *Ancrene Wisse*. The
Lollard adaptor eliminated all references to the nuns for whom
Ancrene Wisse was composed; instead the work is made suitable for
the laity, for whom he expressed considerable admiration. The
purpose of the original was so altered that attacks on the papacy
and the religious orders in general could be introduced. The latter
are unfavourably compared with the aristocracy. While the adaptor
agreed with preaching, he evidently distrusted both learning and
scholars. In his work he employed many words which we think of
as being Lollard and his style, like Wyclif's, is relatively simple.
The resulting work has none of the rhythm and fluency which are
the hallmark of the *Ancrene Wisse*. However, it does contain
references to the sweetness and burning love which are more
characteristic of Rolle's style. We should, therefore, not assume
that medieval religious prose can be neatly divided into several
water-tight compartments. Not only is this book a Lollard version
of an early thirteenth-century homiletic work, but it has also
borrowed from fourteenth-century mysticism; it unites several
strands in religious prose. It reminds us that in their early days the
Lollards had much in common with more orthodox critics of the
Church. Yet although Wyclif, who put so much emphasis on
preaching and simplicity, may have had some impact on later
writers and on the general attitude towards English prose, the
heresies of which he was accused must have made many cautious
of following him, just as John of Gaunt had withdrawn his political
support. Consequently, for this reason and also because it was
developing in a different direction, what we may call courtly prose
was little affected by his style. There, as we shall see, the fashion
was more for rhetoric and augmenting. His Biblical translation was
consulted by later translators, for they were scholars who would
naturally consult earlier works. And writers on religious topics
might well imitate his approach and style. But literary men follow
their own fashion and neglect what is outside it.

Mandeville's Travels is worlds apart from Wyclif and Rolle in both style and subject-matter. The book contains the travels of a certain Sir John Mandeville to the Near and Far East and his impressions and comments upon the peoples and customs he saw. It was one of the most popular books in the Middle Ages and was translated into most West European languages; in this respect it differs from the works of Rolle and Wyclif. Yet its origin and authorship have been the subject of considerable controversy. Some have suggested that the *Travels* was composed in Liège and that Sir John Mandeville never existed. But as the Anglo-Norman version of the *Travels* appears to be the original one and as the style of that version has much in common with fourteenth-century English, it is now believed that the *Travels* was composed in Anglo-Norman about 1356 by an English gentleman called Mandeville. The Anglo-Norman version was soon translated into English, continental French and Latin; it is with the English translation that we are concerned here. Some of the manuscripts in which the *Travels* is found are so magnificently produced and illustrated that they must have been intended for noble purchasers. The *Travels* would have appealed to such an audience since they include the exotic, romance, learning, exploration and an exploitation of the interest in the Holy Lands generated by the crusades. The author may have travelled to some of the lands he mentioned, but for the most part he relied upon, and made excellent use of, various geographical and historical works, like *Godefroi de Bouillon*, romances about Alexander, Charlemagne and Arthur, and legendary material found in such compilations as *Legends of the Cross* and *Legenda Aurea*. Yet the book was a work of fiction designed for entertainment; and it is as fiction that it should be judged.

There are several important aspects of the work which deserve discussion. If the author was an Englishman from St. Albans, his use of French suggests that he and perhaps others in his class felt English to be insufficiently developed to serve as a medium for courtly fiction. Perhaps for him it was not yet a polite literary language. Yet although he wrote in French, he used prose. During the thirteenth and early fourteenth centuries verse romances had been popular. But as the fourteenth century progressed, prose became much commoner as a medium for romance. It allowed for length, a more leisurely development, a more involved style and the introduction of learned words. It is possible that this change to prose also reflects a change in reading habits: private reading was now becoming more usual than public declamation. The *Travels* both reflects and contributed to this trend towards prose. Yet it was a development that was more marked in France and Burgundy than in England, which tended merely to imitate at a later date what happened on the Continent. It was certainly to the Continent that Mandeville looked for his models. This can be seen in his prologue, the very inclusion of which indicates continental borrowing. In it Mandeville uses doublets, proverbs, tags from Latin authors, moral exhortations and clichés, such as the humility formula and the acceptance of correction by those better informed.

Mandeville's style was relatively simple and this simplicity was taken over into the English version which is a literal translation. This passage gives some idea of the comparative lack of rhetoric; the narrative is simple and straightforward.

Wel may that lond be called delytable & a fructuouse lond that was bebledd & moysted with the precyouse blode of oure lord, Jhesu Crist, the whiche is the same lond that oure lord behighte us in heritage.	*delectable/fruitful* *moistened* *promised as an inheritance* *the owner*
And in that lond he wolde dye as seised for to leve it to us his children. Wherfore every gode cristene man, that is of powere & hath whereof, scholde peynen him with all his strengthe for to conquere oure right heritage & chacen out all the mysbeleevynge men. (Prologue)	*has the means* *heathen*

Because the translation was literal, the vocabulary of the English version has a strong French influence: the passage contains such French words as *delytable, precyouse* and *heritage.* The English translation has several doublets, the linking of either two words (*delytable & fructuouse*) or two phrases (*is of powere & hath whereof*) with roughly the same meaning. This form of embellishment was to become a feature of English prose. The literalness of the translation also led to the transference of French idioms to English: in the passage the *hath whereof* corresponds to the French idiom *a de quoi.* Furthermore, because the translator tackled his work either so hastily or so incompetently, he often misread or failed to understand his original. In a description of the Zodiac, for example, he interpreted *signes du ciel* as 'swannes of hevene', perhaps confusing *signes* with *cygnes.* His work is so typical of the vast number of translations which were produced about this time that it is necessary to consider this phenomenon more closely.

Mandeville wrote his *Travels* in French. From this it has been assumed that he considered French a more courtly language than English. But very soon after he wrote his work, it was translated into English. Why should someone else have bothered to make an English translation, if the author himself had decided that he should not compose his work in English? The reason probably lies in the contemporary attitude towards the English and French languages and literatures. English was considered to be barbarous and rude, whereas French was elegant and courtly. Thus although it might be difficult to compose a courtly work in English, it was reasonable to translate a French work into English so long as the translator kept as close to the original as possible. In this way some of the courtly qualities of French prose would be transferred to the English version. A translation into English from French was likely to be in a more elegant style than a work written originally in English. Hence many translations from French were made, and the majority of them are written in a style which is a mixture of French and English. It is not to be understood that the translator of Mandeville started this revolution singlehanded. He reflected, rather than originated, this change. Translation had after all been common in medieval England, though up to this time it had usually been of religious texts from Latin. There was consequently little secular English prose literature. Prose writers had no secular English model they could follow. Hence when the nobles started to take an interest in literary matters, it was natural that they should look to France since secular literature was well established there. The native alliterative prose style in England may have been too closely associated in their minds with religious or mystical tracts; and anyway they looked to French models for their subject-matter, so it was natural that they should also look there for their style. Even Chaucer based his *Tale of Melibee* on a French version, and his poems are likewise largely modelled on foreign sources. The translator of Mandeville was acting like the translators of the *Romaunt of the Rose*: he was making courtly French literature available to Englishmen in a style which was designed to be as elegant as the original. This pre-eminence of the French in secular literature explains why so many French works were translated into various European languages at this time. Though Mandeville's translator did not start the fashion in England, he must have emphasized it. The *Travels* no doubt encouraged a taste for prose fiction. The book must have owed its popularity in England to the fact that it was a courtly tale translated from the

French. Yet the work deserved its success for its own merits, for despite the narration of many marvellous sights, the author remained urbane and tolerant. He was a superb storyteller with a vivid imagination, who was able to combine the novel with the familiar, and moral exhortation with entertainment. It was a formula that was to be widely imitated.

John Trevisa's most famous translation, that of Higden's *Polychronicon*, has much in common with *Mandeville's Travels*. But one must be cautious of assuming that it reflects that same development of courtly translation exhibited by Mandeville. For Higden's book was in Latin and translation from Latin was common at this time. Trevisa, who was born in Cornwall in 1342, studied at Oxford, where he was successively a member of Exeter and Queen's College, until his expulsion from the University in 1378. Even before this event he had had some connexion with the Lords of Berkeley; but after it he became vicar of Berkeley in Gloucestershire and private chaplain to Thomas IV, Lord Berkeley, for he had been ordained priest in 1370. He died prior to 21 May 1402. It is possible that while at Oxford he was associated with the translation of the Bible into English and that it was for this reason he was expelled. Whether this is so or not, his reputation today rests on a series of translations he made for his patron. Besides the *Polychronicon*, these include the *Gospel of Nicodemus*, *Dialogus inter Militem et Clericum*, *Defensio Curatorum*, *De Regimine Principum* and *De Propietatibus Rerum*. Some of these works have original passages added by Trevisa, who also wrote a *Dialogue between the Lord and Clerk on Translation* and an *Epistle to Lord Berkeley on Translation*, which are often printed as prologues to the *Polychronicon*. Although most of the works Trevisa translated have a religious bias, they would also have satisfied the taste for the bizarre, romance and history in much the same way as *Mandeville's Travels* did. These qualities in Trevisa's translation would no doubt have appealed to Lord Berkeley, for although we cannot tell whether Trevisa or his patron chose the texts, we may assume that the choice would not have run counter to Lord Berkeley's taste. He may stand as a representative of the aristocratic class which was beginning to take an increasing interest in literary affairs, both by the acquisition of books and through the patronage of men of letters. Some patronized such poets as the author of *Sir Gawain and the Green Knight*. But there cannot have been sufficient talent of this calibre to go around, so many of the nobility took the easy alternative of getting their chaplain or some other scholar to prepare a translation for them. The translator needed only a knowledge of Latin or French; he did not require much feeling for English style or any talent for original composition. And there were plenty of scholars available to those who could pay. Since translation had always been common and since it was at that time becoming fashionable, to order or accept a translation must have seemed a satisfactory compromise to the nobility. Trevisa's translations do, therefore, reflect the new tendencies in English prose; they cater for more secular tastes. Yet at the same time they are more traditional than the Mandeville translation.

Stylistically as well, Trevisa fills an intermediate position; his English shows similarities with both Rolle and the Mandeville translation. It is with the latter that the style of his translations has most in common. In the translation of *Polychronicon*, for example, he kept closely to the syntax of the Latin, but he introduced many doublets.

By the worthynesse and ensaumple of so worthy	*example*
writeris i-spight and i-egged, nought bostynge of	*urged/incited*
myn owne dedes nother skornynge ne blamynge of	
other men dedes, I have y-kast and y-ordeyned, as I may,	*determined/decided*
to make and to write a tretes, i-gadered of dyverse	*treatise*
bookes, of the staat of the ylonde of Britayne, to	
knowleche of men that cometh after us. (Bk I. i. 5)	*for the information*

The doublets remind one of the translation of Mandeville, but Trevisa's English differs from that work in its relative lack of French loanwords. He was of course translating from Latin; but that alone would not account for his use of English words to make doublets. And though he was writing after Wyclif and Mandeville's translator, his language seems more old-fashioned and provincial, as in his retention of the *i-/y-* prefix. Such features may have been caused by his long residence in the West Country. Apart from his attempt to elevate the style of his original by doublets, Trevisa kept closely to his sources. Since they were written in a straightforward style, his English is usually readily intelligible even though his sentences, as in the example quoted, are too long. The lack of connecting words in his English has meant that the relationship between some of his clauses is imperfectly expressed. They hang together; they are not linked to one another.

In addition to this style which he used in his translations, Trevisa could also write in an alliterative manner. This other style can best be seen in his *Epistle to Lord Berkeley on Translation*, which opens (in modern spelling):

Wealth and worship to my worthy and worshipful Lord Sir   *honour*
Thomas, Lord of Barkley. I, John Trevisa, your priest and
beadsman, obedient and buxom to work your will, hold in   *dutiful*
heart, think in thought, and mean in mind your needful
meaning and speech that ye spake and said, that ye would
have English translation of Ranulphus of Chester's books
of chronicles.

Such passages as these in which Trevisa used the alliterative style are important because they show that some writers were prepared to extend the style to secular composition. Alliteration was not to be confined to religious writing. Yet Trevisa used it more for decoration than as a structural principle. The passage quoted is little more than a string of alliterative doublets; as such it is the logical result of making doublets out of English words. The alliteration merely adds a little more elevation to the style. This use of alliteration varies from Rolle's in much the same way as Wulfstan's Old English prose had differed from Ælfric's; though this does not mean that Trevisa and Wulfstan have anything in common. It is interesting to note that the prologue in which this passage occurs was composed by Trevisa; it was not a translation. It is possible that it represents his own style – a style which he felt unable to achieve in translation. On the other hand, a prologue is usually written in an inflated prose because that is the place where the writer must impress his reader. Perhaps Trevisa chose alliteration to increase the stature and appeal of his preface; and he may have done so because he thought it was the style which would appeal to his patron, whose affiliations with the West Country must have been stronger than his own. Whatever the reason was for his use of alliteration, Trevisa certainly used two styles; but in neither case do his examples reproduce the purer expressions of those styles.

Although this survey has not covered all the writing produced in the fourteenth century, this is a convenient place to pause to consider the development of medieval prose. It has been suggested by R. W. Chambers that Middle English prose developed in an unbroken tradition from Old English through the writing of homiletic literature. This theory assumes that certain works such as Rolle's writings are central, while others such as Wyclif's sermons are peripheral. The latter are not part of the tradition. The theory received considerable support at first, but recently it has been criticized for its simplification of the history of Middle English prose. Investigations in depth of many texts have still to be made, so that we cannot yet say with any definiteness, for example, how much Rolle owed to this posited homiletic prose tradition. But a theory which puts Wyclif, Mandeville and Trevisa on one side can hardly be said to account adequately for the development of English prose. For other scholars have at one time or another called each of these authors the 'Father of English Prose'. The difficulty is that Middle English prose lies between Old English prose and the more modern Tudor prose. It has consequently been considered in relation to these two periods. Chambers, looking at it from the Old English period, naturally assumed that the homiletic prose tradition was the most important feature of the later period as it was of the earlier one. Other critics, however, have looked back at the fourteenth century through the fifteenth and sixteenth centuries. The type of writing a critic has regarded as most prominent in these centuries has led him to invest the protagonist of that style in the fourteenth century with the title 'Father of English Prose'. The solution probably lies between these two approaches, though it has yet to be worked out in a scholarly way. The fourteenth century was a period in which English prose exhibits a diversification in style, subject-matter and geographical distribution. The traditional prose continued, but there were new developments. Different audiences resulted in changes in style and subject-matter. But there was no dramatic change; the many styles existed side by side. We should not, therefore, assume that there was only one style in the fourteenth century or that all who wrote at that time drew on the same stylistic sources. Rolle may have drawn on the traditional homiletic style, but he also made use of Latin rhetorical handbooks. Wyclif no doubt drew his style from the traditional teaching on the plain style in Latin works, which he merely adapted to use in English. Mandeville based his work on French models and copied their style as well, which was faithfully reproduced in the translation. And Trevisa, as we have seen, knew of the alliterative style and the new courtly one. His work reminds us that we should not expect conformity of style in one author, let alone in all fourteenth-century prose. Similarly when we come to the fifteenth-century, although I shall suggest that one style was the fashionable one, it is not to be understood that it was the only one. All the styles we have met had their exponents in that century.

In the fourteenth century we can trace the development of a new fashion in prose. While the Church had been the main patron of letters, it was natural that the homiletic tradition with its alliterative style should flourish. And it continued to do so in the fifteenth century. But when the court began to patronize literature, a new subject-matter and style were introduced from France. The popularity of this new style was the result of two major causes. Firstly, the English aristocracy tended to imitate their French counterparts in many cultural activities, so of course they also copied their literary themes and style. Secondly, Chaucer's reputation and practice contributed to the new style's adoption. Chaucer's work is dealt with elsewhere in this volume, but it is necessary to remind the reader here that his example encouraged writers to turn away from the alliterative style in order to use French metres and a courtly vocabulary which would be suitable for poems on love and chivalry. Courtly writers after his time looked back to Chaucer as the founder of eloquent speech in English; and they tried to emulate his work. Usually this implied the use of a French or Latin vocabulary with some rhetorical figures in allegorical poems on courtly themes. Although his influence was particularly felt by the poets who followed him, his example was also imitated by the prose writers. He had made a certain style fashionable, and consequently those who wanted to be in the fashion had to use it. Naturally, writers near London or those connected with the court were affected first, but the style became more generally popular as the fifteenth century progressed. It should be added that this style may also have been popularized by Latin rhetorical writings such as Thomas Merke's *De Moderno Dictamine* [*On Modern Rules for Writing*]. But insufficient work has as yet been done on texts of this sort for us to be able to assess their influence.

This style, of which we saw the beginnings in the Mandeville translation, was an attempt to raise the English language from its barbarity by using a Latinate vocabulary. The tendency, therefore, was to use an inflated, repetitive, heavy prose; for in this way one elevated the language. Simplicity was scorned. The development of this style may be traced in three areas. Firstly, it unleashed a spate of translation into English from both French and Latin. Since these languages were considered more elegant than English, it was natural that many writers should have pursued the easy alternative of making a translation. In this way a writer was sure that his work would be well received. Not all translations in the fifteenth century are the result of this stylistic development, but those which slavishly follow their sources in the manner of the Mandeville translation probably are. And this is above all the period of literal translation. Secondly, the new style influenced the writing habits of the merchants. They usually provide indications of cultural changes since they try so hard not to be thought uncultured. When they wrote business letters, they were content to use a plain style. But when they wanted to make an impression, as in the following letter from the City of London to Henry V, they used what they thought was the accepted style.

... bisechyng the hevenly kyng of his noble grace and pitee that he so wold illumine and extende upon the trone of your kyngly mageste the radyouse bemys of hys   *radiant* bounteuous grace, that the begunnen spede, by hys   *success now started*

benigne suffraunce and help yn your chivaliruse persoune fixed and affermed, mowe so be continued forth, and   *may/in future* determined so to his plesaunce, your worship, and alle   *pleasure* your reumys proffyt, that ...   *realm's*

Here the three outstanding characteristics of the style can be seen: doublets, a French-Latin vocabulary and a tortuous syntax. In this style a weighty vocabulary takes precedence over an unambiguous syntax. Thirdly, the new style was adopted by the courtly writers. As an example of its effect upon them, let us consider the work of Thomas Usk.

Usk was a contemporary of Chaucer's and he may have known the poet. He was associated with two mayors of London in the 1380s. He was partly responsible by a timely confession for the death of the first; but he met his death together with the second in 1388. In the previous year, however, he had managed to complete a prose treatise, *The Testament of Love*. Its theme and language are modelled closely on Chaucer's works. In the *Testament* Usk is visited in prison by a beautiful lady, Heavenly Love, and she leads him to confess the errors of his youth, which had included a flirtation with Lollardism; she shows him how to do penance for those errors, and she reveals what joys his repentance will lead to. The setting and much of the language are taken straight from Chaucer's translation of Boethius's *De Consolatione Philosophiae*.

But Usk also drew on Chaucerian poems for his language, for some passages in his work are little more than paraphrases of Chaucerian lines. So his vocabulary and style naturally have much in common with Chaucer's, though he perhaps used rhetorical devices a little more frequently than his master. His work included an appeal for considerate attention and correction. Such appeals, often expressed in proverbial or pithy form, had been popularized by Chaucer, though they were common in French works. Usk also introduced a passage in praise of Chaucer:

Quod Love: '. . . Myne owne trewe servaunt, the noble
philosophical poete in Englissh, whiche evermore him   *who*
besieth and travayleth right sore my name to encrese   *labours with zeal*
(wherfore al that willen me good owe to do him   *ought*
worship and reverence bothe; trewly, his better ne
his pere in scole of my rules coude I never fynde) –
he (quod she), in a tretis that he made of my servant   *treatise*
Troilus, hath this mater touched, and at the ful this
question assoyled. Certaynly, his noble sayinges can   *expounded*
I not amende; in goodnes of gentil manliche speche,
without any maner of nycete of storiers im-   *folly/story-teller's*
aginacion, in witte and in good reson of sentence he
passeth al other makers'. (Bk III, 4)   *poets*

Passages like this became commonplace in fifteenth-century prose and poetic works. Chaucer was praised for his moral guidance, for Love calls him 'philosophical'. But the manner of his writing receives equal, if not greater, praise. Earlier writers had provided the same type of moral instruction, but only Chaucer had been able to clothe it in a style suitable for a courtly audience. And Usk is here trying to emulate Chaucer's teaching and his style. Usk's work is important because it shows that Chaucer was immediately regarded as a model, and that his style was emulated by prose-writers as much as by poets. We must remember that Usk was connected with London and the court; and so he would have known of Chaucer's work and its impact. Because he was so quick to follow Chaucer's example, it does not mean that everyone did so either in subject- matter or in style. The further away a writer was from London, the less likely he was to be influenced by Chaucer's example, for writers in the country were often writing for a different audience.

Even when authors wrote prose not far from London, they did not always follow the courtly style if they were writing for a non-courtly audience. This can be seen in a series of tracts, usually known by the name of the Lollard *Jack Upland*, in which questions by this 'Upland' and their answers by 'Friar Daw Topias' are to be found. They were no doubt designed for a humble audience, for whom the courtly style would have been inappropriate. The first tract was written in a simple prose not unlike Wyclif's style. But the last two are in a kind of alliterative prose, which editors have taken as alliterative poetry. The alliteration is too sporadic for us to accept that the tracts were designed as poetry, though they show that alliteration was employed not only for the heightened style of Rolle's mysticism, but also for the more workaday needs of religious controversy. It is interesting to speculate whether *Piers Plowman* might have influenced the style of the alliterative tracts, since it is known that many clerics owned copies of the poem. Perhaps the alliterative style was becoming the one used increasingly by humbler writers, now that the courtly authors had turned away from it. Such writers, particularly the religious ones who had a tradition to look back to, may have used alliteration to give their work some decoration and to give their writings the additional support of a well-known style. Yet the alliterative style here is but a pale imitation of its former self.

But, Jak, do thi won, and lette not to lyene; I have as leef	*habit/do not stop lying*
thi leesing as thi soth saw, for who is oonis suspect, he is	*lies/true report/ once*
half honged. Thou seist that we prechen fallace and fables and not Goddis gospel to good undirstondinge; and we ben more holdun therto than to alle other reulis.	*ought to observe*

(*Friar Daw's Reply*, 597–602)

Alliteration is confined to a phrase or a doublet; it does not extend through a whole clause. It is used here as it had been by Trevisa. It has been grafted onto a style which is otherwise plain and which has a simple vocabulary. There are none of the older words which we associate with alliteration. It is used for decoration and invective; it is not used to heighten the tone or as a structural principle. The style is debased; and this may be another reason why courtly writers were neglecting it. It was suitable only for homely and provincial audiences.

Though the work of the next three writers we must consider, the author of *The Cloud of Unknowing*, Walter Hilton and Julian of Norwich, was composed in the East Midlands, it should not be considered 'provincial' in any derogatory sense. Their writings were not, however, in the courtly style. Since they used one another's work and since they wrote in the same tradition, we shall treat their work as one unit, though it exhibits many differences within itself. As they all wrote in the East Midlands in the late fourteenth century, it is possible that the new style had not reached their part of the country at the time they were active. But as mystics, they naturally followed the tradition developed by Rolle, though Hilton and the author of the *Cloud* were priests who expressed concern at the current misunderstandings of his work. These two were primarily interested in the care of souls, for which end the bulk of their work was written. But all contributed to the development of fourteenth- and fifteenth-century mysticism. The author of the *Cloud*, who also composed several other treatises and made some translations, had a dynamic and austere personality, though with a sympathetic understanding of psychological difficulties. For him, to achieve contemplative perfection it was necessary to pass beyond intellectual effort into the cloud of unknowing, a concept he borrowed from Dionysian mysticism. In this cloud the Christian must cut himself off from physical things to perfect himself for divine union. Although the concept is difficult, it is expressed in a practical manner. Hilton's writing was less esoteric and less personal than that of the author of the *Cloud*, perhaps because *The Scale of Perfection* was written for a woman recluse. In this work humility and Christocentrism are the characteristic features. The *Scale* shows the way to contemplative prayer through the necessary moral and ascetic preparations. The goal of such prayer is Jerusalem, and the second part of the book takes the reader along the road that leads there. Of all English mystics, Hilton is the one who shows himself to be the most human and understanding. The *Revelations* of the anchorite Dame Julian are very different. Her mystical experiences took place in 1373, but were not written down for twenty years. Although Julian considered herself to be a 'simple creature', her book has a formal structure and reveals a knowledge of other mystical writings. The intention of her book was to pass on the benefits of her revelations to her fellow-Christians. It set out to resolve the apparent inconsistency between the nearness of Christ as revealed in her revelations and the gulf between Christ and man springing from the latter's sins. Although Julian was a spiritual director, her work was more concerned with her own experiences than were the writings of the two men.

As will be apparent from this brief sketch the talents and intentions of these three mystics differ considerably; and naturally the language in each text was varied to express the author's different purposes. Yet their style has sufficient in common for it to be considered as an entity. Most of their writings were original compositions, but even in such translations as they produced, the style employed is very different from that of the average fourteenth- or fifteenth-century translator. They looked to Latin rhetorical handbooks for help in composing their treatises – there is no question of their following French idioms or syntax. Although they used Latin rhetorical devices, which in Julian's case may have come through the intermediary of other vernacular texts, they also exhibit a striking sensitivity for the rhythms of English. Their prose does not appear foreign in any way. At the same time they did not use alliteration in the way Rolle had done. Where it occurs, it is woven into the texture of the prose; it does not call attention to itself as it had done in Rolle or even in *Friar Daw's Reply*. This is true also of the other decorative rhetorical devices, like homoeoteleuton. The work of these mystics is methodically built up to show the ordered progression of the Christian mystical experience. Order rather than emotion is an essential part of these texts, even though they try to depict the ineffable. Hence they naturally relied on those rhetorical devices which helped to emphasize that ordered progression; these include antithetical and balanced clauses, and the use of repetitive features such as anaphora, which help to point each new step. Yet the use of antithesis and balance was not pushed to the extremes of absolute isocolon and parison (balance); usually the authors varied one member of the sentence slightly to provide some relief in the rhythm. As an example of this style I shall quote from the opening of *A Tretyse of the Stodye of Wysdome that Men Clepen Beniamyn* by the author of the *Cloud*.

A greet clerk that men clepyn Richard of Seinte   *call*
Victore, in a book that he makith of the studie of
wisdom, witnessith & seith that two mightes ben in a
mans soule, yoven of the Fader of heven, of whome   *given*
alle good comith, the tone is reson, the tother is   *the one/the other*
affeccioun or wille. Thorow reson we knowe, &
thorow affeccioun we fele or love. Of reson springeth
right counselles & goostly wittes, and of affeccioun *spiritual/understanding*
springeth goostly desire and ordeynd felynges. And   *well-ordered*
right as Rachel & Lya weren bothe wyves to Jacob,
right so mans soule, thorow light of knowyng in the
reson & swetness of love in the affeccioun, is
spousid unto God. By Jacob is understonden God;
by Rachel is understonden reson; by Lya is understonden affeccioun. (I–13)

Although this work might be called a translation (it is based on Richard of St. Victor's *Benjamin Minor*), it is in reality a free adaptation. The author expresses Richard's views in his own way. In the passage the alliteration is so subdued that it could easily be overlooked: *mightes ben in a mans soule*. Balance and antithesis make a greater impression, but yet in such a sentence as *Thorow reson we knowe, & thorow affeccioun we fele or love* the two halves have a different rhythm. Here, as elsewhere in medieval prose, doublets are used, though we may doubt whether they were introduced through the influence of courtly prose. The whole paragraph is well arranged and neatly ordered, though the means by which the structure is achieved never become strident. The sentences are varied and culminate in the final balanced sentence with its rhythmic progression of *God: reson: affeccioun*. This prose is of a high technical standard: the medium is finely attuned to express what the author wanted to say.

Quite different in tone and structure is the work of Margery Kempe. She was born about 1373 to a former mayor of Lynn. During her life she underwent mystical experiences and travelled widely either on pilgrimage or to attest to the truthfulness of her experiences. As she had little formal education, her autobiography was first written down by an Englishman living in Germany and then revised by a priest in England. To what extent the final version represents the priest's revision is difficult to say, though much of the autobiography seems to reflect Margery's own voice. While it was influenced by the style of the earlier English mystics, her work comes far short of theirs. Here is a typical passage:

And evyr she was turned ayen abak in tym of temptacyon, lech unto the reedspyr whech boweth wyth every wynd & nevyr is stable les than no wynd bloweth,	*like/reed-stalk* *unless*
unto the tyme that ower mercyfulle Lord Cryst Ihesu havyng pety & compassyon of hys handwerke & hys	*pity*
creatur turnyd helth into sekenesse, prosperyte into adversyte, worshep into repref, and love into hatered.	*honour/reproof*
Thus alle this thyngys turnyng up-so-down, this	*upside-down*
creatur whych many yerys had gon wyl & evyr ben unstable was parfythly drawn & steryd to entren the	*wayward/* *perfectly/stirred*
wey of hy perfeccyon, whech parfyth wey Crist ower Savyowr in hys propyr persoone examplyd. Sadly he	*own/exemplified/* *Soberly*
trad it & dewly he went it beforn. (Prologue)	

Some attempt at balance and antithesis has been made, but the final effect is one of disorganization. This is partly because there are too many parallel phrases, as in the first sentence, and partly because the sentences are insufficiently ordered. Rhetorical devices and alliteration are rarely used. But the extensive use of doublets and loanwords and the artless syntax of her sentences are reminiscent of courtly prose. Her work may therefore suggest that writers in the East Midlands were beginning to feel the pull of this style; but since Margery had travelled widely and had been to court, she may have met with it on her travels. Though the final effect is one of artlessness, as so often with the courtly writers, it is not necessary to think that Margery was ignorant of trends in the development of English prose, though her own place in that development has yet to be worked out fully. Her position is different from that of the letter collections which have survived from the fifteenth century, of which the most famous is that of the Paston letters. Some of the Pastons were undoubtedly better educated than Margery, and books are mentioned in their correspondence from time to time. But they were writing private letters which were not meant for publication. Hence they wrote in a simple, colloquial style. They wanted to convey information rather than to impress their recipient. Occasionally as in a letter from a son to a father (e.g. John Paston II's letter of 5 March 1464), there is a heightening of style. They also resort to pithy aphorisms and even sometimes to rhyme. These cases show that they could have written in the courtly style if they had wanted to; but usually the plain style was suitable for their purpose. Their artlessness does not indicate any inability to write in a more elevated style. But since their letters were private documents, they are not germane to the main story of the development of English prose.

Many of the writers we have considered in the last few paragraphs came from the east of the country; and another who came from the North-East may be mentioned here. Nicholas Love, prior of the Carthusian house of Mount Grace in the early fifteenth century, made several translations from Latin texts. Though they follow the originals fairly closely, they are written in a more idiomatic English than is usual in fifteenth-century translation. Perhaps he followed in the footsteps of the mystical writers. It has been noted that much of the writing in the later medieval period came from the east of the country, which is in sharp contrast to the earlier one. It is possible, therefore, that there was an eastern school of English writing in the later medieval period which flowered in the fourteenth and fifteenth centuries. But we should not forget that there are considerable differences in the translations by Love and those by the author of the *Cloud*, just as there is a gulf between Dame Julian and Margery Kempe. It is perhaps difficult to accept the existence of an eastern school as such. Probably there were various centres at which English prose was being produced vigorously until they began to feel the stifling effects of London in the fifteenth century. Love's prose may represent the writing found in one centre, though it is not necessary to assume that it was related very closely with the prose being produced in other centres. Nor, happily, were his works the last to be produced in this style, for later in the fifteenth century such translations as *The Orcherd of Syon* carry on a similar tradition. However strong the tide of courtly prose was, there were many centres in which a different style was employed. And this applies particularly to those genres such as translations of mystical writings in which there was a native tradition to use as a guide. Nevertheless, many translators of saints' lives or schoolbooks were content to follow the fashion of close translation and all that that implied.

Reginald Pecock has much in common with Wyclif, though he was a staunch anti-Lollard. Born at the end of the fourteenth century in Wales, he was elected to a fellowship at Oriel College, Oxford, in 1414/5. The patronage of Humfrey, Duke of Gloucester, brought him to London, where his support of the Lancastrian party contributed to his rise within the Church. He was Bishop successively of St. Asaph and of Chichester. He made himself the spokesman of the bishops against the new puritan tendencies, though they often felt that his outspoken and tactless utterances harmed rather than helped their cause. He wrote several works in Latin and English. One of his more famous English works, the *Repressor*, an anti-Lollard tract, defended images, pilgrimages, clerical possessions, the religious orders and various other of the Lollard targets. He also wrote several English works which set out to explain the principles of the Christian religion. But one of these, the *Book of Feith* (*ca*. 1456), went too far and his writings were condemned as heretical, though it is possible that his political leanings rather than his theological opinions were responsible for his downfall. He spent the rest of his life confined to the abbey of Thorney, where he was deprived of books and writing materials. He died in 1460.

As a bishop and anti-Lollard it is surprising that Pecock should have used English rather than Latin for his writings; but like 'Friar Daw', he no doubt wanted to repay the Lollards in their own coin. But whereas Wyclif had used a plain style and had consciously strived to avoid the use of logical subtleties and casuistical niceties, Pecock welcomed them and was therefore compelled to use a more sophisticated style. His sentences are frequently long and complex; but because of his knowledge of Latin and syllogistic reasoning, they are always clearly and correctly put together. He was the first to show that English could be used to express subtle shades of meaning and that it could match the complexity of Latin. While his syntax is complicated, his vocabulary is often strange and seemingly old-fashioned. As a pioneer in the use of English for theological disputation, he was faced with the problem of creating a technical vocabulary. To solve this problem he anglicized Latin and French words, he translated Latin and French words by their nearest English equivalent, and he extended the meaning of English words. Thus he called one of his books the *Folewer*, not the *sequel*; he used *outdraught* (*i.e.* 'drawn out') for *extract*. He also constructed long compound words like *un-to-be-thought-upon* in the manner of *Piers Plowman*. Many of his strange words are found in doublets, where he may have placed them to make their meaning clear. But since doublets are used more frequently than was necessary to explain the hard words, and since three or even four words are often grouped together in an extended 'doublet', it is probable that he took over the habit of verbal parallelism from the courtly style. As he spent so much of his life near the court and as he spoke for authority and the bishops, he may well have thought it desirable to use the accepted, elevated style.

Some of the features of his style can be seen in this passage:

These distinccions, o my sone, take thou to thee, and make the myri with hem, and thanke God for thyn so *them* light and esi comyng into hem and into the leernyng of *pertaining to* knowyngal vertues and of moral vertues in her ground *knowledge/their* and fundament, such as is here bifore in this book so *foundation* soon and so redili and promptli yovun to thee. And *given* marke wel heraftir how fer thou myghtist have radde and in how many yeeris, eer thow schuldist have founde document forto lede thee cleerli and feelyngli and com- prehensiveli into hem. (*Folewer*, pt I. ch. 27)

Here then is more order than one usually finds in fourteenth- and fifteenth-century prose. The sentences have a coherent structure and they express the author's thought. But the tautologous nature of the prose becomes tedious, for both words and phrases are varied constantly. This variation is carried to such extremes that it is almost a parody of the courtly style. Such variation can be made pleasing if the author has a feeling for rhythm; but this Pecock lacked. His prose is a praiseworthy attempt to make English a fit vehicle for intellectual argument; it showed that the courtly style could be adapted to theological disputation and that it need not be confined to tales of romance and moral legends. At the same time, it also showed that the courtly style was not the most suitable medium for utilitarian purposes. A simpler style is more appropriate for technical prose. But it may have been more difficult for a fifteenth-century prelate associated with the court to write simple prose than it had been for Wyclif.

Even so, some authors managed to write in a simpler prose in the fifteenth century. One of these was John Capgrave, prior of the Friary at Lynn. He wrote many works in Latin and a few in English. These latter include poetry and prose. Since he wrote verse and had been patronized by Humfrey, Duke of Gloucester, it is surprising that he was so little affected by the courtly style in his prose. Perhaps his almost unbroken residence at Lynn and the fact that his prose consisted largely of historical works counteracted any tendencies towards that style. For English historical works, notably the *Brut*, were written in a simple style, even though many of them were originally translated from French. A chronicle does not allow for much decoration, and Capgrave's *Chronicle* is indeed very plain. Another writer to use a simpler style was Sir John Fortescue, whose work on the differences between an absolute and a limited monarchy is full of good sense. Possibly Fortescue was influenced by Latin prose, for his syntax is admirably clear. But his vocabulary is not difficult and he uses few of the devices found in courtly prose. These two writers are the successors to Wyclif in style in the fifteenth century. But they were isolated examples, whose influence outside their specialist circles was limited.

Of all the writers dealt with in this chapter, Sir Thomas Malory is the one with whom modern readers find themselves most in sympathy. *Le Morte Darthur* is still read with pleasure. Yet the book remains surrounded by a certain mystery. It was written by Malory, a knight prisoner, about 1470. But who this Malory was, where he came from, why he was in prison and where he wrote his work are problems that have remained unsolved, though solutions have been put forward. Caxton printed the work under the title *Le Morte Darthur* in July 1485, and for long his edition was our only source. But in 1934 W. F. Oakeshott discovered the unique manuscript in

Winchester College. Unfortunately the manuscript is incomplete at the beginning and end, so that for these parts Caxton's text remains our source. However, the manuscript that Caxton must have used and the Winchester manuscript cannot have been identical; and apart from this, Caxton also edited the work for publication. His alterations to Malory's style and language will be discussed in our consideration of Caxton. The printer, however, changed his manuscript in a more fundamental way: he imposed an editorial unity upon the eight tales of the manuscript. He did this by eliminating many of the *explicits* and by dividing the whole story into twenty-one books, each in turn sub-divided into chapters. The realization that Malory's original work was divided into eight tales led the modern editor, Vinaver, to argue that each tale was an independent unit. In his opinion Malory began by turning the alliterative poem, *Morte Arthure*, into prose, and continued by translating further tales from French sources. The tales were not designed as one composition, and thus there are chronological inconsistencies; Tristram figures prominently in book seven, though his birth is recorded only in book eight. Hence Vinaver called his edition *The Works of Sir Thomas Malory*. Although this view was argued persuasively by Vinaver, few have accepted it. Today it is widely held that either Malory wrote the eight tales as a unified work or he wrote them as part of a cycle which had an underlying theme even though it allowed for digression and sub-plot. That theme is taken to be the rise and fall of Arthur's court – the fall caused by the sins of the court's members. This underlying thematic unity is suggested by Malory's treatment of his sources. Thus when he turned the alliterative *Morte Arthure* into prose, he did not include Modred's treason and Arthur's death in their rightful place, but he delayed them until the eighth tale, where they form a suitable conclusion to the whole cycle.

In the development of English prose Malory occupies a unique position, and his present popularity has tended to distort our understanding of that development. Firstly, he wrote in an alliterative prose. As we have seen in this chapter, an alliterative style was used by the religious writers such as Rolle and by the popular writers of religious controversy like 'Friar Daw'. In courtly prose alliteration had been used only as a kind of occasional decoration. Yet Malory's story was a courtly story of knights, of 'noble chivalry' as Caxton put it; all such stories had been and were to be written in the courtly style. Secondly, he made a prose version of an alliterative poem. It has been suggested that this gave him his taste for the alliterative style, which he then extended to his translations from French. The adaptation of verse romances to prose was common in France and Burgundy in the fourteenth and fifteenth centuries; but it had not become common among English writers. They usually preferred to translate the French prose versions of the romances. Only one or two prose romances made from English poems are extant, and they were made from poems by Lydgate. So in his prose version of *Morte Arthure*, Malory was unusual both in choosing to make a prose version of an English poem and in his choice of an alliterative poem. The result was magnificent, but nevertheless it remains exceptional.

Here we can do no more than consider Malory's tale of Arthur and Lucius (Book V), which is the prose version of *Morte Arthure*. As an example of Malory's style let us consider the following passage, corresponding to lines 941–54 of the poem.

Than the kynge yode up to the creste of the cragge, and	*went*
than he comforted hymself with the cold wynde; and than	
he yode forth by two welle-stremys, and there he fyndys	*streams*
two fyres flamand full hyghe. And at that one fyre he	*burning*
founde a carefull wydow wryngande hir handys, syttande	*sorrowful*
on a grave that was new marked. Than Arthure salued hir	*greeted*
and she hym agayne, and asked hir why she sate sorowyng.	
(Bk V, 4)	

The passage is not uncharacteristic. The tale is narrated in a straightforward manner so that the pace of the story does not slacken. This has been achieved by cutting out much that was decorative or repetitive in the poem. In this passage the directness is also achieved by the repetition of the simple *yode*, which replaces alliterative words in the poem. This word adds directness and a sense of purpose. Alliteration has been retained, but the words which alliterate have been carefully chosen. Thus the corresponding passage in the poem opens:

The kyng coveris the cragge wyth cloughes full hye,	*reaches/ravines*
To the creste of the clyffe he clymbez on lofte;	*aloft*
Keste upe hys umbrere, and kenly he lukes,	*vizor/boldly*
Caughte of the colde wynde, to comforthe hym selven. (941–4)	

Malory has taken *creste* and *cragge* from two different lines; he was probably attracted by their harsh *cr*-sound. At the same time he has not retained the other words alliterating in *c*-from the first two lines, so that his prose is not overloaded with alliteration. The alliteration has become more emphatic. He continues his next clause with a *c*-alliteration, but the *co*-sound here seems refreshingly different from that of *cr*. He has not jumbled them together as the poet did. In this following clause he has also developed the meaning of the poem. The *comforthe hym selven*, which is little more than a tag in the poem to fill out the alliterative line, has become central in the prose version. It was in ways like this that Malory adapted his source. Yet he also made his version more courtly than the original. Thus the last sentence in which there is a polite salutation between Arthur and the widow has been developed from a simple enquiry on Arthur's part in the poem. In Malory things are more formalized and chivalrous. The *Morte Arthure* was a heroic poem which had the nature of a *chanson de geste*. Malory has toned down the heroism into chivalry; and a heroic poem has become a prose romance. The language of the prose version still retains traces of its origins. In the fifteenth century *creste* and *cragge* were relatively rare and had a Northern flavour. The Northern present participle in *-ande* is retained, though Malory changed *welle-strandez*, another Northernism, into *welle-stremys*. Yet throughout the prose version Malory maintains a rhythm and balance which owe little to his source. His work revealed that it was possible to write romance in an English prose rather than in a mixed French-English style. But his example was not to be followed, since his work was known to most readers only in Caxton's version.

William Caxton, our first printer, is included here not for any personal contributions to literature, but for the evidence he provides us with of literary taste at the end of the fifteenth century. Caxton was a mercer and merchant adventurer, who in 1469 started to translate a French prose version of the history of Troy with a view to printing it. After learning how to print in Cologne, he printed his *Recuyell of the Historyes of Troye* in Bruges in 1473/4. In 1476 he moved the press to Westminster where he continued to translate and print works till his death in 1492. In England his publishing policy was to create a market consisting of the aristocracy and the richer merchants. His output consisted of moral and chivalrous works for the most part, though other types of writing were occasionally published. To many of the texts he printed Caxton added a prologue or epilogue in which he gave his reasons for publishing the work, asked pardon for his limitations, and sometimes commented on the literary life of his time. The style of these original contributions is immature: the sentences are long and rambling. They have not been constructed; they just go on and on with little syntactical framework. But the information they contain is invaluable.

From these prologues and epilogues one can appreciate that in translation Caxton thought it necessary to adhere very closely to his French originals, because French style was more elegant than the English one. The English language was rude and barbarous, but it had been lifted out of this condition to some extent by Chaucer who was its first embellisher. He had elevated the language by using the colours of rhetoric and foreign models. Caxton, therefore, apologized that his prose was not rhetorical enough, even though it was based on French originals. But from his prologue to *Eneydos* it is clear that not everyone accepted the courtly style with its French vocabulary. Some of his readers complained of the 'over-curious terms' he used. Caxton showed little sympathy with them; his books were to be fashionable, and the older style was now outmoded. Old books used an obsolete vocabulary and were not elevated in style as they used no rhetoric. It should be stressed that the words Caxton used to express this attitude to style were borrowed from the English poets of the fifteenth century, particularly Lydgate. Caxton picked up the terminology as part of the fashionable coin; he showed little understanding of what was involved and he was unable to apply these stylistic precepts to his original compositions. He reflects the contemporary trend of the extension of the new poetic style to prose. Caxton himself could do little more than stick closely to his sources and introduce doublets into his prose.

Apart from the prologues and epilogues, Caxton's attitude to style is revealed in his edition of Malory. As we saw, Malory's work was in an alliterative style – and that style was considered old-fashioned by the courtly writers. Consequently Caxton had to adapt Malory's text in order to make it suitable for his courtly clientele. Thus the passage from Malory printed above appeared in Caxton's edition in the following form:

And soo he ascended up in to that hylle tyl he came to a grete fyre, and there he fonde a careful wydowe wryngynge her handes and makyng grete sorowe, syttynge by a grave newe made. And thenne kynge Arthur salewed her and demaunded of her wherfore she made suche lamentacion.

The differences between the two versions are striking. Caxton has eliminated the alliteration: *creste of the cragge* has become *hylle*, and *fyres flamand* is reduced to *grete fyre*. Apart from destroying the rhythm, these changes make the prose less colourful and less specific. Words like *hylle* and *grete* lack individuality. Caxton also replaced many of the simple words by heavy French loanwords. In these two sentences alone we find *ascended, demaunded* and

lamentacion. These words contribute to the impersonal and generalized tone. Caxton's sentences could be from any prose romance,
for all Malory's particular quality has been lost. Caxton created a
doublet for a phrase in Malory: in his 'wryngynge her handes and
makyng grete sorowe' the latter phrase is added. But it merely
repeats what the first phrase had said; it adds nothing new. For
Caxton repetition was a mark of courtly style and therefore one
included doublets; it was not necessary that they should also be
meaningful. Finally, it should be noted that all the dialect qualities
of Malory's prose have been eliminated. The passage has become
good, standard courtly prose; but it has also become dull and
lifeless.

The printing press thus added its support to the style developed
at the court, which had already received material assistance from
the growth of a standard language based on London English. Books
in the courtly style could now be disseminated with ease throughout
the whole country. The way was prepared for that dominance of
London in literary affairs which we regard as characteristic of the
Elizabethan period. And to prove that Caxton was not an isolated
phenomenon, we have only to consider the work of John Skelton,
tutor to the Prince of Wales under Henry VII. His poetry falls
mainly in the following period, but his translation of Diodorus
Siculus was made in the fifteenth century. His style is more extravagant than Caxton's:

Men ar hyghly bounde of a congruence unto these	*as is fitting*
wrytars of maters & histories, that by their laborious	
estudye have pourchaced hye enprowmentes unto	*improvements*
the lyf of man. They manyfeste unto theym that lyste	
to rede, by exemplifyenge of those that ben passed,	*through the example*
what we ought to coveyte & desyre, and what we	*covet*
ought to avoyde & eschewe. (Bk I. i)	

The difference between the two writers is one of degree, not of
kind. But it should be noticed that Skelton's work is a translation of
a classical text in which many loanwords are based on Latin rather
than on French. Both developments became more pronounced in
the sixteenth century, though at first translation of French texts
continued to be made by such people as Lord Berners.

In conclusion, it should be stated that the various texts have been
chosen and discussed in such a way as to bring out the development
of English prose in the late medieval period. The value of a particular text for the clarification of that development is not necessarily

commensurate with whatever literary merit it may possess. But the period is mainly important for the new change in direction which came over English prose. Naturally those who started this change were unable to bring the new style to perfection overnight. They prepared the foundations, upon which writers were to build so well. Whether the change itself was desirable or not, each reader must decide for himself.

BIBLIOGRAPHY

Abbreviations

EETS   Early English Text Society.
NED   *New English Dictionary on Historical Principles*, ed. J. A.
      H. Murray and others, Oxford 1888–1928, 1933,
      supplements 1972–.

1. *The Conditions of Literary Composition in Medieval England*

G. H. Putnam, *Books and their Makers During the Middle Ages*, New
    York, London, 1896, Vol. I, 476–1600.

F. Wormwald and C. E. Wright, edd. *The English Library Before
    1700*, London, 1958.

K. J. Holzknecht, *Literary Patronage in the Middle Ages*, Philadelphia,
    1966.

M. Schlauch, *English Medieval Literature and its Social Foundations*,
    London, 1967.

A. F. Leach, *The Schools of Medieval England*, London, 1916.

H. Rashdall, *The Universities of Europe in the Middle Ages*, Oxford,
    1942, Vol. III: The English University; The Numbers in the
    Medieval Universities; Student-life in the Middle Ages.

R. M. Wilson, *The Lost Literature of Medieval England*, London,
    1952.

C. Brown and R. H. Robbins, *The Index of Middle English Verse*, New
    York, 1943.

W. F. Bolton, *A History of Anglo-Latin Literature, 597–1066*,
    Princeton, 1967, Vol I, 597–740.

M. D. Legge, *Anglo-Norman Literature and its Background*, Oxford,
    1963.

R. W. Ackerman, *Medieval English Literature*, New York, 1968.

H. J. Chaytor, *From Script to Print*, Cambridge, 1945.

R. B. Hepple, *Mediaeval Education in England*, London, 1932.

J. W. Thompson, *The Literacy of the Laity in the Middle Ages*,
    Berkeley, 1939.

J. W. Thompson, *The Medieval Library*, Chicago, 1939.

R. F. Green, *Poets and Princepleasers: Literature and the English Court in the Late Middle Ages*, Toronto, 1980.

J. J. Murphy, *Rhetoric in the Middle Ages*, Berkeley, 1974.

F. P. Pickering, *Literature and Art in the Middle Ages*, Coral Gables, 1970.

P. Piehler, *The Visionary Landscape: A Study in Medieval Allegory*, London, 1971.

B. Boyd, *Chaucer and the Medieval Book*, San Marino, 1973.

J. M. Powell, *Medieval Studies: An Introduction*, Syracuse, 1976.

Walter H. Beale, *Old and Middle English Literature to 1500: A Guide to Information Services*, Detroit, 1976.

David C. Fowler, *The Bible in Early English Literature*, Seattle, 1976.

2. *The Old English Period*

Editions
(those with a translation are marked with an asterisk)

The Anglo-Saxon Poetic Records, Vols I–VI, ed. G. P. Krapp and E. V. K. Dobbie, New York, 1931–42.
*The Exeter Book, Part I, ed. I. Gollancz, 1895; Part II ed. W. S. Mackie, 1934, EETS, London.
*Ælfric's Lives of Saints, ed. W. W. Skeat, EETS, reprinted 1966.
*The Sermones Catholici or Homilies of Ælfric, ed. B. Thorpe, London, 1844, 1846.
*King Alfred's West-Saxon version of Gregory's Pastoral Care, ed. H. Sweet, EETS, reprinted 1958.
*King Alfred's Orosius, ed. H. Sweet, EETS, reprinted 1959.
*The Old English version of Bede's Ecclesiastical History, ed. T. Miller, EETS, reprinted 1959, 1963.
*The Blickling Homilies, ed. R. Morris, EETS, reprinted 1967.

Translations

R. K. Gordon, *Anglo-Saxon Poetry*, London, reprinted 1959.
S. A. J. Bradley, *Anglo-Saxon Poetry*, London, 1982.
J. R. Clark Hall, *Beowulf and the Finnesburg Fragment*, revised by C. L. Wrenn, revised edition, London, 1950.
C. W. Kennedy, *Early English Christian Poetry*, New York, 1952, with critical commentary.
C. W. Kennedy, *The Poems of Cynewulf*, London, 1910.
C. W. Kennedy, *The Cædmon Poems*, London, 1916.
G. N. Garmonsway, *The Anglo-Saxon Chronicle*, London, 1953.
Dorothy Whitelock, *English Historical Documents*, Vol. I, c. 500–1042, London, 1955.

Surveys and bibliographies

W. L. Renwick and H. Orton, *The Beginnings of English Literature to Skelton, 1509*, revised edition, London, 1952.
S. B. Greenfield and F. C. Robinson, *A Bibliography. . . on Old English Literature*, Toronto, Manchester, 1980.
C. W. Kennedy, *The Earliest English Poetry*, London, 1943.
G. K. Anderson, *The Literature of The Anglo-Saxons*, London, 1949.
K. Malone, 'The Old English Period, to 1100' in *A Literary History of England*, ed. A. C. Baugh, New York, 1948.

S. B. Greenfield, *A Critical History of Old English Literature*, New York, 1965.
Continuations and Beginnings, ed. E. G. Stanley, London, 1966.
C. L. Wrenn, *A Study of Old English Literature*, London, 1967.

3. *Early Middle English Literature*

Texts and readers

Almost all writings in early Middle English have been printed in the publications of the Early English Text Society (EETS) in two series (Original Series: os and Extra Series: es) continued as one series from 1921.

There are many Readers of early Middle English containing a range of representative texts, often with useful introductions and notes. Some of the best-known Readers are:

R. Morris and W. W. Skeat, *Specimens of Early English* (Parts I & 2), Oxford, 1867 & later revisions.

O. F. Emerson, *Middle English Reader*, New York, 1905.

J. Hall, *Selections from Early Middle English*, 2 vols, Oxford, 1920.

B. Dickens & R. M. Wilson, *Early Middle English Texts*, Cambridge, 1951.

J. A. W. Bennett & G. V. Smithers, *Early Middle English Verse and Prose* with Glossary by Norman Davis, Oxford, 1966.

Collections of modern renderings

E. Rickert, *Early English Romances in Verse*, 2 vols, London, 1908.

J. L. Weston, *Chief Middle English Poets*, Boston, 1914.

R. S. Loomis & R. Willard, *Medieval English Verse and Prose in Modernized Versions*, New York, 1948.

Editions

The Lay of Havelock the Dane, ed. W. W. Skeat, revised K. Sisam, Oxford, 1950 (EETS, es 4, 1868).

King Horn, ed. J. Hall, Oxford 1901 (EETS, 14, 1901).

Floris and Blauncheflower, ed. A. B. Taylor, Oxford, 1927 (EETS, os 14, 1901).

The Romance of Guy of Warwick, ed. J. Zupitza, Oxford 1875–91 (EETS, es 25, 42, 49, 59).

The Romance of Sir Beves of Hamtoun, ed. E. Kölbing, Oxford 1885–94 (EETS, es 46, 48, 65).

Amis and Amiloun, ed A. Leach, Oxford 1935 (EETS, 203).

King Alisaunder, ed. G. V. Smithers, 2 vols, Oxford 1952–57 (EETS, 227, 237).

Geoffrey of Monmouth, *The Histories of the Kings of Britain*, trans. E. Evans, revised C. S. W. Dunn, London and New York, 1958.

J. S. P. Tatlock, *The Legendary History of Britain: Geoffrey's Historia and its early vernacular versions*, Berkeley, 1950.

Bestiary in J. Hall, *Selections from EME*.

Proverbs of Alfred, ed. O. Arngart (Anderson), Lund, 1942–55.

Proverbs of Hendyng, ed. G. Schleich, *Anglia* 51, 1927.

Vices and Virtues, ed. F. Holthausen, Oxford 1888–1921 (EETS, 89, 159).

The Owl and the Nightingale, ed. J. W. H. Atkins, Cambridge, 1922 (both texts and translation).

The Owl and the Nightingale, ed. E. G. Stanley, Edinburgh, 1960.

The English, French and Latin texts of the *Ancrene Riwle* are appearing in the publications of EETS.

Ancrene Wisse, ed. G. Shepherd, Manchester, 1973.

Ancrene Riwle, trans. M. B. Salu, London, 1955.

Hali Meiðhad, ed. R. M. Wilson, Leeds, 1940.

Sawles Warde, ed. R. M. Wilson, Leeds, 1938.

Þe *Liflade ant te Passiun of Seinte Iuliene*, ed. S.R.T.O. d'Ardenne, Liège, 1936, repre. EETS, 1961.

The Early South-English Legendary, ed. C. Hortsmann, Oxford, 1887.

The Northern Passion, ed. F. A. Foster, Oxford 1913-16 (EETS, 145, 147).

Old English Homilies, ed. R. Morris, Oxford 1867–8 (EETS 29, 34).

Kentish Sermons in J. Hall, *Selections from EME*.

Ormulum, ed. R. M. White and R. Holt, Oxford, 1878.

Genesis and Exodus, ed. R. Morris, Oxford, 1865 (EETS, 87).

Jacob and Josep, ed. A. S. Napier, Oxford, 1916.

Cursor Mundi, ed. R. Morris, Oxford, 1874–92 (EETS, 57, 59, 62, 66, 68).

Handlyng Synne, ed. F. J. Furnivall, Oxford, 1901–3 (EETS, 119, 123).

Charles W. Dunn and Edward T. Byrnes, ed. *Middle English Literature*, New York, 1973.

Layamon: Brutt, ed. G. L. Brook and R. F. Leslie (EETS 250, 277), London, 1963, 1976.

Lewis T. Owen and Nanacy H. Owen, ed. *Middle English Poetry: An Anthology*, Indianapolis, 1971.

Books on literary and social history

J. W. H. Atkins, *English Literary Criticism: the medieval phase*, Cambridge, 1943.

A. C. Baugh, *The Middle English Period,* in *A Literary History of England,* New York, 1948.

J. Bédier, *Les fabliaux,* Paris, 1895.

Marc Bloch, *Feudal Society,* trans. L. A. Manyon, London, 1962.

E. de Bruyne, *Etudes d'esthétique médiévale,* Vols 2 and 3, Bruges, 1946.

J. A. Burrow, *Medieval Writers and their Work: Middle English Literature and Its Background 1100–1500,* Oxford, 1982.

John N. Ganim, *Style and Consciousness in Middle English Narrative,* Princeton, 1983.

J. de Ghellinck, *L'Essor de la littérature latine au XIIe siècle,* Bruges, 1954.

C. H. Haskins, *The Renaissance of the Twelfth Century,* Cambridge, Mass., 1927.

L. A. Hibbard, *Medieval Romance in England,* New York, 1960.

Kathryn Hume, *The Owl and the Nightingale; The Poem and Its Critics,* Toronto, 1975.

R. S. Loomis, *Arthurian Literature in the Middle Ages, A Collaborative History,* Oxford, 1959.

S. Painter, *William Marshal,* Baltimore, 1933.

Velma B. Richmond, *The Popularity of Middle English Romance,* Bowling Green OH, 1975.

C. A. Robson, *Maurice of Sully and the Medieval Vernacular Homily,* Oxford, 1952.

R. W. Southern, *The Making of the Middle Ages,* London, 1953.

R. W. Southern, *Saint Anselm and his Biographer: a study of monastic life and thought 1059–c. 1130,* Cambridge, 1963.

John Stevens, *Medieval Romance: Themes and Approaches,* New York and London, 1973.

R. M. Wilson, *Early Middle English Literature,* London, 1939.

R. M. Wilson, *The Lost Literature of Medieval England,* London, 1952.

James I. Wimsatt, *Allegory and Mirror: Tradition and Structure in Middle English Literature,* New York, 1970.

Susan Wittig, *Stylistic and Narrative Structures in the Middle English Romances,* Austin TX, 1978.

T. Wolpers, *Die englische Heiligenlegende des Mittelalters,* Tübingen, 1964.

Full bibliographical information about early Middle English is available in

J. E. Wells, *A Manual of the Writings in Middle English, 1050–1400,*

New Haven, 1916 and nine Supplements, 1919–51. A complete revision of this work is now beginning to appear: J. B. Severs, *A Manual of the Writings in Middle English 1050–1500*, Fascicule I, Romances, New Haven, 1967.

4. *Alliterative Poetry in the Fourteenth and Fifteenth Centuries*

Texts

In addition to the standard scholarly editions, I have listed where possible some that are perhaps more accessible to non-specialist readers.

Alexander A and B: The Gests of King Alexander of Macedon, ed. F. P. Magoun, Cambridge, Ma, 1929.

The Awntyrs off Arthure at the Terne Wathelyn, ed. R. Hanna III, Manchester, 1974.

Chevalere Assigne, ed. Lord Aldenham, EETS es 6, 1868.

Cleanness, ed. J. J. Anderson, Manchester, 1977; and see *Pearl* below.

Death and Life, ed. Sir I. Gollancz, London, 1930.

The Destruction of Troy, ed. D. Donaldson and G. A. Panton, EETS 39 and 56, 1869 and 1874.

Joseph of Arimathie, ed. W. W. Skeat, EETS 44, 1871.

Joseph of Arimathea, ed. D. A. Lawton, New York, 1983.

Jack Upland, Friar Daw's Reply, and Upland's Rejoinder, ed. P. L. Heyworth, Oxford, 1968.

Morte Arthure, EETS 8, 1865, revised E. Brock, 1871.

Morte Arthure, selections ed. J. Finlayson, London, 1967.

The Alliterative Morte Arthure, ed. V. Krishna, New York, 1976.

King Arthur's Death: The Middle English Stanzaic Morte Arthur and Alliterative Morte Arthure, ed. L. D. Benson, Indianapolis, 1974.

Morte Arthure, ed. M. Hamel, New York, 1984.

Mum and the Sothsegger, ed. M. Day and R. Steele, EETS 199, 1936.

The Parliament of the Three Ages, ed. M. Y. Offord, EETS 246, 1959.

Patience, ed. J. J. Anderson, Manchester, 1969; and see *Pearl* below.

Pearl, ed. E. V. Gordon, Oxford, 1953.

Pearl, Cleanness, Patience, and Sir Gawain and the Green Knight, ed. A. C. Cawley and J. J. Anderson, London, 1976.

The Poems of the Pearl Manuscript, ed. M. Andrew and R. Waldron, London, 1978.

Pierce the Ploughman's Creed, ed. W. W. Skeat, EETS 30, 1867.

Piers Plowman, The Three Parallel Texts, ed. W. W. Skeat, Oxford, 1886, 2 vols.

Piers Plowman, ed. E. Salter and D. Pearsall, London, 1967. Selections from the C-text with a long introduction and notes.

Piers Plowman: The Prologue and Passus I–VII of the B Text, ed. J. A. W. Bennett, Oxford, 1972.

Piers Plowman, ed. A. V. C. Schmidt, London, 1978.

Piers Plowman: An Edition of the C-text, ed. D. Pearsall, London, 1978.

The Quatrefoil of Love, ed. I. Gollancz and M. Weale, EETS 195, 1935.

Saint Erkenwald, ed. R. L. Savage, New Haven, 1926.

Saint Erkenwald, ed. R. Morse, Cambridge, 1975.

Saint Erkenwald, ed. C. Peterson, Philadelphia, 1977.

Scottish Field, ed. J. P. Oakden, Chetham Society Vol. 94, 1934.

Scotish Feilde and Flodden Feilde: Two Flodden Poems, ed. I. F. Baird, 1982.

The Siege of Jerusalem, ed. E. Kölbing and M. Day, EETS 188, 1932.

Sir Gawain and the Green Knight, ed. J. R. R. Tolkien and E. V. Gordon, revised N. Davis, Oxford, 1968.

Sir Gawain and the Green Knight, ed. J. A. Burrow, Harmondsworth, 1972.

See also *Pearl* above.

Susannah, ed. A. Miskimin, New Haven, 1964. See also *The Pistill of Susan* in *Scottish Alliterative Poems* below.

The Wars of Alexander, ed. W. W. Skeat, EETS es 47, 1886.

William of Palerne, ed. W. W. Skeat, EETS es 1, 1867.

Winner and Waster, ed. Sir I. Gollancz, London, 1920, revised M. Day, 1931.

Anthologies and readers

Scottish Alliterative Poems, ed. F. J. Amours, Edinburgh, 1897. This contains *The Awntyrs of Arthur*, *The Book of Howlat*, *Golagros and Gawain*, *Rauf Coilyear*, and *The Pistill of Susan*.

Historical Poems of the Fourteenth and Fifteenth Centuries, ed. R. H. Robbins, New York, 1959. This contains *Fortune* or *Summer Sunday*, *A Satire on the Consistory Courts* and other alliterative satires, some poems by Minot, and *Crowned King*.

Medieval Literature: Chaucer and the Alliterative Tradition, ed. B. Ford, Vol. I, part one, of *The New Pelican Guide to English Literature*, Harmondsworth, 1982. The anthology at the end of this volume includes *Blacksmiths*, *Winner and Waster*, *Pearl*, and extracts from *Piers Plowman*.

Studies I: Alliterative poetry in general

Much work has been done in the field since this chapter first appeared. An excellent picture of current knowledge and opinion will be found in the collection of essays edited by D. A. Lawton, *Middle English Alliterative Poetry and its Literary Background*, Cambridge, 1982.

J. P. Oakden, *Alliterative Poetry in Middle English*, Manchester, 2 vols, 1930 and 1935. Still a standard work to refer to, but not for beginners.

G. Shepherd, 'The Nature of Alliterative Poetry in Late Medieval England', *Proceedings of the British Academy* 56 (1972), pp. 56–76, also published separately, 1971.

T. Turville-Petre, *The Alliterative Revival*, Cambridge, 1977.

Studies II: Individual poems

The list is confined to the works of Langland and the Gawain-poet because so few of the other alliterative poems have as yet been the subject of whole books, but a collection of essays on *Morte Arthure* should also be included:

The Alliterative 'Morte Arthure': A Reassessment of the poem, ed. K. H. Göller, Cambridge, 1981.

R.W. Frank, *Piers Plowman and the Scheme of Salvation*, New Haven, 1957.

J. Lawlor, *Piers Plowman: An Essay in Criticism*, London, 1962.

E. Salter, *Piers Plowman: An Introduction*, Oxford, 1962.

L. D. Benson, *Art and Tradition in 'Sir Gawain and the Green Knight'*, New Brunswick, 1965.

J. A. Burrow, *A Reading of 'Sir Gawain and the Green Knight'*, London, 1965.

P. M. Kean, *'The Pearl': An Interpretation*, London, 1967.

I. Bishop, *'Pearl' in its Setting*, Oxford, 1968.

A. C. Spearing, *The Gawain-Poet: A Critical Study*, Cambridge, 1970.

E. Wilson, *The Gawain-Poet*, Leiden, 1976.

W. A. Davenport, *The Art of the Gawain-Poet*, London, 1978.

D. Fox, ed., *Twentieth-Century Interpretations of 'Sir Gawain and the Green Knight'*, Englewood Cliffs, NJ, 1968.

D. R. Howard and C. K. Zacher, *Critical Studies of 'Sir Gawain and the Green Knight'*, Notre Dame, 1968.

5 (i) *Chaucer's Life*

M. M. Crow and C. C. Olson, *Chaucer Life-Records*, Oxford, 1966.

A. Brusendorff, *The Chaucer Tradition*, London, 1925.

E. P. Hammond, *Chaucer: A Bibliographical Manual*, New York, 1908.

D. D. Griffith, *Bibliography of Chaucer*, 1908–1953, Seattle, 1955.

W. R. Crawford, *Bibliography of Chaucer*, 1954–1963, Seattle, 1967.

M. Bowden, *A Reader's Guide to Geoffrey Chaucer*, New York, 1964.

R. D. French, *A Chaucer Handbook*, New York, 1947.

M. Hussey et al., *An Introduction to Chaucer*, Cambridge, 1965.

C. Spurgeon, *Five Hundred Years of Chaucer Criticism and Allusion*, 1914–1925.

J. S. P. Tatlock and A. G. Kennedy, *A Concordance to the Complete Works of Geoffrey Chaucer*, Washington, 1927.

Derek Brewer, *Chaucer in his Time*, London, 1973.

—— *Geoffrey Chaucer*, London, 1974

R. S. Loomis, *A Mirror of Chaucer's World*, Princeton, 1965.

E. Rickert, *Chaucer's World*, New York, 1948.

G. G. Coulton, *Chaucer and his England*, London, 1927.

M. Hussey, *Chaucer's World*, Cambridge, 1967.

D. W. Robertson, Jr., *Chaucer's London*, New York, 1968.

B. Rowland et al., *Companion to Chaucer Studies*, London, 1968.

Robert B. Burlin, *Chaucerian Fiction*, Princeton, 1977.

David Burnley, *A Guide to Chaucer's Language*, Norman, 1983.

Chaucer Review (journal)

Alfred David, *The Strumpet Muse: Art and Morals in Chaucer's Poetry*, Bloomington, 1976.

Norman Davis, Douglas Gray, Patricia Ingham and Anne Wallace-Hadrill, *A Chaucer Glossary*, Oxford, 1979.

Norman E. Eliason, *The Language of Chaucer's Poetry*, Copenhagen, 1972.

R. V. W. Elliot, *Chaucer's English*, London, 1974.

John C. Gardner, *The Poetry of Chaucer*, Carbondale, 1977.

S. S. Hussey, *Chaucer: An Introduction*, New York, 1972.

Robert P. Miller, ed. *Chaucer: Sources and Backgrounds*, New York, 1977.

John Norton-smith, *Geoffrey Chaucer*, London, 1974.

Studies in the Age of Chaucer (journal).

5 (ii) *The Minor Poems and the Prose*

F. N. Robinson, *The Works of Geoffrey Chaucer*, 2nd edn, Boston, 1957.

B. A. Windeatt, *Chaucer's Dream Poetry, Sources and Analogues*, Cambridge and Totowa, NJ, 1982.

C. Dahlberg (tr.), *The Romance of the Rose*, Princeton, 1971.

H. E. Philips, *The Book of the Duchess*, Durham and St. Andrews, 1982.

Derek Brewer, *The Parlement of Foulys*, London, 1960.

D. J. Price, *The Equatorie of the Planetis*, London, 1955.

J. A. W. Bennett, *Chaucer's Book of Fame*, Oxford, 1968.

—— *The Parlement of Foules: An Interpretation*, Oxford, 1957.

P. Boitani, *Chaucer and the Imaginary World of Fame*, Cambridge and Totowa, NJ, 1984.

Derek Brewer, *An Introduction to Chaucer*, London, 1984.

W. Clemen, *Chaucer's Early Poetry*, London, 1963.

R. W. Frank, *Chaucer and the Legend of Good Women*, Cambridge, Mass., 1972.

S. S. Hussey, *Chaucer: An Introduction*, 2nd edn, London, 1981.

C. S. Lewis, *The Allegory of Love*, Oxford, 1936.

C. Muscatine, *Chaucer and the French Tradition*, Berkeley, 1957.

A. C. Spearing, *Medieval Dream Poetry*, Cambridge, 1976.

5 (iii) *Troilus and Criseyde*

Editions

Troilus and Criseyde, ed. B. A. Windeatt, London and New York, 1983 (the major work on *Troilus*, containing an up-to-date select but large bibliography).
The Works of Geoffrey Chaucer, ed. F. N. Robinson, 2nd edn, London, 1957.

Source

N. R. Havely, *Chaucer's Boccaccio*, Cambridge, 1980.

Collections of essays

S. A. Barney, ed. *Chaucer's Troilus: Essays in Criticism*, London, 1980.
Derek Brewer, *Geoffrey Chaucer: Writers and their Background*, London, 1974.
M. Salu, ed. *Essays on Troilus and Criseyde*, Cambridge, 1979.

General

Derek Brewer, *Tradition and Innovation in Chaucer*, London, 1982.
——*Chaucer: The Poet as Storyteller.* London 1984.
  An Introduction to Chaucer, London, 1985.
C. Muscatine, *Chaucer and the French Tradition*, Berkeley and Los Angeles, 1957.
A. C. Spearing, *Chaucer: Troilus and Criseyde*, London, 1976.

5 (iv) *The Canterbury Tales*

G. L. Kittredge, *Chaucer and his Poetry*, Cambridge, Mass., 1915.

C. Muscatine, *Chaucer and the French Tradition*, Berkeley and L. A., 1957.

E. Talbot Donaldson, *Chaucer's Poetry: An Anthology for the Modern Reader*, New York, 1958: critical commentary, pp. 871–950.

Chaucer: Modern Essays in Criticism, ed. E. Wagenknecht, New York, 1959: especially the articles of Hoffman, Muscatine and Kittredge.

Chaucer Criticism: the Canterbury Tales, ed. R. Schoeck and J. Taylor, South Bend, 1960: especially the articles by Donaldson, Baldwin, Frost, Tatlock and Muscatine.

D. W. Robertson, *A Preface to Chaucer*, Princeton, 1963.

Chaucer and Chaucerians: Critical Studies in Middle English Literature, ed. D. S. Brewer, London and Edinburgh, 1966.

R. M. Jordan, *Chaucer and the Shape of Creation*, Harvard, 1967.

P. M. Kean, *Chaucer and the Making of English Poetry*, London, 1972.

Jill Mann, *Chaucer and Medieval Estates Satire*, Cambridge, 1973.

D. R. Howard, *The Idea of the Canterbury Tales*, Berkeley and Los Angeles, 1976.

Alfred David, *The Strumpet Muse: Art and Morals in Chaucer's Poetry*, Indiana, 1976.

Charles A. Owen, *Pilgrimage and Storytelling in the Canterbury Tales*, Norman, Oklahoma, 1977.

David Aers, *Chaucer, Langland and the Creative Imagination*, London, 1980.

Helen Cooper, *The Structure of the Canterbury Tales*, London, 1983.

V. A. Kolve, *Chaucer and the Imagery of Narrative: The First Five Canterbury Tales*, London, 1984.

Derek Brewer, *An Introduction to Chaucer*, London, 1984.

6. *Later Poetry: The Popular Tradition*

Romances

Middle English Metrical Romances, ed. W. H. French and C. B. Hale, New York, 1964.

Le Bone Florence of Rome, ed. W. Vietor and A. Knobbe, Marburg, 1889.

Ipomadon, ed. E. Kölbing, Breslau, 1889.

Kyng Alisaunder, ed. G. V. Smithers, EETS 227, 237, 1952, 1957.

Le Morte Arthur, ed. J. D. Bruce, EETS, es 88, 1903.

The Seven Sages of Rome, ed. K. Brunner, EETS 191, 1933.

Sir Tristrem, ed. G. P. McNeill, STS 1886.

Ywain and Gawain, ed. A.B. Friedman and N. T. Harrington, EETS 254, 1964.

A. C. Baugh, 'The Middle English Romance, Some Questions of Creation, Presentation, and Preservation', *Speculum* xlii (1967), 1–31.

A. H. Billings, *A Guide to the Middle English Metrical Romances*, New York, 1901.

H. J. Chaytor, *The Troubadours and England*, Cambridge, 1923.

D. Everett, 'A Characterization of the English Medieval Romances', *Essays and Studies* xv (1929), 98–121.

Laura Hibbard, *Medieval Romance in England*, New York, 1960.

George Kane, *Middle English Literature*, London, 1951.

Arthurian Literature in the Middle Ages, ed. R. S. Loomis, Oxford, 1959.

Dieter Mehl, *The Middle English Romances of the Thirteenth and Fourteenth Centuries*, London, 1968.

D. Pearsall, 'The Development of Middle English Romance', *Medieval Studies* xxvii (1965), 91–116.

Lyrics

English Lyrics of the Thirteenth Century, ed. Carleton Brown, Oxford, 1932.

Religious Lyrics of the Fourteenth Century, ed. Carleton Brown, revised by G. V. Smithers, Oxford, 1956.

Religious Lyrics of the Fifteenth Century, ed. Carleton Brown, Oxford, 1939.

Secular Lyrics of the XIVth and XVth Centuries, ed. R. H. Robbins, Oxford, 1952.

The Harley Lyrics, ed. G. L. Brook, Manchester, 1948.

Early English Lyrics, ed. E. K. Chambers and F. Sidgwick, London, 1921.
Medieval English Lyrics, ed. R. T. Davies, London, 1963.
The Early English Carols, ed. R. L. Green, Oxford, 1935.
English Carols, ed. R. L. Green, Oxford, 1962.
Peter Dronke, *The Medieval Lyric*, London, 1968.
Douglas Gray, *Themes and Images in the Medieval Religious Lyric*, London, 1972.
John Stevens, *Music and Poetry in the Early Tudor Court*, London, 1961.
Rosemary Woolf, *The English Religious Lyric in the Middle Ages*, Oxford, 1968.

Mystery and morality plays

The Chester Plays, ed. H. Deimling and J. Matthews, EETS, es 62, 115, 1892, 1916.
Ludus Coventriae, ed. K. S. Block, EETS, es 120, 1922.
The Towneley Plays, ed. G. England and A. W. Pollard, EETS, es 91, 1897.
York Plays, ed. L. Toulmin Smith, Oxford, 1885.
Two Coventry Corpus Christi Plays, ed. Hardin Craig, EETS, es 87, 1957.
The Non-Cycle Mystery Plays, ed. O. Waterhouse, EETS, es 104, 1909.
Everyman, ed. A. C. Cawley, Manchester, 1961.
The Macro Plays, ed. M. Eccles, EETS 262, 1969.
Ten Miracle Plays, ed. R. G. Thomas, London, 1966.
E. K. Chambers, *The Medieval Stage*, Oxford, 1903.
Hardin Craig, *English Religious Drama*, Oxford, 1955.
Harold Gardiner, *Mysteries' End*, New Haven, 1946.
V. A. Kolve, *The Play Called Corpus Christi*, Stanford, 1966.
Robert Potter, *The English Morality Play*, London, 1976.
Eleanor Prosser, *Drama and Religion in the English Mystery Plays*, Stanford, 1961.
Glynne Wickham, *Early English Stages* 1300–1600, vol. I, London, 1959.
Arnold Williams, *The Drama of Medieval England*, East Lansing, 1961.
Rosemary Woolf, *The English Mystery Plays*, Berkeley, 1972.
Karl Young, *The Drama of the Medieval Church*, Oxford, 1933.

7. Later Poetry: The Courtly Tradition

Gower

Works, ed. G. C. Macaulay, Oxford, 1899–1902.
Selections, ed. J. A. W. Bennett, Oxford (Clarendon Medieval and Tudor Series), 1968.

Hoccleve

Minor Poems I and *The Regement of Princes*, ed. F. J. Furnivall, EETS, 1892, 1997.
Minor Poems II, ed. Sir I. Gollancz, EETS, 1925.

Lydgate

Minor Poems ed. H. N. MacCracken, EETS, 1911–34.
The Fall of Princes, ed. H. Bergen, EETS, 1924–7. (Other poems of Lydgate are to be found in volumes of the EETS).
Selections, ed. J. Norton-Smith, Oxford (Clarendon Medieval and Tudor Series), 1965.
Derek Pearsall, *John Lydgate*, London, 1970.

Chauceriana

The Complete Works of Geoffrey Chaucer, ed. W. W. Skeat, Oxford, 1897, volume VII.
The Flour and the Leafe and *The Assembly of Ladies*, ed. Derek Pearsall, London (Nelson's Medieval and Renaissance Library), 1962.

Hawes

The Passetyme of Pleasure, ed. W. E. Mead, EETS, 1928.
A. S. G. Edwards, *Stephen Hawes*, Boston, 1983.

Barclay

The Shyp of Folys, ed. T. H. Jamieson, Edinburgh, 1874.
Egloges, ed. Beatrice White, EETS, 1928.

Skelton

Works, ed. A. Dyce, London, 1843.
John Skelton: *The Complete English Poems*, New Haven, 1983.
Maurice Pollet, *John Skelton: Poet of Medieval England* (tr. John Warrington), London, 1971.

Lyrics and ballads

Secular Lyrics of the XIVth and XVth Centuries, ed. Rossell Hope Robbins, Oxford, 1952.
Historical Poems of the XIVth and XVth Centuries, ed. Rossell Hope Robbins, New York, 1959.
The English and Scottish Popular Ballads, ed. F. J. Child, Boston, 1857–8.

Barbour

The Bruce, ed. W. Mackay Mackenzie, London, 1909.
The Kingis Quhair, ed. W. Mackay Mackenzie, London, 1939.
The Kingis Quhair, ed. John Norton-Smith, Oxford, 1971.

Henryson

Poems and Fables, ed. H. Harvey Wood, Edinburgh, 1933.
Poems, ed. Denton Fox, Oxford, 1981.
Henryson: Poems, ed. Charles Elliott, Oxford, 1974.
Robert L. Kindrick, Robert Henryson, Boston, 1979.

Dunbar

Poems, ed. W. Mackay Mackenzie, London, 1932.
Poems, ed. James Kinsley, Oxford, 1979.
Selections, ed. James Kinsley, Oxford (Clarendon Medieval and Tudor Series), 1958.
Edmund Reiss, *William Dunbar*, Boston, 1979.

Douglas

Aeneid, ed. David F. C. Coldwell, Edinburgh (STS), 1951–64.
Selections, ed. David F. C. Coldwell, Oxford (Clarendon Medieval and Tudor Series), 1965.

Studies

Thomas Warton, *History of English Poetry*, 1774–1778.
C. S. Lewis, *The Allegory of Love*, Oxford, 1936.
H. S. Bennett, *Chaucer and the Fifteenth Century*, Oxford, 1947.
G. H. Gerould, *The Ballad of Tradition*, Oxford, 1932.
J. Stevens, *Music and Poetry in the Early Tudor Court*, London, 1961.
Raymond Oliver, *Poems Without Names: The English Lyric 1200–1500*, Berkeley, 1970.

8. *Late Medieval Prose*

Many Middle English prose works are still unedited, though the Early English Text Society and the Middle English Texts series continue to produce important editions. Many older editions are outdated. Thus T. Arnold, *Select English Works of John Wyclif* (Oxford, 1869–71) and C. Babington and J. R. Lumby, *Polychronicon Ranulphi Higden Monachi Cestrensis* (London, 1865–6) contain no notes or glossary. The former is being replaced by A. Hudson and P. Gradon, *English Wycliffite Sermons* (Oxford, 1983–   ), the first volume of which has so far been published. Caxton's prologues and epilogues are available in N. F. Blake, *Caxton's Own Prose* (London, 1973) and Usk's *Testament of Love* was published in W. W. Skeat's *Chaucerian and Other Pieces* (Oxford, 1897). Two of the projected three volumes of N. Davis's *Paston Letters and Papers of the Fifteenth Century* (Oxford, 1971–   ) are available. P. Hodgson has edited *The Cloud of Unknowing and Related Treatises on Contemplative Prayer* (Exeter, 1982). H. E. Allen has produced a volume of the *English Writings of Richard Rolle Hermit of Hampole* (Oxford, 1931). M. C. Seymour has edited a version of *Mandeville's Travels* (Oxford, 1967), and he and others have edited Trevisa's translation of *On the Properties of Things* (Oxford, 1975). There are informative editions of Lydgate's *The Serpent of Division* by H. N. MacCracken (London, 1911) and of *Jack Upland, Friar Daw's Reply and Upland's Rejoinder* by P. L. Heyworth (Oxford, 1968). E. Vinaver's *The Works of Sir Thomas Malory* is available in a second edition (Oxford, 1967). Two interesting books of selections are N. F. Blake, *Middle English Religious Prose* (London, 1972) and A. Hudson, *Selections from English Wycliffite Writings* (Cambridge, 1978).

Bibliographical guides to Middle English prose are improving. A. S. G. Edwards has edited *Middle English Prose: A Critical Guide to Major Authors and Genres* (New Brunswick, NJ, 1984), which contains full bibliographies. Other helpful aids include P. S. Jolliffe, *A Check-list of Middle English Prose Writings of Spiritual Guidance* (Toronto, 1974) and P. Revell, *Fifteenth Century English Prayers and Meditations* (New York, 1975). An index of Middle English published prose by N. F. Blake, A. S. G. Edwards and R. E. Lewis appeared in 1985, as did a bibliographical guide to William Caxton by N. F. Blake. Handlists of prose in manuscript are being prepared and published: those for the Huntington library (by Ralph Hanna

III) and for the John Rylands and Chetham libraries (by G. A. Lester) have appeared.

No comprehensive literary critical guide to Middle English prose has appeared, for G. P. Krapp's *The Rise of English Literary Prose* (New York, 1915) is principally concerned with prose after the end of our period. There is much of value still in H. S. Bennett, *Chaucer and the Fifteenth Century* (Oxford, 1947). Some modern studies of particular subjects include E. Salter, *Nicholas Love's 'Myrrour of the Blessed Lyf of Jesu Christ'* (Salzburg, 1974); R. K. Stone, *Middle English Prose Style* (The Hague and Paris, 1970); and W. Riehle, *The Middle English Mystics* (London, 1981). Numerous studies on Malory and his prose style have appeared. A *Fourteenth Century English Mystics Newsletter* has been prepared in Iowa for the last decade.

TABLE OF DATES

939	Athelstan d, Edmund becomes king
940	Dunstan begins to refound Glastonbury as a regular monastic house
	Copy made of the *Exeter Book* (?)
946	Edmund d.
959	Edgar becomes king
960	Dunstan becomes Archbishop of Canterbury
970	*Regularis Concordia* is compiled (?)
971	*Blickling Homilies*
973	Edgar is crowned and consecrated
975	Edgar d; Edward 'the Martyr' becomes king
979	Murder of Edward; Æthelred 'the Unready' becomes king
991	Raid at Maldon
1002	Æthelred orders the massacre of all Danes in England
1005	Ælfric becomes Abbot of Eynsham, Oxon.
1023	Wulfstan d.
1035	Cnut d.
1037	Harold becomes king
1040	Harold d.; Harthacnut becomes king
1042	Harthacnut d.; Edward 'the Confessor' becomes king
1066	Edward d.; Battle of Hastings
1067–70	English rebellions
1072	Bishop Leofric d.
1086	Domesday survey carried out
1093	Anselm appointed Archbishop of Canterbury
1100–1200	Early 12th C.: *Durham*
1100	William Rufus d.; accession of Henry I
	Peter Lombard b. (?)
1120	Wreck of the White Ship
1126	Averroës b.
1128	Alan of Lille (*doctor universalis*) b.
1135	Henry I d.; accession of Stephen
1136	Geoffrey of Monmouth, *Historia Regum Britanniae*
1139–53	Civil war in England
1142	Peter Abélard d.
1143	William of Malmesbury d.
1153	St. Bernard d.
1154	Stephen d., accession of Henry II; end of the *Anglo-Saxon Chronicle*

1157	Alexander Neckhan b.
1162	Becket appointed Archbishop of Canterbury
1167	Oxford University organized as a *studium generale* (?)
1169–72	English conquest of Ireland begins
1170	Murder of Becket
	Chrétien de Troyes, *Eric and Enide* (?)
1180	Adam the Scot fl.
1189	Henry II d.; accession of Richard I
1190–92	Richard I on crusade
1190	*Ipomadon* (?)
1199	Richard I d.; accession of John
1200–1300	Early 13th C.: *Floris and Blanchflour*
	Mid 13th C.: *Genesis and Exodus*
	Late 13th C.: *Amis and Amiloun*
1208–14	Interdict in England
1209	First historical trace of Cambridge as a *studium generale*
1210	By now Aristotle's works available in Latin translation
1212	Everard de Béthune, *Grecismus* (Greek grammar)
1215	Magna Carta; civil war in England; Dominicans instituted
1216	John d.; accession of Henry III
1221–4	Arrival of Dominican and Franciscan Friars in England
1230	*Ancrene Wisse* (?)
1247	Odo of Cheriton d.
1249	University College, Oxford, founded, the first college of the University
1250	Earliest MS of *King Horn* (?); *Harrowing of Hell* (?)
1265	Simon de Montfort killed
	Duns Scotus b. (?); Dante b.
1272	Henry III d.; accession of Edward I
	Havelok the Dane written before this date
1274	St. Thomas Aquinas (*doctor angelicus*) d.
1278	Roger Bacon (*doctor mirabilis*) confined (?)
1280	Albert the Great d.
	William of Ockham b. (?)
1294	War with France begins
1300–1400	Early 14th C.: *King Alisaunder; Ywain and Gawain*
	Late 14th C.: *The Cloud of Unknowing; Sir Gawain*

	and the Green Knight; Thomas Chestre, *Sir Launfal*; *Libeaus Desconus*; *Morte Arthure*; *Pearl*; *Wars of Alexander*
1300	Guillaume de Machaut b. (?)
	Sir Tristem (?)
1307	Edward I d.; accession of Edward II
	Dante, *Divina Commedia* begun, or possibly not until 1314 or later
1314–25	*Harley Lyrics* (?)
1314	Scottish victory at Bannockburn
1315–6	Great famine
1320	John Barbour b. (?)
1321–2	Civil war in England
1327	Deposition and death of Edward II; accession of Edward III
1337	The Hundred Years War begins
	Jean Froissart b. (?)
1339–41	Political crisis in England
1341	Petrarch crowned poet in Rome
1346	English victories at Crécy and at Neville's Cross
1347	English capture Calais
1348	First occurrence of plague in England
1349–51	Boccaccio, *The Decameron*, arranged in definitive form
1356	English victory at Poitiers
1361	Second major occurrence of the plague
1367–70	William Langland, *Piers Plowman* (?)
1368	Thomas Hoccleve b. (?)
1373	Margery Kempe b. (?); Dame Julian of Norwich has her mystical experiences
1376	Edward, the Black Prince, d.
1377	Edward III d.; accession of Richard II
1378	John Hardyng b.
1380	Wycliffe begins translation of the New Testament
1381	The Peasants' Revolt
1382	Condemnation of John Wycliffe's works
1385	Chaucer, *Troilus and Criseyde* (?)
1387	Chaucer begins *Canterbury Tales* (?)
1388	Battle of Otterburn against the Scots
1391	Sir John Clanvowe d.
1396	Anglo-French treaty

1399	Deposition of Richard II; accession of Henry IV
1400	Rebellion of Owain Glyndwr begins (to 1410)
	Geoffrey Chaucer d.
1402	John Trevisa d.
1403	Henry Hotspur defeated at Shrewsbury
1405	Execution of Archbishop Scrope of York
1408	Defeat of the earl of Northumberland at Bramham Moor
	John Gower d.
	Jean Froissart d.
1411	Thomas Hoccleve, *The Regement of Princes*
1413	Death of Henry IV; accession of Henry V
1415	English victory at Agincourt; York plays MS written
1419–20	English conquest of Normandy; Towneley Cycle
1420	John Lydgate, *The Siege of Thebes* (?)
1422	Henry V d.; accession of Henry VI
	James I of Scotland, *Kingis Quair*
1430	Christine de Pisan d. (?)
1431	François Villon b.
1440	Eton founded; Gutenberg invents printing with movable type
1450	John Cade's rebellion
	Hoccleve d.; Lydgate d.
1456	Reginald Pecock, *Book of Feith* (?)
1460	John Skelton b.
1461	Deposition of Henry VI; accession of Edward IV
1465	Dunbar b. (?)
1470	Deposition of Edward IV; return of Henry VI
	Thomas Malory, *Le Morte Darthur* (?)
1471	Return of Edward IV; death of Henry VI
1476	William Caxton moves his press from Bruges to Westminster
1477	William Caxton's first book printed in England
1483	Edward IV d.; deposition and death of Edward V; accession of Richard III
1485	Death of Richard III at Bosworth; accession of Henry VII
	Caxton prints Malory's *Le Morte Darthur*
1487	Rebellion of Lambert Simnel
1492	Columbus discovers New World; François Rabelais b.
	William Caxton d.

1501	Gavin Douglas, *The Palice of Honour*
1503	William Dunbar, *The Thrissill and the Rois*
1505	Thomas Tallis b. (?)
1509–19	*Everyman* (?)
1509	Accession of Henry VIII
	Erasmus, *Moriae Encomium* (*The Praise of Folly*); Stephen Hawes, *The Passetyme of Pleasure* printed; Alexander Barclay, *The Shyp of the Worlde* printed
1516	Sir Thomas More, *Utopia* (Latin: English translation, 1551)
1517	Henry Howard, Earl of Surrey b.
1520	William Dunbar d. (?)
1523	John Skelton, *Goodly Garland or Chaplet of Laurel*
1529	Skelton d.
1531	Sir Thomas Elyot, *The Governor*
1533	Ariosto d.; Montaigne b.; More, *Apology*
1535	More executed
1536	Erasmus d.; William Tyndale burnt
1539	The Great Bible
1542	Wyatt d.
1547	Henry VIII d; accession of Edward VI; Earl of Surrey executed
	Cervantes b.
1549	The Book of Common Prayer, largely the work of Cranmer
1552	Sir Walter Ralegh b.; Edmund Spenser b. (?)
1553	Edward VI d.; accession of Queen Mary
	Rabelais d.;
	Gavin Douglas' translation of *Aeneid* (made *ca.* 1513) printed
1554	Sir Fulke Greville b.; Richard Hooker b.; Sir Philip Sidney b.

INDEX